Microsoft®

Extreme Programming Adventures in C#

Ron Jeffries

PUBLISHED BY
Microsoft Press
A Division of Microsoft Corporation
One Microsoft Way
Redmond, Washington 98052-6399

Library of Congress Cataloging-in-Publication Data
Jeffries, Ron, 1939-
    Extreme Programming Adventures in C# / Ron Jeffries.
        p. cm.
    Includes index.
    ISBN 0-7356-1949-2
    1. Computer software--Development.   2. eXtreme programming.   3. C# (Computer
    program language.)   I. Title.

  QA76.76D47J437   2004
  005.1'1--dc22   2003068645

Printed and bound in the United States of America.

1 2 3 4 5 6 7 8 9   QWE   8 7 6 5 4 3

Distributed in Canada by H.B. Fenn and Company Ltd.

A CIP catalogue record for this book is available from the British Library.

Microsoft Press books are available through booksellers and distributors worldwide. For further information about international editions, contact your local Microsoft Corporation office or contact Microsoft Press International directly at fax (425) 936-7329. Visit our Web site at www.microsoft.com/mspress. Send comments to *mspinput@microsoft.com*.

Acquisitions Editors: Linda Engelman and Robin Van Steenburgh
Developmental and Project Editor: Devon Musgrave
Indexer: Julie Kawabata
Interior Artist: Joel Panchot
Desktop Publisher: Carl Diltz

Body Part No. X10-25681

To Kent—without whom none of this would have happened.

To Ricia—without whom none of this would have mattered.

Contents at a Glance

Table of Contents

Foreword

"Sir! Torpedo Lock! God, there are dozens of them!" The tactical officer's eyes stared wide at his display. This couldn't be happening. "Where away, Ensign Farber?" Captain Jeffries' dark penetrating eyes flashed urgency at the young officer. He should have announced torpedo location and trajectory without having to be told. Seconds counted.

"Thirty by minus 50, range 1-6-0 thousand, 10 thousand kps, sir." The radial coordinates and incoming velocity vector snapped out with trained precision. "A Ferengi vessel just came out of warp behind the torpedoes! Cripes, it must have been firing as it made the transition!"

"Hard over, Helm! Full impulse toward that bogey."

"Aye, aye, sir! Damn it!" Commander Langr clearly didn't like that order but immediately turned the ship into the path of the incoming torpedoes and flooded the engines with power. The bridge crew grabbed hold of their consoles as the inertial dampers fought to compensate for the horrific shift in g-forces. First Officer Ch't-Hen locked eyes with the captain and calmly stated, "Sir, heading into the torpedoes gives us approximately 7.23 seconds to impact."

"Full power, Commander Langr." Jeffries' eyes never wavered from Ch't-Hen's.

Ch't-Hen continued unabated. "I count 42 torpedoes with 12 warheads apiece, each with a yield of 200 megatons. The 100.8 gigaton detonation will completely overwhelm our shields... Two seconds... One..." The crew held their breath for an infinitely long second. "Sir," Ch't-Hen continued without breaking rhythm, "it would appear that the torpedoes have failed to detonate."

Jeffries nodded. "Ferengi are too cowardly to arm their torpedoes until they are a safe distance from their ship. I think we managed to squeak inside that radius. Helm, stay on your course! I want you to miss that Ferengi by inches, Langr, inches! Lieutenant Hill, target our rear phasers on their warp nacelles. Wait until we are two klicks past them, then."

OK, now that I have your attention, I want you to know that you have chosen the right book. I presume you picked it up because you wanted to learn something about C# and agile methods. If so, don't put it down now. This book will take you on an adventure that is every programmer's dream. By reading this book you'll learn side-by-side with Ron Jeffries, one of the most talented master programmers in our galaxy. You won't just learn facts about C#—you'll learn a master's principles, patterns, and practices.

In this book, Ron pair programs with *you*. As you read it, you will feel that *you* are sitting next to him, watching him—even helping him—to write C# code. You'll read his thoughts, his fears, his complaints, and his rejoicings. You'll laugh with him, and you'll get mad at him. You'll participate in his mistakes and successes. You'll agree and disagree with him. You'll argue with him, and some of those arguments you'll win. Reading this book is as close to having Ron as a one-on-one mentor as it's possible for print to allow.

Are you new to C#? If so, keep a language reference nearby. Ron will teach you a lot about C#, but he's not going to spoon-feed you. This is not a C# tutorial. There are many things you are going to have to look up for yourself. However, this book will give you an order in which to look those things up. Each chapter will lead you to more and more interesting concepts in C# and to a deeper and deeper understanding of agile methods. Treat this book as a *pathway* instead of as a reference. Do you already know C#, or Java, or C++? If so, read this book for the skills, the attitudes, the practices, and the thrill of discovery. You'll learn along with Ron as he explores C# and .NET. You'll gain deep insights into the thought processes, personal values, and subtle gestures of a master.

Ron Jeffries started his programming adventures in 1961 (*before* the Beatles appeared on Ed Sullivan!) at the age of 21. Through an accident of fortune, he found himself working summers at Strategic Air Command (in a hardened underground installation) and was able to *play* with their computer systems. He learned programming from some of the brightest folks who had been charged with our security, and he could apply that learning with some of the best and most powerful tools in existence. From that auspicious start, Ron went on to learn more about software than there was to know at the time. He wrote compilers, databases, tax systems, payroll systems, obscure mathematical processors, business systems, multi-programming operating systems, etc, etc. He's worked in APL, Basic, C, C++, C#, Commercial Translator, Delphi, Fortran, IPL-V, LISP, Logo, Pascal, Prolog, Smalltalk, Snobol, IBM 704, 7090, 1401, 1620, and 360 series, the DEC PDP-1 and -7, the SDS/Xerox 940, Sigma 7 and Sigma 9, the 6502, 8080.... In short, he's been *around*.

Ron has been fortunate (or devious) enough to work with some of the best in our industry. He's worked with Ward Cunningham (yes, by reading this book you'll have a Ward number of at most 2), Kent Beck, Ken Auer, Bill Wake, Chet Hendrickson, Ann Anderson, Michael Feathers, Jeff Langr, Michael Hill, Robert Koss, and even—er—me. Ron is an outspoken XPer and a founding signatory to the Manifesto of the Agile Alliance.

Ron loves to write code. If he has a spare minute, he wants to spend it coding. He'll go to the Michigan Union to meet a friend, and the two of them will crack their laptops and write code together. More importantly, Ron loves to write *good* code. He's not happy just making the code work. Ron wants to make it *right*. And making code *right* is something that Ron Jeffries knows better than anyone else. Ron takes a rare pride in the code he produces and in the way he produces it. He craves the creation of magnificence.

I first met Ron in 1999. Ron had been doing Extreme Programming (XP) for nearly five years by then. He was the first XP coach ever and had helped many companies improve their practices. Ron drove to my house (in his hatchback Z3) to meet with me to help plan the first XP Immersion course. I wanted Ron to be one of the instructors. This is a decision I have never regretted. Ron is an outstanding instructor who is deeply motivated to share his vast wealth of knowledge. Ron understands software with a rare clarity and has the even rarer ability to share that clarity with others.

If you want to learn how to use C# *well*, if you want your code to be *right*, if you want to learn the skills, disciplines, and attitudes of a true master, then you've done well to pick up this book. Keep reading—you're in for a *wild* adventure. You'll boldly go where you've never gone before.

Robert C. Martin
December, 2003

Introduction

One of the most controversial aspects of Extreme Programming (XP), and of all the "agile" methods, is reduced focus on up-front design. While agile proponents generally do recommend doing some up-front design, the rapidity with which we turn to programming seems dangerous, even foolhardy, to people who don't understand or who have not yet tried what we teach.

For the past few years, I've been experimenting with these ideas. I start with a very simple design idea and implement features in a customer-driven order, using refactoring to keep the design just barely sufficient to the moment. One question I've been interested in was whether the code necessarily becomes brittle, hard to change, and unreliable or whether the process seems to be sustainable. Another key question has been whether more up-front planning and design would give better results, in terms of substantially less rework, faster progress, or a better resulting design.

My findings, for my work, are these:

- I can deliver features that the customer wants, at a consistent rate, over the course of the project.

- I make design improvements all the time, but mechanically they are more like additions and rearranging things, rather than like rework or redesign or starting over.

- I can keep the code clean and fit for its purpose, over the course of the whole project.

- I invest just as much in good infrastructure as I ever did, perhaps even more, but I make that investment over the course of the project, not just at the beginning.

- I deliver more function per unit time, embodied in code that I can be proud of.

This book is a chronicle of a little project done in the style XP recommends, insofar as I'm capable of doing what I teach. The project includes many of the things that befall real projects: people leave the project and come back, new people come in for a while, key people get sick, hard problems crop up, and so on. We even get a difficult "surprise" requirement. To make it even more difficult, I chose a programming language and environment that I had never used before the start of the project, namely C# and Microsoft Visual Studio .NET.

Looking back over it now, I'm amazed at how a one-person book project can look so much like larger "real-life" projects. The project is open to you. I share my thoughts, my mistakes, my little triumphs, and my code, good or bad. When I learn a lesson, for the first or hundredth time, I share it with you (typically in reader aids and sidebars).

For me, the bottom line remains that this approach works for me, and I can also report that it's working well for most of the teams all over the world who are adopting Extreme Programming and agile software development practices.

For you, the opportunity in this book is to see how these practices work in the hands of an aging geek who is one of the most vocal proponents of these ideas. You can observe both what works and where I go off the rails. You can make your own decisions about how to fit the XP/agile ideas into your own development bag of tricks.

Code on the Companion Web Site

My intention in this book is to describe the thought and work practices that I use in creating a program and not to present here every line of code that went into the system. You might find value in being able to see all the code at various states through the project. The book's Web page at *http://www.microsoft.com/mspress/books/6777.asp* includes several snapshots of all the code, taken at various points along the way. To access the code from the book's Web page, click the Companion Content link in the More Information box on the page. This will load the Companion Content Web page, which includes a link to download the sample files.

System Requirements

To get the most out of this book, you will need the following:

- Microsoft Windows (Windows 2000, Windows XP, or Windows Server 2003)

- Microsoft Visual Studio .NET 2002 or Visual Studio .NET 2003

Many of the code samples in the book can also be used with Microsoft Visual C# .NET or with the command-line tools in the Microsoft .NET Framework 1.0 (or 1.1) Software Development Kit (SDK). However, because these tools don't have the same capabilities as Visual Studio .NET, the tasks described in the book will be different from your experience.

Support

Every effort has been made to ensure the accuracy of the book and the companion content. Microsoft Press provides corrections for books and companion content through the World Wide Web at

http://www.microsoft.com/learning/support/

If you have comments, questions, or ideas regarding the book or the companion content, please send them to Microsoft Press by e-mail to *MSPinput@microsoft.com* or by postal mail to

Microsoft Press
Attn: *Extreme Programming Adventures in C#* Editor
One Microsoft Way
Redmond, WA 98052-6399

Please note that product support is not offered through the above addresses. Support for Microsoft products can be found at *http://support.microsoft.com*.

Acknowledgments

It is impossible to properly acknowledge everyone who played an important role in the creation of this book. Here is a short list:

My family, without whom I'd not be here and not be what I am: my parents, Ronald E. and Margaret S. Jeffries; my brothers, Dick, Tom, and Pat; my wife Ricia; my sons Ron and Mike.

My forebears, betters, and colleagues in the XP and agile community: Ward Cunningham, Kent Beck, Martin Fowler, Alistair Cockburn, Jim Highsmith, Andy Hunt and Dave Thomas, Bob Martin, and so many more.

The many people interested in Extreme Programming and agile methods who have helped me to figure out what I was trying to say, by wading through so many ideas on mailing lists all over the Internet.

My pal, pair programmer, and colleague, Chet Hendrickson, and my pair programming partner, Paul Friedman.

My editors Linda Engleman, without whom this book would not have happened; Devon Musgrave, without whom it would have appeared to be in some strange new version of English; my technical editors Lee Holmes and Kyle Cordes; reviewer Dominique Plante; and the many others who have offered ideas, help, and criticism along the way. Jim LeValley at Microsoft Press, who supported the project from the very beginning. And the many people behind the scenes at Microsoft, including Carl Diltz, who paged the book, Julie Kawabata, who created its index, and Joel Panchot, who created its art. Thanks also for the proofreading of Sandi Resnick at Microsoft and the team at NSightWorks: Joe Armstrong, Steve Boudreault, Catherine Cooker, Kerin Foley, Beth Lew, Katie O'Connell, Dan Shaw, Asa Tomash, and Melissa von Tschudi-Sutton.

Extreme Programming

In this second introductory chapter, we'll take a brief look at the XP values and practices as background for how we approach things in the rest of the book.

XP in the Context of This Book

While this isn't a book about Extreme Programming, it is a book about what an XP practitioner does. Some of what we'll see here is right out of the XP body of knowledge, and some comes from the general knowledge we all build up over the years—in my case, over many years.

Team members on XP projects are expected to do the same: to use the specialized XP values and practices and to blend these thoughtfully with all the other skills that they have. And if that isn't enough, we're expected to learn and apply new skills as we go. *That, in fact, is the topic of this book: how we can build useful software in a situation where we have a lot to learn.*

Extreme Programming Values

Kent Beck, the founder of the Extreme Programming movement, says that "XP is a community of software development practice based on values of simplicity, communication, feedback, and courage." Let's look briefly at these values and how they influence our approach to projects. After a look at the values, we'll examine XP's fundamental practices.

Simplicity

Some approaches to software development are quite complex, with many phases, rituals, plans, handoffs, and steps. XP, in contrast, is focused on being "the simplest process that could possibly work." There are no required phases, documents, or steps. Your project situation may well require you to add in some of these complexity-adding elements, and if so, you must do them and do them well. To borrow the words of Einstein, an XP project should be "as simple as possible, but no simpler."

Communication

Most projects have more than one person involved, and communication among these individuals is critical to project success, whether they are developers or some other kind of stakeholders. Extreme Programming emphasizes face-to-face, person-to-person communication. We make this emphasis partly in the spirit of simplicity, but mostly because two-way person-to-person communication is far more effective for reaching understanding and agreement than are colder forms of communication such as writing. You may find it desirable to document a joint understanding or agreement after the fact. Attaining that common view is most important, and that is far better done face to face when possible.

Feedback

Complex efforts such as software projects work far better if we steer them frequently. Steering is a process of observing where we are and where we are heading, and making frequent adjustments. XP is full of practices that provide feedback. Face-to-face communication, already mentioned, provides for quick and effective feedback on how the communication is going. XP also uses extensive automated testing to provide feedback on how well the software is progressing, frequent delivery of running tested software to users to find out how well we are meeting their real needs, and short cycles of development to let us assess progress and accurately predict delivery time and contents.

Courage

Because it is rich in communication and feedback, XP fills project stakeholders with courage and confidence about how things are going. But XP also calls for courage in the first place: the courage to do simple things, to communicate openly and frequently, and to trust our fellow stakeholders on the project.

This is not blind courage; it is informed courage, created by simple feedback mechanisms and clear, open communication. Assessing our level of courage is a valuable flag that gives us feedback on how well we are performing our practices and how well we are living up to our values.

The Values in Concert

As an XP team goes forward, it strives always to make decisions in the light of these values. Team members adjust their practices, always, to have the best blend of simplicity, communication, feedback, and courage.

Extreme Programming Practices

Building on the values of simplicity, communication, feedback, and courage, Extreme Programming is characterized by about a dozen key practices, 13 in the form I use to describe them. I'll describe the practices and then discuss how they are best used and how they "characterize" the Extreme Programming process.

Whole Team

The Whole Team practice calls for all the stakeholders—developers, managers, customers, and users—to form a single team. The practice calls for the team to work together and to be together psychologically and even physically. The ideal situation is to have the whole team together, in one room, to do their work.[1]

The Whole Team practice was originally called "On-Site Customer" to reflect the special importance of a tight connection between the people who need the software, customers and users in the XP "Customer" role, and those developing it, developers and managers, whom we call "Programmers." When customers and programmers are together, information flows freely and rapidly. Perhaps even more important, working together engenders trust and cooperation between these two halves of one project.

This practice, as you can see, supports the values of simplicity, communication, and feedback. It enables the team to use conversation instead of needing so much written material, and because the team members are together, their conversations can be as frequent as needed to keep everyone aligned.

Planning Game

The XP planning practices are called the "Planning Game" to make planning less frightening and to remind us that planning is an activity that works best if we do it willingly and often. XP plans are always produced by the Whole Team, never by a single individual either inside or outside the team. The practices combine the special knowledge of everyone on the team. Customers understand priorities and needs, managers understand time and money budgets, and programmers understand how to build things and how long it will take.

The XP "Release Plan" lays out a picture of the whole project. It looks at all the known requirements in sufficient detail to associate an estimate with each desired feature, or "story," as we call the features. With estimates in hand, customers and managers can put together the best possible schedule given priority and budget. This plan is, of course, subject to revision as the whole team learns more about all the variables: feature definitions, priorities, actual costs,

---

1. When we say "ideal," we mean it. Recent studies at the University of Michigan found that teams working physically together were two times as effective as those working apart.

and changing budgets. An XP Release Plan can give an increasingly accurate picture of what is really going to happen. Wise teams update their Release Plans very frequently.

The XP "Iteration Plan" plans the next iteration. XP teams develop software in short time-boxed periods called iterations, typically spanning one or two weeks. In each iteration, the team plans, builds, and delivers tested new features to the customer. Yes, features are delivered starting with the very first iteration. There's no "three months to set up the framework" in XP, and just how we go about delivering with the first iteration is the real subject of this book.

At the beginning of each iteration, the Iteration Plan is produced. At first, it can be difficult to know how much we can get done in an iteration, but because we repeat the planning process every week or two, we quickly get quite good at it. The customer, based on the programmers' estimates of cost and on the team's observed speed of building features, selects the feature stories to be built. The team puts together a simple plan to get these stories done and then builds, tests, and delivers the software.

These XP planning practices are quite simple. They focus on communication of requirements stories and on feedback about the speed and quality of our implementation. In addition, the customers get good feedback on the quality of their decisions, by seeing the actual results of their requests in tested, running software.

Small Releases

XP teams focus on small releases of tested, running software. With every iteration, the team delivers proven software to its customers. Beyond that, however, we put the software in the hands of real end users as frequently as possible. If an XP project were to run for a year, we would like to ship production versions four or more times during that period.

This practice provides important feedback to stakeholders on how well the team is progressing. Placing the product in real users' hands also provides important feedback on the quality of requirements stories and on priority decisions.

Customer Acceptance Tests

Although requirements stories are written on cards to serve as planning tokens, and although stories are explained in many conversations between programmers and the on-site customers, requirements in XP have a third critical component: confirmation. The customer confirms that every story is correctly understood and implemented by defining one or more automated "Customer Acceptance Tests" (also referred to as "customer tests" throughout this book). Let's underline these points. An XP story includes three aspects: card, conversation, and confirmation. And the story is done when the Customer Acceptance Tests run.

This practice provides important feedback to the customers about the quality of the team's work—and important feedback about the quality of the customers' own tests. The customer tests communicate and document the precise requirements in an unambiguous and verifiable way. Seeing the Customer Acceptance Tests coming on line and continuing to work gives the entire team confidence that things are going well and provides the courage to continue.

Simple Design

As a new program comes into being, it starts out small and grows over time. We want the design of the program to be good always, and we observe that a small program's good design can and should be much simpler than that of a larger program. Because we are building the program incrementally, shipping new and improved versions every couple of weeks, we start with a simple, good, and sufficient design for the small early versions and we grow and improve the design as we add capability to the program. The result is that our design investment is spread over the whole life of the project, rather than loaded at the front. Because of this, we can spread the delivery of features over the life of the project as well, instead of loading feature delivery towards the end. We can even deliver the most important features early in the project lifetime. This practice improves the return on the project investment, and it gives our stakeholders great feedback and courage about the project. We focus on keeping the program as simple as possible but no simpler. We use the rapid feedback of XP's short iterations to improve the design.

This book is about this process. It explores how we can begin a project knowing very little, begin with a simple design, and keep our design good as we grow the program.

Pair Programming

Extreme Programmers write their production code with two programmers sitting side by side at the same machine. This practice provides immediate code review for every line of code, it improves the design every step of the way, it helps us maintain energy and momentum, and it helps us maintain the discipline to work in the most effective way we know how.

Most programmers have worked together on hard or interesting problems, and usually they find it productive and beneficial. Extreme Programmers work together all the time and gain the benefits all the time.

The practice of pair programming provides immediate feedback on the quality of our work. It helps us communicate the design ideas, and it helps us upgrade our skills through sharing. It gives us courage to work on parts of the code we might otherwise be afraid to touch.

In this book, which is mostly a one-person effort, I didn't always get to pair program. This means you'll get a clear look via my efforts in this book at the effects of working with someone else versus working alone.

Test-Driven Development

Because we are growing the program as we go, because we are committed to improving the design, and because we must ship working software so frequently, we need great confidence that our new code, and our design changes, work as we intended them to. We cannot afford to have some design change break existing functionality or slow down the adding of new features.

Extreme Programmers accomplish this using "Programmer Unit Tests" (also referred to as "programmer tests" throughout this book), which we write as we go. We write most of the tests one at a time, immediately before adding the feature being tested. When, as inevitably happens, we do find a defect after the fact, we write new tests that first show that the defect exists and that then confirm we have the problem fixed. The existence of this growing family of tests helps us communicate what the code is supposed to do and how to use it, and it gives us feedback as to whether the code does its job correctly. The automated tests give us concrete feedback, showing that our changes haven't broken anything, and they give us the courage to make the changes needed to keep the program alive and growing.

In this book, you'll see how we write these tests and how they give us courage. You'll also see what happens when we slip and don't write all the tests we should!

Design Improvement

If we're going to start small and simple and to grow the program while keeping its design good, we must improve the design as we go. Extreme Programmers do design improvement using "refactoring," a highly disciplined technique for improving the design of existing code. The definitive book on this subject is Martin Fowler's *Refactoring: Improving the Design of Existing Code* (Addison-Wesley, 1999), and wise programmers everywhere, extreme or not, will study it and learn its lessons.

Refactoring is not about churning the code. It's about keeping the design clean as requirements are added such that the program remains viable—alive—throughout development.

The refactoring practice supports the simplicity of the design and improves the ability of the code to communicate its design and intent. Continuous refactoring on an XP project is safe because we have our extensive automated tests to give us feedback on our changes and to gives us the courage to continue.

In this book, you'll see our simple program's design improve through refactoring, and you'll get a sense for the power of the technique and the pitfalls in its use.

Supporting Practices

The eight practices described so far include the four that help with the customer/programmer interface: Whole Team, Planning Game, Small Releases, and Customer Acceptance Tests. I call these the "Circle of Life." The other four practices make up the central programming cycle, which might be called the "Circle of Code": Simple Design, Pair Programming, Test-Driven Development, and Design Improvement. There are five more supporting practices that we need to consider briefly.

XP teams practice **Continuous Integration**. The program is always integrated, always ready to go. XP teams say that [sb]daily builds are for wimps. (Througout this book, the [sb] superscript indicates the beginning of what I'm calling a "sound bite." See the "Sound Bites" chapter at the back of the book for more on these.) The best XP teams, even quite large ones, integrate and build the entire system many times per day. This practice provides feedback on the quality of our work, and ensures that we will communicate frequently about what we're doing.

Extreme Programmers practice **Team Code Ownership**. Any pair of programmers is empowered to improve any code at any time. This practice is safe because of our many tests and easy to do because we pair program, learning new areas of the system all the time. The practice provides a simple way to put resources where they're needed, provides a platform for communicating design ideas across the team, and gives feedback to us all so that we can benefit from everyone's ideas.

XP teams evolve a **Coding Standard**. Because we work together all the time, a standard is inevitable. We'll have to agree on a few things, like where to put the curly braces, but most of the standard emerges as a natural result of working in pairs and owning all the code as a team. The coding standard adds simplicity to our process by allowing flexibility and by settling many details. It improves our ability to give feedback by keeping the form of all code familiar. It helps us communicate through the code, and it gives us courage to contribute to any area needing our help.

XP teams use a **Metaphor** or **System of Names** to provide a common language for talking about the design of the program. Often a simple metaphor can help us focus on how the system works: "It's like a swarm of bees that go out on the Web and bring information back to the hive." Or "It's like a manufacturing line that manufactures checks instead of cars." Even if we don't have an evocative metaphor, we develop a common terminology that helps us communicate quickly and effectively.

XP teams work at a **Sustainable Pace**. We do not kick way back sometimes and work massive overtime at other times. We strive to go as fast as possible and no faster. While we'll certainly put in extra hours in an emergency, we are very sensitive to the fact that an over-tired team is a stupid team and stupefied programmers write defective programs. Worse yet, they write those defective programs slowly! We work hard, rest well, and come back to work refreshed. Sustainable Pace is not a license to slack off; it is a demand that we always make our best possible forward speed. This practice provides consistent velocity feedback, which communicates how we're doing to our customers and other stakeholders. It requires that we know what our best pace is and that we have the courage to stick to it.

Is It XP?

People often ask us if it's still XP if we don't have a customer with us, or work in cubes instead of together, or don't pair program, or don't write many tests. It's natural to ask this question, but in fact it isn't that helpful.

Software development is a complex business, and it requires all the skill we can bring to bear and all the good practices we know. The Extreme Programming practices represent important skills in software development. They are rich—they represent many skills, not just a dozen. They work together in ways that are fairly obvious, like the way that testing supports improving the design without breaking things. They also work together in subtle ways, ways that you'll recognize only when you encounter them. People who learn and use all the practices, together, all the time, often report that the development experience has been one of the best of their lives.

My advice to you is to try all the practices, mindfully, until you are skilled with them. Use them in all the combinations you can, and integrate them fully into your skill set. Eventually, it won't matter then whether you're "doing XP" or not. You'll be better equipped to do the best work of which you are capable in a style that is what it should be: a style all your own.

1

XML Notepad Stories

My colleague Chet Hendrickson and I are working with .NET and C#, to learn it, with the intention of writing the book you're holding in your hands. Our chosen application is the "XML Notepad." Here's the initial vision and some stories.

Building an Application Extreme-Programming Style

In this book, we'll be working on a real application. Although the app will be small enough to fit in the book, it will be large enough, and tricky enough, to offer some important lessons about how a real application might go.

As you know, I am a strong proponent of Extreme Programming and "agile" software development, so there will be a lot of XP-related discussion in the book. I'll also be drawing on my years of programming experience (much of it good), with the hope of bringing out some generally useful techniques. Finally, I'll be discovering, as we go, how to use the C# language and the Microsoft .NET tools.

The book, therefore, is a journey of discovery, a journey led by an experienced guide who is nonetheless new to this specific territory. If we're lucky, I won't make a complete fool of myself!

Our project begins, as most do, as a vague initial idea, followed shortly by an optimistic dream of what might be possible, followed by a long period of progress toward a goal that changes along the way. Extreme Programming has taught me some ways of dealing effectively with such things, and that's part of what we'll be looking at as we go along.

As I mentioned in the "Extreme Programming" preliminary chapter, a real XP project team includes two separate roles, called "Customer" and "Programmer." The XP Customer team members have the business responsibility for the project. They decide what the desired features are, what the value of each feature is, and at what point in the project to build that feature, based on its value and its expected cost. The XP Programmer team members are the individuals who build the software. They determine the design, estimate the cost of all features for input into the planning process, and deliver running, tested features throughout the course of the project. I'll be addressing most of the XP-defined Customer and Programmer behaviors as the book goes on, but it's that last one that is the core topic of the book.

XP teams deliver running, tested software, building features—"stories," as we call them—that the Customers see as real progress, from the first week of the project to the last. XP teams don't take a few months at the beginning of the project to set up the "infrastructure"; they get right down to delivering features that reflect value to the Customers. The big question, of course, is how we manage to do these things. How do we ship features without a lot of up-front design and infrastructure and still avoid building an ill-designed program that can't be maintained and can't do the job? That's what our example application—the XML Notepad—is about. It's big enough to give us a look at how this is possible. With that warmup, let's join the project at the beginning.

Initial Vision

The "team" in this book is mostly me, Ron Jeffries. I'm getting help both in ideas and programming from Chet Hendrickson, one of my co-authors on *Extreme Programming Installed* (Addison-Wesley, 2001). Chet will be pair programming with me at times throughout the book and helping me figure out what to do next. I'll be programming alone much of the time—which as an Extreme Programmer I'd rather not do—and I'll be getting other pairing help when I can. Acting as XP Customers for a while, Chet and I came up with a vision for a project.

My Web site, *http://www.XProgramming.com*, is mostly generated from XML input, processed through some Ruby code to produce the indexes and through XSLT to generate the Web pages in a consistent format. (An example of the format appears at the end of this chapter.) The XML format is pretty simple and straightforward, but it's a bit awkward to type in, because you have to embed all your paragraphs in <p></p> tags and use other tags for sections and headings and the like. Our starting idea is for a tool to help with this job. Our amazing dream vision goes like this:

> *There's this WYSIWYG editor that looks just like an*
> *XProgramming.com Web page. You can type anywhere*
> *and edit the page. With a few simple control characters,*
> *you can select any of the special format items that the site's*
> *XML can contain. The page takes shape as you watch.*

Now this is a grand vision. However, while it might be a decent initial idea, it's neither specific enough nor practical enough to build in XP style. To build a product in XP style, we need to break it down into small features that can be built in a week or so. On a real project, this would be a collaborative effort between the Customers and the Programmers, talking about what's possible, understanding the vision, understanding what the important aspects of that are, and so on.

The good news is that since I'm acting as both Customer and Programmer (with Chet's help), there won't be much disagreement. But the bad news is that it will be easier to lose track of delivering value. As programmers, we often get excited about some technical problem and we start working on that prematurely or too much, at least from the viewpoint of delivering features. Of course, we always say "your features will be easier and cheaper if we work on this first." In my very experienced opinion, this is almost never really true, and as you read along in the book you'll find out why I believe that and the extent to which I'm right.

Anyway, in a bit of a split personality kind of way, we immediately started working as programmers (that's us) with our customers (that's us too), talking about feature stories, value, and cost estimates. Since we didn't know how to program in C# at all, our cost estimates were pretty rough. But on the other hand, our customer (that's us) trusts us.

We fear[1] that WYSIWYG editing will be expensive, because of the difficulty we expect in figuring out where the cursor is, when typing into a formatted Web page. When an XP team is too ignorant to estimate the difficulty of something and afraid that it might be expensive, it's time for an experiment. So with this initial vision in mind, Chet and I undertook a few simple experiments.

Learn from the Best

Before deciding anything about what to recommend, I like to do some reading and some simple programs, to get a feel for the situation. In this case, I bought a number of books on C# and .NET that looked useful. I started my first experiments using Charles Petzold's book, *Programming Windows with C#* (Microsoft Press, 2002). I have used his books in the past, and I like his "close to the iron" approach. You might prefer a different teacher, but working through some examples is always a good idea.

---

1. We like to use the word "fear" where other people might say "concern" or "worry." We find that the sooner we acknowledge that we are afraid of something, the better equipped we are to deal with it. You should use the terms that work best for you.

Following Petzold, I created a new solution from the menu File/New/Blank Solution. I gave the project the name Petzold and put the files in my directory C:/Data/csharp. Next I added an empty C# project to the solution, using File/Add Project/New Project. Petzold likes to have us type in all the code on our own. You might prefer to create a C# Console Application or a Windows Form. In this book, we're creating Console Applications as a rule, because we can view debug output more readily, and they are easy enough to convert to pure Windows Forms when the time comes. For this first example, I created an empty project as instructed. Then I added a new C# file to the project, using Project/Add New Item and selecting Code File. I named it ConsoleHelloWorld. Then I typed in the program, much as Petzold had suggested:

```
class ConsoleHelloWorld {
  public static void Main() {
    System.Console.WriteLine("Hello, world!");
  }
}
```

This program compiles. (I use Ctrl+Shift+B, Build Solution.) When I run it, using the menu Debug/Start, it opens a black DOS kind of window, displays "Hello, world!", and says "Press any key to continue." After the traditional brief search for the "Any" key, I press enter and the window disappears. Success!

For our next trick, I tried a Windows Dialog version of Hello World, after skimming through Petzold's very good description of C#'s namespaces, console I/O, and general language information. Depending on the languages you already know, you might choose to do a few more experiments using the console, but it all looked familiar enough, so I moved on.

Lesson   We're doing experiments to get a sense of how to do things and how hard they are to do. Often there is more value in trying a very different kind of experiment, rather than digging deeply into the current one. Since our application is supposed to be a Windows Forms kind of thing, it's probably best to move in that direction early and to fill in some of the unknowns about C# as we go. As always, you'll want to find your own balance on this, but my practice is to move to a simple experiment that will teach something very new—in this case, a Dialog.

We'll add a new empty project, named DialogHelloWorld, and a new C#
file of the same name, with these contents:

```
class MessageBoxHelloWorld {
  public static void Main() {
    System.Windows.Forms.MessageBox.Show("Hello, world!");
  }
}
```

Now this won't even compile. The compiler says "The type or namespace
name 'Windows' does not exist in the class or namespace 'System'." This is one
of the irritating aspects of building things entirely by hand, as Petzold teaches
us. The good news is that we learn the details, but it's much easier to use some
of the more advanced templates, rather than empty project and so on. I'll come
back to that in a moment. What's going on here is that we have to add the references needed by this program.

In the Solution Explorer, right-click the References line under DialogHelloWorld and select Add Reference. This brings up a dialog with a tabbed window offering .NET, COM, and Projects. In .NET, we'll choose
System.Windows.Forms.dll, press the Select button, and then OK. Now the
program should compile, and it does. And it will run, bringing up a little message box that says "Hello, world!" (Depending on which solution you're using,
you may need to right-click the DialogHelloWorld project and select Set As
Start Project. In a solution, there can be many projects, but only one of them
will be started when you choose Debug/Start.)

Now if you're like me and this is your first time with C# and Microsoft
Visual Studio, these two simple things might not seem quite so simple. I'm too
embarrassed to take you through all the fumbling I did to find those simple
steps, even with the book right in front of me. If you're more experienced now
than I was then, I'm sure you're thanking me for not going through that painful
experience.

When we start from a blank project, we have to set up the references
more on our own than if we used one of the built-in projects.

(The first time I tried this, I was using the limited Visual Studio that comes
with C# at your local computer store, and it didn't offer the options that Petzold
was using. That caused me to fumble around more than I would like to. If
you're using that version of Visual Studio or working with a text editor and the
command line, you're on your own for a bit here. What you see here is based
on a full edition of Visual Studio.)

Petzold Notepad Version 1

Petzold's book includes a number of interesting yet simple form examples, showing how forms are displayed and closed, how to change some text, and so on. I worked through a couple of those just for fun. Petzold talks about the Application object, about events, and so on. Those concepts were familiar to me and probably are to you as well. And in the spirit of learning something about my real topic, which is an XML editor, I moved on to experiment with Petzold's example that builds a clone of the famous Windows Notepad application. (This was quite a jump—it's on page 847 of his book—but it's still a simple program.) And here it is, as I typed it into a new solution and project:

```
using System;
using System.Drawing;
using System.Windows.Forms;

namespace Notepad1
{
  class NotepadCloneNoMenu : Form
  {
    protected TextBox txtbox;

    public static void Main()
    {
      Application.Run(new NotepadCloneNoMenu());
    }

    public NotepadCloneNoMenu() {
      Text = "Notepad Clone No Menu";

      txtbox = new TextBox();
      txtbox.Parent = this;
      txtbox.Dock = DockStyle.Fill;
      txtbox.BorderStyle = BorderStyle.None;
      txtbox.Multiline = true;
      txtbox.ScrollBars = ScrollBars.Both;
      txtbox.AcceptsTab = true;
    }
  }
}
```

That's the program as Petzold provided it. In his book, he goes on to do things with the registry and then with menus. That's not my interest at the moment. I'm more interested in learning how to make a simple action at the keyboard insert XML characters. The action I have in mind is typing a control character. I'll experiment with that by creating a new class, XMLNotepad, that inherits from the NotepadCloneNoMenu class:

```
using System;
using System.Drawing;
using System.Windows.Forms;

namespace Notepad1
{
  class XMLNotepad : NotepadCloneNoMenu
  {
    [STAThread]
    static void Main(string[] args)
    {
      Application.Run(new XMLNotepad());
    }

    public XMLNotepad() {
      Text = "XML Notepad";
    }
  }
}
```

To make this work, I fumbled around in Visual Studio a fair amount, trying to learn about solutions and projects. And I had to remove the Main() method from the NotepadCloneNoMenu class to put it in mine. I'm trying to spare you the painful report of every mistake I made so that we can get down to the real work. The end result is a program with the same functionality as the original, except with a new Text property set into the top bar of the window. This is enough to show me that my subclass is up and running.

> **Lesson**   There's great value to reading the books and examples written by other people. I prefer books, in general, because they tend to hang together better than the separate articles we can find on the Web. Books are kind of expensive sometimes, but ask yourself what you'd pay for a good idea when you need one. Fifty bucks or so might be a bargain. On the other hand, when it gets down to learning how to do something more specific, you may not have a book that talks about that subject and it's very likely out there on the Web somewhere. See this book's Bibliography for a list of some of the resources I found along the way.

(continued)

There's some art to selecting spikes[2] to do, especially when working from a book. I skipped all over Petzold's book, trying things I didn't know, but always trying to focus on things that led me in the direction I was heading in: an editor for XML. When the book started to lead me off into menus, I could have continued, but it seemed like time to start adapting the ideas in the books to my own program. In general, I think it pays off to put things into the context of the problem we're trying to solve, as soon as we reasonably can.

I could have started modifying the original Petzold program instead of creating my own subclass. I chose to create the subclass for a few reasons. First, it allowed me to preserve Petzold's running code without change. I felt safer in doing that, in part because I haven't set up any code management software yet. Second, I frankly wanted to try subclassing in C#, just to get a feeling for it. Third, Petzold, in his later examples, uses subclasses based on this original class, so I assumed that it was a good idea, without a clear understanding of why. Later on in the book, you'll see that I reverse that decision and get rid of the Petzold class.

Lesson And here's a lesson about the previous lesson. As we go forward in this book, you'll see again and again that we try things. Some of them work and we keep them forever. Some of them work for a while and then get changed. Some don't work at all, and of course we don't keep them at all. I learned long ago that I make mistakes in designing things; I'd encounter trouble in programming when the design didn't bear up under the weight of reality. For a long time, I assumed that I needed to do more and better design. That's no longer my view. My view today is that it's better to start delivering useful software with a simple, clear design and to evolve the design as I go forward.

If you're like me, at first you'll fear that evolving the design will be inefficient or that you might reach some corner you can't get out of. This book is exploring what will happen if we do very little *design up front* and instead lots of *design all the time*. Please note that distinction: I'm not saying no to design. I'm saying to design all the time.

---

2. "Spike" is an Extreme Programming term meaning "experiment." We use the word because we think of a spike as a quick, almost brute-force experiment aimed at learning just one thing. Think of driving a big nail through a board.

Handling Keyboard Events

Building from the success thus far, I'm going to extend the XMLNotepad class to have a keyboard handler. As soon as I get the handler to fire and let me put something into the text, I'll consider this spike done and start working test first.[3] After this one little spike to learn about the keyboard, I think I'll be at a good point to stop and rest. Here goes...

Well, Petzold seemed to be suggesting that I could override OnKeyDown, but I couldn't make that work. What did work, after some more reading, is to set up a handler. The program now looks like this:

```
using System;
using System.Drawing;
using System.Windows.Forms;

namespace Notepad1
{
  class XMLNotepad : NotepadCloneNoMenu
  {
    [STAThread]
    static void Main(string[] args)
    {
      Application.Run(new XMLNotepad());
    }

    public XMLNotepad() {
      Text = "XML Notepad";
      txtbox.KeyDown += new KeyEventHandler(XMLKeyDownHandler);
    }
    void XMLKeyDownHandler(object objSender, KeyEventArgs kea) {
      if (kea.KeyCode == Keys.P && kea.Modifiers == Keys.Control) {
        txtbox.Text += "controlP";
        kea.Handled = true;
      }
    }
  }
}
```

---

3. "Test-first programming," or "test-driven development," is the phrase we use for a style of programming where we write new code only in response to a test we have written that does not work. Much of the work in this book will use that technique. Often, when doing a spike, I do not use test-driven style. You can help me decide, as we go forward, whether I should.

Lesson   This goofy little program just does one new thing. It works just like our previous notepad examples, unless you type Ctrl+P. In that case, the string "controlP" is appended to the textbox. Not very impressive, is it? And yet, this little spike embodies the essence of how the XML Notepad will work for most of this section of the book. You'll see that the Key Down handler will survive for a long time, providing more and more functionality to the program. So this trivial example has forged a link between the almost complete ignorance in which we started this chapter and a living, breathing program.

That's the essence of the spike concept. We try to hammer through our ignorance, not by building a complex, well-crafted program for the ages, but by finding something simple, ideally trivial, that bridges gaps in our knowledge. As we'll see, the experiments above told us enough to give our customer (that's us) some good information about what we can do now, and what we cannot as yet do.

Shaping the Release

An Extreme Programming team works in very small requirement chunks that we call stories. The best XP teams today are breaking work down into stories that can be accomplished in a couple of days yet that offer visible bits of business value to the customer. There can be a lot of skill to this, and while it isn't the main theme of this book, you'll get a feeling as we go forward for how to turn a large and complex requirement into small, simple things you can actually do.

Recall our initial vision of a wonderful WYSIWYG editor where you are editing right inside your browser. How do we begin to help the customer decide what our first release of software should be? The basic rule in XP is this: the customer decides what features would be of "business value." The programmers help the customer break down features into stories that are small enough to estimate, test, and implement. Then the programmers estimate the cost in time of doing each story. Based on her understanding of the value and the cost, the customer decides what will be worked on, in "iterations" of a week or two. At the end of each iteration, the programmers deliver to the customer running, tested code that implements the stories for that iteration.

Now we can't fully simulate that process here, and in fact our purpose is to explore how to build software in that short, iterative style and yet have a good design right along, not to simulate all the aspects of XP. But to do that, we had to select some stories to start with.

We did some reading and Web searching to find out about editing in a browser and about Rich Text Format. We believe that WYSIWYG editors such as Microsoft FrontPage are probably editing in a RichTextBox, or else they are rendering everything directly in graphics. The Petzold book shows code that displays various fonts with direct graphics, so we got a good sense of how hard that would be. Our conclusion was that direct rendering would be difficult and time consuming but not impossible. Our conclusion on Rich Text Format was that the specification is huge and hard to understand, but that the RichTextBox can surely do everything we would need for WYSIWYG display if that's what the customer wants. So we suggested to ourselves that a Rich Text Format pane might be a good approximation and perhaps much easier to implement, and we did a brief spike with an RTF pane to get a sense for what's possible. We found that the RTF format itself is far more complex than either XML or HTML.

Now the point of our software product is to deliver business value, which in this case means easier editing of the XML that makes up the Web pages of XProgramming.com. On the basis of what we know from our experience, including these spike experiments, we want to work out some detailed stories with our customer.

Stories for Initial Release

Extreme Programming teams deliver running, tested software to their customer frequently. How frequently? Every iteration,[4] which means every week or two weeks, depending on the chosen iteration size. Obviously we cannot implement the customer's vision in a week. What we can do is pull out the essential ideas that make up business value in the customer's mind and focus on implementing the most valuable and important features, or the features where the customer will learn the most about what he really wants.

We begin by summarizing for our customer what we have learned so far.

◼   **Rich Text Format is difficult.** We do not know how to edit a page that looks just like the target Web page, in place. We have two approaches that might work. We can use the RichTextBox control in .NET. This has the ability to display most anything we could want. The Rich Text Format language is complex and not easy to understand, though we can probably do most of what we need somewhat by rote, just putting canned text items into the page. The results

---

4. XP developers develop software in "iterations," fixed time boxes that are typically one or two weeks long. In every iteration, the team produces running, tested software that can be understood as offering business value to the customer. Not just infrastructure; real, running, somewhat useful software.

wouldn't look just like the resulting Web page, but it could be made to look pretty good. We believe that it will take a week or two of our time to get a credible example running and probably three days to do enough experimentation to provide a better estimate.

- **Direct rendering is also difficult.** In the Petzold book, we found lots of information about rendering various kinds of text directly into a simple form, and there is even information about how to draw lines and curves. We could use that approach to put together a simulated Web page. Like the Rich Text Format approach, it wouldn't look perfect, but it should be pretty good. We would need about three days to experiment with this, and we think it would take a week or two to get it running.

- **Editing the file.** Our experiment included the basic connection between the form and the keyboard. We just made the program enter "controlP" when a Ctrl+P was typed, but that was enough to tell us that we could readily make it insert <P></P> or other XML tags. We think we could build a little XML Notepad clone that did smart things as you type; each feature that was just a text edit would take a day or less. This wouldn't give a fancy display, but the user could use the existing approach of generating the HTML and looking at the results. An easier way to see the display could be done later. We think that would take a few days as well.

> **Lesson**   Notice the vagueness of these estimates, which is typical when we're starting out. Also notice that we have some easy stories and some stories that are much harder. Three times harder, perhaps even five or ten times harder. This level of understanding is usually enough to enable a team to figure out the next couple of weeks' effort at the beginning of a project.

Our basic recommendation to our customer is that we can make the editing job a lot easier by using a simple notepad approach, and that we can address the vision of the more beautiful WYSIWYG format later on. We're willing to go ahead with the graphical part first, but if we do we'll have to break it down into smaller one-week chunks. We think the simple editor approach is a good way to start, because the XML editing approach we are replacing is a neat little product named *TextPad* (*http://www.textpad.com/*) that we use to enter our XML. I'm typing into TextPad right now. We have a few TextPad macros defined such that getting to the next paragraph or heading isn't too hard. But TextPad doesn't understand what we're really up to.

We propose a starting version of the customer's vision that works like a smarter TextPad, one that understands a little more about what's going on and is more helpful with the editing. We talk about it and come up with the following stories:

- When we're typing a paragraph inside P tags and we hit Enter, create another P tag underneath this one and put the cursor in between the new tags in the right typing location.

- When we're typing inside P tags and we want the line to be, say, Heading 2, typing Ctrl+2 will remove the P tags and replace them with H2. When we hit Enter inside H2, create a P tag underneath the H2 line and put the cursor inside it.

- Same as H2 for H3.

- Start the editor (File/New) not on an empty page but on an empty template for my Web site. Put the cursor inside the first unfilled tag so that we can just start typing the title or whatever it is.

- When we type Tab in the editor, move the cursor to the next tag (or maybe the next unfilled tag). We'll have to try it to see what works best. Think of it as tabbing from field to field in a form.

At this point, we're not estimating these stories in much more detail beyond "OK" or "too hard." We think each of these can be done in about a day of work. Certainly none of the above are "too hard," unlike some of the ones in the initial vision. These stories are more than enough, we think, for our first iteration and first release. We agree with our customer to work on these.

Our customer is now imagining a product like TextPad. It's a Notepad-like product, but when the user types into it, the editor automatically updates the XML in ways that are more convenient, and more intelligent, than NotePad can do. We all know that the desire to view what the page will look like will come back. We also know, however, that the customer has a perfectly good, but not entirely convenient, way to do that now. We agree that the best first task is to get some editing working so that the customer can see that we're making progress.

Lesson   Now in a real XP project, with a live customer, full-time programmers, and so on, we would put together two plans at this point. The "Release Plan" would consist of looking at all the stories in the whole product, estimating each one, and laying them out on a table to see how long the whole project might take. We wouldn't be very accurate in the first couple of days, of course, but we'd be able to get a good sense of the project right away. And over time we would review and revise that Release Plan by using the results of our work so far to improve estimates.

In addition, we'd do an "Iteration Plan" at the beginning of each two-week iteration. That plan would include a bit more detail on each story, our envisioned tasks, who was planning to work on each one, and so on. Not a big deal, but some notes on the whiteboard to make sure the whole team has the same understanding.

The focus of this book, however, is on how the programmers develop useful software while learning. So we'll remark on things like the Iteration Plan, but our focus will be on figuring out what stories we can do, estimating them closely enough to be sure they're small enough, and then building the software in a way that shows value to the customer and keeps the design good and improving.

Subsequent Iterations and Releases

It's appropriate on every project to look ahead, and this one is no exception. We have just scratched the surface of what the customer might want. There will be the usual file operations: save, open, close, and so on. There will be edit operations like copy and paste, as well as lots of XML-oriented commands. We know that the customer will want to see the resulting Web page.

Like any other user, our customer has a long list of features he'd like to have. We'll learn to estimate how hard they are, and using that plus a sense of value, our customer will decide what's best for the Web site and for this book. All those things might be useful. They're all the sort of thing you'd find in a typical Marketing product plan. We think that some of these ideas might have value and some might not. As the project moves along, we'll keep you up to date on how our customer (one last time: that's us) thinks about investing in these features.

Tracking all the features of a complete product, even one as simple as the XML Notepad, would require a book much longer than this one. We'll limit ourselves here to enough stories to make the product seem real and to teach the lessons we want to offer.

Lesson: What Have We Learned So Far?

Even this early on, there are some lessons to call to your attention:

- **Simple estimation.** We did some simple estimation of the things our customer wanted. We suggested things to implement that should surely look like progress to our customer, while allowing us to focus on learning important and central things about how the app works. We steered away from fancy GUI stories that would look good but wouldn't focus on the real guts of the application.

- **Collaborate with our customer.** Now this was easy in our case, but the principles are the same. Make the customer aware of the cost of features and the risk associated with them. Then let them decide what we should work on.

- **Focus on delivery.** Even in our first iteration, we'll be delivering a customer story. We really don't know .NET or C# at this point. We could make a case that we need training and time to learn. And surely we'll go more slowly now than we will when we're more adept. But still, we focus each week's work on delivering something—anything—that the customer can see as progress.

- **Balance ambition with reality.** Everyone, when envisioning some new product idea, sees good things that will never happen. We just can't have everything—as Chet asks, where would we keep it? As programmers who have to deliver this stuff, we want to balance our customer's enthusiasm, and our own, with some reality. We do that not by being pessimistic and pushing back, but by estimating as accurately as we can and communicating our estimates, and our results, with the customers. We trust, based on long experience, that faced with the best possible information, they'll make the best possible decisions.

The XProgramming Format

Here's what part of this chapter looks like in the XProgramming XML format:

```xml
<?xml version="1.0"?>
<!DOCTYPE page SYSTEM "ron.dtd">
<page>

  <header index="yes">
  <topic name="acs"/>
  <date updated="no">20020710</date>
    <title>XML Notepad Stories</title>
    <author>Ron Jeffries</author>
    <precis>My colleague Chet Hendrickson and I are working with .NET and C#,
    to learn it, with the intention of writing the book you're holding in your
    hands. Our chosen application is the "XML Notepad." Here's the initial
    vision and some stories.</precis>
  </header>
  <contents/>
  <sect1><title>Building an Application Extreme-Programming Style</title>
  <P>In this book, we'll be working on a real application. Although the app
  will be small enough to fit in the book, it will be large enough, and tricky
  enough, to offer some important lessons about how a real application might
  go.</P>
  <P>As you know, I am a strong proponent of Extreme Programming and "agile"
  software development, so there will be a lot of XP-related discussion in the
  book. I'll also be drawing on my years of programming experience (much of it
  good), with the hope of bringing out some generally useful techniques.
  Finally, I'll be discovering, as we go, how to use the C# language and the
  Microsoft .NET tools.</P>
  <P>The book, therefore, is a journey of discovery, a journey led by an
  experienced guide who is nonetheless new to this specific territory. If we're
  lucky, I won't make a complete fool of myself!</P>
  <P>Our project begins, as most do, as a vague initial idea, followed shortly
  by an optimistic dream of what might be possible, followed by a long period
  of progress toward a goal that changes along the way. Extreme Programming has
  taught me some ways of dealing effectively with such things, and that's part
  of what we'll be looking at as we go along.</P>
  ...
  </sect1>
</page>
```

2

Testing with NUnit

Some tips and techniques for using NUnit, the testing framework used in this book.

Testing: A Core Practice

As you read this book, you'll see that we do a lot of testing. We write most of our tests before we write the code, one test at a time. A little test, a little code to make it work, and so on. We work that way for some good reasons, which you'll see as we go along:

- Most important, well-tested code works better. Customers like it better.

- Testing as we write means we spend less time debugging. We get our programs done faster.

- Testing as we write means that we don't have those long testing cycles at the end of our projects. We like working without that death march thing.

- Our tests are the first users of our code. We experience what it is like to use our code very quickly. The design turns out better.

- Tests support refactoring. Since we want to ship useful function early and often, we know that we'll be evolving the design with refactoring.

- Tests give us confidence. We're able to work with less stress, and we're not afraid to experiment as we go.

- Testing before coding is more interesting than testing after we code. Because it's interesting, we find it easier to maintain what we know is a good practice.

But I'm not here to sell testing; I'm here to tell you how we do it. Let's move along. We're going to start here with a moderately advanced example using regular expressions and the .NET Regex class. In the next chapter, which relates our first real efforts on the XML Notepad, you'll see that we return to an approach that is even simpler than Regex. Here, we're just experimenting with NUnit and learning a bit about Regex.

As we work with the XML Notepad, I'm expecting that we'll have to look at text strings a lot and figure out whether they have any XML tags in them. XML tags, as you probably know, come in matched pairs of strings embedded in squiggles: <SomeTag>like this</SomeTag>. Now .NET includes some powerful features for working with XML, and later on in the book we'll look at some of them. But we're here to learn C#, and part of that will mean digging down a little deeper into how things work. Since C# has some powerful support for regular expressions, I decided to learn a little about them.

Often when I experiment with something new, I just write some throwaway code that prints results to the console. Some good angel inspired me to do it this time by writing tests using NUnit, the .NET testing framework. The result, as you'll see, is some permanent information instead of just something that goes into my head, perhaps later to be forgotten. And something that others can learn from, making their job just a bit easier. Read on.

NUnit

In this book, we're testing with NUnit, a .NET testing framework written by Jim Newkirk, Michael Two, Alexei Vorontsov, and Charlie Poole, based on the original NUnit by Philip Craig. You can find it at *http://www.nunit.org*. NUnit is much the same as all the Extreme Programming test frameworks (xUnits), with two important differences:

1. NUnit uses the "attribute" feature of .NET to identify tests. As you'll see, test fixtures are identified by the attribute [TestFixture] and individual tests by [Test]. This means that you can write tests that don't inherit from a fixed TestCase superclass and NUnit can still find them. At first I thought this was just gratuitously different, but I'm finding that it works just fine and I rather like it.

2. NUnit allows you to write tests in any .NET language. So even though NUnit itself is written in C#, you can write your tests in Microsoft Visual Basic or C++ or, I suppose, even in ML or Eiffel. Language interoperation is a key characteristic of .NET and one that I consider to be quite important.

When you write tests using NUnit, you can run the NUnit application and it will run and report on your tests. There are two versions of the app, one that runs at the command prompt and a GUI version. I prefer the GUI version and will be using it throughout most of this book. When I say NUnit, I'm usually talking about that GUI, which looks like this:

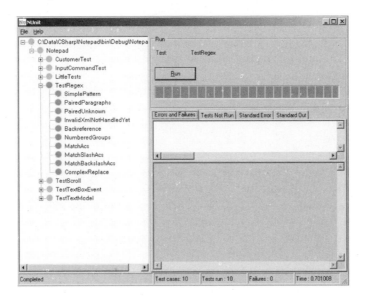

When you press the Run button, NUnit looks at your program, finds all the tests, and runs them. Each test fixture in your program has its own setup and tear-down methods, and each test case runs with a fresh setup. This means that your tests are all automatically independent and that NUnit will run them all. If the tests all run correctly, NUnit displays a green bar, as just shown. (Trust me, the bar in the graphic above is green.) If any of the tests don't run, the bar is red.

Extreme Programming teams write lots of tests, and the rule is that we release code back to the repository only if all the tests run correctly. This may seem like a big burden, but it turns out not to be. And imagine how confident you can be in your code if you have lots of tests and every one of them is working correctly!

But enough warmup. Let's take a look at what it's all about.

Setting Up NUnit

To write tests using NUnit, your project needs to reference the nunit.framework.dll. In Visual Studio, you click on the project and choose Add Reference. Then navigate to the nunit.framework DLL and select it. I keep nunit.framework.dll in the directory that holds all my .NET project directories, to make it easy to find.

The usual way to write tests is to set up a "test fixture," which is a class. The convention is to use a separate fixture for every test topic—for example, we'll have a fixture for our Regex tests. Since each fixture has only one setup and one teardown, all the tests in the class want to be somewhat alike, and usually we wind up with one or a few fixtures for each important class in our system. The basic test fixture class looks like this:

```
using System;
using NUnit.Framework;
using System.Text.RegularExpressions;

namespace Notepad
{
  [TestFixture] public class TestRegex : Assertion{
  }
}
```

The [TestFixture] is one of those attributes I was telling you about. It tells NUnit that this class has tests in it.

NUnit tests allow us to write "assertions," and it checks those assertions to see if they are true. So if we wanted to test whether 2+2 is 4, we might write

```
[Test] public void TwoPlusTwo {
  AssertEquals(4, 2+2);
}
```

NUnit has a number of different assertion methods for your convenience. We'll see more of them as we move on in the book. By far, the most commonly used one is AssertEquals().

We don't have to have the test fixture inherit from Assertion, as shown previously, but I prefer that because it means I can say AssertEquals rather than Assertion.AssertEquals. Note also in this example that I'm already showing the reference to System.Text.RegularExpressions. I have to do that to write any references to the Regex class. So we're all set to go.

Finding a Simple Pattern

Our mission in the grand scheme of things is to find XML tags in text. So our first test will just look for a paragraph tag, <p>, in a string.

```
[Test] public void SimplePattern() {
  Regex r = new Regex("<p>");
  Match m = r.Match("contains <p> here");
  Assert(m.Success);
  m = r.Match("contains no para");
  Assert(!m.Success);
}
```

So. There's the [Test] attribute, telling NUnit this is a test method. We create a Regex that searches for <p>, then test it against two strings. We expect the first to succeed and the second to fail. (As far as I can tell, the Match class doesn't have a Failure property, only a Success property.)

If you're not familiar with C#, notice that the code says m.Success, not m.Success(). C# has methods, which take parenthesized lists of arguments (sometimes null), and "properties," which act like instance variables, with setters and getters. They can be implemented with member variables or any other way you might like. They aren't member variables, they just act that way.

OK, we get a Green Bar, and we have a running Regex test now. The reality was almost that easy, even though the only documentation I had was the C# Help, which is comprehensive but not easy to dig through.

Lesson   Now, to some people, that test may seem too simple. You'll want to find your own balance, but I always make my first test really simple. Sometimes I even write a test that just says `Assert(true)` to get things going. I do that for a few reasons. First of all, it takes a little discipline to do testing, even when I do them first. So I like to make it easy to get started. Second, for me, the first tests usually include a lot of learning about something new, and rather than spend time debugging, I'm perfectly happy to start with something trivial. It takes only a moment to do, and it starts me off on the right foot. Third, sometimes even the simplest test I can think of doesn't work. The simpler it is, the sooner I'll figure out what it is I'm missing about whatever I'm testing. I'd suggest that you try tests ranging from very simple to more difficult and see what works best for you. But please do try trivial tests— they're surprisingly useful.

Lesson   It occurs to me as I write this that in the course of this book, you'll probably encounter examples of doing things in ways that seem almost obtusely simple. I assure you that I'm not doing it to make the book suitable for third-graders, nor because I myself am also simple. I work that way because in the half-dozen years I've been doing Extreme Programming, I've been working in simpler and simpler ways, and my work seems to be getting better and better. So, please, when you see something here that looks odd, give it a try. Often I think you'll find it interesting.

Paired Tags

OK, enough advertising. Let's do another test.

In XML, tags must always be paired and properly nested, unlike HTML, which is more liberal. So in a legal paragraph in XML, we have a leading <p> and a trailing </p>. We'll write a test to see if we can recognize such a string.

```
[Test] public void PairedParagraphs() {
  Regex r = new Regex("<p>.*</p>");
  Match m = r.Match("<p>this is a para</p>");
  Assert(m.Success);
}
```

So there we are. The Regex looks for a p tag, an un-p tag, as I call them, and anything in between. (In Regex, dot means "any character," and star means "any number of the preceding.") Again, we get the green bar. I'm having good luck so far, maybe because I've done some stuff with regular expressions in Ruby and read most of the famous regular expressions book, *Mastering Regular Expressions*, by Jeffrey E. F. Friedl (O'Reilly & Associates, 2002). The next problem, though, gets a bit trickier, and as we'll see, I have some problems with it.

Paired Unknown Tags

OK, tags come in pairs, and there's stuff in between them. I want to see if I can recognize two tags at once and pull out the stuff in the middle. Here's the test as it wound up; we'll talk about how it got that way.

```
[Test] public void PairedUnknown() {
  Regex r = new Regex("<(?<prefix>.*)>(?<body>.*)</(?<suffix>.*)>");
  Match m = r.Match("<p>this is a para</p>");
  Assert(m.Success);
  AssertEquals("p",m.Groups["prefix"].Value);
  AssertEquals("p",m.Groups["suffix"].Value);
  AssertEquals("this is a para",m.Groups["body"].Value);
  m = r.Match("<H2>this is a heading</H2>");
  Assert(m.Success);
  AssertEquals("H2",m.Groups["prefix"].Value);
  AssertEquals("H2",m.Groups["suffix"].Value);
  AssertEquals("this is a heading",m.Groups["body"].Value);
}
```

Here I got into a little trouble trying to build this up. I knew that I wanted three "groups" in regular expressions, one for each section of the input: the leading tag, the content, the closing tag. In the kinds of expressions I'm used to, the expression would have been something like this:

```
"(<.*>)(.*)(</.*>)"
```

That means there are three groups, in the parens. The first is a less than, any sequence of characters, and a greater than. The second is any sequence of characters. The third is a less than, any sequence, and a greater than. This isn't good enough to last for the ages. We'll probably want to have the sequences inside the tags not include a greater than, and so on. But it seemed enough to start with. So I tried that sequence exactly. I couldn't figure out how to make it work. I was trying things like

```
AssertEquals("p", m.Groups(0).Value);
```

which turns out not to be right. I finally dug through the help and found an example. .NET Regex allows you to specify the groups to have names, as shown in the ?<prefix> and similar strings. It still didn't work. The only example I had was in Visual Basic. I guess that Visual Basic does subscripting with parentheses, not square brackets. When I finally figured out what the C# compiler was complaining about and entered the syntax as shown in the example, the test worked.

So the Groups property is a collection of groups. It is indexable by name (and it turns out, by integer) and returns a Group when you index into it. That Group has a Value attribute, which is the string matched.

> **Lesson**   A key thing is happening in this test. We might have been doing this experimentation with print statements. In fact, I actually did some to find out what was coming out of these methods, when all else failed. But then I turned them back into tests. These tests are documenting for me (and for you) what I've learned so far about how to work Regex. It's not the whole story, but the story begins to take shape. I can look back at these tests and remind myself how things are supposed to work, in a way that actual code using the Regex might not. Here, I see what the exact inputs are and what the outputs are. Very clear, no need to deduce what's up.

OK, now we have a regular expression that includes opening and closing tags, and we can extract which tag it found and what was between the tags. Good stuff. Still not robust enough, but nearly enough for now. To make it more robust, what we might want is to ensure that the closing tag matches the opening one (H2 and /H2, and so on). I think there's a way to do that with .NET Regex, but I've not gotten there yet. One last test for now. I still want to understand a bit better how those Groups work. I think that if I leave the names off, I should be able to index by integers. After a little fiddling around, and some more printing as I went, I got this test to work:

```
[Test] public void NumberedGroups() {
    Regex r = new Regex("<(.*)>(.*)</(.*)>");
    Match m = r.Match("<p>this is a para</p>");
    Assert(m.Success);
    // foreach(Group g in m.Groups){
    //     Console.WriteLine(g.Value);
    // }
    AssertEquals("<p>this is a para</p>",m.Groups[0].Value);
    AssertEquals("p",m.Groups[1].Value);
    AssertEquals("p",m.Groups[3].Value);
    AssertEquals("this is a para",m.Groups[2].Value);
}
```

You see what I learned. Group 0 is the whole matched string. I believe that if there was extra stuff outside the tags, it wouldn't be included in this. Maybe I'll write another test to verify that, or modify this one. And the groups are then in order, 1, 2, 3. It all makes sense. I can't remember for sure, but I think my original problems, solved with the named groups in the preceding test, all came from not knowing the syntax for the Groups methods. So I got the more sophisticated way to work first and then backed into the simple solution I had been working toward to begin with.

Unmatched Tags

In the previous matching tag examples, my input has matched p and H2 tags, and the Regex finds them just fine. However, there's nothing in the regular expression itself that requires the opening and closing tags to match. I'm going to add a test that shows that unmatched tags will still pass this Regex, and then see if I can figure out how to require them to match. I seem to remember that there's a way to do that with the Regex class. Here's the new test:

```
[Test] public void InvalidXmlNotHandledYet() {
    Regex r = new Regex("<(?<prefix>.*)>(?<body>.*)</(?<suffix>.*)>");
    Match m = r.Match("<p>this is a para</H2>");
    Assert(m.Success);
    AssertEquals("p",m.Groups["prefix"].Value);
    AssertEquals("H2",m.Groups["suffix"].Value);
}
```

Just as expected, the same Regex matches a p followed by an H2. Not what we really want, but we want to be sure we understand what our code does. This test now motivates the next extension, to a Regex that does force the tags to match. I'm not sure we will need this—we may already have gone beyond our current need for regular expressions, but my mission here is to learn as much as I can, in a reasonable time, about how Regex works. Now I'll have to search the Help a bit. Hold on...

The documentation seems to suggest that you can have named backreferences, using \k. I'll write a test. Hold on again... All right! Worked almost the first time: just a simple mistake away from perfect. Here's the new test:

```
[Test] public void Backreference() {
    Regex r = new Regex("<(?<prefix>.*)>(?<body>.*)</\\k<prefix>.*>");
    Match m = r.Match("<p>this is a para</p>");
    Assert(m.Success);
    m = r.Match("<p>this is a para</H2>");
    Assert(!m.Success);
}
```

In this test, notice that we had to type \\k to get the \k into the expression. This is because C# strings, like most languages' strings, already use the backslash to prefix newlines and other special characters. We have to type two of them to get one backslash into the string. The amazing thing is that I actually remembered to do that the first time! The mistake? I left the word "suffix" there instead of saying \k<prefix>, as was my intent.

What's Left?

We're in pretty good shape for regular expressions now, though there are a number of things we might want to learn about. One complication is that you can apparently get all the matches that are possible when a pattern matches several times on one string. I have no immediate use for that, so probably won't go there. Another complication is that Regex has a Replace method that will produce a new string with a replacement done based on the pattern. We'll probably need that one, when we replace a p-tagged string with an H2-tagged string. I'm bored with this game right now, so will leave the Replace tests until I get that story.

Wait! I Just Thought...

In the example above, I have the \k, but it's followed by a .* left over from the original pattern. I bet that's redundant in this case. I'll change the test to remove that and see if it still runs. Sure enough, it still works. The backreference eats all the characters, given the pattern we have. I bet you could do some tricky things with that feature, such as embedding backreferences in other patterns, but I'm not going to mess with that for now. For the record, here's the final version of the test. The only difference is the removal of the .* after the second occurrence of <prefix>.

```
[Test] public void Backreference() {
  Regex r = new Regex("<(?<prefix>.*)>(?<body>.*)</(\\k<prefix>)>");
  Match m = r.Match("<p>this is a para</p>");
  Assert(m.Success);
  m = r.Match("<p>this is a para</H2>");
  Assert(!m.Success);
}
```

> **Lesson**   That's enough playing with Regex for now. What have we learned? What we have here is a small set of tests that were used to learn how to use Regex, and that now document that learning so that I can refer to it later and so that other programmers, like Chet when he sees this, can learn from it as well. It took a little more discipline to start testing Regex instead of just doing little experiments with printing, but to me the payoff is clear: this material can be used to pass on the learning to others and to my future forgetful self. I think it's worth it, and I commend the idea to your attention.

A Short Look at Debugging Under NUnit

My standard way of using NUnit is in its stand-alone GUI form. The NUnit GUI runs as a separate program that is looking at your program. When you press the button, NUnit runs your tests and displays the results in its panes. My usual work cycle is to write or enhance a test, make it work, run the tests, and repeat. The cycle, for me, is quite short: usually less than ten minutes, often only two.

Working this way, I really don't get many bugs and I don't often get confused. That's good, because I don't like hunting for bugs and I don't like being confused. Both slow me down. Sometimes, though, it's hard to write a test for something. Often this happens when I'm using some .NET object that I'm not familiar with and I don't know what kind of result it's going to give me back.

My first reaction is often to do a Console.WriteLine to see what is going on. NUnit displays the console output right in one of its panes, and I build my software—even forms software—in console mode, so this works pretty well. But it has its limitations, as we'll see.

Now of course Visual Studio has strong debugging capabilities, and you can set breakpoints, run your program, stop at the breakpoints, and look around. You can inspect variables, step the program, and so on. It's all good. Sometimes in working with the XML Notepad, I've done that to figure out what was going on. But I always lean away from using the debugger. For me, it is a potential trap, a slippery slope. All too many times in the past, I have written vast amounts of code and then spent hours in the debugger trying to make it work. The test-driven style I use now, which you're seeing in this book, allows me to work at a more constant rate of progress, without those long, frustrating, high-pressure debugging sessions. I'm afraid that if I get too good at using the debugger, I might fall back into bad habits. So I've held off on learning to use debuggers. I've been programming in Ruby for two years or more, don't know how to use its debugger at all, and don't miss it a bit. Still, Visual Studio's debugger can be helpful at times, and you can use it a few ways in conjunction with NUnit. Let's look at a couple of them.

The Debug Startup Program

Visual Studio understands a number of configurations of your program. In particular, it understands a "production" configuration and a "debug" one. You can set up your debug configuration to start up a new copy of NUnit. So if you set a breakpoint and then start with debugging, NUnit will run. You can select the test of interest in the NUnit GUI, then run, and—voila!—you get the breakpoint you were interested in.

To set up your startup program, check the Help in Visual Studio for Modifying Project Properties And Configuration Settings. Don't expect it to be entirely accurate, however. It's not in my version, though it is close. Here's how to do it in my Visual Studio, "Microsoft Development Environment 2002, Version 7.0.9466."

Select the project in the Solution Explorer. Bring up the project Properties, via a right-click on the project name or via the Project menu. Click Configuration Properties, Debugging. You'll get a window like this:

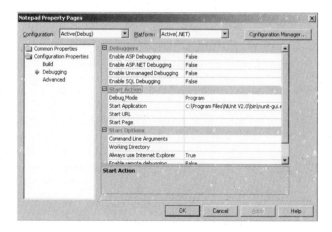

Set the window as shown. Under Debug Mode, select Program. Then, under Start Application, use the little "..." button to browse to the NUnit-GUI.exe file and select it. Apply or OK the window. From now on, when you do Debug/Start, or press F5, NUnit will start up. Works fine.

Attach to the NUnit Process

Visual Studio can attach to a running process and debug it. At this writing, I have no idea how this works, but I can tell you how to make it do something you might want. Start the NUnit GUI if it isn't already running. Select the Visual Studio menu item Debug/Processes. This will bring up a Processes window:

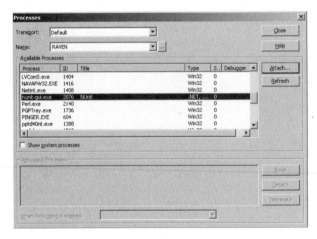

Scroll to find nunit-gui.exe, click it, and press Attach. This will bring up a window that looks like this:

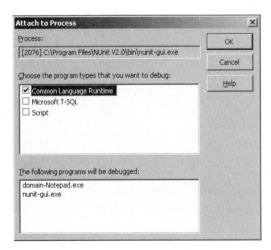

Select Common Language Runtime (at least), press OK, and close the Debug Processes window. Now you can set a breakpoint in Visual Studio, go to the NUnit GUI, run a test, and, badda-bing badda-boom, you're at your breakpoint.

Using this technique, if you rebuild your app, the connection to the NUnit process is broken, so you'll have to reset it.

Choosing a Technique

The Debug Startup technique takes more clicks to set up, but once it's done, you can always set a breakpoint and start a new NUnit by using Debug/Start. Attaching to the process is a bit easier, but it works only until the next time you build the project. I prefer the first way but often work for days without using either one. Try them both, and choose your favorite.

Summary

Almost all the code in this book will be developed with associated tests in NUnit. I expect that you'll see that working this way serves well to keep the problems small, keep the code working, and make the code easy to improve. Once in a while, we'll be working without tests, either because we can't figure out how to write a test or because we get lazy. If that happens, I bet there will be bugs in the code.

Because this is a book about learning, if there are bugs, we're going to let you see them. Assess whether our bugs would have been reduced by writing more or better tests. My bet right now is that you'll come to see how effective the testing approach is. That's not all we're here to learn, but it's one thing that will come out.

Installing NUnit into your .NET development process is quite easy. It should take only an hour or so to write your first test. And I hope you'll try it and never stop.

3

A Pressing Matter

Today Chet and I spent a couple of hours working on the XML notepad GUI. We learned a lot, some of it useful.

The First Story

When Chet came over today, we decided to begin our work on the first story for the XML Notepad. We had a running sample that fields events, and our plan was to implement the following story:

> *When the user types Enter, space down an extra line, create an empty P tag pair, and place the cursor in the middle of the tag, as shown here:*

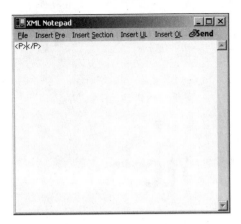

It seemed easy enough: our prototype already fields several control characters, which we used to display values from the TextBox control on the console, to get a better sense of what is happening in the XMLNotepad form code. (We could perhaps have used tests, as we did in Chapter 2, "Testing with NUnit," but the TextBox was more of a spike to learn to make the GUI code work.) Here's the code we started with, inheriting from the Petzold notepad spike we showed you in the previous chapter:

```
using System;
using System.Drawing;
using System.Windows.Forms;
using Nunit.Framework;
using System.Collections;
namespace Notepad
{
  class XMLNotepad : NotepadCloneNoMenu
  {
    [STAThread]
    static void Main(string[] args)
    {
      Application.Run(new XMLNotepad());
    }
    public XMLNotepad() {
      Text = "XML Notepad";
      txtbox.KeyDown += new KeyEventHandler(XMLKeyDownHandler);
    }
    void XMLKeyDownHandler(object objSender, KeyEventArgs kea) {
      if (kea.KeyCode == Keys.P && kea.Modifiers == Keys.Control) {
        txtbox.Text += "controlP";
        kea.Handled = true;
      }
```

```
if (kea.KeyCode == Keys.L && kea.Modifiers == Keys.Control) {
  String[] lines = txtbox.Lines;
  foreach ( String s in lines) {
    Console.WriteLine(s);
  }
  kea.Handled = true;
    }
  }
 }
}
```

We talked about how to do it. I had been experimenting with a TextManipulator object that I thought could wrap a TextBox control and let us write methods against it. I'd been thinking the TextManipulator would then become the model for the Notepad. As I tried to explain to Chet what I had done, it became clear that while I had probably learned some useful things, it wasn't time to commit to using that object, because the code didn't need it, nor did it point in just that direction. So our plan was to work directly in the Windows.Form, right inside the event handlers, until the code told us what it wanted to be like.

Lesson   If you're like me, you can't stop writing chunks of code that seem like they will be useful someday. And if you're like me, they often seem good enough to start using them, even if they don't exactly fit into the system, because we're sure they'll be useful later. I believe that the better thing to do is to keep the learning in our head, and maybe even in our file directories, but generally not in the system. The system should always have in it just the functionality that has been delivered to the customer and the simplest well-designed code needed to support that functionality. We should try not to put in generality before it's needed.

We've probably all said something like "It will be cheaper if we put in this generality now; it will be harder to put in later." XP practices teach us that this isn't as true as we think. In this book, as we go forward, be watching for two things. First, watch to see if we get in trouble later because we didn't put in something more general than we needed at the moment. Second, watch to see what happens when we do put in more generality than is strictly needed. See whether we make mistakes and need to change it later. Then find your own balance.

(continued)

> There's another advantage to you, the reader, taking the approach of putting things into the GUI at the beginning. This application is almost all GUI. It's nothing but a little text editor, with practically no interesting functionality, at least not yet. So what you'll get to see is how we write the code, test it, refactor it, and even write acceptance tests for our customer. We expect to wind up with a good design that separates GUI functionality from "model"—text manipulation—functionality. We expect that good design to emerge, gradually and naturally. We may be crazy, so watch carefully to see what happens.

Handling the Enter

All that glorious emergent design comes later. Here's what happened in our first couple of hours.

We had some starting code for handling events, which we moved into our XMLNotepad class from the Petzold prototype discussed previously. Here's our handler:

```
void XMLKeyDownHandler(object objSender, KeyEventArgs kea) {
  if (kea.KeyCode == Keys.P && kea.Modifiers == Keys.Control) {
    txtbox.Text += "controlP";
    kea.Handled = true;
  }
  if (kea.KeyCode == Keys.L && kea.Modifiers == Keys.Control) {
    String[] lines = txtbox.Lines;
    foreach ( String s in lines) {
      Console.WriteLine(s);
    }
    kea.Handled = true;
  }
}
```

> Lesson   The highlighted if statement referring to "Keys.P" is the code that handles Ctrl+P for our prototype. All it does is add the string "controlP" to the text, when you type Ctrl+P. You probably remember that from Chapter 1, "XML Notepad Stories." As dumb as it looks, I'd like to remind us again that this is a good example of a well-chosen "spike." (A "spike" is what we call a simple experiment aimed at learning how to do something. Think of driving a big spike through a board.) The other if

statement is one we put in to display the TextBox contents on the console, for fun and for debugging.

This simple code does at least four valuable things in just a few lines:

1. It teaches us how to hook a KeyDown event.
2. It teaches us how to distinguish a Ctrl+P from a regular P.
3. It teaches us how to programmatically add text to the TextBox.
4. It teaches us how to tell Microsoft Windows that we have handled the key—or at least we thought it did.

When we're trying to learn how something works, we don't fiddle around trying to get something important implemented. Instead, we take little tiny bites, trying to learn the most while typing the least. Since we don't know what we're doing, by definition, the less code we write, the less we'll confuse ourselves. And we're easily confused when we're trying something we've never done before. Maybe you are, as well.

So, based on that spike, the handling of Enter for our story gave us these simple tasks:

1. Write an Enter KeyDown handler just like the Ctrl+P one.

2. Figure out what line has the cursor.

3. Create a new line array with all the lines up to that one, followed by a blank line, followed by a line with <P></P>, followed by all the remaining lines.

4. Set the cursor in between those P tags.

It seemed easy enough. We wrote the handler in the obvious way, referring to kea.KeyCode==Keys.Enter. No problem. Only thing was, we needed the code to get the CursorLine. I had written some experimental code to figure out which line had the cursor, and I was going to extract that into a method, but Chet had a better idea: "Just write the CursorLine method to return a constant. That will tell us if the code works." So we had the handler, and a CursorLine method, like this:

```
if (kea.KeyCode == Keys.Enter) {
  String[] lines = txtbox.Lines;
  int cursorLine = CursorLine();
```

```
      String[] newlines = new String[lines.Length+2];
      for(int i = 0; i <= cursorLine; i++) {
        newlines[i] = lines[i];
      }
      newlines[cursorLine+1] = "";
      newlines[cursorLine+2] = "<P></P>";
      for (int i = cursorLine+1; i < lines.Length; i++) {
        newlines[i+2] = lines[i];
      }
      txtbox.Lines = newlines;
      kea.Handled = true;
    }
    ...
private int CursorLine() { return 3; }
```

This code is pretty straightforward. We get the lines from the TextBox and get the cursor line, by cheating for now. We copy the lines from the beginning up through the cursor line, add our two new lines, and copy the rest of the lines. Then we slam the lines back into the TextBox and report that we handled the event.

As I look at that code now, it doesn't express our intention very well. It would have been better to write it expressing intention because it had a few bugs in it before we got it right: various off-by-one errors. We'll give some examples of that later on, but that's not the core of tonight's tale.

(Note during editing: Looking at this code much later, as I edit the book, I realize that there are surely ways that ArrayList or Array class could have helped with this. We didn't know it at the time. Let's watch to see whether we write better code later and whether this code ever gets cleaned up.)

It Didn't Work!

Well, it almost worked, but it didn't. What happened was that the text was added in the right place, but an extra newline was added. We saw quickly that it must be the newline that would have been added in a normal TextBox. But we're signaling that we handled the key, with that kea.Handled = true. Why are we getting an extra return?

We fiddled around a bit. We thought maybe that when we typed Enter, Windows was sending an Enter character and a LineFeed character, so we wrote a handler for that. That wasn't it. We thought maybe the TextBox used KeyUp instead of KeyDown, so we converted to that. That didn't help: we kept getting that extra newline. At some point we realized that whenever we typed any control character into our original prototype, the "bell" would ring, even when it was one of the characters that we were handling. That told us that our handlers were really not suppressing the handling of things by the TextBox. That realization didn't solve the problem, but it told us that either we had a generic kind of bug in our code or something was going on we didn't understand.

A bunch of digging through the TextBox documentation showed us that there was another event besides KeyUp and KeyDown, namely KeyPress. It turns out that Microsoft has this other event that abstracts the idea of key up and down into "this key was pressed" and produces three events for each key action: Down, Press, then Up. Wonderful. It also turns out that KeyPress doesn't use those nice mnemonic key definitions: it returns a char type. We suppose that's some historical deal, since the Up and Down events are so nicely object-oriented.

Anyway, we wrote a KeyPress event handler that checks for Enter and indicates that we had handled the event. It makes the extra line go away, and it looks like this:

```
void XMLKeyPressHandler(object objSender, KeyPressEventArgs kea) {
    int key = (int) kea.KeyChar;
    if (key == (int) Keys.Enter) {
        kea.Handled = true;
    }
}
```

From now on, when you see that second handler, you'll know why it's there. We decided to use the KeyDown handler for the bulk of our work because we prefer the interface that lets us refer to the keys by name. Still, this "solution" is fairly ugly, and we posted a note on the C# newsgroup (microsoft.public.dotnet.languages.csharp) for a better way to do it. If we get an answer, we'll change it and let you know. All that the code actually does, however, is indicate to Windows that the Enter has been handled. The result was the code working as expected: hit Enter and it inserts the two desired lines, after line 3, because CursorLine() always returns 3. So we went back and wrote a real CursorLine() method:

```
private int CursorLine() {
    String[] lines = txtbox.Lines;
    txtbox.SelectionLength = 0;
    int start = txtbox.SelectionStart;
    int length = 0;
    int lineFound = 0;
    int lineNr = 0;
    foreach ( String s in lines) {
        if (length <= start && start <= length+s.Length + 2 ) {
            lineFound = lineNr;
        }
        length += s.Length + 2;
        lineNr++;
    }
    return lineFound;
}
```

This isn't pretty, but it works. It's looping over the lines and checking to see if the cursor position is between the beginning and end of each line. The +2 handles the CrLf at the end of each line. We suspect there might be a better algorithm, and cleaner C# code, and we'll try to clean it up before we're done. If we don't, you can write us an email and ask why we didn't. But for now it works, so we're going with it.

We were quite tired by now, since we had been going at it for a couple of hours and had been beating our heads against some unknown API thing for much of it, and we decided to call it a day.

Lesson: What Have We Learned?

Quite a bit. We have code, rough as it is, to figure out what line the cursor is on. We have code, rough as it is, to compute a new line collection. We have handled the keyboard events, and although we don't like what we had to do, we're now sure that we can do all the control sequences that the application needs to do, at least for the basic editing stories.

So far, this code isn't very good, and that needs to be improved. But our story isn't done: we still have to set the cursor to the correct new location, task 4. We've done only a couple of hours' work so far, so we feel it's OK that it isn't sweet yet. More important, though, is the fact that we've been running without tests, other than visual ones. We feel a lot of fear when we work without tests, but we didn't know how to do the GUI stuff test first, and we felt it was better to learn how to do what we had to do. We'll rectify the testing problem tomorrow, I expect.

I'd feel much better if we had known how to do today's exercise test first, but we didn't. If you have any ideas, let us know and we'll try it next time. As the book goes on, I'm sure you'll see some better examples of how to test this sort of thing. At this point, we just didn't know enough C# to do it.

What's Next?

We'll start cleaning up this code. And we'll show you how to extract this GUI code off to a testable space. And—watch for this—we'll do an acceptance test. That's right: an automated acceptance test for a GUI application. Can we do it? Stay tuned.

4

Extracting the Model

Our XMLNotepad spike worked well enough to make us think we should start putting it in the right shape. That didn't turn out quite like we expected...

Where We Were

We had a little XMLNotepad prototype working: we could edit in the window, and when we hit Enter, we got a new section with paired P tags. We hadn't yet put the cursor where we wanted it, between the tags, but we knew how to do that. Now we thought we should put the code in better order. Here's what it looked like when we started, with a few debugging additions compared to the last time you saw the code:

```
using System;
using System.Drawing;
using System.Windows.Forms;
using Nunit.Framework;
using System.Collections;
using System.Text.RegularExpressions;
namespace Notepad
{
  class XMLNotepad : NotepadCloneNoMenu
  {
    static void Main(string[] args)
    {
      Application.Run(new XMLNotepad());
    }
    public XMLNotepad() {
      Text = "XML Notepad";
      txtbox.KeyDown += new KeyEventHandler(XMLKeyDownHandler);
      txtbox.KeyPress += new KeyPressEventHandler(XMLKeyPressHandler);
    }
```

```
private int CursorLine() {
  String[] lines = txtbox.Lines;
  txtbox.SelectionLength = 0;
  int start = txtbox.SelectionStart;
  int length = 0;
  int lineFound = 0;
  int lineNr = 0;
  foreach ( String s in lines) {
    if (length <= start && start <= length+s.Length + 2 ) {
      lineFound = lineNr;
    }
    length += s.Length + 2;
    lineNr++;
  }
  return lineFound;
}
void XMLKeyPressHandler(object objSender, KeyPressEventArgs kea) {
  int key = (int) kea.KeyChar;
  if (key == (int) Keys.Enter) {
    kea.Handled = true;
  }
}
void XMLKeyDownHandler(object objSender, KeyEventArgs kea) {
  if (kea.KeyCode == Keys.P && kea.Modifiers == Keys.Control) {
    txtbox.Text += "controlP";
    kea.Handled = true;
  }
  if (kea.KeyCode == Keys.Enter) {
    String[] lines = txtbox.Lines;
    Console.WriteLine("LineCount {0}", txtbox.Lines.Length);
    int cursorLine = CursorLine();
    String[] newlines = new String[lines.Length+2];
    for(int i = 0; i <= cursorLine; i++)  {
      newlines[i] = lines[i];
    }
    newlines[cursorLine+1] = "";
    newlines[cursorLine+2] = "<P></P>";
    for (int i = cursorLine+1; i < lines.Length; i++) {
      newlines[i+2] = lines[i];
    }
    txtbox.Lines = newlines;
    kea.Handled = true;
    Console.WriteLine("LineCount {0}", txtbox.Lines.Length);
  }

  // debugging keys
  if (kea.KeyCode == Keys.L && kea.Modifiers == Keys.Control) {
    String[] lines = txtbox.Lines;
```

```
    foreach ( String s in lines) {
      Console.WriteLine(s);
    }
    kea.Handled = true;
  }
  if (kea.KeyCode == Keys.S && kea.Modifiers == Keys.Control) {
    txtbox.SelectionLength = 0;
    kea.Handled = true;
  }
  if (kea.KeyCode == Keys.Q && kea.Modifiers == Keys.Control) {
    Console.WriteLine("cursor: {0}", CursorLine());
    kea.Handled = true;
  }
    }
  }
}
```

You'll note a few debug lines just above. Ctrl+S sets the selection length to zero, and Ctrl+Q displays the current cursor position. I used these to get an understanding of how the TextBox handles the cursor position and the selection. Nothing to see here, move on.

This isn't a very good design. All our operational code is in the Form object, in the KeyDownHandler, and we're working directly with the TextBox. The single Form object is handling the display of the data, the keyboard processing, and the actual text processing. Objects should have one and only one purpose, so this is two too many. Chet and I set out to create a new object to serve as the "model" in a Model View Controller (MVC) triad.[1] Our problems turned out to be many. First, we are too new with C# to be sure how (or even whether) to set up MVC in .NET. Second, we aren't facile enough yet with events and delegation to be sure how to proceed. Still, we need to clean up this code, and this will be a chance to show you how we clean up a design without having a grand design objective in mind.

The Basic Plan

Take a look at that XMLKeyDownHandler method. It is fielding and decoding the keys typed to see if it likes them, but it's also doing actual work for the application. Most of it now is just debugging and information-providing methods, but take a look at the highlighted Keys.Enter case, for example. This code is manipulating the contents of the Textbox as follows:

---

1. MVC is one of a handful of well-known patterns for separating GUI functionality from system functionality. Its details are out of scope for us here, especially since we didn't use the pattern. As you'll see, we do wind up, over time, with a fairly good separation of functionality.

1. Get the lines from the Textbox.

2. Figure out where the cursor is.

3. Allocate a new line buffer with room for two more lines.

4. Copy all the lines up to the cursor line.

5. Insert a blank line and one with a P tag.

6. Copy the rest of the lines into the buffer.

7. Set the Textbox text to the new lines.

Look at the code; can you see where it does those seven things? You'll be able to figure it out. But why should we have to figure out what code does? Why doesn't the code *say* what it does? We call that [sb]"expressing intention."

We look at this code, and we realize that we haven't clearly expressed our intention in writing it. Perhaps even worse is that this functionality is all about manipulating the Textbox and not at all about being part of the form. That suggests that we want a new object, which we'll call a TextModel, to start handling the text processing.

Reflecting on what we would have to do to build this, one issue that Chet and I worried about was that the way it works now, the TextModel would have to have a reference to the view, or else the Form would have to rip stuff out of the Textbox and jam it into the TextModel and rip stuff out of the TextModel and jam it into the view. Both of these seemed wrong.

Lesson   We could have stopped at this point and done some heavy design to figure out a really good way to do this. That would have stopped our progress on the actual project, which is to get the Enter key working and to have an acceptable design. We aren't entirely comfortable continuing with everything jammed together, but we don't feel that we should delay progress while we figure out a perfect design. This is a tradeoff we have to make every day: is our work good enough but not so good that we are wasting time?

It will turn out, as the code evolves, that a good design will emerge, and if we had more experience, we might have seen it right away. Our unfamiliarity with .NET and the way that events work caused us not to see the solution, so watch as we go forward to see how the design continues to improve. For now, Chet and I decided to do the refactoring we could see, because we're sure that breaking this function out into a separate TextModel object will help.

One more thing: if you know more C# than we did at the time we wrote the code above, you're probably wondering why we weren't using an ArrayList or some other more capable data structure. At the time, we didn't know much about ArrayList, and since the TextBox uses an array, we had gone down that path. Of course it's always good to know more, but this book isn't about what we should have known, or what you should know—it's about what we do with what we know, to make the code better and better and better.

Chet and I actually fiddled with this a couple of different ways. I'll spare you our false starts. What we finally decided was that our TextModel wanted to think of the text as an array of lines, and that it would be fed the lines by the Form and have the lines taken back by the Form when processing was done. We realized that every time we called the model, we'd have to give it the lines, and although that is grossly inefficient, we had no measurement that showed it was even noticeable in the real world. So we decided to live with it. This gets changed, for a while, a long time from now—in Chapter 22, "The Delegate from Troy."

The Refactoring

With a plan in hand—have a TextModel that is given the lines and has them taken back—we created an empty TextModel class, just *public class TextModel {}*. Then we gave the Form a member variable containing a TextModel, with *private TextModel model;*. And when we initialized the form, we created an instance of TextModel. It looks like this:

```
class XMLNotepad : NotepadCloneNoMenu
{
  private TextModel model;
...
  public XMLNotepad() {
    Text = "XML Notepad";
    textbox.KeyDown += new KeyEventHandler(XMLKeyDownHandler);
    textbox.KeyPress += new KeyPressEventHandler(XMLKeyPressHandler);
    model = new TextModel();
  }
...
}
```

With that, we're ready to start refactoring the code. The idea is to move functionality out of that big KeyDownHandler method and over to the Text-Model class. We started by moving the original Ctrl+P code that just echoed "controlP" to the Textbox. That was enough to get us going. It looked like this:

```
void XMLKeyDownHandler(object objSender, KeyEventArgs kea) {
  model.Lines = textbox.Lines;
  model.SelectionStart = textbox.SelectionStart;
  if (kea.KeyCode == Keys.P && kea.Modifiers == Keys.Control) {
    model.InsertControlPText();
    kea.Handled = true;
  }
  ...
  textbox.Lines = model.Lines;
  textbox.SelectionStart = model.SelectionStart;
}
```

And the first TextModel class looked like this:

```
class TextModel {
  private String[] lines;
  private int selectionStart;

  public TextModel() {
  }

  public void InsertControlPText() {
    lines[lines.Length-1] += "ControlP";
  }

  public String[] Lines {
    get {
      return lines;
    }
    set {
      lines = value;
    }
  }

  public int SelectionStart {
    get {
      return selectionStart;
    }
    set {
      selectionStart = value;
    }
  }
}
```

Lesson   Let me emphasize that technique for a moment. Even though, as we'll see in a moment, the real code might have been easy enough to write immediately, I always like to start a new path with something abysmally simple. If it really is simple, it will take only a moment to do. And if, as so often happens, it isn't quite as simple as I thought, the learning is isolated to whatever's not right. In this case, what's in question is whether the TextModel and the Form are wired together correctly and whether the Form is properly loading the Text-Model with the current Textbox contents and putting the model's final contents back in the Textbox. Doing this in the simple case lets us focus on the central idea of the two objects intercommunicating, without complicating the situation with a complex method inside one of them.

However, we have no tests. We're still verifying this code manually. This is very risky, and you'll probably see, as we go forward, that working without tests will often trip us up. Still, we're slow to learn, and sometimes we just can't think of a test or we get too excited about a coding idea to wait. Bad programmers. Go to your room.

Next we worked on the code we really cared about, the Enter method. We moved it over to the TextModel class as a unit. It doesn't compile because it calls CursorLine. At first we were going to copy CursorLine over as well, but then we realized that was a pretty big change. [sb]Twenty lines without a successful test is a pretty big change! So we just implemented a stub method for CursorLine(), returning 2. The result would be that when you type Enter, the TextModel would always insert a blank line and a P-tagged line after line 2. Not what we really want, but easy to test. Pretty soon it worked, and we had this method in TextModel:

```
private ArrayList lines;
private int selectionStart;

public void Enter() {
  int cursorLine = CursorLine();
  String[] newlines = new String[lines.Length+2];
  for(int i = 0; i <= cursorLine; i++)  {
    newlines[i] = lines[i];
  }
  newlines[cursorLine+1] = "";
  newlines[cursorLine+2] = "<P></P>";
```

```
      for (int i = cursorLine+1; i < lines.Length; i++) {
        newlines[i+2] = lines[i];
      }
      lines = newlines;
      selectionStart = NewSelectionStart(cursorLine + 2);
    }

    private int CursorLine() {
      return 2;
    }
```

With that working (on cursor line 2), we then moved over the CursorLine method, which, completed, looks like this:

```
    private int CursorLine() {
      int length = 0;
      int lineNr = 0;
      foreach ( String s in lines) {
        if (length <= selectionStart && selectionStart <= length+s.Length + 2 )
          break;
        length += s.Length + Environment.NewLine.Length;
        lineNr++;
      }
      return lineNr;
    }
```

Recall that we have to load and unload the TextModel each time we use it, and recall also that we decided to ignore the efficiency issue and do the most straightforward thing. That implied adding a few lines to the KeyDownHandler, so it now looks like this:

```
    void XMLKeyDownHandler(object objSender, KeyEventArgs kea) {
      model.Lines = textbox.Lines;
      model.SelectionStart = textbox.SelectionStart;

      // key down handlers here

      textbox.Lines = model.Lines;
      textbox.SelectionStart = model.SelectionStart;
    }
```

As you can see, we just rip the lines and selection start out of the Textbox at the beginning of the key down handler and jam them back in at the end. Rough but straightforward.

> **Lesson**   Again, a comment on the technique. We're doing an inefficient and ugly thing here, ripping the guts out of our Textbox and jamming them back. Our mission at this stage is to learn how to build the basic structure of the system, and we're pretty sure that this separate TextModel is the right way to do it, but we don't as yet know the best detailed way to do it. So we're blocking it in: [sb]we start new features with large bold strokes. We'll clean up the details as we go along.

Now I'm famous for saying that when we say "we'll clean it up later," later never comes. And yet, in this chapter we've recommended putting in code that's clearly not up to our standards of craftsmanship. What's up with that? Are we being inconsistent, or are we taking a risk that things won't get cleaned up? We're sure we're not inconsistent: we're intentionally building from rough toward smooth, as you've already seen. We put the code in the Form, and now we're moving it to a better place. We'll keep doing that as we go forward. However, there's a risk that we'll leave some bad code lying around. Watch as we go along, and make your own decision on where the balance lies for you. Chet and I have worked together a lot, and we're pretty comfortable with the balance we've found. We probably will leave some bad code somewhere, but what I predict is that it will be in a place we never visit again during the course of this story. What I hope you'll see is that everything we *do* visit we make a little better each time we pass through. Again, you need to make your own decision, based on your experience with the techniques and on your own projects.

As you'll see later in the book, we did clean up a lot of code. We never did get a better idea than just saving and restoring all the text and status between the Textbox and our TextModel. I suspect that as long as we stick with using the simple Textbox control, it's the best thing to do.

One Last Thing

Now then, we never did set the cursor back where we want it. Maybe you noticed the lines about selection start in the XMLKeyDownHandler method and a corresponding one in the Enter code, where we call NewSelectionStart. We just wrote those methods in a straightforward way, based on a spike we had done earlier. It looks like this:

```
private int NewSelectionStart(int cursorLine) {
  int length = 0;
```

```
    for (int i = 0; i < cursorLine; i++)
      length += lines[i].Length + Environment.NewLine.Length;
    return length + 3;
  }

  public int SelectionStart {
    get {
      return selectionStart;
    }
    set {
      selectionStart = value;
    }
  }
}
```

What's Next?

At the end of every session, we like to take a few minutes to reflect on what has happened: what we've learned, what went well, what went poorly. This time, things went rather well. However, the code still isn't expressing intention very well. I'd like to improve that in an upcoming chapter. This will also help us hone our skills in C#, which, with only about eight hours' experience, we really need. Also, the connection between our Textbox and TextModel is pretty ugly. Thanks to our pals on the XP mailing list, we received some suggestions on how to use events to make this look smoother and maybe even work better. So watch for that in the future.

5

Expressing Ideas

Just for something to do, I decided to clean up some code. Here's what happened—not all of it good!

Something to Do

I think I'll refactor the code a bit, just for something to do. Let's take a look. Here's the method that handles Enter:

```
public void Enter() {
  int cursorLine = CursorLine();
  String[] newlines = new String[lines.Length+2];
  for(int i = 0; i <= cursorLine; i++)  {
    newlines[i] = lines[i];
  }
  newlines[cursorLine+1] = "";
  newlines[cursorLine+2] = "<P></P>";
  for (int i = cursorLine+1; i < lines.Length; i++) {
    newlines[i+2] = lines[i];
  }
  lines = newlines;
  selectionStart = NewSelectionStart(cursorLine + 2);
}
```

Here are some of the ideas that went into this code:

- Handle the Enter key.

- Change the lines table to include a blank line and a P tag line after the line that contains the cursor.

- Figure out which line contains the cursor.

- Copy the lines from the beginning through the cursor line to the output.

- Put a blank line into the output.

- Put a P tag line into the output.

- Copy the lines from after the cursor through the end to the output.

- Place the cursor in the middle of the P tag.

- Remember the output lines.

You might be wondering why I'm mentioning the inclusion of the blank line and the P tag twice. The first mention is the purpose of the whole method. The second is a description of what some lines of code do.

Commenting for "Clarity"

Often we're told to comment our code to make it more clear. I think just for fun, I'll comment this code to show where these ideas are hiding. We'll see whether this makes the code better. Then we'll see whether we can do better than just putting comments in to make things more "clear."

```
//
// Handle the Enter Key
//
public void Enter() {
//
// On Enter, we change the TextModel lines to insert, after the line
// containing the cursor, a blank line, and a line with <P></P>. We set the new
// cursor location to be between the P tags: <P>|</P>.
//
// calculate which line has the cursor
    int cursorLine = CursorLine();
// allocate a new line array with two more lines
    String[] newlines = new String[lines.Length+2];
// copy line 0 through cursor line to output
    for(int i = 0; i <= cursorLine; i++)  {
        newlines[i] = lines[i];
    }
// insert blank line
    newlines[cursorLine+1] = "";
// insert P tag line
    newlines[cursorLine+2] = "<P></P>";
// copy lines after cursor lein to output
```

```
    for (int i = cursorLine+1; i < lines.Length; i++) {
        newlines[i+2] = lines[i];
    }
// save new lines as result
    lines = newlines;
// set cursor location
    selectionStart = NewSelectionStart(cursorLine + 2);
}
```

If your eyes are sharp, you noticed a typo in (at least) one of those comments. I noticed that while typing it in but decided to leave it to remind us all that I might *not* have noticed it. Comments aren't checked by the compiler, and they don't have to reflect reality. However—and you'll have to take my word for this—I did rebuild the program and run the tests after putting these comments in, and it did compile and run even with that mistake in the comment.

> **Lesson**   This is a message from the Ron Jeffries of the future. You should know something that the Ron Jeffries writing this chapter does not: The tests he is running don't test the TextModel at all; the only tests for it are currently manual. The manual tests do run, but he has been very lucky! Watch what happens!

Is This *Really* More Clear?

In addition, we need to ask ourselves whether this is better code. Frankly, I'd rather deal with this method in its first form rather than the second. Your mileage may vary on that. But let's see where we wind up before we finally decide.

Commenting Means "Not Done"

Kent Beck taught me that if the code needs a comment, we should take that as a sign that the code isn't done yet: either it doesn't work, or it isn't good enough. Let's see whether we can get rid of some of those comments, making the code so good that it doesn't need them.

Easy Pickins

Let's start with something easy, that first comment: "Handle the Enter Key". We're trying to express the idea that the method named Enter handles the processing of the Enter key. I like the word "process" better than "handle." So I think maybe I should remove that first comment, and rename the method from

Enter to ProcessEnterKey. But wait, the next comment points out that what we do on Enter is insert a blank line and a P tag. Maybe we should deal with that instead. The code that calls Enter, in the KeyDownHandler, looks like this:

```
if (kea.KeyCode == Keys.Enter) {
  model.Enter();
  kea.Handled = true;
```

I'm torn between two ways to handle this issue. One is to rename the Enter method to ProcessEnterKey, but that will leave the next concern to be expressing insertion of the P tag. And we need to decide who should know that Enter means to do that. I'm inclined to think that the TextModel doesn't know *why* it is doing this and that we should rename this method for what it does, not why or when it does it. So I'm going to rename the method to InsertParagraph-Tag, at least for now. So the KeyDownHandler code becomes

```
if (kea.KeyCode == Keys.Enter) {
  model.InsertParagraphTag();
  kea.Handled = true;
```

And the Enter method looks like this:

```
public void InsertParagraphTag() {
//
// On Enter, we change the TextModel lines to insert, after the line
// containing the cursor, a blank line, and a line with <P></P>. We set the new
// cursor location to be between the P tags: <P>|</P>.
//
// calculate which line has the cursor
  int cursorLine = CursorLine();
  ...
}
```

My first inclination was to remove that whole first comment because I expect to express all those facts by the time I'm done. But I'm looking ahead, based on a lot of experience. Let's just see how much of the comment we can legitimately remove. I've already removed the part about processing the Enter key. That fact is expressed in the code from KeyDownHandler, which pretty clearly says that if the key code is enter, we should InsertParagraphTag. I feel that a comment saying that wouldn't help anyone. In the InsertParagraphTag method itself, can we remove some or all of the long comment? What if we named the method like this?

```
InsertBlankLineAndParagraphTagAndSetCursorBetweenParagraphTag
```

Frankly, I don't think that would help.

I feel that the essence of this method is insertion of the paragraph tag and that the details don't need to be in the name. We might decide not to include the blank line, for example. So let's wait and see.

Well, the easy pickin's turned out to be easy enough, but you see the thinking that went into just that simple Rename Method refactoring. We had a couple of approaches we could have taken, and we're still not entirely satisfied we've got it good enough. Let's reflect a moment and then move on.

> **Lesson**   Names trump comments. Faced with a method name that communicates intent or a cryptic name with a comment, I prefer the intention-revealing name every time. You should, too. It will help those who have to read your code later. And remember: the most likely "those who will have to read your code later" is you!

The Cursor Line

Well, the next line and comment are about calculating which line has the cursor. I like the variable name OK, cursorLine, but I'm not so happy with the method name, CursorLine. How about we call that method FindLineContainingCursor or LineContainingCursor or something like that? I think I'll call it LineContainingCursor. I'll change the line that sends the message and the line that defines the method. So now the line has no comment, and it reads

```
int cursorLine = LineContainingCursor();
```

Things are a bit better now. I'll show the code as it now looks, and then I'm going to bed. Important point here:

> **Lesson**   Release early and often. I know I'm not done refactoring this code, but on a real project, rather than hold it out of the code base overnight, I could, and should, release it. The code is better than it was, and it's running all the tests. I might wish to hold it out, but if I were working in a team environment, it would be better to keep the code in the repository in case someone else needed to work on it or understand it. I believe the best approach is to keep the best possible code, and the most current code, in the repository at all times.

Anyway, here's where we are:

```csharp
public void InsertParagraphTag() {
//
// On Enter, we change the TextModel lines to insert, after the line
// containing the cursor, a blank line, and a line with <P></P>. We set the
// new cursor location to be between the P tags: <P>|</P>.
//
  int cursorLine = LineContainingCursor();
// allocate a new line array with two more lines
  String[] newlines = new String[lines.Length+2];
// copy line 0 through cursor line to output
  for(int i = 0; i <= cursorLine; i++)  {
    newlines[i] = lines[i];
  }
// insert blank line
  newlines[cursorLine+1] = "";
// insert P tag line
  newlines[cursorLine+2] = "<P></P>";
// copy lines after cursor lien to output
  for (int i = cursorLine+1; i < lines.Length; i++) {
    newlines[i+2] = lines[i];
  }
// save new lines as result
  lines = newlines;
// set cursor location
  selectionStart = NewSelectionStart(cursorLine + 2);
}
```

Here's what I'll be thinking about for next time. The next few patches of code are dealing with creating a new line array and then filling it in. I'll want to be using Extract Method to make them more meaningful, with names like CopyThroughCursor, InsertPTag, CopyAfterCursor, or something like that. I note that to do that, I probably won't want "newlines" to be a local variable because the individual methods will each want to process the newlines array. I can make it a member variable easily enough, but I don't feel entirely comfortable with that: a guideline that I use is that all the variables in an object should change at the same frequency, and it feels to me that "lines" changes at the beginning and end, and "newlines" changes a lot, in the middle.

Also, C# includes a class called ArrayList, which is like an array except that you can insert into it and such. I'm tempted to change TextModel to use ArrayList. But I would have to know more about ArrayList before I can decide on that.

Lesson: Digression—Doing It Right

At this point, some readers are probably saying something like, "If you had spent more time thinking about this at the beginning, you wouldn't have to be doing all this changing now." And it's true: if we had thought a long time at the beginning, and if we were very smart, I might not be doing this changing now. We might also not have any running code at all. Chet and I are very comfortable working this way, through lots of practice. I like it that I can walk away tonight and not address this problem again until I'm home two days from now, maybe with Chet's help, and that the code is working fine now, so that what I'm working on is cosmetic, not functional. But you might find comfort working with more thought up front.

I'd urge you, though, to push the refactoring approach all the way to the limits, like we're doing here, at least for a while. That way, you'll know what it really feels like rather than be guessing. You may be feeling that I'm doing a lot of rework, but that's not what's really happening. Chet and I didn't do much thinking up front about what to call these methods and lines of code—we deferred that thinking almost entirely, and we're doing it now. We agree that time must be spent thinking about these matters. We're just saying that we can defer that thinking until later. Later (that is, now), we know more about what the code really wants to be, so we're better qualified to give things good names and arrange things for best effect.

If we were to stop with the code as originally written, that could be bad: it's not very clear and it might be hard to maintain. If we were to think more up front, we might make better decisions, but they would be made in the absence of the learning we gained by making this code work.

There's an old saying in programming: "Make it work, make it right, make it fast." That's what's happening here. We have made it work. Now we're in the process of making it right, and if we need to, later, we'll make it fast. There's nothing new under the sun: the XP programming style is "Make it work, make it right, make it fast." We just know a bit more about how to go about it.

You think on that. I'm going to bed now, and I'll work on this more when I get back to Michigan.

> **Lesson**   Ron of the future here again. Upon waking up (literally and figuratively), I realized that I had gotten lucky. My tests weren't really there to support my refactoring. Here's what I wrote next:

We Need Some Tests Here!

I did a little simple refactoring just above, just some renaming and method extraction, and got away with it. I was running the tests, but I had forgotten that none of them tested the TextModel that I was working on. No excuse, sir: we should have written the tests first, but sometimes even we nod. We've decided that these chapters won't be sanitized: you'll see us learning, making mistakes, and, we hope, ultimately producing some pretty nice code. In what follows, we get down to writing the tests we should have written before.

We're still working on our first story:

When I'm typing a paragraph inside P tags and hit a return, create another P tag underneath this one, and put the cursor in between the new tags, in the right typing location.

We have this functionality working in the GUI and therefore in the Text-Model, which drives the GUI. We should have written tests for the TextModel already, but we couldn't figure out how. Now we know enough to do it, and we sorely need to write those tests. We'll start with simple ones, and move forward.

Our first test just checks to make sure that a TextModel that hasn't actually done anything answers an empty array of strings. Our purpose with this test is mostly to check that we are correctly set up.

```
[SetUp] public void CreateModel() {
  model = new TextModel();
}

[Test] public void TestNoLines() {
  model.Lines = new String[0];
  AssertEquals(0, model.Lines.Length);
}
```

Next we test that a TextModel given three lines, with no processing, returns three lines. Again, a pretty simple test. We like to go in tiny steps, especially because these tests usually run, giving us a little jolt of success. Even so, once in a while we get a surprise. In addition, remember that we're just learning

C#. We hadn't worked much with arrays of strings and such, so we take extra small steps, knowing that we're likely to write code that doesn't work. Anyway, here's the no-processing test:

```
[Test] public void TestNoProcessing() {
  model.Lines = new String[3] { "hi", "there", "chet"};
  AssertEquals(3, model.Lines.Length);
}
```

OK, so far so good. Now we'll actually do some work. This test takes a Text-Model with one line of content, "hello world", and tells it to insert a paragraph tag. We expect to find three lines in total: the original, a blank line, and a paragraph tag pair. The cursor should be between the Ps of the P tag. That's 18 characters in: 11 for hello world + 2 for newline + 2 for blank line + 3 for *ltP>.

```
[Test] public void TestOneEnter() {
  model.Lines = new String[1] {"hello world" };
  model.SelectionStart = 5;
  model.InsertParagraphTag();
  AssertEquals(3, model.Lines.Length);
  AssertEquals(18, model.SelectionStart);
}
```

Because we're confident in the content, we're not checking it. A case could be made that we should be checking it. In a later test, we actually do that. As always, it's a judgment call what to test when you're testing after the fact. Testing before the fact usually gives us better tests. Try it both ways yourself and see what you discover.

Some Additional Tests

Let's summarize some additional tests that we wrote. We'll review the code that supports them later on.

We implemented a new feature that handled the special case of hitting Enter in a TextBox containing nothing. It just inserts a single paragraph tag pair (not the blank line). Here's the test we wrote for that:

```
[Test] public void TestEmptyText() {
  model.Lines = new String[0];
  model.InsertParagraphTag();
  AssertEquals(1, model.Lines.Length);
  AssertEquals(3, model.SelectionStart);
}
```

This test didn't work, because it was a new feature, and it took us a little while to make it go, because we had a subtle defect in our code that figures out which line the selection is on. It turns out that if the cursor was at the beginning of a line, our code thought it was in the previous line. There were a couple of offsetting errors making that happen, and it took us some time to find the second problem.

To show this bug and make sure it was fixed, we wrote another test, to handle the cursor being at the start of the line. It looks like this:

```
[Test] public void InsertWithCursorAtLineStart () {
    model.Lines = new String[3] { "<P>one</P>", "", "<P>two</P>"};
    model.SelectionStart = 14;
    model.InsertParagraphTag();
    AssertEquals("<P>two</P>", model.Lines[2]);
}
```

In this test, the cursor is ahead of the P tag on line two. We had discovered while working on the previous test that when we hit Enter there, the blank line and paragraph tag pair was inserted in front of the two line, instead of after it as we expected. So we wrote this test in preparation for fixing the problem.

Lesson [sb]Find a bug—write a test. This is a standard Extreme Programming recommendation: if you find a defect, first write a test that will work when the defect is fixed, and only then fix the defect. This idea has at least three advantages:

- It helps focus our attention on the exact circumstances that cause the problem.
- It gives us a clear indication when we have it fixed.
- It subtly teaches us a little about how to test better and where our mistakes tend to be.

I think it's the last advantage that really makes the recommendation worthwhile. By having the discipline to write this test and fix it, we have a sharper focus on what kinds of situations we make mistakes in and on the kind of test we should write to avoid those mistakes. We always try to reflect just a bit—"What have we learned from this?"—but even if we forget, this little ritual pounds a little sense into our heads. Try the practice out—we think you'll like it.

This test gave us a bit of an extra problem: when I originally counted the characters to figure out where the selection start should be, I got 13. So we thought the code was wrong, changed it back to the way it had been before the TestEmptyText, and then finally figured out that our test was wrong by printing the output and counting it again.

Still, all this rigmarole took us only about an hour, and now we feel that the TextModel is pretty well protected for further refactoring to express its ideas better. Now we can get back to it.

The Starting Code

With the tests in place, it's time to use our next session to improve the code's ability to express our intention. At this point, the code looks like this:

```
public void InsertParagraphTag() {
//
// On Enter, we change the TextModel lines to insert, after the line
// containing the cursor, a blank line, and a line with <P></P>. We set the
// new cursor location to be between the P tags: <P>|</P>.
//
  int cursorLine = LineContainingCursor();
// allocate a new line array with two more lines
  String[] newlines = new String[lines.Length+2];
// copy line 0 through cursor line to output
  for(int i = 0; i <= cursorLine; i++)  {
    newlines[i] = lines[i];
  }
// insert blank line
  newlines[cursorLine+1] = "";
// insert P tag line
  newlines[cursorLine+2] = "<P></P>";
// copy lines after cursor lien to output
  for (int i = cursorLine+1; i < lines.Length; i++) {
    newlines[i+2] = lines[i];
  }
// save new lines as result
  lines = newlines;
// set cursor location
  selectionStart = NewSelectionStart(cursorLine + 2);
}
```

Lesson   Do you find those comments to be helpful? Chet and I do not. They do tell a bit about the intention of the various bits of code, and that's good. But they also make the code seem choppy and hard to read. This code is a good example of Kent's suggestion that a comment is the code's way of telling us that it wants to be more clear.

To make this code better, we just kept pecking away at it, changing things around to make the code more expressive and, in some cases, to use approaches that seemed better to us in C#. The first of these ideas was the best. This version uses two arrays of strings, creating a new array, "newlines", to be two more lines than the existing "lines" array. We knew there was an object in C#, ArrayList, which is basically an array that can grow, have insertions, and so on. So our first step was to change the object to use two ArrayLists instead of two arrays. To do this, we needed to change the Lines property:

```
public String[] Lines {
  get {
    // there must be a way to cast this??
    String[] textlines = new String[newlines.Count];
    for (int i = 0; i < newlines.Count; i++) {
      textlines[i] = (String) newlines[i];
    }
    return textlines;
  }
  set {
    lines = new ArrayList(value);
    newlines = lines;
  }
}
```

There's nothing magical about this. The interface we chose expects arrays of string, so we're converting to and from ArrayList internally. There might be a better way to do the get operation, but at the Michigan Union, with no C# books, we sure couldn't find it. So we create an array whose size matches newlines.Count. (For reasons known only to Microsoft, ArrayList uses Count where Array uses Length.) Then we copy the newlines ArrayList into the array. We're hoping to find a way to just "cast" the ArrayList to an array of String, and when we do, we'll change this code to be more clean.

We also had to change the TextModel constructor to initialize the lines and newlines variables to ArrayLists. (I think we had actually written the constructor during the testing phase described previously, when we built the test of an empty TextModel.)

```
public TextModel() {
  lines = new ArrayList();
  newlines = lines;
}
```

It also turns out that the InsertParagraphTag method includes some special case code, handling the empty case. I'll just show it here for completeness.

We're hoping that when the refactoring is done, it will fall into the general case, but for now it's separate:

```
// handle empty array special case (yucch)
if ( newlines.Count == 0 ) {
  newlines.Add( "<P></P>" );
  selectionStart = 3;
  return;
}
```

Slowly, things are getting better. We are now really set up to do some better work. ArrayList has a method, AddRange, that lets you add a section of one ArrayList into another, so we can rewrite all that array copying this way:

```
newlines = new ArrayList();
newlines.AddRange(LinesThroughCursor());
newlines.AddRange(NewParagraph());
newlines.AddRange(LinesAfterCursor());
```

Note that we extracted two methods, LinesThroughCursor and LinesAfterCursor. They look like this:

```
public ArrayList LinesThroughCursor() {
  return lines.GetRange(0,LineContainingCursor()+1);
}


public ArrayList LinesAfterCursor() {
  int cursorLine = LineContainingCursor();
  return lines.GetRange(cursorLine+1,lines.Count - cursorLine - 1);
}
```

And we wrote a NewParagraph method to answer the blank line and paragraph tag pair:

```
public ArrayList NewParagraph() {
  ArrayList temp = new ArrayList();
  temp.Add("");
  temp.Add("<P></P>");
  return temp;
}
```

The net result of all this is to replace this code:

```
// allocate a new line array with two more lines
  String[] newlines = new String[lines.Length+2];
// copy line 0 through cursor line to output
  for(int i = 0; i <= cursorLine; i++)  {
    newlines[i] = lines[i];
  }
// insert blank line
  newlines[cursorLine+1] = "";
```

```
// insert P tag line
  newlines[cursorLine+2] = "<P></P>";
// copy lines after cursor lien to output
  for (int i = cursorLine+1; i < lines.Length; i++) {
    newlines[i+2] = lines[i];
  }
```

with this:

```
newlines = new ArrayList();
newlines.AddRange(LinesThroughCursor());
newlines.AddRange(NewParagraph());
newlines.AddRange(LinesAfterCursor());
```

The Current Code

We think that's a lot more expressive. Here's the whole method. See whether you agree that we have made it more expressive and whether we're justified in taking out the comments we removed:

```
public void InsertParagraphTag() {
  //
  // On Enter, we change the TextModel lines to insert, after the line
  // containing the cursor, a blank line, and a line with <P></P>. We set the
  // new cursor location to be between the P tags: <P>|</P>.
  //
  // handle empty array special case (yucch)
  if ( newlines.Count == 0 ) {
    newlines.Add( "<P></P>" );
    selectionStart = 3;
    return;
  }

  newlines = new ArrayList();
  newlines.AddRange(LinesThroughCursor());
  newlines.AddRange(NewParagraph());
  newlines.AddRange(LinesAfterCursor());

  // set cursor location
  selectionStart = NewSelectionStart(LineContainingCursor() + 2);
}
```

This code still isn't done, as we'll suggest in a moment, but you can see what's happened: we've taken code that *clearly* needed some explanation and we've replaced it with code that surely needs less explanation. You might prefer a bit more than we do, but we'll wager that most readers won't want one line of comment per line of code anymore.

What's Next?

As I said, the code doesn't look done to us: we have a sense of duplication from that special case that inserts the paragraph tag and such. We'd like to consolidate the special case and the general case. Furthermore, now that we're more familiar with ArrayList, we think we can probably do the editing right in the "lines" ArrayList and get rid of "newlines" altogether. We're going to leave that for another day, because...

Our Story Works!

That's right. Our first story is now working. Remember, it was

> *When I'm typing a paragraph inside P tags and I hit a*
> *return, create another P tag underneath this one and*
> *put the cursor in between the new tags, in the right*
> *typing location.*

So, we're finished and can move on to the next story, right?

WRONG! Where's Our Customer Acceptance Test?

We don't have a customer test for this story. We've satisfied ourselves as programmers that it works, but how can we satisfy our customer? We owe our customer a customer test. In the next chapter, we'll show how we create a customer test for this, our very first story. No framework, no waiting for QA to show up; we'll just create a test we think our customer will be able to understand. Watch for it!

A Little Refactoring: That Ugly Get

I posted for help on converting the newlines ArrayList to an array of String and got a reply that showed how to do it. The trick was the typeof function, which I had forgotten about since C days so long ago. I promised to fix it when I learned a better way and had nothing else to do after dinner, so I decided to clean up the code a bit more. Remember that we had this:

```
public String[] Lines {
  get {
    // there must be a way to cast this??
    String[] textlines = new String[newlines.Count];
    for (int i = 0; i < newlines.Count; i++) {
      textlines[i] = (String) newlines[i];
    }
    return textlines;
```

```
    }
    set {
      lines = new ArrayList(value);
      newlines = lines;
    }
  }
```

It's that ugly get of the Lines property that I'm trying to fix. Sure enough, this approach works just fine:

```
public String[] Lines {
  get {
    return (String[]) lines.ToArray(typeof(String));
  }
  set {
    lines = new ArrayList(value);
  }
```

You would think that a reasonable language wouldn't have needed two hints that both say, "Hey, this is an array of strings." Still, this is much better.

Get Rid of the Text Copy

Recall that the InsertParagraphTag method makes a copy of "lines" into "new-lines" with this code:

```
newlines = new ArrayList();
newlines.AddRange(LinesThroughCursor());
newlines.AddRange(NewParagraph());
newlines.AddRange(LinesAfterCursor());
```

We should be able to do this edit directly into the "lines" variable, by using InsertRange instead of AddRange. To make it work completely, however, is a pretty big edit: there might be various places that rely on "newlines". So I decided that first I would make the InsertRange work and only then remove "newlines". To accomplish that, I wrote this code:

```
newlines = new ArrayList(lines);
newlines.InsertRange(LineContainingCursor()+1, NewParagraph());
```

That leaves the result in the newlines variable, so this is the only code that has to change to test things. And sure enough, it worked just fine! The next step was just to replace all references to "newlines" with references to "lines". I did a few of those with a quick text find—where, oh where, is Smalltalk's "Browse References"? Then I removed the instance variable "newlines", compiled (finding one more reference), and the program still runs all the tests, even the acceptance test that we haven't told you about yet.

Observations and Conclusions

Take a look at the InsertParagraphTag method as it now stands:

```
public void InsertParagraphTag() {
  //
  // On Enter, we change the TextModel lines to insert, after the line
  // containing the cursor, a blank line, and a line with <P></P>. We set the
  // new cursor location to be between the P tags: <P>|</P>.
  //
  // handle empty array special case (yucch)
  if ( lines.Count == 0 ) {
    lines.Add( "<P></P>" );
    selectionStart = 3;
    return;
  }

  lines.InsertRange(LineContainingCursor()+1, NewParagraph());

  // set cursor location
  selectionStart = NewSelectionStart(LineContainingCursor() + 2);
}
```

Frankly, I think that's getting rather clean. And each step from the original ugly version to this one was a simple refactoring, supported by tests that told us that we weren't breaking anything. (Well, OK, the first couple of refactorings weren't test-supported. That was risky, but I got away with it this time.) Since then, things have gone faster and we've been much more confident. I even felt pretty safe working alone on this chapter, because the tests Chet and I had devised were working for us even when he was home with his wife, where he belongs on a Saturday. Here's the thing to remember: [sb]automated tests record our intelligence for use later!

Now, the most irritating part that still remains in the InsertParagraphTag method is that special case for an empty array. I'd like to clean that up sometime, but not right now. And the selectionStart doesn't satisfy me entirely. I'm tempted to move that searching code to the get method that returns the variable. That would let me remove this line. But I'm not sure that will work, because the cursor setting depends on the size of the tag inserted. I'll talk about that with Chet next time we get together. It's a pretty small wart, I think.

Reflecting Back

Think back, if you will, to how we built this method. Originally it was written inline in the OnKeyDown method of the Form. It was pretty ugly then, and we put all those comments in it hoping to make it better. Then, in a few short sessions—none of them over two hours—we cleaned it up, using these techniques:

■   Extract Class—to create the TextModel class.

■   Extract Method—to give good names to the loops that copied and added.

■   Extract Method—was also used to clean up a few other things.

■   Substitute Algorithm—to move to ArrayList, and again to get rid of newline.

■   Replace Magic Number with Symbolic Constant—to move the return and paragraph tag out of the mainline.

And probably more. Each change was pretty simple, and almost all of them worked the first time. The resulting code is much improved.

> **Lesson**   It is possible to *imagine* having done better with forethought. Hindsight is like that. What we'd like you to take away from this experience is that—believe us—it almost always works out this way. We begin with simple, straightforward, almost procedural code. At this point we're working to understand how to do the thing at all. We usually write more tests up front, as you'll see in later chapters, and we usually express intention a bit more than we did here. But we always wind up with code that wants a bit of refactoring to be really nice. And the refactoring always goes like it did this time: one little step after another, each one going along quite well. Once in a while, a refactoring won't work or will be a bad idea. Since it's a small step, we just back it out.
>
> We've been working on this application only a couple of hours at a time. There isn't much time in it at all, and it's looking pretty good!

Lesson: The Key Lesson

This style of programming works better for us—and for most people who try it—than doing a whole lot of design up front and trying to get it all right the first time. The lesson to take home is that this approach is worth trying. Push it as far as you can, especially when you're doing things where you're comfortable. We think you'll find that the optimal point has far less up-front design than you would expect and that the whole process is easy and stress-free.

Current Code

```
using System;
using System.Collections;
using System.Text;

namespace Notepad {
  class TextModel {
    private ArrayList lines;
    private int selectionStart;
    public TextModel() {
      lines = new ArrayList();
    }

    public void InsertControlPText() {
    }

    private int LineContainingCursor() {
      int length = 0;
      int lineNr = 0;
      int cr = Environment.NewLine.Length;
      foreach ( String s in lines) {
        if (length <= selectionStart
          && selectionStart < length+s.Length + cr )
          break;
        length += s.Length + cr;
        lineNr++;
      }
      return lineNr;
    }

    public void Enter() {
      InsertParagraphTag();
    }
```

```
public void InsertParagraphTag() {
  //
  // On Enter, we change the TextModel lines to insert, after the line
  // containing the cursor, a blank line, and a line with <P></P>. We set
  // the new cursor location to be between the P tags: <P>|</P>.
  //
  // handle empty array special case (yucch)
  if ( lines.Count == 0 ) {
    lines.Add( "<P></P>" );
    selectionStart = 3;
    return;
  }

  lines.InsertRange(LineContainingCursor()+1, NewParagraph());

  // set cursor location
  selectionStart = NewSelectionStart(LineContainingCursor() + 2);
}

private int NewSelectionStart(int cursorLine) {
  int length = 0;
  for (int i = 0; i < cursorLine; i++)
    length += ((String)lines[i]).Length + Environment.NewLine.Length;
  return length + "<p>".Length;
}

public ArrayList LinesThroughCursor() {
  return lines.GetRange(0,LineContainingCursor()+1);
}

public ArrayList NewParagraph() {
  ArrayList temp = new ArrayList();
  temp.Add("");
  temp.Add("<P></P>");
  return temp;
}

public ArrayList LinesAfterCursor() {
  int cursorLine = LineContainingCursor();
  return lines.GetRange(cursorLine+1,lines.Count - cursorLine - 1);
}

public String[] Lines {
  get {
    return (String[]) lines.ToArray(typeof(String));
  }
  set {
    lines = new ArrayList(value);
  }
}
```

```csharp
      public String TestText {
        get {
          StringBuilder b = new StringBuilder();
          foreach(String s in lines) {
            b.Append(s);
            b.Append(System.Environment.NewLine);
          }
          b.Insert(SelectionStart,"|");
          return b.ToString();
        }
      }

      public int SelectionStart {
        get {
          return selectionStart;
        }
        set {
          selectionStart = value;
        }
      }
    }
  }
}

using System;
using Nunit.Framework;

namespace Notepad {

  [TestFixture] public class TestTextModel : Assertion {
    private TextModel model;

    [SetUp] public void CreateModel() {
      model = new TextModel();
    }

    [Test] public void TestNoLines() {
      model.Lines = new String[0];
      AssertEquals(0, model.Lines.Length);
    }

    [Test] public void TestNoProcessing() {
      model.Lines = new String[3] { "hi", "there", "chet"};
      AssertEquals(3, model.Lines.Length);
    }

    [Test] public void TestOneEnter() {
      model.Lines = new String[1] {"hello world" };
      model.SelectionStart = 5;
```

```
      model.InsertParagraphTag();
      AssertEquals(3, model.Lines.Length);
      AssertEquals(18, model.SelectionStart);
   }

   [Test] public void TestEmptyText() {
      model.Lines = new String[0];
      model.InsertParagraphTag();
      AssertEquals(1, model.Lines.Length);
      AssertEquals(3, model.SelectionStart);
   }

   // Chet comments that he hates the comments

   [Test] public void InsertWithCursorAtLineStart () {
      model.Lines = new String[3] { "<P>one</P>", "", "<P>two</P>"};
      model.SelectionStart = 14;
      model.InsertParagraphTag();
      AssertEquals("<P>two</P>", model.Lines[2]);
   }

   [Test] public void TestLineContainingCursorDirectly() {
      // todo?
   }
 }
}
```

6

The First Customer Acceptance Test

Sometimes, too often, XP teams don't have Customer Acceptance Tests or they leave them until "later." The result is a less confident customer and problems when you least need them. **Here's our first customer test.** *See? That wasn't hard.*

Do We Need a Customer Test?

In the previous chapter, I mentioned, in a screaming sort of tone of voice, that we need a customer test. Extreme Programming teams use at least two levels of testing: programmer tests, like we've already been writing, and customer tests. The main distinguishing characteristic of a customer test is that it belongs to the customer. That ownership is important.

The basic cycle of the project is that the customer says what she wants and the programmers build it. For the cycle to work, the programmers have to become clear on what the customer wants, so that they can build it, and the customer needs to be sure whether the programmers have built what she asked for. Thus, the customer test is born. We say sometimes that an XP story has three aspects:

- **Card** A sentence or two, written on a ^{sb}card, used as a token in planning what is to be done. Teams typically write estimates on cards and often carry them around or post them on the walls when the stories they represent are being worked on.

- **Conversation**   A series of discussions between the programmers and the customer, building understanding of what the story really means. This conversation is often supported with paper or electronic documentation, but the character of conversation—two-way communication—is always present.

- **Confirmation**   One or more concrete, executable, automated Customer Acceptance Tests. These tests are written in an unambiguous language, either a conventional programming language, or a scripting language, or a little table language. Preferably, the language is one that the customer can understand, ideally one that the customer can produce herself.

The rule is: [sb]The story's not done till the customer tests run. Unfortunately, it's common for teams to leave acceptance tests until later or sometimes to skip them altogether, often for reasons the team considers good ones. Maybe they think that testing should be done by the QA people, or maybe they think that the system is GUI-based and that automated tests are not necessary. Maybe they are waiting for a testing framework that has not yet been created or not yet arrived in the mail.

None of these reasons are good enough, in my opinion. Customer tests are a critical aspect of the process. The tests amount to an unambiguous written requirements document! And they constitute the best possible kind of requirements document, because they can be verified by the computer. So don't go skipping your acceptance tests. Don't make me come over there!

Still, it might be difficult to do the customer tests, and it takes a little discipline. In this book, we're not going to ship the first story until we have automated Customer Acceptance Tests, and we'll show you how we got ours. With luck, they'll help you get yours.

OK, We Need a Test

We accept that we need customer tests. How can we do them? This is a GUI app: there's no obvious way to test it in an easy automated way. We could buy some screen-scraping software or something like that, but that seems wrong. Besides, we need a test right now.

Each of the customer stories for this application actually specifies a text translation that should take place and be shown in the GUI: "User hits Enter. A new line containing P tags appears, after the end of the current line." And we have just built this TextModel object, which takes the input lines and a command and produces the output lines. So Chet and I thought we would do a little scripting language that allowed the customer (or us) to define customer tests in files: the input, the command, and the output. We thought a script might look like this:

```
*input
<P>Here is some input in the editor already.</P>
*end
*enter
*output
<P>Here is some input in the editor already.</P>

<P>|</P>
```

The idea is that a little script would define the input, all the lines between "*input" and "*end". Then it would take various commands, like "*enter", meaning "user types Enter," and it would show what text should then be in the editor, from "*output" to the end of the script (or to "*end", not shown here).

You might feel that the customer may not find this scripting language completely convincing. And you will be right. But they will almost certainly find it more convincing than nothing, and they'll find it far more repeatable than typing in the same old stuff into each new version. We've found, again and again, that by producing some little language like this to make requirements concrete and check that they're implemented, we've built a stronger relationship with our customer. And we've found that the simple little idea soon grows into a stronger framework, but that instead of guessing what might be needed in the future and waiting until we have it, we get the real benefit right away. The bottom line is this: [sb]We don't need a testing framework; we need tests.

Having decided that we wanted this little script to run, we started by creating a new test file to contain this test and the customer tests that we were sure would follow. We called the file CustomerTest.cs, and the first test looked like this:

```
    [Test] public void ArrayInput() {
      String commands =
*input
some line
*end
*enter
*display
*output
some line

<P>|</P>";
      InterpretCommands(commands);
    }
```

As always, we start with something simple. Some text in the window, type Enter, and see the result. We made up a new command while we were at it, *display, that will display the text to the console. We were certain that when tests failed, as they surely would, we would want to see what the text looked like.

The "InterpretCommands"? That's the method, as yet unwritten, that will go through the string "commands" line by line, setting up and executing the test. We wrote InterpretCommands this way:

```
private void InterpretCommands(String commands) {
  StringReader reader = new StringReader(commands);
  String line = reader.ReadLine();
  while ( line != null) {
    if ( line == "*enter")
      model.Enter();
    if (line == "*display")
      Console.WriteLine("display\r\n{0}\r\nend", model.TestText);
    if (line == "*output")
      CompareOutput(reader);
    if (line == "*input")
      SetInput(reader);
    line = reader.ReadLine();
  }
}
```

Lesson   For some readers, this is something you've done many times. But for those who haven't done this sort of thing much, take a moment to look at how simple this command interpreter is. We don't need lex or yacc or some compiler generator. We don't need a powerful scripting framework. We just read lines, see whether they represent a command, and if they do, process the command. In this version, we're not even handling errors. When that starts to bother us, we'll improve the code.

The idea here, just as in our application, is to get going as soon as possible. We just wrote down our intention: if the line says "*enter", tell the model to do Enter(). If the line says "*input", set the input into the model. And so on.

Of course, we had to implement the SetInput() and CompareOutput() methods. They look like this, with the associated helper methods:

```
private void SetInput(StringReader reader) {
  String[] input = ArrayToEnd(reader);
  model.Lines = input;
}

private String[] ArrayToEnd(StringReader reader) {
  ArrayList result = new ArrayList();
  String line = reader.ReadLine();
  while (line != null && line != "*end") {
   result.Add(line.TrimEnd());
    line = reader.ReadLine();
   }
  String[] answer = new String[result.Count];
  result.CopyTo(answer);
  return answer;
}

private void CompareOutput(StringReader reader, String message) {
  String expected = ExpectedOutput(reader);
  AssertEquals(message, expected, model.TestText);
}

private String ExpectedOutput(StringReader reader) {
  return ReadToEnd(reader);
}

private String ReadToEnd(StringReader reader) {
  String result = "";
  String line = reader.ReadLine();
  while (line != null && line != "*end") {
    result += line;
    result += System.Environment.NewLine;
    line = reader.ReadLine();
  }
  return result;
}
```

In this code, you probably see some evidence that we're not very good yet with C#. That's part of the learning process in action. As the chapters wear on, you'll see that we use better techniques that we've learned. In some cases, we'll go back and improve the old code. Usually we do that only when we come across something really awful, in the course of maintenance. If the code never needs changing, we're not as likely to go after it. As always, you have to find your own balance between keeping things clean and shipping useful code to your customer.

The Test Runs!

With little difficulty, we made this array-driven test run. To us, this was the core of the scripting problem. If we can run a script from an array, we can surely run it from a file. If we can run it from a file, we can surely run scripts in a batch of files. And if we can run scripts from a batch of files, we can store customer tests in files and run them automatically.

Imagine a Long Delay...

With our conflicting schedules, Chet and I haven't worked on our XML Notepad for over a week. After a delicious lunch at *California Pizza Kitchen* (*http://www.cpk.com/*), we went to the Michigan Union to write a little code. A quick review of the tests was all it took to get us back on track. The last test in the code base was this one, a precursor to a real customer test, in CustomerTest.cs:

```
    [Test] public void ArrayInput() {
        String commands =
*input
some line
*end
*enter
*display
*output
some line
<P>|</P>";
        InterpretCommands(commands);
    }
```

What we remembered was that we were on the path of setting things up so the customer could type in files containing little scripts like the one in "commands" and there would be a generic test method that would run them all. We hadn't, as yet, figured out how to do that: we started by just writing a script as a string and making it run.

Reviewing this test, we noticed that it isn't array input, it's string input, so we renamed it:

```
[Test] public void StringInput()
```

Let's review what we've done so far. This test takes a series of little commands: "*input", "*enter", and "*output". The input command primes a Text-Model with the provided input, the enter command causes the model to do its keyboard Enter action, and the output command reads the text from the Text-Model and compares it to the provided output. We have written a tiny command interpreter, using just a bunch of if statements, to handle this language. I plan to come back to this topic, but just a mention here: We could have been saying here that we can't even unit test this object because the program is just a GUI program. Instead, we extracted the functional logic to a TextModel, for which we could write tests. We're not very good at C# yet, and we'll probably wind up making the connection between the Form and the TextModel better as we learn, but we got it extracted and tested with no big problems. Review Chapter 4, "Extracting the Model," for that story.

Similarly, we are programming this for ourselves—because, as you know, we are the customer—and we could have skipped the customer tests, using unit tests instead. But we have a purpose here, which is to show you how we'd write a real application, and that would include customer tests. So we wrote this simple command interpreter that supports the test StringInput, which you just saw. To save you looking back, here's that code:

```
private void InterpretCommands(String commands) {
  StringReader reader = new StringReader(commands);
  String line = reader.ReadLine();
  while ( line != null) {
    if ( line == "*enter")
      model.Enter();
    if (line == "*display")
      Console.WriteLine("display\r\n{0}\r\nend", model.TestText);
    if (line == "*output")
      CompareOutput(reader);
    if (line == "*input")
      SetInput(reader);
    line = reader.ReadLine();
  }
}
```

Not a very sophisticated or beautiful interpreter, but it works just fine. We'll see whether it needs to be improved—later.

Lesson: Remarks on Technique

Before we move along, we'd like to underline what we did. Our real purpose is to have a directory full of customer test scripts, to run them all automatically with NUnit, and to have them report results in some useful way. We could have started by finding out how to read file names from a directory and how to read lines from a file—these are things that we don't know how to do in C# and that are necessary to the process. But we didn't do that. Why? you might ask.

(continued)

We didn't do those things because, although we don't know exactly how to do them, there's clearly no big mystery. I can tell you right now what the code will look like:

```
Get a list of files matching test names from some directory.
Loop over the list.
Read each file.
Treat it as a test
    accept input
    accept editor commands like Enter
    check output, i.e. the current contents of the TextModel
```

There's no mystery to the directory and file part of that, even though we don't know any of the details. The mystery is in how we'll process the file contents to do commands. Therefore, that's the part we solved first. The result was the ArrayTest. This is, we suggest, a good general rule:

The Learning Rule

When creating a new capability, work first on the part where you'll learn the most about the real shape of the problem.

There's only one problem with this rule. There's another rule that goes this way:

The Difficulty Deferral Rule

[sb]Solve what you know; leave the parts you don't know until later.

Maybe later on we'll use that rule. We'll try to see if we can give some guidelines about when to do that. Right now, the learning rule seems more important.

Moving right along...

Test from a File

Since we're trying to write a customer test here, we envision that the customer will give us little scripts, like the one in StringInput, in files. We created a file by pasting the StringInput data into a text file, and we wrote this new test:

```
[Test] public void FileInput() {
    StreamReader stream = File.OpenText("c:\\data\\csharp\\notepad
    \\fileInput.txt");
```

```
      String contents = stream.ReadToEnd();
      stream.Close();
      InterpretCommands(contents);
   }
```

We had to look up some file stuff, because we haven't done much file reading, but the test above worked the first time. Sophisticated C#ers will notice that we didn't use the @"string" technique to avoid doubling those backslashes. That's because we didn't know it. I just read about it last night, and I promise to use it in the future.

Test a Lot of Files

Well, OK, now our customer can type test files and the system can run them, except that we don't want to have to write a new test like FileInput every time the customer adds a test. So we have one more test in mind: one that finds all the files and runs them. We decided that using ".txt" as the test file suffix was a bad idea, so we resaved the file as ".test" and changed the FileInput test accordingly. Then we fiddled around until we found the Directory class and we wrote this test:

```
[Test] public void TestAllFiles() {
   String[] testFiles = Directory.GetFiles("c:\\data\\csharp\\notepad
      \\", "*.test");
   AssertEquals(1, testFiles.Length);
   foreach (String testFile in testFiles) {
      InterpretFileInput(testFile);
   }
}

private void InterpretFileInput(String fileName) {
   StreamReader stream = File.OpenText(fileName);
   String contents = stream.ReadToEnd();
   stream.Close();
   InterpretCommands(contents);
}
```

We worked up to this with an intermediate assert in the test, which is still shown. Since we weren't sure what would come back from the Directory.Get-Files, we asserted that it would be of length one. Sure enough it was, and we'll need to take that test out shortly. This test worked quite well, except that something odd happened.

We had originally named InterpretFileInput as TestFileInput. It made sense at the time. However, even though NUnit finds tests that have the [Test] attribute, it also finds all methods in subclasses of Assertion that start with "Test". So the TestFileInput method was being run, even though I didn't intend it to be a test, and it would loop instead of throwing an exception or failing. We didn't see that it wasn't our new TestAllFiles method (can't read, I guess), and we spent a bunch of time trying to figure out why it was looping. Once we saw the problem, we just renamed the method and everything was just fine.

Lesson: What We Learned

We have a customer test! Now a non-programmer (us, the way we're doing here) can enter files named something.test and put little scripts in there, to test things. It wasn't difficult, only a couple of hours of work all together, and now with our customer hat on, we can test the system. There were only a few necessary steps:

Extract the Model

We elected to break out the functional part of the program into a separate object that is "just code" and no GUI. Some people talk about instantiating forms and talking to them, and maybe we'll experiment with that as well. But it seems right to break out the model anyway. You've seen that article and we hope it seemed as natural and easy to you as it did to us.

Work Up to It

We started with that DirectInput test, which was nearly trivial. It just sent Enter to an empty TextModel and checked the output directly. That was enough to drive us to build the basic connections. The trickiest bit was the little command language. And notice how we skipped all the things that could make a command language difficult. We have no syntax to speak of, just lines that start with * and have a command word. We have no parser, just code that looks at the line to see if it is a command. A loop and some if statements.

Then we went a step further and wrote the ArrayInput test (renamed to TestInput) that worked from a string. Naturally, we were thinking we'd get the string from a file some time soon. Then read one file, then read them all. Step by step, inch by inch, slowly we turned—an empty program into a customer test.

And you can, too.

Still to Come

This is just one test, but we can hand the tool to our customer now (that's us with our customer hat on, but an actual human could do it) and the customer can write more tests. We know that when he does, we'll get some requests. We'll have a need to set the cursor position. We might have a need to have incorrect files report an error, such as files that do no checking of *output. And, of course, there will be new editing instructions and new commands.

We already know what the next story will be. Our customer wants us to implement a File menu, with Save and New and Open. We'll probably split that story and do Save first. Probably before that happens, however, the customer will write some more tests and break our tiny framework. But that's OK, because we don't have a framework—we have tests. And that's the bottom line:

We don't need a testing framework. We need tests!

7

Warts and All

Sometimes the bear bites you. Today it bit Ron and Chet. But we learned some lessons, and we'll share them with you.

Enhancing the Customer Tests

In the preceding chapter, we got our first Customer Acceptance Test working, and it was clear that our customer could do more tests. So we did a couple more and sure enough they all ran. But we knew there was something we couldn't test, so we came up with this test as an example:

```
*input
<P>This is the first p|aragraph.</P>
<P>This is the second paragraph.</P>
*end
*enter
*output
<P>This is the first paragraph.</P>
<P>|</P>
<P>This is the second paragraph.</P>
```

The tricky bit is in the first line: *<P>This is the first p|aragraph.</P>*. See that vertical bar? The customer wants to write a test that shows that if the cursor is in the first line and he presses Enter, the editor inserts a blank paragraph tag in between the first and second lines, with the cursor in the middle of it. Now, it turns out that the TextModel actually works that way: we can run the GUI and show it. But we can't *test* that feature of the TextModel, because we don't set the SelectionStart property when we read the input.

Our mission is simple. We need to parse the input lines a little bit, remove the vertical bar from the input (because it isn't really there, it's just a cursor), and remember where it was so that we can set the SelectionStart property.

The following are the results of that trial, and trial it was.

Do You Have a Test for That?

We wrote that customer test, and sure enough it didn't work. No surprise there. I was all for fixing it, but Chet asked, "Should we write a failing programmer unit test first?" Well, of course we should. So we looked at our SetInput method, the one that reads the input from the input stream and sets it into the Text-Model. It goes like this:

```
private void SetInput(StringReader reader) {
  String[] input = ArrayToEnd(reader);
  model.Lines = input;
}
```

We figured it needed to go something like this:

```
private void SetInput(StringReader reader) {
  String[] input = ArrayToEnd(reader);
  model.Lines = CleanLines(input);
  model.SelectionStart = CursorLocation(input);
}
```

CleanLines would return a new array of lines with the line containing the vertical bar fixed. And CursorLocation would return the cursor location by counting characters up to the vertical bar. No problem.

The First Test Worked

We wrote a little unit test, right in the CustomerTest file, that tested a new method, CursorLocation, which answered the cursor location given an array of lines. It just went over the array and counted characters until it found the vertical bar character. It took a little while to get that running, but just a little. Then we went to lunch, at the Lazy Lizard. (No, we aren't getting paid for these plugs.)

At lunch, I was complaining because that new SetInput method was going to loop over the lines twice, once to get the clean lines and once to get the cursor location. Obviously, that was inefficient. Where was my partner??? What were we thinking??? Everyone knows you don't work on efficiency until you have the code working. Besides that, the candidate code for doing it in a single function looks worse, not better:

```
private void SetInput(StringReader reader) {
    String[] input = ArrayToEnd(reader);
    int cursorLocation;
    String[] newLines;
    CleanInput(input, out cursorLocation, out newLines);
    model.Lines = newLines;
    model.SelectionStart = cursorLocation;
}
```

We just sketched this code, however, rather than typing it in, so we didn't really see how ugly it was. And we couldn't see how to write a decent unit test for it, and we had this perfectly good acceptance test, so we pushed ahead. Mostly I pushed ahead. I think after a while Chet was being swept along, while I kept thinking I was just a few more lines away from making it work. The breakdown came when I converted one method to return the new records, thus destroying its ability to be used for whatever it had done before. It was too much. And since we're working without much of a code manager and we hadn't backed up the files, we were doomed. I knew that if I would just write one more method, I could make it work. But I realized that even if I did, I could never explain it to you tonight.

Two hours of work, and that sinking feeling that you were better off before you started. What do you do?

There's Only One Thing to Do

Well, when the code is well and truly ruined, there's just one thing to do: back it out. The easiest way was to hold down Ctrl+Z (undo) until the code was backed up to a known good point. So we did that and then took a little time to reflect. It's important to reflect when things go wrong. You won't always have the right idea for what's next, but often you will.

I like to think that Chet and I are pretty calm about throwing code away. (We've thrown away so much!) It always hurts but only until you do it. Then it's like putting down a big bucket of water: a great relief. So we thought, and Chet reflected back on something he had said earlier in the process. We kept having to write procedural code inside the CustomerTest to manipulate the strings that make up a test. He had commented that the object wasn't helping us much, but we never followed up on it. We decided to think about it a little bit before we stopped for the day.

We Need an Object

Look at that code up there for SetInput. Either we have a two-pass algorithm or we have a complex setup to call a function that will be hard to write and that might still have a two-pass algorithm in it. Maybe I wasn't so wrong after all. The two-pass thing isn't as much a concern about speed, perhaps, as about our ability to express ourselves: we can't say what we want when we do it this way.

So we imagined some new object that holds input. We called it an Input-Command, and our proposed code looks like this:

```
private void SetInput(StringReader reader) {
  InputCommand input = InputCommand(reader);
  model.Lines = input.CleanLines();
  model.SelectionStart = input.SelectionStart();
```

If we can do something like that, it will be quite clean! So we imagine an object that will take the input from the reader that holds the whole script. It will know how to produce the clean lines (the ones without the vertical bar), and it will know how to say where the SelectionStart (cursor location) is. We think we like this. And we're pretty sure it will be easy to write. Tomorrow we're going to start on it.

Lesson: Lessons Relearned Today

If You Can't Test It, It's Wrong

When we realized we couldn't readily test this code, we should have stopped coding. The lack of testability was telling us, long before anything else did, that there was at least one missing object.

Procedural Code Is a Very Bad Smell

When you find yourself writing procedural methods and utility methods and railing at how the objects aren't helping you, this, too, is telling you that there's a missing object.

Too Long Between Green Bars

After we made our one new unit test work, we went for a long time without a new test or a new green bar—basically, all the time after lunch. This is at least a sign that you're stuck, and it should be used to trigger a rewind and a start in some new direction. Or even to start over in the same direction.

Conclusions for Today

We messed up. We finally figured out that we had. We backed up to last known good, maybe even going a little further back than we felt we had to. We did a quick retrospective and then called it a day. Maybe we wasted two or three hours, but we were confident that when we started over, everything would go much more smoothly.

Further Reflection

The next day, before starting the day's effort, Chet and I did a quick retrospective of the last day's, um, experience. We drew a couple of additional lessons over those above.

Program by Intention

We try always to write code that expresses our intention. (See, for example, the "Test First, by Intention" chapter in *Extreme Programming Installed* [Addison-Wesley, 2001].) Good code has methods with names that reveal their intention. And a good method that does two things "procedurally" needs to be refactored, using Extract Method, to express what those things are.

When we program, we all generally have some intention in mind: "First, I'll scan through all the files, looking for the ones that are updated. Then I'll make copies of those." When programming by intention, we make ourselves aware of these intentions as they come to us. Sometimes we then immediately write, first, a few lines of code to get the files and then a few more to make the copies. When we do this, the code does not express our intention. Here's an example of some code, from our CustomerTest.cs, that doesn't express intention as well as it might:

```
private String[] ArrayToEnd(StringReader reader) {
  ArrayList result = new ArrayList();
  String line = reader.ReadLine();
  while (line != null && line != "*end") {
    result.Add(line.TrimEnd());
    line = reader.ReadLine();
  }
  String[] answer = new String[result.Count];  result.CopyTo(answer);
  return answer;
}
```

Let's figure out this code. First we build an ArrayList containing all the lines of the input StringReader, up to "*end" or the end of the reader. Then we allocate an array of Strings of the right size and copy the ArrayList into it. Then we return the array.

That code might be better if it looked something like this:

```
private String[] ArrayToEnd(StringReader reader) {
  ArrayList result = ArrayListToEnd(reader);
  return ArrayListToArray(result)
}
```

It might be even better with better names—we could discuss that. In any case, we could argue that we should use Extract Method to refactor out those two methods, and Compose Method to create the new version of ArrayToEnd.

Programming by intention goes a step further than expressing intention after the fact. When we program by intention, we reflect on what we intend to do and we write the simple method first. If we know that we're going to create the array of strings by first creating an ArrayList and then copying it into an array of Strings, we say so. We write the short version of the method first, and then we write the two submethods.

Proceeding this way has a number of advantages. First, we don't have to remember so much. As soon as we know what we intend to do, we write it down. Then we just refine it until the code is there. Second, the code comes out well-factored without as much refactoring. We get better code, and it takes less time!

So why don't we do that all the time? We're not sure. We think it has to do with unfamiliarity with the language. We're so focused on how we might write legal statements in C#, and on which objects in C# might help us, that we forget to play our best game. Our first resolution is to return to programming by intention. Keep an eye on us, and see if we live up to our resolution.

Better Code Management

I might not have mentioned it before, but we have a simple code manager that we use as we develop this application. It's written in Ruby, and all it does is this: whenever we type **cm** in a command window, all the files of the source directory are copied to an archive directory. The file foo.cs, if dated today at 3:47:21 PM, will be named foo.cs.20020821154721 in the archive. All we have to do is type **cm** once in a while, and all our code is backed up. Works well enough for most of what we do, which is typically small programs. We have a little restore function, of course, that copies all the files back, with their value as of some given time.

You're probably asking yourself, if they used this cm thing, why did they have to Ctrl+Z yesterday to get back to a safe point? Did they have six saved versions or only five? Well, to tell you the truth, in all the excitement, we lost count ourselves. We forgot to type **cm** at crucial points in the development, so we didn't have a good point to restore to, other than the beginning of the day.

That was today's second resolution: have more points to back up to. That will make it easier to back up when we make a mistake, and we'll be less encouraged to keep plunging on, deeper and deeper into the depths of coding depravity.

Upgrading the Code Manager

Our little code manager is written in Ruby, so the actual code doesn't matter here. Here's a quick look at what we did with it. We decided that we wanted it to just hang in a loop, checking for files that change. When they change, poof, it copies them to the archive.

So we put our Ruby hats on and wrote a test to find changed files in the CodeManager's source directory. That worked pretty quickly, once Chet figured out that I was checking the wrong directory for changes. We paused for lunch with some friends at Red Hawk and finally we got back to work. We quickly made a test for backing up changed files, made that work, and refactored the code a bit. Then we wrote a simple timer loop method that sleeps, checks for changes, backs up if there are any, and sleeps again. From now on, we'll use that cm to watch our work.

We know we'll want some new features. The first few times we have to restore, we won't mind doing it manually, but we know we'll get tired of that. So we wrote a few new stories for the code manager, while we were thinking of them:

1. Build a restore GUI, probably in C#, that lets us pick a version to restore and puts it all back. That'll be interesting, not least because Visual Studio probably has some of the files reserved, given some other odd things we've seen. We'll burn that bridge when we come to it.

2. Change NUnit to write a file recording test results into the source directory. The cm program will back this file up, just like any other. We can make our GUI show us the red bar/green bar status, using that file. It'll be easy to decide how far to back up.

3. Integrate starting the cm into Visual Studio, so we won't forget to run it. Right now we have to remember to start it up, and we could forget, if past performance is any predictor of future results.

> **Lesson** We could have spent more time making this tool more capable, but, wisely for once, we stopped with just enough. We may or may not need those additional features, and we and our customer will schedule those if and when they're needed.

Just for fun, we made a couple of little changes to the Notepad project and watched the code manager put them in the archive. Then we broke for the day.

8

The InputCommand Object

We thought the code was telling us that it wanted another object, so we gave it another object. Was the code then happier? Were we? Read and find out...

Recap

In Chapter 7, "Warts and All," we set up an acceptance test that allowed the customer to say where the cursor was in the input and to condition the output based on that result. Then we went down a rat hole and backed out the code. We had identified that we needed an object, and we sketched the way that object would be used. The object we wanted was called InputCommand, and the idea was that it would be able to answer the clean input (the input except with the cursor position indication removed) and the selection start (the location of the input cursor). The code we wanted to make work looked like this:

```
private void SetInput(StringReader reader) {
  InputCommand input = new InputCommand(reader);
  model.Lines = input.CleanLines();
  model.SelectionStart = input.SelectionStart();
}
```

At this point, there was no InputCommand class, so this was all just speculation. We set out to create this class. Therefore, we needed a test. Here's the first test we wrote:

```
[Test] public void EmptyCommand() {
  command = new InputCommand();
  Assert(1==1);
}
```

Once we made that work, by creating an empty class named InputCommand, we extended the test to say

```
[Test] public void EmptyCommand() {
  command = new InputCommand();
  AssertEquals(0, command.CleanLines().Length);
}
```

The idea is that there's no input, so CleanLines will return an array of String of length zero. We built a CleanLines method that returned new String[0], which made that work. So far, so good.

We like writing these trivial tests. It's tempting to really "do" something, but, as we learned in "Warts and All," we get into trouble when we try to do too much. Starting every class this same way gives us a nice rhythm, and we rarely get into trouble. We've found it's better to keep things simple. Try it—it might work well for you also.

But sooner or later we have to do some work, and now's the time. Looking at the place where we actually intend to use this code, we see that the InputCommand wants to be driven from a StringReader. So we wrote a new test requiring a StringReader:

```
    [Test] public void OneLineCommand() {
      String oneLineString =
@"one line
*end";
      StringReader reader = new StringReader(oneLineString);
      command = new InputCommand(reader);
      AssertEquals(1, command.CleanLines().Length);
    }
```

This seems pretty simple. We're getting better at knowing how to work C#, although there's probably a better way to do this. We create a string that matches some legal input, create a StringReader on it, create an InputCommand on that, and assert that we get one line back from CleanLines(). That test doesn't even compile, because InputCommand doesn't have a constructor on StringReader. We debated whether to write a second constructor, to learn about overloads, but decided that would be a digression. So we changed our first test to use a StringReader also, like this:

```
[Test] public void EmptyCommand() {
  command = new InputCommand(new StringReader(""));
  AssertEquals(0, command.CleanLines().Length);
}
```

Fine. We have two tests that won't compile, because there's no such constructor, and we build the constructor:

```
private ArrayList lines;
public InputCommand(StringReader reader) {
  lines = new ArrayList();
  String line = reader.ReadLine();
  while (line != null && line != "*end") {
    lines.Add(line.TrimEnd());
    line = reader.ReadLine();
  }
}
```

(One of my editors noticed that we have InputCommand tied unnecessarily to StringReader, and he suggested that Reader would have been a better choice. It would have been; in our inexperience, we just didn't think of it.)

We decided to use an ArrayList for the member variable lines, which was what we were using internally in the original CustomerTest. We just read to "*end" and add the lines to ArrayList. And we implemented CleanLines to return the ArrayList. There was a little discussion on that: the rest of the code isn't clear on whether it wants arrays of strings or ArrayLists, and we decided that we like ArrayList better and we'd deal with any changes that we needed. The first change we needed was to change the .Length calls in our tests to .Count because the number of items in an ArrayList is .Count, while the number of items in an array is .Length. Now our two tests look like this:

```
[Test] public void EmptyCommand() {
  command = new InputCommand(new StringReader(""));
  AssertEquals(0, command.CleanLines().Count);
}
[Test] public void OneLineCommand() {
  String oneLineString =
@"one line
*end";
  StringReader reader = new StringReader(oneLineString);
  command = new InputCommand(reader);
  AssertEquals(1, command.CleanLines().Count);
}
```

And now the InputCommand CleanLines method looks like this:

```
public ArrayList CleanLines() {
  return lines;
}
```

The earlier version was answering an empty array of String. At this point, all our tests run. We did a little Ann Anderson goal line victory dance[1] and then

---

1. It's valuable to celebrate our small victories. Ann likes to jump up and do a little dance. Some teams have a little bell that they ring. Others are satisfied with a high five.

got back to work. The thing is, the lines aren't really clean. CleanLines() is supposed to strip out any vertical bars (the cursor location indicator) that are in the input. We haven't written a test that calls for that, so we write it:

```
[Test] public void OneDirtyLine() {
  command = new InputCommand(new StringReader("a|b\n*end"));
  AssertEquals("ab", command.CleanLines()[0]);
}
}
```

That should be enough to do it. We put in "a|b" and expect "ab" back.

> **Lesson**   Let's emphasize again how simple and tiny our tests have been. Certainly we could have put the vertical bar into the second test. If we had, however, we would not have been able to just answer lines back as the result. Now, returning lines is simply wrong, as we'll see in a minute, but in fact we had lots of work to do, with the constructor and adjusting .Length to .Count and so on.
>
>   We didn't *foresee* that there would be enough to do without the added complexity of the vertical bar; we just try *always* to take tiny little steps. It usually makes the job easier, by requiring us to worry about less and keep less in mind. This was just one of those times.

Cleaning the Lines

Anyway, now that we have the OneDirtyLine test, our mission is to produce an ArrayList of lines with no vertical bars in them. (Here again, we're skipping something. We also need to be answering where the cursor-indicating vertical bar was. But we're not thinking about that, so stop thinking about that!) We played a bit with how to do CleanLines. One idea was to calculate the ArrayList right in the CleanLines method. I was going that route, but Chet suggested that we just create the clean lines right as we built the input. With our test not running, we changed the constructor to look like this:

```
public InputCommand(StringReader reader) {
  lines = new ArrayList();
  String line = reader.ReadLine();
  while (line != null && line != "*end") {
    lines.Add(line.TrimEnd());
    line = reader.ReadLine();
  }
  CleanTheLines();
}
```

Note that we added the method CleanTheLines. We're expressing intention here. We also discussed that the constructor needs refactoring now.
Because it has two things that it does—setting up lines, which it does manually,
and setting up the clean lines, which it does by sending a message—we should
make that first bit of code into a method also. But that's not for now: we have
our adding functionality hat on, not our refactoring hat. So we wrote CleanThe-
Lines, like this, adding a new member variable to hold the clean lines:

```
private ArrayList cleanLines;

private void CleanTheLines() {
  cleanLines = new ArrayList();
  foreach ( String line in lines) {
    cleanLines.Add(CleanTheLine(line));
  }
}
```

(By the way, the member variables aren't spread around in the code like
I'm showing them here: they're up at the top of the class. I just didn't want you
to worry about that.)

Lesson   I just mentioned [sb]two hats: the adding functionality hat and
the refactoring hat. Kent Beck taught us to be aware when we're adding functionality, and he suggested that we should not try to clean up,
or refactor, the code at that time. Likewise, when we're refactoring, we
shouldn't try to add functionality. This is good advice, which we do well
to follow. When we mix things together, we seem to get confused more
easily. So we always try to do first one and then the other. Try it, you
might like it.

Notice that we expressed intention again in the previous method. We went
over each line and added a clean version of that line to the ArrayList. Let's underline that for a moment. By expressing intention here, we produce code that is
more expressive, but we also limit what we have to think about all at the same
time. When I'm in C programmer mode, I'd be more inclined to write the foreach
loop there, and then, inside it, try to expand out what CleanTheLine would be.
I'm sure I'm up to that challenge, most of the time, but sometimes I'm not. And,
again, when we work in these tiny steps, we find that we're more relaxed and
we're more able to deal with the distractions that inevitably occur, especially
when we're sitting in the Michigan Union. So now to write CleanTheLine(). We

got smart and typed **line**. (line dot) in the editor. The dot brings up the list of methods on the object—thanks, Visual Studio—and we scrolled through the list until we found Replace, whose write-up says: "Replaces all occurrences of a specified string in this instance, with another specified string." That sounds just right. We coded CleanTheLine this way:

```
private String CleanTheLine(String dirty) {
  return dirty.Replace("|", "");
}
```

That makes our test run! We've now got CleanLines() working, and we decide to put the InputCommand into the CustomerTest class as well:

```
private void SetInput(StringReader reader) {
  InputCommand input = new InputCommand(reader);
  model.Lines = input.CleanLines();
}
```

Note also that we didn't put the SelectionStart stuff in, since it isn't built yet, but we wanted to check whether the string part of the customer tests still worked. Surprisingly, all our customer tests worked, including the following one, which we thought shouldn't have:

```
*input
<P>This is the first p|aragraph.</P>
<P>This is the second paragraph.</P>
*end
*enter
*output
<P>This is the first paragraph.</P>
<P>|</P>
<P>This is the second paragraph.</P>
```

We were surprised by this, because we expected that we needed the selection start logic to figure out where the cursor was. But the default cursor location is zero, so because we didn't set it explicitly, our TextModel assumed that the cursor was on the first line and worked correctly. Oops. We wrote another customer test to verify this theory, and sure enough this test does not run:

```
*input
<P>This is the first paragraph.</P>
<P>This is the second| paragraph.</P>
*end
*enter
*output
<P>This is the first paragraph.</P>
<P>This is the second paragraph.</P>
<P>|</P>
```

Good. We thought we were wrong, and it turns out we were. Does that make us right?

Building SelectionStart

I wanted to go ahead and build SelectionStart, but Chet asked if I was going to write a programmer unit test first. I of course agreed.

> **Lesson**   This is a good habit to have, and especially in this new language we should try to practice good habits. In the larger scheme of things, customer tests might take longer to run. When this happens, we might tend to run customer tests less frequently than programmer tests. Furthermore, programmer tests generally point more directly to the problem when they fail. Therefore, when a customer test fails, the wise programmer writes a failing programmer test and then makes it work.

We added a line to our OneDirtyLine test, like this:

```
[Test] public void OneDirtyLine() {
  command = new InputCommand(new StringReader("a|b\n*end"));
  AssertEquals("ab", command.CleanLines()[0]);
  AssertEquals(1,command.SelectionStart());
}
```

This is enough to drive a trivial implementation of SelectionStart that returns 1, and then we added a line to our OneLineCommand test. We figured that because it didn't have a cursor indicator, the answer should be at the end of the lines.

```
    [Test] public void OneLineCommand() {
      String oneLineString =
@"one line
*end";
      StringReader reader = new StringReader(oneLineString);
      command = new InputCommand(reader);
      AssertEquals(1, command.CleanLines().Count);
      AssertEquals(10,command.SelectionStart());
    }
```

That was enough to get us to write the following, with some help from similar code that's elsewhere in our little system:

```
public int SelectionStart() {
  int charactersSoFar = 0;
  foreach (String line in lines) {
    int index = line.IndexOf("|");
    if (index != -1)
      return charactersSoFar + index;
    else
      charactersSoFar += line.Length + Environment.NewLine.Length;
  }
  return charactersSoFar;
  }
```

Now we really did type this in in one go. We had written a bunch of line-tracking loops recently, and this one just fell trippingly from my fingers. We keep track of how many characters we have read so far (which will be the number of characters in all the lines ahead of the line containing the vertical bar cursor indicator). When we find the first line with a vertical bar, we return the characters so far, plus the index of the cursor. That'll be the position in the whole "file" of the vertical bar. If the line doesn't contain the vertical bar, we update charactersSoFar.

Both our unit tests ran. However, most of the customer tests threw exceptions: index outside array. We fumbled with this a bit and then figured out how to tell from NUnit where the exception was thrown. We finally realized that when we run off the end of the list without finding the vertical bar, we set the selection start *after* the newline on the last line. Bad things happen because the TextModel thinks the cursor is in the next line after the last line. We realized that if SelectionStart finds no cursor, it should assume the cursor is in the last line, not after it. So we have to back out the last NewLine. The new Selection-Start is therefore

```
public int SelectionStart() {
  int charactersSoFar = 0;
  foreach (String line in lines) {
    int index = line.IndexOf("|");
    if (index != -1)
      return charactersSoFar + index;
    else
      charactersSoFar += line.Length + Environment.NewLine.Length;
  }
  return charactersSoFar - Environment.NewLine.Length;
}
```

And the tests all run! We think our story is actually running now and that all the customer tests imaginable for this feature will work. We'll probably write a few more, but for today, we're finished.

Lesson: What We Learned

Backing out our code earlier was pretty scary, but we learned that—as usual—it was a good idea. We guessed that we weren't using objects wisely, and our success with the InputCommand object confirms that. And from experience we learned that this approach is far less error-prone.

We learned that our reflexes to create new objects need to be more sensitive. A lot more work is required in C# (and Java) when building a new class, compared to what we're used to in Ruby and Smalltalk, but the need for new objects is just as strong, so we have to be more sensitive to that need.

Considering the time it takes to build it—just a couple hours' work—the payoff for the new object is large: simple code, nicely partitioned off, easy to test and write. We certainly hope you can sense, both from our expression of the experience and from the code steps themselves, how much easier it was this time. It took only about half the original time, by the way, with far less stress.

Cruft Buildup

However, there's some cruft[2] buildup in the system now. A general confusion between arrays of strings and ArrayLists exists, although we cleaned some of this up as we went by virtue of having chosen ArrayList as the preferred object in InputCommand. Somewhere earlier, I didn't mention a couple of edits, where we matched up the interfaces. The Text-Model used to take an array of strings in its Lines method and convert it to an ArrayList—now it takes an ArrayList. And because the TextForm wants an array of Strings, we had to convert the ArrayList to strings in a new place. We didn't want to go into that, because it interrupted the flow of the narrative more than it interrupted the coding progress. Which brings me to my next point.

(continued)

---

2. Cruft is an unpleasant substance, the results of shoddy construction. Look it up in one of the jargon dictionaries on the Web for more information.

Precompile Checking for Watts Humphrey

I had dinner with Watts Humphrey at XP/Agile Universe. Watts is very much into desk checking code, and I said that we'd try going over our code by eyeball before compiling, shooting for clean compiles. We haven't started doing that yet, but we did talk about it a few times as we went along. The standard XP thing to do is to type in a test, or some code, and then compile and run the tests. You let the compiler, or the failed test, direct your attention to the next thing. We were still doing that. We noticed that we would quite typically do something like the following:

We changed the return type of CleanLines from String[] to ArrayList. We could have looked through the code to see where the changes needed to be made. Instead, we compiled and then clicked on the compiler errors, which took us in the editor to the lines that needed changing. We fixed them and went on. Few if any of the compiler errors surprised us. And the very few logic problems we had, we believe, we would have detected by eyeball.

So we haven't done the experiment yet, but we remain committed to doing so. My subjective impression is that while in the olden days we might have printed a listing and looked at it, marking what we saw, the modern tools change the cost/benefit equation. To scrunch through the code looking for places that assume String[] would be time-consuming and subject to human error. To let the compiler do it is faster and completely accurate. The downside, of course, is that while scanning for those errors, we might well find other errors the compiler cannot help with. This time, we had very few such errors, and as far as we know, there are none that weren't detected by the tests. (I still have to look at that Replace method, though.)

Right now, our tentative conclusion is that the tools are different enough to move the best strategy in the direction of automation, especially in the presence of so many tests.

9

Story One Is Done!

We've got a story working, Customer Acceptance Test and all! It's time to reflect a bit and refactor before we call it done.

Lesson: Retrospectives

Whenever we reach a pause in our work, we like to reflect on what has happened and to try to learn from it. We look forward and think about what we should work on and how we should adjust our practices for better results. In the agile software community, these sessions are usually called "Retrospectives." In other realms they're called "After Action Reviews," "Reviews," and sometimes "Postmortems." We don't like that last term because we aren't dead yet. Sit back and observe our little retrospective and planning session.

Planning Our Next Session

As we generally do but haven't reported, Chet and I discussed what we should do in this session before starting. We'll report it this time because there was a lot more discussion than just "Let's get the code manager running" and "OK." We quickly agreed that we have all the Customer Acceptance Tests for our first story running. So it's time to ship it, right?

Wrong. It's time to be sure the code is clean. We talked for maybe 10 minutes about what we might want to do. Here's what we touched on:

Pushing the Command Metaphor

We needed the InputCommand, primarily because we turned out to be too stupid to make things work without it. The code called out for an object, and we wrote it. InputCommand turned out very nice—so nice that it's clear that we should have an OutputCommand and that ultimately all the operation of the CustomerTest would be embodied in Commands.

We also notice that the InputCommand, though it has some smarts, is just a utility object. We feed it some text, it processes the text, and we rip the text back out and stuff it into the model for testing. It might make sense to tell the InputCommand something like input.execute(model) and have it do its own stuffing. It might also make sense to tell the model to execute the command. But the model doesn't have that kind of functionality now. Still, the model *does* suck the text out of the TextBox and put it back, so maybe the InputCommand is trying to grow up into some more advanced kind of object.

However, we have no driving need to do that. We're not maintaining the CustomerTest class right now, and we have no story that would drive us to do these improvements; our only reason would be to add functionality later. Our discipline is not to make this kind of change unless the code is really asking for it. And our view is that it is not asking...yet.

Chet also pointed out that the Command hierarchy, if we built it, would be in some way parallel to the TextModel, and/or parallel to the CustomerTest. He felt that there isn't enough functionality there for that to come out. Summing it all up, we decided not to do anything about pushing the Command metaphor further at this time.

Duplicate Reading Logic

Because InputCommand reads the input file up to "*end" to get input, and because CustomerTest reads input up to "*end" to get output, the system has some very similar-looking code. In InputCommand we have

```
private void ReadLines(StringReader reader) {
  lines = new ArrayList();
  String line = reader.ReadLine();
  while (line != null && line != "*end") {
    lines.Add(line.TrimEnd());
    line = reader.ReadLine();
  }
}
```

And in CustomerTest we have this:

```
private String ReadToEnd(StringReader reader) {
  String result = "";
  String line = reader.ReadLine();
```

```
  while (line != null && line != "*end") {
    result += line;
    result += System.Environment.NewLine;
    line = reader.ReadLine();
  }
  return result;
}
```

These both have the same kind of loop, and they're doing the same kind of thing, although one of them creates an ArrayList and one appends everything into a String. We see this as duplication, even though it's certainly not as obvious as if all the lines were exactly equal. We don't like duplication, so we don't like this. Possibly we need another utility class that wraps StringReader. Or maybe InputCommand is actually what we want here, just with the wrong name because we don't see its "real" function yet. Either way, we're a bit torn by this duplication because we're afraid that if we don't fix it, we'll forget because we're not likely to remember these two classes as clearly later as we do now. But fixing the problem seems too large, and we don't have a clear sense of direction. Again, we defer the change.

Code Manager Needs Autorun

At this point, we turned to coding. Chet reminded me to start the code manager running so that it would snapshot all our changes. We need a tool for this, so we're reflecting on it for a moment. We're not going to write the tool, but we are reinforcing the idea in our minds a bit.

Watts Stuff

We reflect briefly on our chat with Watts Humphrey and our promise to scan the code trying for clean compiles, in hopes of finding other errors. We're still not ready to do this, and frankly we're not sure it's a good idea in this environment, but we keep thinking about it. As you'll see, we paid a little attention to it this time.

Cleaning the Code

Now we're finished reflecting, and we're ready to clean up the code. We're going to go over most of the modules, and we begin with ones where we're sure there's something to do.

CustomerTest: ArrayToEnd

CustomerTest has a method ArrayToEnd that we think isn't used any more. We ask Microsoft Visual Studio to give us references to it. It says there are none. We remove the method and compile; the compiler doesn't complain. We run the tests; the tests all run. We're quite sure it was OK to remove ArrayToEnd.

Scaffolding Tests

There are some "scaffolding" tests left in CustomerTest. Remember that we did a couple of trivial tests on an empty model, and on a constant string, before making the leap to reading a test from a file. We could remove those tests right now, but we don't, for two reasons:

1.   We enter tests in chronological order in the file. Reading down through the tests gives insight into our thinking as we' built the object. We think that history is potentially valuable. The tests are harmless, and there's no reason to remove them.

2.   These tests are of very fine grain compared to the customer tests. In a sense, they're like unit tests. If something goes wrong in the innards of CustomerTest, the failure of these tests might well identify the problem more quickly than debugging through a customer test.

We generally think this way: if a test is made a bit redundant by a following test but isn't doing any harm and could perhaps point more sharply to a problem, we tend to leave it in. Probably you could match our behavior to 95 percent by just *never* deleting a test. We like to reflect on why we do things, to sharpen our own skills and to share our thinking with you.

Rename a Test

One of the early tests is named DirectInput. We had in mind just giving some input to the model and testing it. But in fact, we tested the model without giving it any input, so we decided to rename the test EmptyModel. It looks like this now:

```
[Test] public void EmptyModel() {
  model.Enter();
  AssertEquals("%lt;P>|</P>\r\n", model.TestText);
}
```

We compiled, built, looked at NUnit and marvelled that it had picked up the new name, and ran the tests. Not that we had any doubt—it's just what we do. Every time. It's fascinating when things work the way they are supposed to.

Rename a Variable

Take a look at the following code:

```
[Test] public void TestAllFiles() {
  String[] testFiles = Directory.GetFiles(@"c:\data\csharp\notepad\", "*.test");
  foreach (String testFile in testFiles) {
    InterpretFileInput(testFile);
  }
}
```

The variable testFile isn't a file; it's the name of a file. We decided to rename it to testFileName. We did that, compiled, ran the tests, and then thought better of the change. We think it's the name of the test file. It's the file name of the test file. So we renamed it testFilename, without the camel cap on "name". Maybe we were right to think it was better, maybe we weren't. Your choices will vary, but do spend the moment it takes to give the thing a good name. Don't give it an hour, not even a few minutes, but a moment? Yes.

InterpretFileInput

We have an issue with the InterpretFileInput method and the way it interacts with InterpretCommands. Take a look at it:

```
private void InterpretFileInput(String fileName) {
  StreamReader stream = File.OpenText(fileName);
  String contents = stream.ReadToEnd();
  stream.Close();
  InterpretCommands(contents, fileName);
}
private void InterpretCommands(String commands, String message) {
  StringReader reader = new StringReader(commands);
  String line = reader.ReadLine();
...
```

Do you see what's happening? InterpretFileInput reads the file into a string, and then InterpretCommands makes a StringReader on that string. Why not just pass a StreamReader on the file into InterpretCommands? That would seem to make more sense.

We decided not to do the change, however. It felt a little larger than the refactorings we were doing, and it would throw off our rhythm to do it. And it's mostly harmless the way it is. Maybe we should have changed it; maybe we'll change it later.

The Read Loops

We have a pattern of code where we read a line from an input stream and then loop while the line isn't null. ReadToEnd, which we already looked at, is an example:

```
  private String ReadToEnd(StringReader reader) {
String result = "";
String line = reader.ReadLine();
while (line != null && line != "*end") {
result += line;
result += System.Environment.NewLine;
line = reader.ReadLine();
  }
  return result;
}
```

We think there should be a way to do this loop without the duplicated reads, one outside and one inside the loop. Without the check for *end, we could do it with reader.Peek(), which returns -1 if nothing's left to read. (Thanks for saving that feature from C, Microsoft!) But in this case, if we use Peek(), we still have to test for *end and we have to break the loop in that case as well. We typed in the code and it looked worse, so we're living with what we have until we have a better idea.

We're about out of ideas for how to clean up CustomerTest.

InputCommand Refactoring

Now we look at InputCommand. The first thing we notice is something we noticed the other day. Here's the code that concerns us:

```
public InputCommand(StringReader reader) {
  lines = new ArrayList();
  String line = reader.ReadLine();
  while (line != null && line != "*end") {
    lines.Add(line.TrimEnd());
    line = reader.ReadLine();
  }
  CleanTheLines();
}
```

The problem here is that the code is at two levels of abstraction. It does two things: first it reads the input into lines, and then it creates the "clean lines," the lines with the vertical bar that represents the cursor position removed. But it does the first thing with a patch of code and the second with a method call.

The "right" structure for a method that does more than one thing is called "Composed Method." Always create a method that is composed of nothing but method calls, all at the same level, rather than expanding any of the ideas out in line. So we did the Extract Method refactoring, to produce this result:

```
public InputCommand(StringReader reader) {
  ReadLines(reader);
  CleanTheLines();
}
private void ReadLines(StringReader reader) {
  lines = new ArrayList();
  String line = reader.ReadLine();
  while (line != null && line != "*end") {
    lines.Add(line.TrimEnd());
    line = reader.ReadLine();
  }
  reader.Close;
}
```

We added the reader.Close because it seems like a good idea to close a reader when you're done with it. As always, we compile, preparing to run the tests. Oops! Doesn't compile! We left the () off Close. We think it's a bug in C# to require parens on methods with no parameters, but Bill isn't here to complain to, so we fix the code to say Close(). That compiles fine, and we run the tests.

BANG! The tests fail. They're trying to read from a closed StringReader. Doh! We were passed this open StringReader. It's no business of ours to close it. This was a bum idea all around, so we remove the Close.

Would Watts Have Helped Us?

We stopped for a moment to chat about whether doing what Watts recommended would have helped us, since this was the first compile error and the first test error we had. Our answer is no, because we were entirely sure we wanted to do this thing. We did think about it: it was exactly what we were thinking about. Our thinking was wrong—but our tests were not. Very interesting...

CleanTheLines

We don't like the method CleanTheLines. We don't usually use "The" as part of a method name. CleanLines would be a better name. We almost change it but then realize that the accessor to the clean lines from outside is called Clean-Lines. That's probably why we named the method so oddly to begin with. We try various ideas in our minds, like renaming the outside method to Cleaned-Lines, and the like. None of the ideas appeal to us. What we do instead is remove the method altogether. We do that by moving the line-cleaning code directly into the CleanLines access method. The old method just returned the instance variable cleanLines:

```
private ArrayList cleanLines;
public ArrayList CleanLines() {
  return cleanLines;
}
```

The new version eliminates the member variable and looks like this:

```
public ArrayList CleanLines() {
  ArrayList cleanLines = new ArrayList();
  foreach ( String line in lines) {
    cleanLines.Add(CleanTheLine(line));
  }
  return cleanLines;
}
```

This compiles, and the tests run fine. The world is a slightly better place.

Smaller Details

We've covered the big things we noticed, either fixing them or deciding consciously not to fix them yet. Now for some small things:

CommandTest

We look back at Command Test. The InterpretCommand method has a bunch of if statements in it. These should at least be if/else, shouldn't they? The code isn't very good, but we think it's clear enough and we decide to let it lay:

```
private void InterpretCommands(String commands, String message) {
  StringReader reader = new StringReader(commands);
  String line = reader.ReadLine();
  CreateModel();
  while ( line != null) {
    if ( line == "*enter")
      model.Enter();
    if (line == "*display")
      Console.WriteLine("display\r\n{0}\r\nend", model.TestText);
    if (line == "*output")
      CompareOutput(reader, message);
    if (line == "*input")
      SetInput(reader);
    line = reader.ReadLine();
  }
}
```

TextModel Method: TestText

The TextModel object has a method named TestText that's there only for testing. It looks like this:

```
public String TestText {
  get {
    StringBuilder b = new StringBuilder();
    foreach(String s in lines) {
      b.Append(s);
      b.Append(System.Environment.NewLine);
    }
    b.Insert(SelectionStart,"|");
    return b.ToString();
  }
}
```

Some people would wonder about having a test method there at all or whether it should be public or private or what. We don't worry about it. We needed a test method that allowed our customer to compare the TextModel's state with what's expected. Possibly that method could be on some other object, but we decide it's not doing any harm where it is. We'll keep an eye on it.

Comments

We have a few comments in TextModel. We make a note to go over those and determine whether the code can be cleaned up to make them unnecessary.

LinesAfterCursor and LinesThroughCursor

The method LinesAfterCursor in TextModel isn't used any more. We check with Visual Studio References, compile, and test. Everything works. Same for the method LinesThroughCursor: check with Visual Studio, compile, test. Everything is OK.

Lessons

Here are a few lessons we learned today that I'd like to pass on to you:

Delete It

Somewhere along the way—I don't even remember where—those methods became useless. Maybe they were always useless. We noticed, removed them, tested, and let them fall into the bit bucket. This is, I suggest, usually your best practice: if it's not used, delete it. The methods are there in the code manager, in case we ever need them. And we write simple, clear code, so they'll be easy to write again if we have to. So get 'em outta there, that's my advice.

No GUI Testing

We haven't even run the GUI for a couple of days! We so completely trust our CustomerTests that we haven't had the slightest temptation to run the GUI. This is a miracle, and we'll come back to it in the next chapter.

Reflection on Watts's Ideas

We still aren't "desk-checking" our code. All day today, however, we had only one compile error (the missing parens on Close) and one test error (the Close itself), so if desk-checking were to help us today, it would have had to find errors not found by our unit tests or our customer tests. We'll keep watching for bugs that show up as we use the program, when we get around to actually using it. For now, we're not seeing where the benefit could be.

In fairness to Watts's ideas, though, we wouldn't expect to see them. His suggestion is that in desk-checking we'll find bugs that (at least) the compiler won't find and (possibly) that our tests won't find either. We had only one case where our tests found anything, and desk-checking wouldn't have helped that and would have taken longer if it had, because compiling and running takes...wait a minute, I'll do it...six seconds. Hard to beat that with the human brain. But we'll keep paying attention to errors and see what happens.

Conclusions

We think our first story now runs; certainly all our tests run and the acceptance tests run. We are open to the possibility that the next story will show a defect that's already here, but that's why we do lots of small releases: so that we, and our customer (hat), can learn. We just hope our customer hat is smarter than we are.

In a final retrospective chapter—Chapter 31, "Project Retrospective"—we'll take a look back at all the book's chapters and we'll draw some overall lessons and conclusions. And you'll notice that we look back frequently, on a smaller scale, just like we did this time. For now, we're ready to ship our first story. The code is pretty clean—we're honestly happy with it—and the tests all run. Maybe we're being too kind to ourselves in not cleaning up some of the things we looked at, but we looked at all of them and consciously decided. If they bite us later, we'll remember and adjust our behavior based on what we learn. We figure that's the best a person can do.

Ship It!

Because our story was done and our customer's acceptance tests run, we asked the customer what to do next. The customer decided that the team should package up the software and ship it as an installable application.

It turns out that Visual Studio has the ability to "deploy" the software, so Chet and I read the help files and set up deployment for our XML Notepad. It took us a couple of hours. Most of the problems were in figuring out how to cause the deployment builder to set up shortcuts to the XML Notepad on the desktop and in the Start menu. We're still not sure we did it exactly right, but now there's a deployment project built in to the solution and it does create a directory with the install files in it.

We were using my modestly priced version of Visual Studio, so there weren't many options: maybe there are more in the bigger versions. The setup program that we got doesn't offer a bunch of options to the user either: it just installs the app in a known location, requiring that you manually remove any previous copies, and puts icons unconditionally in the Start menu and on the desktop.

But we didn't have a story requiring any more than that. Our shipping story—made up on the spot—was to produce a shipping package that would install the system on a suitably preconfigured machine. We're sure that as the project goes on, there will be lots of stories about making the installation more beautiful, flexible, and bulletproof. That's what iterations are all about. The thing is, now we have completed a full cycle of product development, all the way from nothing but an idea, to running, tested, shippable software.

And one more important detail: I'm using the application right now to write up this chapter! It turns out that the TextBox includes copy, cut, and paste, so I can transfer this report to the existing scheme whenever I want to. Typing the raw text here is easier than using TextPad, my usual editor, because here, when I hit return, I get a new paragraph, already in paragraph tags. In TextPad, I have to press Alt+P to create a new paragraph. This is better!

> **Lesson**   I'd like to call your attention to something. This project is between ten and 20 hours old in terms of work on it. For all practical purposes, it is nothing but a GUI app. Nonetheless, it already has an automated Customer Acceptance Test, in addition to a bunch of automated Programmer Unit Tests.
>
> Furthermore, our program is deployed as a shippable, running application.
>
> We did it. You can do it, too.

Iteration Planning

After shipping the product—or at least making the Install file—the customers took the programmers to lunch at Red Hawk for a little celebration. "There must be food" is a core XP principle, and Chet and I have our dials set to ten on that one. During lunch, we discussed what the stories should be for the next iteration or two.

Save a File

One popular idea was to have a File/Save menu so that the customers can use the program and save the output for use in TextPad. We pointed out that we could use copy and paste, if we wanted to defer that story.

Scrolling After Enter

I just noticed a "bug": when I am typing low down in the window and hit Enter, the window doesn't scroll up to show the cursor. I have to use the scroll bars to make it do that.

Except, of course, it *isn't* a bug. There was no story for that behavior, and there was no test. It was an oversight, on both the customers' part and the programmers'. This is actually an important distinction for XP teams to make. Yes, it would have been nice had some programmer thought of making this work. Should the programmer have just done it? Not in our opinion, unless the change was trivial. If it would take any work to do, that work wasn't included in the current story's thinking, and therefore there's a new allocation of effort to be made. Allocation of effort always belongs to the customer. Therefore, if we had thought of it as programmers, we would have asked our customers (who are always on site, by the way) and let them decide.

In addition, the customers didn't think of it either. There's no point in finger pointing and name calling over whether this is a bug. It wasn't asked for, it wasn't tested, and it doesn't work. We'd like it to work: therefore, write a story for it and the team will do it when the customer schedules it.

(I have figured out that the scrolling is actually even more odd than I first noticed. It actually scrolls the window to the *top* of the page every time I hit Enter. I'm making a note of it because it might be a clue for the programmers.)

XML Conversion

(This scrolling problem is getting irritating. I might have to give it priority. But I digress.)

This program is intended to be used to enter articles into the XProgramming.com Web site, which is where initial versions of these chapters first appeared. That process includes an XSLT transformation of the articles in XML into HTML for the site. Customers and programmers talked about this at lunch and agreed that it was of high value. We had been thinking that the story would come a bit later on, after more editing commands, after File/Save, and so on. And we were thinking that it might be a big story.

But with our programmer hats on, we got to thinking that almost certainly there are XSLT objects built into .NET and that it might not be that hard to set up a translator and translate a simple file. We already have the valid XSL that we want to use for the translation, in the "old" manual Web site generation code, so maybe it wouldn't be too hard.

And then we thought about the customer tests for the product so far. Text in, command, expected text out. So why couldn't the test be to put in a simple XML page formatted like an XProgramming.com article, translate it according to the existing XSL file, and check the output to make sure it looks just like the HTML that we get from the old "legacy" process?

All we'd have to do to make that test run would be to set up an XSLT translator, feed it the string, run it, and read out the answer for comparison. The programmers recommended to the customers that the XSLT story be scheduled fairly soon. We felt we could do it in two or three days and that we would learn a lot in that time. We're sure that we can do the File/Save in a couple of hours and that we won't learn much at all. We can do some new control characters to make headers or to insert complex XML structures like those used on XProgramming's Web site, but those won't involve any deep learning either. So, in terms of making the program more useful and in terms of learning as much as possible, we recommended a small XSLT story.

Conclusion

It has been a good iteration. We've learned a lot, and we can tell that our C# code is better and more facile now than it was at the beginning of this effort. We've figured out how to test and how to deploy, and we did it in a very small amount of time. No infrastructure, no warming up, just test, design, and code.

> **Lesson**   One more thing I've noticed that might help you. Because we know that every day's work has to be written up for the Web site, we make a point of doing little retrospectives all the time, basically going over what has happened and what we have learned. I think it's helping us learn faster and remember more. You might want to try that technique yourself.

10

Find a Bug, Write a Test

*Last time out, I found a bug. Our rules of engagement require us to write a test, first to show that the bug exists and later to verify that we have fixed it, **but we don't know how to write that test!** We get by with a little help from our friends.*

Oh No, There's a Bug!

In the previous chapter, I found a defect in the program: when insertion of a new set of paragraph tags takes you below the bottom of the window, the text doesn't scroll up to keep the cursor on the screen. You have to keep clicking on the scroll bars to bring the line back up.

It took me only a little while to find and fix the defect. Here's the code, from the XMLNotepad class, with the fix. That's what we're going to work on today:

```
void XMLKeyDownHandler(object objSender, KeyEventArgs kea) {
  model.SetLines(textbox.Lines);
  model.SelectionStart = textbox.SelectionStart;
  if (kea.KeyCode == Keys.Enter) {
    model.Enter();
    kea.Handled = true;
  }
  if (kea.KeyCode == Keys.L && kea.Modifiers == Keys.Control) {
    String[] lines = textbox.Lines;
    foreach ( String s in lines) {
      Console.WriteLine(s);
    }
    Console.WriteLine("model");
    //Console.WriteLine(model.Text);
```

```
      kea.Handled = true;
    }
    if (kea.KeyCode == Keys.S && kea.Modifiers == Keys.Control) {
      textbox.SelectionLength = 0;
      kea.Handled = true;
    }
    textbox.Lines = model.LinesArray();
    textbox.SelectionStart = model.SelectionStart;
    textbox.ScrollToCaret(); // keep cursor on screen. no test.
}
```

It turns out that when you set the text into a TextBox and then set the cursor, it doesn't force the cursor onto the screen. You have to call the ScrollToCaret method to get that to happen. Finding that method and sending the message was the fix, but only the beginning of my pain.

Find a Defect, Write Tests

The XP discipline that Chet and I follow is that when we find a defect, we write a test that shows the defect and then fix it. The reasoning is that if our tests were good, there would be no defects. Therefore, our tests at this point are inadequate. We write the necessary tests, not so much for this defect, but instead to teach ourselves what kind of tests we need to add.

Here's the problem: this code is in the GUI, and we have no tests for the GUI. Our normal practice is to write very thin GUIs that don't require tests. If you never get a bug in the GUI, you can claim that this practice works. But we *have* a bug in the GUI. Now what?

I made the mistake of asking for advice on the Yahoo extreme programming mailing list. It was Dog Pile On Ron time! People from all over the world berated me for not having tests for this, calling my orthodoxy into question, threatening me with expulsion from the community. They even offered some advice on what to do, when I protested that I didn't know *how* to write this test.

I think much of the advice is good. However, even after a couple of short attempts, I haven't been able to find steps that seem small enough to be safe. This is, for better or worse, untested code, and I don't feel comfortable making significant changes without tests. This morning I've got an idea for something to try. It's a bigger step than I'd like, but maybe it's not too big.

Mock the TextBox

There's a fairly standard technique for testing whether some system object is used correctly. You build a "Mock Object," an object that mimics the system object just enough to detect whether it's being sent the right messages. I've never used the technique in a strongly typed language, so it's time to find out what it takes.

Dave Thomas and Andy Hunt, the "Pragmatic Programmers," published an article about mock objects in *IEEE Software* in May/June 2002. An online copy can be found at *http://www.pragmaticprogrammer.com/articles/may_02_mock.pdf*.

My intention is just this, based on a couple of experiments that I haven't written up. The KeyDownHandler uses only a couple of the features of the TextBox, so I should be able to mock up just those features. In a reasonable language, that would be easy: just plug in a MockTextBox that responds to those messages and let it go. In a strongly-typed language, we can't just do that: the language wants us to support all the known methods of the original object's type. Therefore, I'm going to do this in two steps:

1. **Isolate the usage.**   Note in the code above that the KeyDownHandler really only refers to the textbox in a couple of important places: it reads the data at the beginning, and it sets the data back at the end. (The uses in the middle of the method are just there for early manual testing. I should take them out anyway.)

2. **Build and test the Mock Object.**   Then, my idea is to write a test on my MockTextBox that will check to be sure that the handler sets the cursor.

The Payoff?

Frankly, I expect the payoff on this exercise not to be in the test. After all, I already know that the code works. I expect to learn something about how to do Mock Objects in C#, and I'm hoping that the refactoring will lead to some better ideas for how this part of the program should be done.

Well, enough chit-chat, let's get to work.

Extract Method

I'm going to extract the code that talks to the TextBox from the KeyDownHandler. I think I'll begin with just the last few lines that set the TextBox. I plan two steps, more for purposes of explaining than anything else. First, let's make a new method:

```
public void PutText() {
  textbox.Lines = model.LinesArray();
  textbox.SelectionStart = model.SelectionStart;
  textbox.ScrollToCaret(); // keep cursor on screen. no test.
}
```

And we'll call it from the handler, replacing the last three lines. I removed the debugging stuff as well, so the new handler looks like this:

```
void XMLKeyDownHandler(object objSender, KeyEventArgs kea) {
  model.SetLines(textbox.Lines);
  model.SelectionStart = textbox.SelectionStart;
  if (kea.KeyCode == Keys.Enter) {
    model.Enter();
    kea.Handled = true;
  }
  PutText();
}
```

Normally, I'd just compile now and run the tests. But my tests don't test this! I'll have to test it manually. This is awful! But it seems to work. Now for the second step.

The PutText method refers to the instance variable textbox. I want to pass it in as a parameter instead. This may seem odd at first, but remember that I want to use this thing with my Mock Object.

However, thinking about this tells me that I don't have a clear picture of what my test will look like, so I'm speculating about what I want. And surely so are you. I should be writing the test first. So I'll do that now.

The Scroll Test

You can start a new test class in a number of ways. Lee Holmes of Microsoft uses a keyboard macro to convert a new class file into a test class. See my Web site for an article about how to build a new template for a test class and install it into Microsoft Visual Studio. Often I just manually edit a new class, and I often write a first test that just runs trivially so that I can be sure that it is hooked up:

```
using System;
using NUnit.Framework;
namespace Notepad
{
  [TestFixture] public class TestScroll: Assertion
  {
    [Test] public void HookUp() {
      Assert("hooked up", true);
    }
  }
}
```

Once that works—and it does—I'll proceed to write the test I actually want:

```
[Test] public void ScrollHappens() {
  MockTextBox mock = new MockTextBox();
  XMLNotepad notepad = new XMLNotepad();
  Assert("no scroll", !mock.Scrolled);
  notepad.PutText(mock, lines, selectionStart);
  Assert("scroll happens", mock.Scrolled);
}
```

I just sketched my intention here, and look what happened. I want to set up a MockTextBox, have it declare that it isn't scrolled, then put some text into it, and have it respond that now it is scrolled. My idea is that the MockTextBox will just set a flag when sent the ScrollToCaret. But look at the PutText message. I realized that I don't want to go through the Form if I don't have to, because the Form is doing all kinds of things to the model and textbox that I can't control. So I want not only the textbox parameter but also the lines and selectionStart to be parameters as well.

The test is telling me things about how the object should work.

However, I'm getting in a bit deep here. It's time to dig out and make sure things are running. I'm going to comment out a few lines of this test and then get it running:

```
[Test] public void ScrollHappens() {
  MockTextBox mock = new MockTextBox();
  // XMLNotepad notepad = new XMLNotepad();
  Assert("no scroll", !mock.Scrolled);
  // notepad.PutText(mock, lines, selectionStart);
  // Assert("scroll happens", mock.Scrolled);
}
```

So I write a quick MockTextObject:

```
using System;
namespace Notepad
{
  public class MockTextBox
  {
    public MockTextBox()
    {
    }
    public Boolean Scrolled {
      get {
        return false;
      }
    }
  }
}
```

That test runs. Now I'll uncomment the commented test lines and get to work. The program doesn't compile because lines and selectionStart aren't defined. We can fix that:

```
[Test] public void ScrollHappens() {
  int selectionStart = 1;
  string[] lines = new String[] { "hello", "world" };
  MockTextBox mock = new MockTextBox();
  XMLNotepad notepad = new XMLNotepad();
  Assert("no scroll", !mock.Scrolled);
  notepad.PutText(mock, lines, selectionStart);
  Assert("scroll happens", mock.Scrolled);
}
```

The compiler tells us that no overload for method PutText() takes three arguments. We knew that; that's what we are here to fix. So Back to XMLNotepad to fix PutText:

```
void XMLKeyDownHandler(object objSender, KeyEventArgs kea) {
  model.SetLines(textbox.Lines);
  model.SelectionStart = textbox.SelectionStart;
  if (kea.KeyCode == Keys.Enter) {
    model.Enter();
    kea.Handled = true;
  }
  PutText(textbox, model.LinesArray(), model.SelectionStart);
}
public void PutText(TextBox textbox, string[] lines, int selectionStart) {
  textbox.Lines = lines;
  textbox.SelectionStart = selectionStart;
  textbox.ScrollToCaret(); // keep cursor on screen. no test.
}
```

This nearly works, except (of course) that MockTextBox isn't a TextBox. I'm tempted to have it subclass TextBox, but that's not likely to be a good idea: it would be inheriting lots of behavior that I don't understand, and the PutText method would be sending it messages. Instead, I'm going to comment out the line that sends to it, and I'll test the GUI manually to be sure my new PutText is working. And it seems to be. The next step shouldn't be too hard, but it's a bit of a big one.

Build an Interface

We want our MockTextBox to be able to plug into the PutText method just like a TextBox would. To do that, it has to respond reasonably to just three messages: Lines, SelectionStart, and ScrollToCaret. So first we'll define that interface and then we'll use it. For now, I'm going to do that in the Notepad object, the superclass of our XMLNotepad. That's where the TextBox gets set up. The file looks like this, with the interface done:

```
using System;
using System.Drawing;
using System.Windows.Forms;
namespace Notepad {
  interface ITestTextBox {
    string[] Lines {get; set;}
    int SelectionStart { get; set;}
    void ScrollToCaret();
  }
  class TestableTextBox: TextBox, ITestTextBox {
  }
  class NotepadCloneNoMenu : Form
  {
    public TestableTextBox textbox;
    public NotepadCloneNoMenu() {
      Text = "Notepad Clone No Menu";
      textbox = new TestableTextBox();
      textbox.Parent = this;
      textbox.Dock = DockStyle.Fill;
      textbox.BorderStyle = BorderStyle.None;
      textbox.Multiline = true;
      textbox.ScrollBars = ScrollBars.Both;
      textbox.AcceptsTab = true;
    }
  }
}
```

I'm skipping over a small amount of pain here. Setting up the interface was a bit tricky because I didn't know the syntax for the properties (Lines and SelectionStart) and it took a while to find it. But the result is fairly simple: We define an interface ITestTextBox with the three methods. Then we create a new class TestableTextBox that inherits from TextBox and from ITestTextBox. This is the first time I've done this, but what I'm told is that this is the standard way of setting up for using a Mock Object. You define the methods that you want to mock in a separate interface, and then you have the object you plan to test on inherit from the original object (which already defines those methods) and from the interface. Since the object defines the methods, using the interface just allows you to refine access later.

And we'll do that now. First a build to be sure this all works...and it does. Now I should be able to change the parameters of PutText() to allow me to use my Mock Object in it:

```
public void PutText(ITestTextBox textbox, string[] lines, int selectionStart) {
  textbox.Lines = lines;
  textbox.SelectionStart = selectionStart;
  textbox.ScrollToCaret(); // keep cursor on screen. no test.
}
```

The only change is that the textbox is now declared as an ITestTextBox. We just have to make our MockTextBox use that interface, and we should be golden. Here are the stages:

```
public class MockTextBox: ITestTextBox
{
  public MockTextBox()
  {
  }
  public Boolean Scrolled {
    get {
      return false;
    }
  }
}
```

This doesn't compile yet, because MockTextBox doesn't implement the methods of the interface. So I'll add Lines, SelectionStart, and ScrollToCaret, all trivially. (I am told that Visual Studio 2003 provides some automated help with this.) First SelectionStart:

```
public int SelectionStart {
  get { return 1; }
  set {}
}
```

That compiles, so I must be doing it right. I'll do the others:

```
public string[] Lines {
  get { return new string[0]; }
  set {}
}
public void ScrollToCaret() {
}
```

That should be enough to get the TestScroll to compile with all the comments off. It looks like this:

```
[Test] public void ScrollHappens() {
  int selectionStart = 1;
  string[] lines = new String[] { "hello", "world" };
  MockTextBox mock = new MockTextBox();
  XMLNotepad notepad = new XMLNotepad();
  Assert("no scroll", !mock.Scrolled);
  notepad.PutText(mock, lines, selectionStart);
  Assert("scroll happens", mock.Scrolled);
}
```

It does compile, and the test fails, as expected, on the scroll happens call. The flag isn't set. Now to fix the MockTextBox to detect whether it's scrolled. I'll add a variable, set it to false, and return it. Inside the ScrollToCaret method, I'll set it to true. That should do the job and make the test run.

```
public class MockTextBox: ITestTextBox
{
  private Boolean scrolled = false;
  public MockTextBox()
  {
  }
  public int SelectionStart {
    get { return 1; }
    set {}
  }
  public string[] Lines {
    get { return new string[0]; }
    set {}
  }
  public void ScrollToCaret() {
    scrolled = true;
  }
  public Boolean Scrolled {
    get {
      return scrolled;
    }
  }
}
```

And the test runs! Let's think back and assess what has just happened.

Lessons: Lots of Learning, Not Much Testing

We got only one test out of the deal, but it's at least good enough to check that the PutText method never loses its ScrollToCaret. And breaking out the PutText gives us a better chance of not making the same mistake again by accidentally duplicating the code. What we learned is more important.

Feature Envy

Take a look at the code for PutText again:

```
public void PutText
  (ITestTextBox textbox, string[] lines, int selectionStart) {
  textbox.Lines = lines;
  textbox.SelectionStart = selectionStart;
  textbox.ScrollToCaret();
}
```

This is a method in XMLNotepad class, and it's sending messages only to textbox! This is a major case of Feature Envy, a greater interest in some other class than in one's own. When we look at this code, we see that what we really want is that the text box have the ability to take the data and selection all at once and that it keep its cursor set properly.

We could do something about that if we wished. Because the TextBox class was subclassed to create our TestableTextBox, we could move this function over there. Maybe in a separate chapter we'll do that, although I have something else in mind for the next step.

Object Being Born

Look also at the header for that method. It has the lines and the selection start together. In our usage, we are always dealing with both at once. The code may be telling us that we need a different kind of object here, one that binds the text and the selection together. We have other signs that things are odd in this area, including some bouncing back and forth between string[] and ArrayList. When a program is switching back and forth between data representations, we need to consider whether the objects are quite right.

Building and Using an Interface

We learned how to build an interface. To you Java folks, or people more experienced with C# than I am, that's no big deal, but to a dynamic typing person like me, that's a bit of learning. It's good to have it under my belt, and now I'll know how to do it for next time.

And I implemented an object matching the interface, which netted me a few compiler errors that I spared you. So now I've done both sides of the interface/implementation equation, in a pretty simple form and driven at least partly by tests.

Building a Mock Object

This is the first time I've ever consciously used a Mock Object. It certainly did the job perfectly: it told me whether the text box was getting sent the message ScrollToCaret(), though of course reading the code made it clear that it was. But now we have a test, which feels more secure to me.

I broke the Mock Object out into a separate class for simplicity of learning. But it puts a new class in the system, and I'm inclined to combine the TestScroll class and the MockTextBox class into one class, using a technique called "Self Shunt." (At *http://www.objectmentor.com/resources/articles/Self-ShunPtrn.pdf*, you can find an article by Michael Feathers about Self Shunt. The tag line is "Let's say that you are a test case. One of the things that you can do is pass yourself to the objects you are testing so that you can get more information." Read Michael's article for more detail.)

Tests, Tests, We Need More Tests

You probably can't feel this as clearly as I do, but I am actually relieved to have this new test. Not that it tests anything that didn't work, nor did it find a bug. What it does, though, is extend my ability to test things a bit further, allowing me to work more quickly by avoiding manual tests, and more reliably by extending my testing in new directions.

At the same time, I don't find this particular test to be very satisfying. We have learned a technique that we can use to be sure that our code calls a particular method at the right time. But the test doesn't really show us that the text is displayed on the screen as we might wish, and, besides, we already knew that our change worked from the manual testing. The value of the specific test itself is pretty low. Still, I'm glad we had this time together to look into how we might test this kind of thing, and I think the learning was worth it.

Miles to Go...

Looking at where we are, we can see that things are left to do. In a book with a different perspective, an author might take you from zero to the perfect design in one amazing magical act. But our purpose here is to show you that it's OK to experiment and OK to start from something rough, so long as you keep testing and keep making it better.

Notice that most of our time, even when we're "reworking" the code, has been spent learning new things and putting in new capability. From time to time we do pause and regroup, but the bulk of the work is productive and provides us with more concrete understanding of what to do and how to do it. That's what program design, and programming, are about: learning how best to do the job at hand, given all the things we already know and using well the things that we learn along the way.

Conclusions

I'm glad I asked all those questions on the mailing list, and I'm almost glad everyone hassled me so hard about not having this silly test. And I'm very grateful for all the ideas folks sent, which in some way added up to these changes and this chapter. The blame for any mistakes, of course, lies with Chet.

Code Summary

We've made a lot of changes. Here, for your review, is all the code as it currently stands.

CustomerTest.cs

You'll notice here some code to implement customer tests and some code to test customer tests. The testing code might better be factored out into another class, CustomerTestTest. We built the CustomerTest up to be a [TestFixture], however, so I decided to leave the tests in there.

```csharp
using System;
using System.IO;
using System.Collections;
using NUnit.Framework;
namespace Notepad
{
  [TestFixture] public class CustomerTest : Assertion {
    private TextModel model;
    [SetUp] public void CreateModel() {
      model = new TextModel();
    }
    [Test] public void EmptyModel() {
      model.Enter();
      AssertEquals("<P>|</P>\r\n", model.TestText);
    }

    [Test] public void StringInput() {
      String commands =
```

```
@"*input
some line
*end
*enter
*output
some line
<P>|</P>";
      InterpretCommands(commands, "");
    }
    [Test] public void FileInput() {
      InterpretFileInput(@"c:\data\csharp\notepad\fileInput.test");
    }
    [Test] public void TestAllFiles() {
      String[] testFiles = Directory.GetFiles(@"c:\data\csharp\notepad\",
        "*.test");
      foreach (String testFilename in testFiles) {
        InterpretFileInput(testFilename);
      }
    }
    private void InterpretFileInput(String fileName) {
      StreamReader stream = File.OpenText(fileName);
      String contents = stream.ReadToEnd();
      stream.Close();
      InterpretCommands(contents, fileName);
    }
    private void InterpretCommands(String commands, String message) {
      StringReader reader = new StringReader(commands);
      String line = reader.ReadLine();
      CreateModel();
      while ( line != null) {
        if ( line == "*enter")
          model.Enter();
        if (line == "*display")
          Console.WriteLine("display\r\n{0}\r\nend", model.TestText);
        if (line == "*output")
          CompareOutput(reader, message);
        if (line == "*input")
          SetInput(reader);
        line = reader.ReadLine();
      }
    }
    private void CompareOutput(StringReader reader, String message) {
      String expected = ExpectedOutput(reader);
      AssertEquals(message, expected, model.TestText);
    }
    private String ExpectedOutput(StringReader reader) {
      return ReadToEnd(reader);
    }
```

```
        private String ReadToEnd(StringReader reader) {
          String result = "";
          String line = reader.ReadLine();
          while (line != null && line != "*end") {
            result += line;
            result += System.Environment.NewLine;
            line = reader.ReadLine();
          }
          return result;
        }
        private void SetInput(StringReader reader) {
          InputCommand input = new InputCommand(reader);
          model.Lines = input.CleanLines();
          model.SelectionStart = input.SelectionStart();
        }
      }
    }
```

InputCommand.cs

```
using System;
using System.IO;
using System.Collections;
namespace Notepad
{

  public class InputCommand
  {
    private ArrayList lines;
    public InputCommand(StringReader reader) {
      ReadLines(reader);
    }
    private void ReadLines(StringReader reader) {
      lines = new ArrayList();
      String line = reader.ReadLine();
      while (line != null && line != "*end") {
        lines.Add(line.TrimEnd());
        line = reader.ReadLine();
      }
    }
    public ArrayList CleanLines() {
      ArrayList cleanLines = new ArrayList();
      foreach ( String line in lines) {
        cleanLines.Add(CleanTheLine(line));
      }
      return cleanLines;
    }
    private String CleanTheLine(String dirty) {
```

```
      return dirty.Replace("|", "");
    }
    public int SelectionStart() {
      int charactersSoFar = 0;
      foreach (String line in lines) {
        int index = line.IndexOf("|");
        if (index != -1)
          return charactersSoFar + index;
        else
          charactersSoFar += line.Length + Environment.NewLine.Length;
      }
      return charactersSoFar - Environment.NewLine.Length;
    }
  }
}
```

InputCommandTest.cs

```
using System;
using NUnit.Framework;
using System.IO;
namespace Notepad
{
  [TestFixture] public class InputCommandTest : Assertion
  {
    private InputCommand command;
    [Test] public void EmptyCommand() {
      command = new InputCommand(new StringReader(""));
      AssertEquals(0, command.CleanLines().Count);
    }
    [Test] public void OneLineCommand() {
      String oneLineString =
@"one line
*end";
      StringReader reader = new StringReader(oneLineString);
      command = new InputCommand(reader);
      AssertEquals(1, command.CleanLines().Count);
      AssertEquals(8,command.SelectionStart());
    }
    [Test] public void OneDirtyLine() {
      command = new InputCommand(new StringReader("a|b\n*end"));
      AssertEquals("ab", command.CleanLines()[0]);
      AssertEquals(1,command.SelectionStart());
    }
  }
}
```

ITestTextBox.cs

```csharp
using System;
namespace Notepad {
  interface ITestTextBox {
    string[] Lines {get; set;}
    int SelectionStart { get; set;}
    void ScrollToCaret();
  }
}
```

MockTextBox.cs

```csharp
using System;
namespace Notepad
{
  public class MockTextBox: ITestTextBox
  {
    private Boolean scrolled = false;
    public MockTextBox()
    {
    }
    public int SelectionStart {
      get { return 1; }
      set {}
    }
    public string[] Lines {
      get { return new string[0]; }
      set { scrolled = false; }
    }
    public void ScrollToCaret() {
      scrolled = true;
    }
      public Boolean Scrolled {
      get {
        return scrolled;
      }
    }
  }
}
```

Notepad.cs

```csharp
using System;
using System.Drawing;
using System.Windows.Forms;
```

```
namespace Notepad {
  class NotepadCloneNoMenu : Form
  {
    public TestableTextBox textbox;
    public NotepadCloneNoMenu() {
      Text = "Notepad Clone No Menu";
      textbox = new TestableTextBox();
      textbox.Parent = this;
      textbox.Dock = DockStyle.Fill;
      textbox.BorderStyle = BorderStyle.None;
      textbox.Multiline = true;
      textbox.ScrollBars = ScrollBars.Both;
      textbox.AcceptsTab = true;
    }
  }
}
```

TestableTextBox.cs

```
using System;
using System.Windows.Forms;
namespace Notepad
{
  /// <summary>
  /// Dummy class allowing use of the ITestTextBox interface in testing.
  ///    (See TestScroll.cs and MockTextBox.cs)
  /// </summary>
  class TestableTextBox: TextBox, ITestTextBox {
  }
}
```

TestScroll.cs

```
using System;
using NUnit.Framework;
namespace Notepad
{
  [TestFixture] public class TestScroll: Assertion
  {
    [Test] public void HookUp() {
      Assert("hooked up", true);
    }
    [Test] public void ScrollHappens() {
      int selectionStart = 1;
      string[] lines = new String[] { "hello", "world" };
      MockTextBox mock = new MockTextBox();
```

```
        XMLNotepad notepad = new XMLNotepad();
        Assert("no scroll", !mock.Scrolled);
        notepad.PutText(mock, lines, selectionStart);
        Assert("scroll happens", mock.Scrolled);
      }
    }
  }
```

TextTextBox.cs

You might note an inconsistency in the coding style here. I used "bool" rather than "Boolean." It would be better to be consistent, but in this case I fell short of that goal. You'll probably find other examples as you go through the book. They're part of my learning process, and I'll point them out when I notice them.

Also notice the commented-out code here. It's the result of an attempt to write a test that I later decided was a dead end. I should have had the courage to delete the code, but I must have decided to keep it in case I needed it. As far as I can tell from here, I never needed it. You can draw the obvious lesson from that and delete such things. Trust your code manager to keep a copy, or print the code and keep a big stack of paper in your bottom desk drawer.

```
using System;
using System.Windows.Forms;
using NUnit.Framework;
namespace Notepad
{
  [TestFixture] public class TestTextBoxEvent : Assertion {
    bool changed;
    [SetUp] public void ClearChanged() {
      changed = false;
    }
    [Test] public void CheckEvent() {
      TestableTextBox text = new TestableTextBox();
      text.Text = "some text";
      Assert(!changed);
      text.TextChanged += new EventHandler(Text_Changed);
      text.Text = "more text";
      Assert(changed);
    }
//    [Test] public void HookForm () {
//      TestableTextBox text = new TestableTextBox();
//      text.TextChanged += new EventHandler(Text_Changed);
//      XMLNotepad xn = new XMLNotepad();
//      xn.textbox = text;
//      text.Text = "some text";
```

```
//      xn.PutText();
//      AssertEquals("hello", text.Lines[0]);
//      Assert("changed flag", changed);
//    }
    void Text_Changed(object source, EventArgs args) {
      changed = true;
    }
  }
}
```

TestTextModel1.cs

Here you'll notice a test, ControlTwo, that verifies that the XML Notepad will insert an H2 tag. We haven't talked about this, as there wasn't much to learn from it, but it's a feature that I put in as an early experiment in how to make things work. At least I wrote a test for it!

```
using System;
using System.Collections;
using NUnit.Framework;
namespace Notepad {
  [TestFixture] public class TestTextModel : Assertion {
    private TextModel model;
    [SetUp] public void CreateModel() {
      model = new TextModel();
    }
    [Test] public void TestNoLines() {
      model.SetLines(new String[0]);
      AssertEquals(0, model.Lines.Count);
    }
    [Test] public void TestNoProcessing() {
      model.SetLines(new String[3] { "hi", "there", "chet"});
      AssertEquals(3, model.Lines.Count);
    }
    [Test] public void TestOneEnter() {
      model.SetLines(new String[1] {"hello world" });
      model.SelectionStart = 5;
      model.InsertParagraphTag();
      AssertEquals(3, model.Lines.Count);
      AssertEquals(18, model.SelectionStart);
    }
    [Test] public void TestEmptyText() {
      model.Lines = new ArrayList(new String[0]);
      model.InsertParagraphTag();
      AssertEquals(1, model.Lines.Count);
      AssertEquals(3, model.SelectionStart);
```

```
      }
      // Chet comments that he hates the comments
      [Test] public void InsertWithCursorAtLineStart () {
        model.Lines = new ArrayList(new String[3] { "<P>one</P>", "",
          "<P>two</P>"});
        model.SelectionStart = 14;
        model.InsertParagraphTag();
        AssertEquals("<P>two</P>", model.Lines[2]);
      }
      [Test] public void TestLineContainingCursorDirectly() {
        // todo?
      }
      [Test] public void ControlTwo() {
        model.SetLines(new String[1] {"<P>The Heading</P>" });
        model.ChangeToH2();
        AssertEquals("<H2>The Heading</H2>", model.Lines[0]);
      }
    }
  }
```

TextModel.cs

One of my technical editors commented, upon seeing this code, that he likes to arrange his "using" statements in order of increasing length. That good idea notwithstanding, I suspect that alphabetical might be better. Random is probably worst, and I can't honestly promise that you won't see that here before we're done.

This same individual also rudely pointed out the internal variable "lineNr" used in this method, asking if it was "so much better than lineNumber." It's a good point. I plead a leftover brain cell from back when variables could only be six characters long. Inside a method, you'll often feel a need to trade off the time to type a name with its ability to communicate. When I become aware of the tradeoff, I always try to favor communication: I'll type it only once, but I might read it many times. Unfortunately, I don't always notice.

```
using System;
using System.Collections;
using System.Text;
using System.Text.RegularExpressions;
namespace Notepad {
  class TextModel {
    private ArrayList lines;
    private int selectionStart;
    public TextModel() {
      lines = new ArrayList();
    }
```

```
private int LineContainingCursor() {
  int length = 0;
  int lineNr = 0;
  int cr = Environment.NewLine.Length;
  foreach ( String s in lines) {
    if (length <= selectionStart
      && selectionStart < length+s.Length + cr )
      break;
    length += s.Length + cr;
    lineNr++;
  }
  return lineNr;
}
public void Enter() {
  InsertParagraphTag();
}
public void InsertParagraphTag() {
  //
  // On Enter, we change the TextModel lines to insert, after the line
  // containing the cursor, a blank line, and a line with <P></P>.
  // We set the new cursor
  // location to be between the P tags: <P>|</P>.
  //
  // handle empty array special case (yucch)
  if ( lines.Count == 0 ) {
    lines.Add( "<P></P>" );
    selectionStart = 3;
    return;
  }
  lines.InsertRange(LineContainingCursor()+1, NewParagraph());
  // set cursor location
  selectionStart = NewSelectionStart(LineContainingCursor() + 2);
}
private int NewSelectionStart(int cursorLine) {
  int length = 0;
  for (int i = 0; i < cursorLine; i++)
    length += ((String)lines[i]).Length + Environment.NewLine.Length;
  return length + "<p>".Length;
}
public ArrayList NewParagraph() {
  ArrayList temp = new ArrayList();
  temp.Add("");
  temp.Add("<P></P>");
  return temp;
}
public ArrayList Lines {
  get {
    return lines;
```

```
      }
      set {
        lines = value;
      }
    }
    public void SetLines(String[] lines) {
      this.Lines = new ArrayList(lines);
    }
    public String[] LinesArray() {
      String[] result = new String[lines.Count];
      lines.CopyTo(result);
      return result;
    }
    public String TestText {
      get {
        StringBuilder b = new StringBuilder();
        foreach(String s in lines) {
          b.Append(s);
          b.Append(System.Environment.NewLine);
        }
        b.Insert(SelectionStart,"|");
        return b.ToString();
      }
    }
    public int SelectionStart {
      get {
        return selectionStart;
      }
      set {
        selectionStart = value;
      }
    }
  public void ChangeToH2() {
  ArrayList linesList = Lines;
  String oldLine = (String) linesList[LineContainingCursor()];
  Regex r = new Regex("<(?<prefix>.*)>(?<body>.*)</(?<suffix>.*)>");
  Match m = r.Match(oldLine);
  String newLine = "<H2>" + m.Groups["body"] + "</H2>";
  linesList[LineContainingCursor()] = newLine;
  Lines = linesList;
    }
  }
}
```

XMLNotepad.cs

```
using System;
using System.Drawing;
```

```
using System.Windows.Forms;
using NUnit.Framework;
using System.Collections;
using System.Text.RegularExpressions;
namespace Notepad
{
  class XMLNotepad : NotepadCloneNoMenu
  {
    private TextModel model;

    static void Main(string[] args)
    {
      Application.Run(new XMLNotepad());
    }
    public XMLNotepad() {
      Text = "XML Notepad";
      textbox.KeyDown += new KeyEventHandler(XMLKeyDownHandler);
      textbox.KeyPress += new KeyPressEventHandler(XMLKeyPressHandler);
      model = new TextModel();
    }
    private void InitializeComponent() {
      this.SuspendLayout();
      //
      // textbox
      //
      this.textbox.Visible = true;
      //
      // XMLNotepad
      //
      this.AutoScaleBaseSize = new System.Drawing.Size(5, 13);
      this.ClientSize = new System.Drawing.Size(292, 266);
      this.Controls.AddRange(new System.Windows.Forms.Control[] {
      this.textbox});
      this.Name = "XMLNotepad";
      this.ResumeLayout(false);
    }
    void XMLKeyPressHandler(object objSender, KeyPressEventArgs kea) {
      if ((int) kea.KeyChar == (int) Keys.Enter) {
        kea.Handled = true;
        // this code is here to avoid putting extra enters in the window.
        // if removed, when you hit enter, the new <P> line breaks in two:
        // <P>
        // |</P>  like that.
      }
    }
    void XMLKeyDownHandler(object objSender, KeyEventArgs kea) {
      model.SetLines(textbox.Lines);
      model.SelectionStart = textbox.SelectionStart;
```

```
      if (kea.KeyCode == Keys.Enter) {
        model.Enter();
        kea.Handled = true;
      }
      PutText(textbox, model.LinesArray(), model.SelectionStart);
    }
    public void PutText(ITestTextBox textbox, string[] lines,
      int selectionStart) {
      // this is Feature Envy big time.
      textbox.Lines = lines;
      textbox.SelectionStart = selectionStart;
      textbox.ScrollToCaret();
    }
  }
}
```

11

Adding the Section Tag, Part I

It's time to add a new feature to the XML Notepad. This time it's a multiline "section" tag. Since Chet has found honest work, I'll have to do a lot of this alone. I'll get in trouble—and [sb]*it's Chet's fault!*[1]

Looking at the Next Few Stories

The XML Notepad is actually fairly useful as it stands. The biggest hassle in producing one of these articles (which were later updated and turned into these chapters) is needing to type something special to get a new set of P tags created, and the notepad solves that problem. But there are a number of candidate things to do next. Here's a list of stories that seem potentially interesting:

- Add sect1 tag. Each section of text that shows up in the TOC appears inside sect1 tags. Inside the sect1 is a title tag where you put the title. The ability to create a new section would be nice. Then inside the section we go back to typing paragraphs like always. The sect1 tag should be inserted after one we're currently in.

- When the user types Tab, move the cursor somewhere reasonable. This probably means to the end of the next opening tag, or the beginning of the next closing tag, whichever is closer. This sounds weird, but what it'll do is position the cursor at the beginning of the

---

1. Chet has assumed responsibility for all problems everywhere. If there is a problem in your project or your life, it's Chet's fault. Now stop assigning blame and get on with solving the problem!

next paragraph, then at its end, and so on and so on. It should be a quick way to click through the document. We'll want Shift+Tab to go backwards, I suppose.

- Save a file. Open a file.

- Prime a new file with a starting document, with headers and such. This will help create the "boilerplate" needed to support an article.

Of these, the sect1 story seems most useful and will probably involve the most learning in doing it. One of the issues is that the sect1 involves nesting—that is, it looks like this:

```
<sect1><title></title>
</sect1>
```

There's the title inside there, and of course there will be paragraphs as well. It might turn out to be a bit tricky getting it to work right and look right. I'll start, however, by assuming it's going to work. No need to borrow trouble from the future.

Also, I had a really neat technical idea. If the TextModel used a simple tree structure, where each node knew its tag and had contents that were a collection of other nodes (or raw text), then rendering the text into the TextPane, even in a nice indented form, would be really easy. I don't have a story that requires me to build that model, but I'm interested in it and excited to try it.

Now this could be a good idea, but I also know I'm on a slippery programmer slope, putting in some cool technical gadget that the program doesn't really need. I'm not going to put it in now, but I may well do a spike on it later. I'd advise you to do the same: leave the cool techie stuff for when it's really needed. My experience is that things go better and faster if I stick to simple design with refactoring.

A Quick Look Around

First, I'll review the code, since it has been a couple of weeks since I've worked on this. It shouldn't take long. I'll start with the Customer Acceptance Tests. Look at them with me:

Trivial Test

```
*enter
*output
<P>|</P>
```

File Input Test

```
*input
some line
*end
*enter
*output
some line
<P>|</P>
```

Para After Para Test

```
*input
<P></P>
*end
*enter
*output
<P></P>
<P>|</P>
```

Insert Para Test

```
*input
<P>This is the first p|aragraph.</P>
<P>This is the second paragraph.</P>
*end
*enter
*output
<P>This is the first paragraph.</P>
<P>|</P>
<P>This is the second paragraph.</P>
```

Insert After Para Test

```
*input
<P>This is the first paragraph.</P>
<P>This is the second| paragraph.</P>
*end
*enter
*output
<P>This is the first paragraph.</P>
<P>This is the second paragraph.</P>
<P>|</P>
```

These are all pretty straightforward. And it seems like it would be easy to write a few more customer tests for the sect1 story. I'm thinking that it might be better to drive this whole story from its customer test, but I'm afraid that might be laziness talking. It might just be a way to cheat on my Programmer Unit Tests. Let's look at some of those.

Input Command Test

There's a test for the InputCommand class. I remind myself that the InputCommand handles the customer test aspect where it starts *input and goes through *end. It takes all the lines after *input, through *end, and packs them into an object that can give back the lines without the vertical bar (|) that represents the cursor and that can say where the cursor should be in terms of its position from the beginning of the file. Interesting, but it probably won't be affected by what we're doing.

ITestTextBox and MockTextBox

These classes were built to let me test that irritating problem where the cursor wasn't visible. Again, that probably won't affect us here.

Test Text Model

Now this looks interesting. This is the class that tests all the text manipulation that goes on in the TextModel. Surely we're going to have to add to TextModel to do the insertion of the sect1 tag. Let's look at these tests:

```
using System;
using System.Collections;
using NUnit.Framework;
namespace Notepad {
  [TestFixture] public class TestTextModel : Assertion {
    private TextModel model;
    [SetUp] public void CreateModel() {
      model = new TextModel();
    }
    [Test] public void TestNoLines() {
      model.SetLines(new String[0]);
      AssertEquals(0, model.Lines.Count);
    }
    [Test] public void TestNoProcessing() {
      model.SetLines(new String[3] { "hi", "there", "chet"});
      AssertEquals(3, model.Lines.Count);
    }
    [Test] public void TestOneEnter() {
      model.SetLines(new String[1] {"hello world" });
      model.SelectionStart = 5;
      model.InsertParagraphTag();
      AssertEquals(3, model.Lines.Count);
      AssertEquals(18, model.SelectionStart);
    }
    [Test] public void TestEmptyText() {
      model.Lines = new ArrayList(new String[0]);
      model.InsertParagraphTag();
      AssertEquals(1, model.Lines.Count);
      AssertEquals(3, model.SelectionStart);
    }
```

```
[Test] public void InsertWithCursorAtLineStart () {
  model.Lines = new ArrayList(new String[3] { "<P>one</P>", "",
    "<P>two</P>"});
  model.SelectionStart = 14;
  model.InsertParagraphTag();
  AssertEquals("<P>two</P>", model.Lines[2]);
}
[Test] public void TestLineContainingCursorDirectly() {
  // todo?
}

[Test] public void ControlTwo() {
  model.SetLines(new String[1] {"<P>The Heading</P>" });
  model.ChangeToH2();
  AssertEquals("<H2>The Heading</H2>", model.Lines[0]);
}
  }
}
```

Browsing that, I see that there's a "todo" test, something about testing a line directly that contains the cursor. The intention was to remind myself (and Chet?) of a test that we might want to write, but in fact, now I can't remember what was meant. This wasn't enough of a clue. Little lesson learned here about documenting ideas a bit better. I think I'd still do it right here in the code, but longer comments about what was needed might have helped me remember. For now I'll ignore it and I'll leave the test there in case I can get together with Chet later. He might remember, or chatting about it might help.

Lesson   One of my editors commented that the test should be refactored out. He's probably correct. But the fact is, I left it here, useless, hoping that it would remind me of something. But it never did. I'm not sure whether to advise you not to do this, to write better comments, or what.

As we work, there are so many ideas that we get. Many of them are good, but we just can't do them all. Sometimes something pops into our mind and we don't want to forget it, so we're inclined to write it down. Yet, months or years later, we have perforce had to pass over most of those ideas. My practice has been to write them on cards sometimes, or to write them in a notebook that I carry, or to write them into the code or document I'm working on. None of these approaches works perfectly, but I think that the closer the idea is to where I might next need it, the better. So I leave code ideas in the code. It's not perfect, but it's the balance I've chosen.

There's also that test, ControlTwo(), that we haven't talked about. It's supporting some experimental code that changes the tag of the current line from P to H2. There's this test, a customer test, and model support. I didn't talk about it in the narrative because there was no particular lesson to be drawn. We'll be using it shortly as a prototype for another test, however.

Looking at these tests, we can see that we could produce Programmer Unit Tests for the sect1 idea. It would be easier to use Customer Acceptance Tests, because with the programmer tests we seem to have to do a lot of counting and such.

Here's what I'm going to do. These tests are a lot harder to write than the customer ones. We learned a lot doing the customer ones, and that learning hasn't shown up here yet. So I'm going to write a customer test and see that it doesn't work. Then, using that test as a model, I'll write some programmer tests, but I'm going to focus not just on the testing but also on improving the testing. Let's see what happens.

The New Customer Test

Hey! When I went to set this test up, I noticed that we don't have a customer test for the H2 capability. We haven't talked about the H2 feature, as it wasn't very interesting, but you may have noticed it in the code snippets. Basically when the user types Control-2, we change the tag containing the caret to H2, a heading tag that I use commonly. We'll have to work on that! Should I keep my head down on this task or move to writing the old test? Well, I've got my programmer hat on now. I'm going to keep my head down. Maybe Chet and I will work on the other test this afternoon if we can get together. OK, here's my first test:

```
*controlS
*output
<sect1><title>|</title>
</sect1>
```

Starting from a blank file, typing Ctrl+S will cause the file to contain the sect1 stuff shown above, with the cursor in the middle of the title tags. Of course this won't work. I'll run it to be sure. Right. Everything else works. The sect1 test fails, with no content. That's because the controlS command has no meaning to the testing framework. I think I'll push down this path a little bit. I need a new command. Here's the relevant existing code, from CustomerTest:

```
private void InterpretCommands(String commands, String message) {
  StringReader reader = new StringReader(commands);
```

```
String line = reader.ReadLine();
CreateModel();
while ( line != null) {
  if ( line == "*enter")
    model.Enter();
  if (line == "*display")
    Console.WriteLine("display\r\n{0}\r\nend", model.TestText);
  if (line == "*output")
    CompareOutput(reader, message);
  if (line == "*input")
    SetInput(reader);
  line = reader.ReadLine();
  }
}
```

Clearly what I need here is to add a check for controlS and pass it on to the model. I notice that this command interpreter is getting a bit tricky and it might want to be improved. But not yet, I'm on a mission. So we'll add this:

```
if ( line == "*controlS")
  model.ControlS();
```

We could compile this to see that it doesn't work, but when typing the ControlS message send, I saw that it wasn't defined yet (and of course I knew it anyway), so let's go add it to the TextModel before we go any further. Now, I do have a failing test to drive this code, but I'm feeling a bit guilty about the test being so far from the code. I know that I get the most benefit from test-driven development when the test and the code are conceptually close. I'd better buckle down and add a programmer test.

Adding the Programmer Test

All right, the plan is to add a test to TestTextModel, at least if it doesn't look too hard. Take another look at that class earlier in the "Test Text Model" section. Check out that ControlTwo test right there at the bottom. We need a test like that, except that it tests ControlS. Let's write it; it doesn't look too hard.

```
[Test] public void ControlS() {
  model.Lines = new ArrayList(new String[0]);
  model.ControlS();
  AssertEquals("<sect1><title></title>", model.Lines[0]);
  AssertEquals("</sect1>", model.Lines[1]);
}
```

> **Lesson** Are you wondering why, with a perfectly good customer test, I'm going to write a programmer test? I try to do it as a matter of discipline and good practice. On a real Extreme Programming project, the Customer Acceptance Tests would belong to the customer, and they might not come along in quite as timely a way as this one did. And as a programmer, my main responsibility is the Programmer Unit Tests. In addition, it's not common that customer tests are quite so well-targeted as this one. Usually when a customer test fails, there's some debugging to do. Adding all this up, when I find myself thinking that maybe I don't need a test, I try always to go ahead and write one anyway. It pays off more often than not.

Compiling, I find that TextModel has no ControlS method. No surprise. Let's write that; it'll be a lot like the Enter method or InsertParagraghTag, as I think it's called. Those methods look like this:

```
public void Enter() {
  InsertParagraphTag();
}
public void InsertParagraphTag() {
  if ( lines.Count == 0 ) {
    lines.Add( "<P></P>" );
    selectionStart = 3;
    return;
  }
  lines.InsertRange(LineContainingCursor()+1, NewParagraph());
  // set cursor location
  selectionStart = NewSelectionStart(LineContainingCursor() + 2);
}
```

I'm going to begin in sb."fake it before you make it" mode and just add the lines directly, as we do in the first part of the method above. I expect this to be enough to make this test run, and I expect it to lead to some discoveries in the code. Here's my first cut at the new methods:

```
public void ControlS() {
  InsertSectionTags();
}
public void InsertSectionTags() {
  if ( lines.Count == 0 ) {
    lines.Add( "<sect1><title></title>" );
    lines.Add( "</sect1>");
    selectionStart = 14;
    return;
  }
```

The code compiles, and both tests run, the new programmer test and the first customer test. It's time for a break! I'll see you after lunch!

After Lunch Comes a Bit Late

In our last episode, we implemented a simple ability to add a section tag to the XML Notepad. It turns out I wasn't able to work on it after lunch, and in fact it's now almost a week since I made that test run. The test points right to the code, and the code is simple, so I've had no trouble catching up. Chet will be joining me in just a few minutes, and I'll bring him up to speed. I'll record here what we talk about: it will give you a sense of what it takes to bring a new pair up to date.

Meanwhile, I'm going to clean up the code a little before getting down to things. I've learned from experience that it doesn't pay to let it go too long before cleaning things up. Here comes Chet now; I'll bring him up to speed as we go.

In reviewing the code, we discovered that I had copied a bit of extra stuff into the InsertSectionTags(). We also "discovered" that the Ctrl+S wasn't yet implemented in the GUI. It didn't interfere with the test, but it should have. So Chet said: "What we have learned is that when I'm not here, you leave things out, your code isn't as good, and your tests didn't find the problem." All true: I need a pair. Anyone in the Ann Arbor area want to volunteer?

We noticed that, at least offhand, we don't know how to test whether the GUI implements a particular control character. I'm arguing to defer that issue and go to the core issue of getting things done. A couple of ways exist to check that the key is correctly implemented in the GUI. We both thought independently of the "cool" way: use reflection to check the class, and see to it that it implements what it needs to. That's way too deep in the bag of tricks to be a good idea, but it could be an interesting learning experiment at some time. The simplest thing to do is just to build a notepad object in the Customer Acceptance Tests (which now test against the TextModel) and to send KeyPress events to it. That's probably a good way to do it, but Chet and I both have fear of creating GUI classes during tests. That's probably not a good fear, but it's holding us back right now.

We're going to defer solving this problem. But we know it is a real problem: there's nothing that stops us from writing a good customer test, making it work with lots of good programmer tests, and then having the GUI not show up with the feature. We made a mental note to notice when it happens again, in case we don't get to this test early on. Right now, though, we're going forward with finishing the feature.

Adding Ctrl+S—Almost

We added Ctrl+S code to the GUI, just to see it work, and to cement in our minds that we needed to do it. It looks like this:

```
void XMLKeyDownHandler(object objSender, KeyEventArgs kea) {
  model.SetLines(textbox.Lines);
  model.SelectionStart = textbox.SelectionStart;
  if (kea.KeyCode == Keys.Enter) {
    model.Enter();
    kea.Handled = true;
  }
  if (kea.KeyCode == Keys.S && kea.Alt) {
    model.AltS();
    kea.Handled = true;
  }      PutText(textbox, model.LinesArray(), model.SelectionStart);
}
```

Note that it says AltS, not ControlS. Chet noticed that Ctrl+S is usually used for Save, and he suggested that we didn't want to overload that meaning. So we switched to AltS throughout. Here's the code in TextModel:

```
public void AltS() {
  InsertSectionTags();
}
public void InsertSectionTags() {
  if ( lines.Count == 0 ) {
    lines.Add( "<sect1><title></title>" );
    lines.Add( "</sect1>");
    selectionStart = 14;
    return;
  }
}
```

With this implementation, the notepad correctly displays the section at the beginning of the window, which is the only place it's implemented. However, the notepad is ringing the "bell" on every Alt+S. We're not sure what's causing that. We made a note of it and are moving on.

Test for More of Alt+S

The current implementation of Alt+S works only when the text buffer is empty. We'll write a Programmer Unit Test to handle the other case:

```
[Test] public void AltSWithText() {
  model.SetLines (new String[1] {"<P></P>"});
  model.SelectionStart = 7;
  model.AltS();
  AssertEquals("<sect1><title></title>", model.Lines[1]);
```

```
AssertEquals("</sect1>", model.Lines[2]);
AssertEquals(23, model.SelectionStart);
}
```

Only at this point did I remember a simplifying assumption I'd been making. In this first implementation, I'm assuming that the user will position the cursor at the end of the current sect1 before asking for another one. I'm doing that because the sect1 tag is multiple lines long and I don't want to worry about finding the end of the current one as part of what I'm doing now. Let me comment on that a bit more.

> I find that working in tiny little bites makes things go better. By the end of this subject—perhaps in this chapter, perhaps in the next—I think you'll agree that we're in a good place in both features and code. It would be possible to include the setting to the end of the sect1 tag as part of this phase of the implementation, but then I'd have to solve two problems: getting the stuff inserted and the cursor set, and also finding where to insert. I want to solve one problem at a time, and I want to see the program do something useful, so my next step is "insert the section tag at the current location so that it will work right if the users sets the location first."

The test above therefore takes the smaller step, assuming that the user sets the location for us. Easy does it. It adds a P tag, just to have something there, and then sets the cursor to the end of it. Then it calls for an Alt+S and checks to see if the lines are right and the cursor is set right. Note the 23 as cursor position. That's the 7 characters of the first line plus the CrLf, plus 14 characters into the second line (Lines[1]). I actually got that wrong the first time I wrote the test, and used 21, forgetting the CrLf. Except for this little comment, I'll save you that detail.

Implementing More of Alt+S

Here's how the code for the P tag looks:

```
public void InsertParagraphTag() {
    //
    // On Enter, we change the TextModel lines to insert, after the line
    // containing the cursor, a blank line, and a line with <P></P>.
    // We set the new cursor
    // location to be between the P tags: <P>|</P>.
    //
    // handle empty array special case (yucch)
    if ( lines.Count == 0 ) {
```

```
      lines.Add( "<P></P>" );
      selectionStart = 3;
      return;
    }
    lines.InsertRange(LineContainingCursor()+1, NewParagraph());
    selectionStart = NewParaSelectionStart(LineContainingCursor() + 2);
  }
  private int NewParaSelectionStart(int cursorLine) {
    int length = 0;
    for (int i = 0; i < cursorLine; i++)
      length += ((String)lines[i]).Length + Environment.NewLine.Length;
    return length + "<p>".Length;
  }
  public ArrayList NewParagraph() {
    ArrayList temp = new ArrayList();
    temp.Add("");
    temp.Add("<P></P>");
    return temp;
  }
```

Note those comments, especially the "yucch." We hate that special case for lines.Count == 0, and in a minute we're going to hate it more. Watch what happens. For now, look at what happens in the non-zero case, which is what we need to implement for the section tag. If there are lines, we insert the lines in NewParagraph()—namely a blank line and a P-tag line—into the TextModel lines, right after the line containing the cursor. Then we set the selectionStart.

The NewParaSelectionStart code is almost straightforward. It adds up the length of all the lines up to the line that should contain the cursor (including the CrLfs), and then it adds in the width of the <P> tag. That will position the cursor right after that tag. You might think that lacks generality. So do we, and we're going to go after it. But we're going to go after it in a special way, so hold on and see what happens.

We implement the Alt+S feature in almost exactly the same way. Here's the code for Alt+S:

```
public void AltS() {
  InsertSectionTags();
}
public void InsertSectionTags() {
  if ( lines.Count == 0 ) {
    lines.Add( "<sect1><title></title>" );
    lines.Add( "</sect1>");
    selectionStart = 14;
    return;
  }
  lines.InsertRange(LineContainingCursor()+1, NewSection());
```

```
    selectionStart = NewSectionSelectionStart(LineContainingCursor() + 1);
}
public ArrayList NewSection() {
  ArrayList temp = new ArrayList();
  temp.Add("<sect1><title></title>");
  temp.Add("</sect1>");
  return temp;
}
private int NewSectionSelectionStart(int cursorLine) {
  int length = 0;
  for (int i = 0; i < cursorLine; i++)
    length += ((String)lines[i]).Length + Environment.NewLine.Length;
  return length + "<sect1><title>".Length;
}
```

See that we basically cut and pasted the code for the P tag here and modified it with the new strings we wanted to use for the section tag. Isn't cut and paste bad? Yes, but only if we leave the code that way. We're not going to do that, as you'll see in a moment.

It's time to compile and test. And the tests all run! OK, now let's see about this ugly code.

Improving the Code

In the middle of that discussion, Chet's wife Sue showed up and we had dinner; then they went home. I'm on my own again now. Keep an eye out for the mistakes that I'd have avoided if I'd had him to pair with.

Lesson   You may be tempted to "design" something better to take care of all these special cases. Frankly, a while back in our programming experience, so would we. But we've learned something powerful and interesting about simple code: if we simply find and remove duplication in obvious ways, we usually wind up with code that's much cleaner and clearer. [sb]Removing duplication is your friend. So let's just do that and see what happens.

First let's scan for duplications:

■   In the section-related code, the strings for the first and second line of the section tag are duplicated, in the NewSection() method and in the special case code of the InsertSectionTags() method. We could clearly get rid of the latter by calling the former and looping. That might lead to further consolidation when we do the same thing for the paragraph tag.

```
public void InsertSectionTags() {
  if ( lines.Count == 0 ) {
    lines.Add( "<sect1><title></title>" );
    lines.Add( "</sect1>");
    selectionStart = 14;
    return;
  }
  lines.InsertRange(LineContainingCursor()+1, NewSection());
  selectionStart = NewSectionSelectionStart(LineContainingCursor() + 1);
}
public ArrayList NewSection() {
  ArrayList temp = new ArrayList();
  temp.Add("<sect1><title></title>");
  temp.Add("</sect1>");
  return temp;
}
```

■ The paragraph code has almost the same duplication, except that we double-space before each paragraph tag in all but the empty-lines case. Otherwise, the same strings would appear in analogous places there. That makes it tempting to remove the double-spacing feature to consolidate the strings. We'd have to check with the customer, but I happen to know that they don't double-space their paragraph tags now, so they'd probably go for it.

```
public void InsertParagraphTag() {
  // handle empty array special case (yucch)
  if ( lines.Count == 0 ) {
    lines.Add( "<P></P>" );
    selectionStart = 3;
    return;
  }
  lines.InsertRange(LineContainingCursor()+1, NewParagraph());
  // set cursor location
  selectionStart = NewSelectionStart(LineContainingCursor() + 2);
}
public ArrayList NewParagraph() {
  ArrayList temp = new ArrayList();
  temp.Add("");
  temp.Add("<P></P>");
  return temp;
}
```

- The paragraph code and the section code have exactly the same structure. They check the special case of the model being empty, add some stuff, and set the cursor explicitly. Otherwise, they insert basically the same stuff and set the cursor (somewhat) programmatically. There are three kinds of duplication here:

  - ❏ Paragraph and section have the same shape. That suggests consolidating across them.

  - ❏ Paragraph and section have duplicated function, the insertion, implemented in two different ways. That suggests removing the special case.

- There are, of course, many duplicated individual lines between these two implementations. We could attack them singly.

In the end, it's all a matter of taste what you go after. You'll likely wind up with much the same code in every case, and you'll wind up with much *better* code for sure.

Removing Duplication

It's late in the evening, and I'm getting tired. I want to make a little more progress before I call it quits, so I'll do something very simple. Normally I would try something bigger, probably unwisely. See the following two loops that go over the lines up to cursorLine, adding up their lengths? I'm going to remove that duplication.

```
private int NewParaSelectionStart(int cursorLine) {
  int length = 0;
  for (int i = 0; i < cursorLine; i++)
    length += ((String)lines[i]).Length + Environment.NewLine.Length;
  return length + "<p>".Length;
}

private int NewSectionSelectionStart(int cursorLine) {
  int length = 0;
  for (int i = 0; i < cursorLine; i++)
    length += ((String)lines[i]).Length + Environment.NewLine.Length;
  return length + "<sect1><title>".Length;
}
```

The result looks like this:

```
private int NewSectionSelectionStart(int cursorLine) {
  return SumLineLengths(cursorLine) + "<sect1><title>".Length;
}
```

```
private int SumLineLengths(int cursorLine) {
  int length = 0;
  for (int i = 0; i < cursorLine; i++)
    length += ((String)lines[i]).Length + Environment.NewLine.Length;
  return length;
}
```

I just extracted the loop code into a new method, SumLineLengths(), and used it in NewSectionSelectionStart. I ran the tests and they work. Now I'll use the method in the other location:

```
private int NewParaSelectionStart(int cursorLine) {
return SumLineLengths(cursorLine) + "<p>".Length;
  }
```

The tests still work—wahoo! The code is a little bit nicer. This gives me an idea. Look at those two methods—they are almost completely duplicated except for the string. Recall how they're used. Here's one example:

```
public void InsertSectionTags() {
  if ( lines.Count == 0 ) {
    lines.Add( "<sect1><title></title>" );
    lines.Add( "</sect1>");
    selectionStart = 14;
    return;
  }
  lines.InsertRange(LineContainingCursor()+1, NewSection());
  selectionStart = NewSectionSelectionStart(LineContainingCursor() + 1);
}
```

The other usage looks the same except that it calls NewParaSelectionStart. Let's consolidate those two methods by passing in the string as a parameter from the methods that use them. This is a common situation in removing duplication: we extract the common elements to a method that takes one or more parameters, and we leave the parameters—the differences—in the code that uses the new method. In this case, our calling methods know that string anyway, so let's put all knowledge of it in the callers:

```
public void InsertSectionTags() {
  if ( lines.Count == 0 ) {
    lines.Add( "<sect1><title></title>" );
    lines.Add( "</sect1>");
    selectionStart = 14;
    return;
  }
  lines.InsertRange(LineContainingCursor()+1, NewSection());
  selectionStart = NewSelectionStart(LineContainingCursor() + 1,
    "<sect1><title>");
}
```

And NewSelectionStart gets the obvious implementation:

```
private int NewSelectionStart(int cursorLine, string tags) {
  return SumLineLengths(cursorLine) + tags.Length;      }
```

Tests run! Now I'll use that same method in the paragraph code:

```
public void InsertParagraphTag() {
  if ( lines.Count == 0 ) {
    lines.Add( "<P></P>" );
    selectionStart = 3;
    return;
  }
  lines.InsertRange(LineContainingCursor()+1, NewParagraph());
  selectionStart = NewSelectionStart(LineContainingCursor() + 2, "<P>");
}
```

Now the specialized methods NewParaSelectionStart and NewSectionSelectionStart can be removed. I'll do that and run the tests. Sure enough, they run!

What's Next?

> **Lesson**   As you'll see in a moment, the TextModel code is quite a bit improved by this simple refining. It always seems to turn out this way. We repeatedly comb over the code, and little by little the snarls come out and it gets nicer and nicer. We're not done yet, but there's enough already to see that it's getting better.

I'll include the whole TextModel code here now. My wife Ricia is home, so I'll leave it at that. Note especially that the lines.InsertRange and selectionStart = code looks very similar. We'll go after that in Chapter 12, "Adding the Section Tag, Part II." For now, amuse yourself by reviewing the TextModel and observing that, by gosh, it *is* better:

```
using System;
using System.Collections;
using System.Text;
using System.Text.RegularExpressions;
namespace Notepad {
  class TextModel {
    private ArrayList lines;
    private int selectionStart;
    public TextModel() {
      lines = new ArrayList();
    }
```

```
private int LineContainingCursor() {
  int length = 0;
  int lineNr = 0;
  int cr = Environment.NewLine.Length;
  foreach ( String s in lines) {
    if (length <= selectionStart
      && selectionStart < length+s.Length + cr )
      break;
    length += s.Length + cr;
    lineNr++;
  }
  return lineNr;
}
public ArrayList Lines {
  get {
    return lines;
  }
  set {
    lines = value;
  }
}
public void SetLines(String[] lines) {
  this.Lines = new ArrayList(lines);
}
public String[] LinesArray() {
  String[] result = new String[lines.Count];
  lines.CopyTo(result);
  return result;
}
public String TestText {
  get {
    StringBuilder b = new StringBuilder();
    foreach(String s in lines) {
      b.Append(s);
      b.Append(System.Environment.NewLine);
    }
    b.Insert(SelectionStart,"|");
    return b.ToString();
  }
}
public int SelectionStart {
  get {
    return selectionStart;
  }
  set {
    selectionStart = value;
  }
}
```

```
public void Enter() {
  InsertParagraphTag();
}
public void InsertParagraphTag() {
  if ( lines.Count == 0 ) {
    lines.Add( "<P></P>" );
    selectionStart = 3;
    return;
  }
  lines.InsertRange(LineContainingCursor()+1, NewParagraph());
  selectionStart = NewSelectionStart(LineContainingCursor() + 2, "<P>");
}
public ArrayList NewParagraph() {
  ArrayList temp = new ArrayList();
  temp.Add("");
  temp.Add("<P></P>");
  return temp;
}
public void AltS() {
  InsertSectionTags();
}
public void InsertSectionTags() {
  if ( lines.Count == 0 ) {
    lines.Add( "<sect1><title></title>" );
    lines.Add( "</sect1>");
    selectionStart = 14;
    return;
  }
  lines.InsertRange(LineContainingCursor()+1, NewSection());
  selectionStart = NewSelectionStart(LineContainingCursor() + 1,
    "<sect1><title>");
}
public ArrayList NewSection() {
  ArrayList temp = new ArrayList();
  temp.Add("<sect1><title></title>");
  temp.Add("</sect1>");
  return temp;
}
 private int NewSelectionStart(int cursorLine, string tags) {
  return SumLineLengths(cursorLine) + tags.Length;
}
private int SumLineLengths(int cursorLine) {
  int length = 0;
  for (int i = 0; i < cursorLine; i++)
    length += ((String)lines[i]).Length + Environment.NewLine.Length;
  return length;
}
}
}
```

12

Adding the Section Tag, Part II

We'll continue refactoring our TextModel. Stand back, I don't know how good this thing gets!

Reviewing the Code

The TextModel.cs file was posted at the end of Chapter 11, "Adding the Section Tag, Part I." We can still see lots of duplication in that code. There seems to be a general confusion between whether we want the lines to be an Array or an ArrayList, for example. That should be cleaned up. And here are two methods that are clearly duplication and that I think we should go after:

```
public void InsertParagraphTag() {
  if ( lines.Count == 0 ) {
    lines.Add( "<P></P>" );
    selectionStart = 3;
    return;
  }
  lines.InsertRange(LineContainingCursor()+1, NewParagraph());
  selectionStart = NewSelectionStart(LineContainingCursor() + 2, "<P>");
}

public void InsertSectionTags() {
  if ( lines.Count == 0 ) {
    lines.Add( "<sect1><title></title>" );
    lines.Add( "</sect1>");
    selectionStart = 14;
    return;
  }
```

```
lines.InsertRange(LineContainingCursor()+1, NewSection());
selectionStart = NewSelectionStart(LineContainingCursor() + 1,
  "<sect1><title>");
}
```

See how similar those two methods look? That, boys and girls, is duplication. Let's see how we might reduce it. We could write a new method, Insert-Tag(...), with a few string args and an integer. We might even get rid of the integer by passing in the strings in a "first part"/"last part" pair and then use the length of the first part to set the selectionStart. That looks like fun. But I think I'd rather get rid of that special case code for Count == zero. I see it as the world's most radical form of duplication removal: it should exist zero times rather than just once.

I'm concerned with what will happen if we just remove it. Probably some kind of exception. But in principle, why can't we just do the insert directly? One issue is the blank line between the paragraph tags. I think I'll start by removing that requirement and making the code work. Then maybe I'll put the blank line back when we're done. Step one, remove the blank line from the NewParagraph method and see what breaks:

```
public ArrayList NewParagraph() {
  ArrayList temp = new ArrayList();
  temp.Add("");
  temp.Add("<P></P>");
  return temp;
}
```

changed to this:

```
public ArrayList NewParagraph() {
  ArrayList temp = new ArrayList();
  temp.Add("<P></P>");
  return temp;
}
```

A bunch of tests break. Index out of range. InsertParagraphTag has the phrase LineContainingCursor() + 2, and it should be 1 since now there's just one line being added. I'll change that to 1. Now the tests are breaking because they are wrong. For example:

```
[Test] public void TestOneEnter() {
  model.SetLines(new String[1] {"hello world" });
  model.SelectionStart = 5;
  model.InsertParagraphTag();
  AssertEquals(3, model.Lines.Count);
  AssertEquals(18, model.SelectionStart);
}
```

Because we've removed the blank line, the line count should be 2 now, and the SelectionStart, let's see, I'm betting 16 because we're just removing a CrLf. I'll change that; that works. All the other failures are in Customer Acceptance Tests, each showing multiple lines where there shouldn't be any. I'll change them to remove the blank lines. Here's one example:

```
[Test] public void StringInput() {
    String commands =
@"*input
some line
*end
*enter
*output
some line
<P>|</P>";
        InterpretCommands(commands, "");
    }
```

That blank line above the <P> tags needs to be removed. When I take it out, the test works fine. The rest of the errors are in the .test files. I'll fix them without troubling you here, unless removing blank lines isn't enough, in which case we'll be learning something. Be right back. OK, everything runs.

Lesson   Note in passing that we've *increased* the duplication between the InsertParagraphTag and InsertSectionTags methods—they both refer now to LineContainingCursor() + 1. Sometimes making code that is nearly alike look even more alike, then removing the duplication, and then putting the differences back, is a good refactoring move. We'll see how that works out here. But right now, our mission is to remove the special cases for Lines.Count == 0. I'm going to remove that clause from the following code and see what happens:

```
public void InsertParagraphTag() {
  if ( lines.Count == 0 ) {
    lines.Add( "<P></P>" );
    selectionStart = 3;
    return;
  }       lines.InsertRange(LineContainingCursor()+1, NewParagraph());
  selectionStart = NewSelectionStart(LineContainingCursor() + 1, "<P>");
}
```

converting to this:

```
public void InsertParagraphTag() {
  lines.InsertRange(LineContainingCursor()+1, NewParagraph());
  selectionStart = NewSelectionStart(LineContainingCursor() + 1, "<P>");
}
```

Three tests break: EmptyModel and the TestAllFiles in the customer tests, and TestEmptyText in TestTextModel. They are all throwing an index out-of-range exception in the InsertRange method. The message says: "Index out of range. Must be non-negative and less than the size of the collection." Clearly what's happening is that the insert is getting one as the parameter and the size of the array is zero. The reason is that LineContainingCursor() returns zero if there are no lines. That's wrong, because there is no line zero. What would happen if we initialized lineNr to -1 instead of zero in the following code? I'll try it.

```
private int LineContainingCursor() {
  int length = 0;
  int lineNr = 0;
  int cr = Environment.NewLine.Length;
  foreach ( String s in lines) {
    if (length <= selectionStart
      && selectionStart < length+s.Length + cr )
      break;
    length += s.Length + cr;
    lineNr++;
  }
  return lineNr;
}
```

Even before trying that, I was sure it wouldn't work, because if the cursor is in line zero, the foreach is going to break. I tried it anyway, and lots of things broke. That's not the fix. But TestEmptyText started to work, so it liked the -1. That at least moves the glitch to one location (removing duplication).

> **Lesson**   Just a tiny lesson here. Even though I was sure the change wouldn't work, I ran the tests to see. The test I was concerned about started running, although others broke. That gave me important information: that the -1 is the right answer in that case. Sometimes it's worth trying something that we know won't work for all cases, just to learn something.

Let's make LineContainingCursor return -1 only if the array is empty. The code I tried was this:

```
private int LineContainingCursor() {
  if (lines.Count == 0)
    return -1;
  int length = 0;
  int lineNr = 0;
  int cr = Environment.NewLine.Length;
  foreach ( String s in lines) {
    if (length <= selectionStart
      && selectionStart < length+s.Length + cr )
      break;
    length += s.Length + cr;
    lineNr++;
  }
  return lineNr;
}
```

But it doesn't work! The TestEmptyText still fails, as do the customer tests! But wait, I almost didn't notice that the TestEmptyText method fails in a new way. It says "Expected 3 but was 12." It didn't blow up on the index out of range any more. Let's look at that test:

```
[Test] public void TestEmptyText() {
  model.Lines = new ArrayList(new String[0]);
  model.InsertParagraphTag();
  AssertEquals(1, model.Lines.Count);
  AssertEquals(3, model.SelectionStart);
}
```

We have the line count right, and now it's the SelectionStart that's wrong; we're making progress. Let's look at the InsertParaTag method again and the methods it calls:

```
public void InsertParagraphTag() {
  lines.InsertRange(LineContainingCursor()+1, NewParagraph());
  selectionStart = NewSelectionStart(LineContainingCursor() + 1, "<P>");
}

private int NewSelectionStart(int cursorLine, string tags) {
  return SumLineLengths(cursorLine) + tags.Length;
}
private int SumLineLengths(int cursorLine) {
  int length = 0;
  for (int i = 0; i < cursorLine; i++)
    length += ((String)lines[i]).Length + Environment.NewLine.Length;
  return length;
}
```

I'm really not sure where that 12 is coming from. One possibility is that we're somehow counting the added line twice. It contains "<P></P>CrLf". Yep, that's 9, plus 3 equals 12. The loop in SumLineLengths is running once and should be running zero times. Gack! I think I see the problem, do you?

We fixed the LineContainingCursor() to return -1 if the line array is empty. After we've done the InsertRange, it isn't empty any more and will return zero, which will cause us to count the first line. Here's the code. Notice that the highlighted second use of LineContainingCursor() will be wrong:

```
public void InsertParagraphTag() {
  lines.InsertRange(LineContainingCursor()+1, NewParagraph());
  selectionStart = NewSelectionStart(LineContainingCursor() + 1, "<P>");
}
```

Let's buffer the LineContainingCursor() value in InsertParagraphTag:

```
public void InsertParagraphTag() {
  int cursorLine = LineContainingCursor();
  lines.InsertRange(cursorLine+1, NewParagraph());
  selectionStart = NewSelectionStart(cursorLine + 1, "<P>");
}
```

Now TestEmptyText works. I'll run all the tests...and they *all* run! So we've removed the special case from InsertParagraphTag (though we've added it to LineContainingCursor). It should be possible to remove the glitch now from InsertSectionTags and have it work as well, should it not? From

```
public void InsertSectionTags() {
  if ( lines.Count == 0 ) {
    lines.Add( "<sect1><title></title>" );
    lines.Add( "</sect1>");
    selectionStart = 14;
    return;
  }
  lines.InsertRange(LineContainingCursor()+1, NewSection());
  selectionStart = NewSelectionStart(LineContainingCursor() + 1,
    "<sect1><title>");
}
```

to this:

```
public void InsertSectionTags() {
  lines.InsertRange(LineContainingCursor()+1, NewSection());
  selectionStart = NewSelectionStart(LineContainingCursor() + 1,
    "<sect1><title>");
}
```

Arrgh, the tests don't run: that's wrong. Naturally, I forgot to buffer the cursor line in the new one, and the tests showed me. The correct code is

```
public void InsertSectionTags() {
  int cursorLine = LineContainingCursor();
  lines.InsertRange(cursorLine+1, NewSection());
  selectionStart = NewSelectionStart(cursorLine + 1, "<sect1><title>");
}
```

> **Lesson**   Here we see why it's so important to remove code duplication. When we have duplicate code and need to change things, we have to make the same kind of change in multiple places. When we finish this refactoring, we'll see that we wind up with only one occurrence of this buffering of LineContainingCursor. Maybe, in retrospect, we should have removed the duplication first and then the special case of Count == zero. But no harm done: let's get rid of the duplication.

The Tests All Run

The tests all run, and the code is much better. It's time for a break. Let's see what we've accomplished. We had these two methods:

```
public void InsertParagraphTag() {
  if ( lines.Count == 0 ) {
    lines.Add( "<P></P>" );
    selectionStart = 3;
    return;
  }
  lines.InsertRange(LineContainingCursor()+1, NewParagraph());
  selectionStart = NewSelectionStart(LineContainingCursor() + 2, "<P>");
}

public void InsertSectionTags() {
  if ( lines.Count == 0 ) {
    lines.Add( "<sect1><title></title>" );
    lines.Add( "</sect1>");
    selectionStart = 14;
    return;
  }
  lines.InsertRange(LineContainingCursor()+1, NewSection());
  selectionStart = NewSelectionStart(LineContainingCursor() + 1,
    "<sect1><title>");
}
```

And now we have these:

```
public void InsertParagraphTag() {
  int cursorLine = LineContainingCursor();
  lines.InsertRange(cursorLine+1, NewParagraph());
  selectionStart = NewSelectionStart(cursorLine + 1, "<P>");
}

public void InsertSectionTags() {
  int cursorLine = LineContainingCursor();
  lines.InsertRange(cursorLine+1, NewSection());
  selectionStart = NewSelectionStart(cursorLine + 1, "<sect1><title>");
}
```

Much better. Of course, we can see that these two methods are almost exactly the same, so there's duplication to remove. We'll catch that next time.

The Lesson

I'll include all the code for TextModel below for your comparison. But already we can see that it's much better now, and you can probably see how to make it even better. We have a much better design now—but where did that design come from? We never sat down, reasoned about the program as a whole, or drew any diagrams, nor did we use any arcane incantations. We just removed duplication. Writing the words for this chapter was ten times harder than changing the code.

The power of removing duplication, in the presence of tests, is amazing. It turns programming from a process of building a mental house of cards into a simple code-crafting enterprise. It's rather relaxing. There was one moment there that got a little tense, and usually there is. But even there we didn't panic and didn't resort to the debugger. The problem was right in front of us, we fixed it, and we moved on.

> **Lesson**   Brushing the knots out of the code, one at a time, results in a smooth design, with little effort. We can see design improvements emerging here, and we aren't done yet. Let's review the code and then come back and see what else we can improve.

The TextModel Code

```
using System;
using System.Collections;
using System.Text;
using System.Text.RegularExpressions;
namespace Notepad {
  class TextModel {
    private ArrayList lines;
    private int selectionStart;
    public TextModel() {
      lines = new ArrayList();
    }
    private int LineContainingCursor() {
      if (lines.Count == 0)
        return -1;
      int length = 0;
      int lineNr = 0;
      int cr = Environment.NewLine.Length;
      foreach ( String s in lines) {
        if (length <= selectionStart
          && selectionStart < length+s.Length + cr )
          break;
        length += s.Length + cr;
        lineNr++;
      }
      return lineNr;
    }
    public ArrayList Lines {
      get {
        return lines;
      }
      set {
        lines = value;
      }
    }
    public void SetLines(String[] lines) {
      this.Lines = new ArrayList(lines);
    }
    public String[] LinesArray() {
      String[] result = new String[lines.Count];
      lines.CopyTo(result);
      return result;
    }
    public String TestText {
      get {
        StringBuilder b = new StringBuilder();
        foreach(String s in lines) {
```

```
        b.Append(s);
        b.Append(System.Environment.NewLine);
      }
      b.Insert(SelectionStart,"|");
      return b.ToString();
    }
  }
  public int SelectionStart {
    get {
      return selectionStart;
    }
    set {
      selectionStart = value;
    }
  }
  public void ChangeToH2() {
    ArrayList linesList = Lines;
    String oldLine = (String) linesList[LineContainingCursor()];
    Regex r = new Regex("<(?<prefix>.*)>(?<body>.*)</(?<suffix>.*)>");
    Match m = r.Match(oldLine);
    String newLine = "<H2>" + m.Groups["body"] + "</H2>";
    linesList[LineContainingCursor()] = newLine;
    Lines = linesList;
  }
  public void Enter() {
    InsertParagraphTag();
  }
  public void InsertParagraphTag() {
    int cursorLine = LineContainingCursor();
    lines.InsertRange(cursorLine+1, NewParagraph());
    selectionStart = NewSelectionStart(cursorLine + 1, "<P>");
  }
  public ArrayList NewParagraph() {
    ArrayList temp = new ArrayList();
    temp.Add("<P></P>");
    return temp;
  }
  public void AltS() {
    InsertSectionTags();
  }
  public void InsertSectionTags() {
    int cursorLine = LineContainingCursor();
    lines.InsertRange(cursorLine+1, NewSection());
    selectionStart = NewSelectionStart(cursorLine + 1, "<sect1><title>");
  }
```

```
public ArrayList NewSection() {
  ArrayList temp = new ArrayList();
  temp.Add("<sect1><title></title>");
  temp.Add("</sect1>");
  return temp;
}
private int NewSelectionStart(int cursorLine, string tags) {
  return SumLineLengths(cursorLine) + tags.Length;
}
private int SumLineLengths(int cursorLine) {
  int length = 0;
  for (int i = 0; i < cursorLine; i++)
    length += ((String)lines[i]).Length + Environment.NewLine.Length;
  return length;
}
}
}
```

Looking Around

Let's continue to clean up the TextModel. How good can this get? When I opened the file, here's what the window happened to open on for me:

```
public void InsertSectionTags() {
  int cursorLine = LineContainingCursor();
  lines.InsertRange(cursorLine+1, NewSection());
  selectionStart = NewSelectionStart(cursorLine + 1, "<sect1><title>");
}
public ArrayList NewSection() {
  ArrayList temp = new ArrayList();
  temp.Add("<sect1><title></title>");
  temp.Add("</sect1>");
  return temp;
}
```

That NewSection code is pretty ugly. It's left over from a time earlier in our learning of C#, when we didn't understand arrays and ArrayList very well. I think we can get that down to a data declaration, but let's do it step by step to be sure that we understand how things work. We'll cement our understanding of arrays and ArrayList a bit as well. First, let's create the ArrayList in one step by using a literal string array:

```
public ArrayList NewSection() {
  return new ArrayList(
    new String[] {"<sect1><title></title>","</sect1>" });
}
```

That works. Now, why do we need an ArrayList? It looks like InsertRange will take any collection, so let's just return an array of strings:

```
public string[] NewSection() {
  return new String[] {"<sect1><title></title>","</sect1>" };
}
```

That works just fine also. If that's the case, we should be able to just create that string array as a constant member in the class. We'll make it static, so there will be only one array created. And we'll rename it newSection, because fields are typically lowercase in C#:

```
public void InsertSectionTags() {
  int cursorLine = LineContainingCursor();
  lines.InsertRange(cursorLine+1, newSection);
  selectionStart = NewSelectionStart(cursorLine + 1, "<sect1><title>");
}

private static string[] newSection =
  {"<sect1><title></title>","</sect1>" };
```

That works just fine as well. Now we're noticing that the string passed in to the NewSelectionStart looks a lot like the first element of our input array—but we don't see what would be good to do about it yet. At least I don't. Instead, I'm going to make the same change to the InsertParagraphTag method, from

```
public void InsertParagraphTag() {
  int cursorLine = LineContainingCursor();
  lines.InsertRange(cursorLine+1, NewParagraph());
  selectionStart = NewSelectionStart(cursorLine + 1, "<P>");
}
public ArrayList NewParagraph() {
  ArrayList temp = new ArrayList();
  temp.Add("<P></P>");
  return temp;
}
```

to this:

```
public void InsertParagraphTag() {
  int cursorLine = LineContainingCursor();
  lines.InsertRange(cursorLine+1, newParagraph);
  selectionStart = NewSelectionStart(cursorLine + 1, "<P>");
}
private static string[] newParagraph = { "<P></P>" };
```

That works just fine as well. Let's see what still needs improving. The class now looks like this:

```
using System;
using System.Collections;
using System.Text;
using System.Text.RegularExpressions;
namespace Notepad {
  class TextModel {
    private static string[] newParagraph = { "<P></P>" };
    private static string[] newSection =
      {"<sect1><title></title>","</sect1>" };
    private ArrayList lines;
    private int selectionStart;
    public TextModel() {
      lines = new ArrayList();
    }
    private int LineContainingCursor() {
      if (lines.Count == 0)
        return -1;
      int length = 0;
      int lineNr = 0;
      int cr = Environment.NewLine.Length;
      foreach ( String s in lines) {
        if (length <= selectionStart
          && selectionStart < length+s.Length + cr )
          break;
        length += s.Length + cr;
        lineNr++;
      }
      return lineNr;
    }
    public ArrayList Lines {
      get {
        return lines;
      }
      set {
        lines = value;
      }
    }
    public void SetLines(String[] lines) {
      this.Lines = new ArrayList(lines);
    }
    public String[] LinesArray() {
      String[] result = new String[lines.Count];
      lines.CopyTo(result);
      return result;
    }
```

```
    }
    public String TestText {
      get {
        StringBuilder b = new StringBuilder();
        foreach(String s in lines) {
          b.Append(s);
          b.Append(System.Environment.NewLine);
        }
        b.Insert(SelectionStart,"|");
        return b.ToString();
      }
    }
    public int SelectionStart {
      get {
        return selectionStart;
      }
      set {
        selectionStart = value;
      }
    }
    public void Enter() {
      InsertParagraphTag();
    }
    public void InsertParagraphTag() {
      int cursorLine = LineContainingCursor();
      lines.InsertRange(cursorLine+1, newParagraph);
      selectionStart = NewSelectionStart(cursorLine + 1, "<P>");
    }
    public void AltS() {
      InsertSectionTags();
    }
    public void InsertSectionTags() {
      int cursorLine = LineContainingCursor();
      lines.InsertRange(cursorLine+1, newSection);
      selectionStart = NewSelectionStart(cursorLine + 1, "<sect1><title>");
    }
    private int NewSelectionStart(int cursorLine, string tags) {
      return SumLineLengths(cursorLine) + tags.Length;
    }
    private int SumLineLengths(int cursorLine) {
      int length = 0;
      for (int i = 0; i < cursorLine; i++)
        length += ((String)lines[i]).Length + Environment.NewLine.Length;
      return length;
    }
  }
}
```

What Do We See Now?

There are a number of things that I don't like much. There is still evidence of confusion between arrays and ArrayLists, and I don't like the look of that highlighted LineContainingCursor method. Also, the AltS and Enter methods just call the InsertParagraphTag and InsertSectionTags methods. I'm not entirely fond of that but it is a well-honored coding pattern, "Explaining Method Name." We could just copy the code for InsertSectionTags in there, but if we did, then when we read the AltS code we would have to figure out its purpose. Using the other method name says "Alt+S is InsertSectionTags". If the code didn't say it, then a comment would have to. I'd rather have the code say it.

Another thing I notice is that the highlighted InsertSectionTags and Insert-ParagraphTag methods look a lot alike. Duplication! We have to get rid of it. How to do it? Extract a new method called, say, InsertTags, giving it parameters for the variable bits, the tags. We'll do them one at a time, first InsertSection-Tags, for no particular reason. The new code is

```
public void InsertSectionTags() {
  InsertTags(newSection, "<sect1><title>");
}
private void InsertTags(string[] tagsToInsert, string tagsPrecedingCursor) {
  int cursorLine = LineContainingCursor();
  lines.InsertRange(cursorLine+1, tagsToInsert);
  selectionStart = NewSelectionStart(cursorLine + 1, tagsPrecedingCursor);
}
```

Tests all run. I'll make the same change to InsertParagraphTag:

```
public void InsertParagraphTag() {
  InsertTags(newParagraph, "<P>");
}
```

Tests still run. Now, looking at those Insert methods, it's clear that their tagsPrecedingCursor strings should be converted to static constants, just like the tagsToInsert. Let's do that:

```
private static string[] newParagraph = { "<P></P>" };
private static string paragraphSkip = "<P>";
private static string[] newSection =
  {"<sect1><title></title>","</sect1>" };
private static string sectionSkip = "<sect1><title>";

public void InsertParagraphTag() {
  InsertTags(newParagraph, paragraphSkip);
}
public void InsertSectionTags() {
  InsertTags(newSection, sectionSkip);
}
```

Again, the tests all run. There's a little duplication in those strings, but we'll let it go for now: I like the way the strings communicate what's inserted and what is skipped to set the caret.

Judgment Call

Earlier I was complaining about the AltS method having just that simple Insert-SectionTags method call. Take a look at the InsertSectionTags method now. We could eliminate that method entirely, by putting its InsertTags call up in AltS. That would change this

```
public void AltS() {
  InsertSectionTags();
}
public void InsertSectionTags() {
  InsertTags(newSection, sectionSkip);
}
```

and would give us this:

```
public void AltS() {
  InsertTags(newSection, sectionSkip);
}
```

We need to decide if that code communicates sufficiently what's going on. My judgment is that it does, so I'll leave it that way. On the other hand, I'm working without a pair, who might not agree. And you might not agree: that's why I call it a judgment call. For now, I like it, and I'll do the other method the same way:

```
public void Enter() {
  InsertTags(newParagraph, paragraphSkip);
}
```

I run the tests...and they don't run!!! It turns out there are three tests that were calling InsertParagraphTag directly. Now the decision is harder. If I change this one back, I really should change the other one, or else the code here will look odd. Or I can change the tests to send Enter instead of InsertParagraphTag. That's not clearly the right thing to do. Let's look at the tests to see whether doing that will make them more confusing.

```
[Test] public void TestOneEnter() {
  model.SetLines(new String[1] {"hello world" });
  model.SelectionStart = 5;
  model.InsertParagraphTag();
  AssertEquals(2, model.Lines.Count);
  AssertEquals(16, model.SelectionStart);
}
```

```
[Test] public void TestEmptyText() {
  model.Lines = new ArrayList(new String[0]);
  model.InsertParagraphTag();
  AssertEquals(1, model.Lines.Count);
  AssertEquals(3, model.SelectionStart);
}
[Test] public void InsertWithCursorAtLineStart () {
  model.Lines = new ArrayList(new String[3] {
    "<P>one</P>", "", "<P>two</P>"});
  model.SelectionStart = 14;
  model.InsertParagraphTag();
  AssertEquals("<P>two</P>", model.Lines[2]);
}
```

Again, judgment. I feel that I like the compression of the TextModel class enough to live with the slightly less clear tests. And the first one is called "Enter" and then calls InsertParagraphTag, so it will actually be improved.

But wait! There's another reason why this should NOT be done, however. The InsertParagraphTag and InsertSectionTags methods are *logical* behavior, and the AltS and Enter methods are *physical*: they represent the particular choice of which keystroke should do which function. And I'm reminded that we have already changed AltS once, from ControlS. That's enough to convince me to go back to the previous arrangement with AltS calling InsertSectionTags and so on. A little undo, and we should be all right. Hold on...bunch of Ctrl+Zs, compile and run tests...all back the way it was.

Lesson   Is there a lesson here? Well, probably a few (in no particular order):

- Too tight a linkage between user actions and system actions is probably a bad idea.

- A partner might have helped me not make the mistake.

- My tests already embodied the logical/physical distinction and gave me an important clue.

- It was easy to do the experiment, and easy to undo it, because I was going in tiny steps.

- Don't be afraid to change your mind.

   Depending on your original view, you might also offer another lesson: don't fall too much in love with tight code at the expense of clarity.

Enough for Now

I feel that that's enough clean up for now, a couple/three hours' work, probably less if I weren't writing chapters as I go. There's still some confusion between ArrayList and Array, but that's mostly a function of the TextBox needing Array and our own classes looking better with ArrayList. We might look at that later, but more likely we'll move on to improving the tool and its tests. As an example of what has changed, here's what this code looked like when we started this exercise:

```
public void InsertParagraphTag() {
  //
  // On Enter, we change the TextModel lines to insert, after the line
  // containing the cursor, a blank line, and a line with <P></P>.
  // We set the new cursor location to be between the P tags: <P>|</P>.
  //
  // handle empty array special case (yucch)
  if ( lines.Count == 0 ) {
    lines.Add( "<P></P>" );
    selectionStart = 3;
    return;
  }
  lines.InsertRange(LineContainingCursor()+1, NewParagraph());
  selectionStart = NewParaSelectionStart(LineContainingCursor() + 2);
}
private int NewParaSelectionStart(int cursorLine) {
  int length = 0;
  for (int i = 0; i < cursorLine; i++)
    length += ((String)lines[i]).Length + Environment.NewLine.Length;
  return length + "<p>".Length;
}
public ArrayList NewParagraph() {
  ArrayList temp = new ArrayList();
  temp.Add("");
  temp.Add("<P></P>");
  return temp;
}

public void AltS() {
  InsertSectionTags();
}
public void InsertSectionTags() {
  if ( lines.Count == 0 ) {
    lines.Add( "<sect1><title></title>" );
    lines.Add( "</sect1>");
    selectionStart = 14;
    return;
```

```
  }
  lines.InsertRange(LineContainingCursor()+1, NewSection());
  selectionStart = NewSectionSelectionStart(LineContainingCursor() + 1);
}
public ArrayList NewSection() {
  ArrayList temp = new ArrayList();
  temp.Add("<sect1><title></title>");
  temp.Add("</sect1>");
  return temp;
}
private int NewSectionSelectionStart(int cursorLine) {
  int length = 0;
  for (int i = 0; i < cursorLine; i++)
    length += ((String)lines[i]).Length + Environment.NewLine.Length;
  return length + "<sect1><title>".Length;
}
```

And here's what it looks like now:

```
public void Enter() {
  InsertParagraphTag();
}
public void InsertParagraphTag() {
  InsertTags(newParagraph, paragraphSkip);
}
public void AltS() {
  InsertSectionTags();
}
public void InsertSectionTags() {
  InsertTags(newSection, sectionSkip);
}
private void InsertTags(string[] tagsToInsert, string tagsPrecedingCursor) {
  int cursorLine = LineContainingCursor();
  lines.InsertRange(cursorLine+1, tagsToInsert);
  selectionStart = NewSelectionStart(cursorLine + 1, tagsPrecedingCursor);
}
 private int NewSelectionStart(int cursorLine, string tags) {
  return SumLineLengths(cursorLine) + tags.Length;
}
private int SumLineLengths(int cursorLine) {
  int length = 0;
  for (int i = 0; i < cursorLine; i++)
    length += ((String)lines[i]).Length + Environment.NewLine.Length;
  return length;
}
```

Remember that all that code was duplicated for the Enter/InsertParagraph-Tag, and now it's all using the same methods. Very little duplication. I think it's a noticeable improvement and hope that you do as well.

> **Lesson**   The big learning here is worth underlining: we have very much improved the design of this class. Almost everything that was specific is general now. Things that were cut and pasted or duplicated are now almost all centralized. The code looks like it was designed, and designed fairly well.
>
> But we know differently. This code was not designed: it was refined, and refined, by looking always at little chunks, not by looking at the overall picture. To me, this is the big programming lesson of XP: simple design, solid tests, and continuous refactoring make a program come into being that is well-designed—without having to make any big design decisions. Of course, if you like making big (and risky) design decisions, you might not like this outcome. I like it a lot, because it lets me focus on delivering what my customer wants and needs, without concern that I'll mess up the design by going too fast.
>
> And don't forget those tests. They saved me a number of times—and I learned that I need a few more. We'll address that concern as we go along.

Code Summary

The class, with things rearranged a bit, looks like this now:

```
using System;
using System.Collections;
using System.Text;
using System.Text.RegularExpressions;
namespace Notepad {
  class TextModel {
    private static string[] newParagraph = { "<P></P>" };
    private static string paragraphSkip = "<P>";
    private static string[] newSection =
      {"<sect1><title></title>","</sect1>" };
    private static string sectionSkip = "<sect1><title>";
    private ArrayList lines;
    private int selectionStart;
    public TextModel() {
```

```
      lines = new ArrayList();
    }
    public ArrayList Lines {
      get {
        return lines;
      }
      set {
        lines = value;
      }
    }
    public void SetLines(String[] lines) {
      this.Lines = new ArrayList(lines);
    }
    public String[] LinesArray() {
      String[] result = new String[lines.Count];
      lines.CopyTo(result);
      return result;
    }
    public String TestText {
      get {
        StringBuilder b = new StringBuilder();
        foreach(String s in lines) {
          b.Append(s);
          b.Append(System.Environment.NewLine);
        }
        b.Insert(SelectionStart,"|");
        return b.ToString();
      }
    }
    public int SelectionStart {
      get {
        return selectionStart;
      }
      set {
        selectionStart = value;
      }
    }
    public void Enter() {
      InsertParagraphTag();
    }
    public void InsertParagraphTag() {
      InsertTags(newParagraph, paragraphSkip);
    }
    public void AltS() {
      InsertSectionTags();
    }
    public void InsertSectionTags() {
      InsertTags(newSection, sectionSkip);
```

```
    }
    private void InsertTags(string[] tagsToInsert, string tagsPrecedingCursor)
      {
      int cursorLine = LineContainingCursor();
      lines.InsertRange(cursorLine+1, tagsToInsert);
      selectionStart = NewSelectionStart(cursorLine + 1, tagsPrecedingCursor);
    }
     private int NewSelectionStart(int cursorLine, string tags) {
      return SumLineLengths(cursorLine) + tags.Length;
    }
    private int SumLineLengths(int cursorLine) {
      int length = 0;
      for (int i = 0; i < cursorLine; i++)
        length += ((String)lines[i]).Length + Environment.NewLine.Length;
      return length;
    }
    public void ChangeToH2() {
      ArrayList linesList = Lines;
      String oldLine = (String) linesList[LineContainingCursor()];
      Regex r = new Regex("<(?<prefix>.*)>(?<body>.*)</(?<suffix>.*)>");
      Match m = r.Match(oldLine);
      String newLine = "<H2>" + m.Groups["body"] + "</H2>";
      linesList[LineContainingCursor()] = newLine;
      Lines = linesList;
    }
    private int LineContainingCursor() {
      if (lines.Count == 0)
        return -1;
      int length = 0;
      int lineNr = 0;
      int cr = Environment.NewLine.Length;
      foreach ( String s in lines) {
        if (length <= selectionStart
          && selectionStart < length+s.Length + cr )
          break;
        length += s.Length + cr;
        lineNr++;
      }
      return lineNr;
    }
  }
}
```

By the way, you may have noticed that ChangeToH2 and LineContain-ingCursor. They're part of an experiment that I haven't written up, in how to change a <P> tag to an <H2>. If I were entirely brave, I'd delete the code and the test that uses it until I need it. But I'm only human...

13

Discovering the Menu

Our addition of the "section" feature worked fine, except for an irritating beep every time we insert a section. A bit of learning suggests that this is a menu-related problem, even though we don't have a menu—yet.

Exploring the Problem

As soon as we added the new section logic to the GUI, using Alt+S, and began using the software through the GUI, Chet and I discovered an irritating beep every time we typed the Alt+S. We tried to be sure that we were properly telling Microsoft Windows that we had consumed the character, but that didn't suppress the beep. So we did a little experimenting: we added a couple of Console.WriteLine sends to the KeyPress and KeyDown handlers, to print out what was happening and when. In the course of that, we learned some interesting things. For example, all typed characters seem to go through KeyDown, but some never show up in KeyPress. It isn't too much of a surprise to find out that Alt and Shift do that, since they are basically key modifiers. It's more interesting to know that the arrow keys—up, down, left, right—also do not show up in KeyPress. We'll have to remember that in case we want to specialize them.

Perhaps the most interesting thing, however, is the behavior of the Alt key. I noticed right away that it repeats in KeyDown until you type the S or whatever you're trying to Alt. No surprise. But the code I was using was this:

```
Console.WriteLine(
  "KeyPress\n  char {0}\n int {1}",
  kea.KeyChar, (int)
  kea.KeyChar);
```

What prints as the character? The Alt key is named "Menu". Furthermore, when I typed one Alt, the screen displayed this:

```
KeyDown  char Menu int 18
```

But the second Alt you type doesn't print. Then the third one does, and so on. So, Holmes on the case here finally makes the connection: Alt is doing something about going to the Form's menu.

Therefore, I finally figured out, if the form had a menu item whose accelerator key was Alt+S, the menu item would trigger and probably that annoying beep would go away. I decided to do a little research on Menu. In my reading, I found Charles Petzold telling me that Microsoft .NET has changed the conventions a bit for how menus work, compared to conventional Microsoft Windows. I'll not go into details here, but it was enough to make me sure that trying the menu was probably interesting.

Other Issues

Recall that in my pairing session with Chet, we realized that though we have a set of programmable Customer Acceptance Tests, they aren't testing end to end as well as they should. We can forget to handle a new keystroke in the GUI and the Customer Acceptance Tests will run. On the C3 project, we had a saying, sb"end to end is further than you think," and this is an example of that.

So I also did a little research on how GUI programs can be made more testable. I came across Michael Feathers's article on the Humble Dialog Box, at *www.objectmentor.com/resources/articles/TheHumbleDialogBox.pdf.* The article is in C++, so it helped me along but also left me unsure about how to connect the ideas into our XML Notepad. I also chatted with Michael, and with Brian Button, who wrote a C# program along the lines of Michael's Humble Dialog Box notion.

I realized after a while that what I was trying to do was to get a sense of the future. Now as an XPer, I'm not supposed to care about the future, at least not to the extent of putting the future into my code. So what's up with that?

I realized that since I don't have much experience building GUIs the .NET C# way, I was sensing things that were wrong with the code—"code smells" as Beck and Fowler would have it—but I didn't know what to do about those smells. I was feeling nervous, and the feeling was telling me that I needed to understand more about what might happen.

> **Lesson**   So I'd offer that lesson to the reader, as well: when you're looking at part of the system that doesn't seem just right, trust that feeling. If you know what to do to improve it, do so the next time you're working in that area. And if you *don't* know what to do, take it as a signal that it's time to do some research, time to add a few things to your bag of tricks. Don't use those things, necessarily, in the real program, although you might well want to experiment. But do take the occasion to learn.

Preparing the Ground

OK, enough preaching. Let's try the menu idea and see what happens. Here's my prediction on what will happen, given my reading of some examples:

- The menu code will be long, but not particularly difficult. I plan to start with an incredibly simple menu and go from there.

- The menu code will contain substantial duplication, which will irritate us as time goes on.

- The menu code will require me to link the menu item to a separate handler, which will originally duplicate code in the keyboard handler.

- It should be possible to remove the code from the keyboard handler after the menu works.

- The breakout of the menu handler will make the code a bit nicer. This may lead to further improvement using the same technique.

This is all speculation, of course. I'm sharing it with you so that you'll know that in XP we do speculate, and so that we can see how it turns out. Let's look at the code we're starting with for the Form:

```
using System;
using System.Drawing;
using System.Windows.Forms;
using NUnit.Framework;
using System.Collections;
using System.Text.RegularExpressions;
namespace Notepad
{
```

```
class XMLNotepad : Form {
  public TestableTextBox textbox;
  private TextModel model;

  static void Main(string[] args)
  {
    Application.Run(new XMLNotepad());
  }
  public XMLNotepad() {
    Text = "XML Notepad";
    textbox = new TestableTextBox();
    textbox.Parent = this;
    textbox.Dock = DockStyle.Fill;
    textbox.BorderStyle = BorderStyle.None;
    textbox.Multiline = true;
    textbox.ScrollBars = ScrollBars.Both;
    textbox.AcceptsTab = true;
    textbox.KeyDown += new KeyEventHandler(XMLKeyDownHandler);
    textbox.KeyPress +=
      new KeyPressEventHandler(XMLKeyPressHandler);
    model = new TextModel();
  }
  private void InitializeComponent() {
    this.SuspendLayout();
    //
    // textbox
    //
    this.textbox.Visible = true;
    //
    // XMLNotepad
    //
    this.AutoScaleBaseSize = new System.Drawing.Size(5, 13);
    this.ClientSize = new System.Drawing.Size(292, 266);
    this.Controls.AddRange(new System.Windows.Forms.Control[] {
                                  this.textbox});
    this.Name = "XMLNotepad";
    this.ResumeLayout(false);
  }
  void XMLKeyPressHandler(object objSender, KeyPressEventArgs kea) {
    Console.WriteLine(
      "KeyPress\n  char {0}\n int {1}",
      kea.KeyChar,
      (int) kea.KeyChar);
    if ((int) kea.KeyChar == (int) Keys.Enter) {
      kea.Handled = true;
      // this code is here to avoid putting extra enters
      // in the window.
      // if removed, when you hit enter, the new <P> line breaks
```

```
        // in two:
        // <P>
        // |</P>  like that.
      }
    }
    void XMLKeyDownHandler(object objSender, KeyEventArgs kea) {
      Console.WriteLine(
        "KeyDown  char {0} int {1}", kea.KeyCode, (int) kea.KeyCode);
      model.SetLines(textbox.Lines);
      model.SelectionStart = textbox.SelectionStart;
      if (kea.KeyCode == Keys.Enter) {
        model.Enter();
        kea.Handled = true;
      }
      if (kea.KeyCode == Keys.X)
        kea.Handled = true;
      if (kea.KeyCode == Keys.S && kea.Alt) {
        model.AltS();
        kea.Handled = true;
      }
      PutText(textbox, model.LinesArray(), model.SelectionStart);
    }
    public void PutText(ITestTextBox textbox, string[] lines,
      int selectionStart) {
      // this is Feature Envy big time.
      textbox.Lines = lines;
      textbox.SelectionStart = selectionStart;
      textbox.ScrollToCaret();
    }
  }
}
```

I've left the Console.WriteLines in there so that you can see where I put them. I also think that when the menu goes in, we might see something interesting in the key handlers. You might also notice that I've taken out the inheritance of this Form from the earlier NotepadCloneNoMenu Form. I just moved the textbox stuff down to this class, because the other Form wasn't helping and seemed to be making things hard to understand.

Furthermore, based on my reading of code that Microsoft Visual Studio generates, there's a bit of confusion between creating and initializing things like the textbox in the object constructor (XMLNotepad()) and in the InitializeComponent() method. Visual Studio .NET seems to put most of the stuff in the InitializeComponent. Petzold, on the other hand, puts everything in the constructor. I consider our current mixed approach to be a bit of a code smell, but I'm not going to worry about it yet. Well, on the other hand, why not. Let's experiment; that's what this book is about. I'm going to move all the code from the InitializeComponent up to the constructor and remove the method. My reading says that the SuspendLayout calls are probably a red herring, so I'm going to remove that altogether. The result, after a little rearrangement, looks like this:

```
public XMLNotepad() {
  model = new TextModel();
  Text = "XML Notepad";
  textbox = new TestableTextBox();
  textbox.Parent = this;
  textbox.Dock = DockStyle.Fill;
  textbox.BorderStyle = BorderStyle.None;
  textbox.Multiline = true;
  textbox.ScrollBars = ScrollBars.Both;
  textbox.AcceptsTab = true;
  textbox.KeyDown += new KeyEventHandler(XMLKeyDownHandler);
  textbox.KeyPress += new KeyPressEventHandler(XMLKeyPressHandler);
  this.textbox.Visible = true;
  this.AutoScaleBaseSize = new System.Drawing.Size(5, 13);
  this.ClientSize = new System.Drawing.Size(292, 266);
  this.Controls.AddRange(new System.Windows.Forms.Control[]
    { this.textbox});
  this.Name = "XMLNotepad";
}
```

This compiles, and the tests all run. I know that the GUI testing is still a little weak, though, so I'm going to run the actual application...and it works fine.

> **Lesson**   I don't like this feeling of fear. When we run our tests, we should feel almost completely confident that the system is going to work correctly. Something will have to be done about this. Right now, however, we're working on the menu.

Adding the Menu

For my initial cut at the menu, I'll add InsertSection right at the top. The code looks like this:

```
public XMLNotepad() {
  model = new TextModel();
  Text = "XML Notepad";
  MenuItem insertSection = new MenuItem (
```

```
    "Insert &Section",
  new EventHandler(MenuInsertSection));
Menu = new MainMenu(new MenuItem[] {insertSection} );
textbox = new TestableTextBox();
textbox.Parent = this;
textbox.Dock = DockStyle.Fill;
textbox.BorderStyle = BorderStyle.None;
textbox.Multiline = true;
textbox.ScrollBars = ScrollBars.Both;
textbox.AcceptsTab = true;
textbox.KeyDown += new KeyEventHandler(XMLKeyDownHandler);
textbox.KeyPress += new KeyPressEventHandler(XMLKeyPressHandler);
this.textbox.Visible = true;
this.AutoScaleBaseSize = new System.Drawing.Size(5, 13);
this.ClientSize = new System.Drawing.Size(292, 266);
this.Controls.AddRange(new System.Windows.Forms.Control[]
  { this.textbox});
this.Name = "XMLNotepad";
}
void MenuInsertSection(object obj, EventArgs ea) {
  Console.WriteLine("Insert Section");
}
```

I just created a new MenuItem, with an accelerator of Alt+S (signified by the &S in Section). When clicked, it will invoke the handler MenuInsertSection, which I've got set up just to display something to the console. Sure enough, the menu comes up on the screen, as shown here, and the console is printing the message.

You might be wondering about that @Send thing showing up in the menu bar. That's from my fax software, eFax. It adds that icon to any window that it thinks contains text that you might want to fax. I'm not sure why it chose to appear in this app, but it's perfectly OK with me that it did, at least for now.

Now it's time to make the menu item work. I'll just extract the code from the AltS in the key handler and move it over to the MenuInsertSection. Cleverly, I'm going to remember to move the lines that read and reset the TextBox:

```
void MenuInsertSection(object obj, EventArgs ea) {
  model.SetLines(textbox.Lines);
  model.SelectionStart = textbox.SelectionStart;        model.AltS();
  PutText(textbox, model.LinesArray(), model.SelectionStart);
}
```

It works! The tests all run, Alt+S inserts the section tags, and the irritating beep is gone. But there's a pretty obvious problem with that code. Note that it sends the AltS message to the TextModel. This code makes it clear, if it wasn't already, that we have some confusion between the human factors gestures, Enter and Alt+S, and the model's logical behavior, InsertParagraphTag and InsertSectionTags.

We might choose not to worry about it. The new menu approach, carried forward, will probably help us provide isolation between the keystroke gestures and the actions. The menu item names will be the actions, which is good enough for now. For now I'll change the code to send InsertSectionTags, which makes more sense to me. This might not be good enough for all time. If this application were going to be internationalized, for example, the menu items might change. We'll definitely not worry about that for now: we don't have a story for it.

Enough For Now?

This might be almost enough for now. We've shown that we can get rid of the beep, and we've learned a little bit about menus. Our Insert Section Tags story is working fine. There are, however, some things to worry about:

- Looking at that MenuInsertSection, we can see that there's some code duplication coming. Every one of the commands we send will have to read the TextBox into the TextModel, execute the model, and then read the model back into the TextBox. We'll have to deal with that—but not until it happens.

- We don't have decent testing of the GUI. This all started when we implemented the section logic in the model and tested it but forgot to put any way to access it into the GUI. So we need to be on the alert to improve that testing.

■   I just noticed that my references to the textbox in the constructor don't start with "this.", while the ones generated by Windows do. Those need to be consistent. I'll change them all to use "this."—because although the textbox variable is local to this class, the other things being referenced are in the superclass and without the "this.", it wouldn't be clear what was going on. This could be wrong; we'll find out as time goes on.

Now let's review our predictions from above.

■   The menu code isn't long yet, but we can see that it's going to take a lot of words to say very little. It's not very difficult, though, as I had hoped.

■   We moved the code to the handler and removed the duplication at the same time. A little use of foresight, but not too much, I feel. What would have happened had I not removed it? I suspect it would have inserted the section tags twice. Anyway, we dodged that bullet.

■   The code did get removed from the keyboard handler.

■   The code is a tiny bit nicer, I think. The function is a bit more clear, because the menu handler is more explicit and doesn't confuse the AltS and InsertSectionTags notions. Just a small improvement, but I think a real one.

■   We haven't seen duplication across menu items yet, but it seems clear that each one is going to look much like the previous ones. We'll keep watching for this, and if it crops up as we expect, we'll deal with it.

So this time, most of the predictions came true. Overall, my prediction record isn't quite that good; that's why I don't make many predictions.

What's Next?

We're in good condition to take on some new stories. New tags are possible, and our customer might ask for some other interesting features.

But we're weak on Customer Acceptance Tests. I'm a bit worried about that: the lack of tests has slowed me down and created at least one bug that might have slipped through to my customer. That would be bad.

So, for next time, I'll be thinking of new stories that would add value to the product and I'll be thinking of better ways to test it.

14

Don't Try This at Home

Concern over potential code duplication in menus led me to do a little research. That led me to a really cool feature. I think I went down a rat hole—what do you think?

The Idle Brain Is the Devil's Playground

In looking at the menu method from last time, I can foresee duplication of code. The method looked like this:

```
void MenuInsertSection(object obj, EventArgs ea) {
  model.SetLines(textbox.Lines);
  model.SelectionStart = textbox.SelectionStart;
  model.InsertSectionTags();
  PutText(textbox, model.LinesArray(), model.SelectionStart);
}
```

Now I foresee that lots of insertion methods are coming; I've seen the stories. There will be one to insert plain code like the method here, one for those precis things at the top of the articles/chapters, and a bunch of little utility ones for articles and so on. I see duplication coming! Every one of those menu items will have a method like this one, and the only difference between those methods will be that instead of saying InsertSectionTags, a method will say something like InsertCode or InsertPrecis. Duplication, running wild! As you know, the primary coding technique we use for keeping the code clean is to remove duplication, and although I usually know what I'd do to get rid of duplication, this time I'm not so sure. So I'm worried.

YAGNI

Now, there's an XP "rule" called [sb]YAGNI: You Aren't Gonna Need It. This rule reminds us not to borrow trouble from the future and not to implement a feature today that we don't need today. If I'm not mistaken, I actually coined that rule back in the days of the original XP project, C3, when one of us would say "We're gonna need ..." and start suggesting that we should build something for the future. That's what makes this chapter such a sin: I'm going to break that rule. We'll see what happens.

Sketching the Solution

One way to eliminate the duplication would be to send all the menu commands to the same handler method, look at the menu item that was actually clicked, and decide what to do then. The code might look sort of like this (untested):

```
void MenuAllInserts(object obj, EventArgs ea) {
  model.SetLines(textbox.Lines);
  model.SelectionStart = textbox.SelectionStart;
  string item = MenuItem(obj);
  if (item == "Insert &Section" )
    model.InsertSectionTags();
  else if (item == "Insert &Code" )
    model.InsertCode();
  PutText(textbox, model.LinesArray(), model.SelectionStart);
}
```

In this code, the fiddling with the textbox and model would occur only once. Mission accomplished, if it can be made to work.

I did some experimenting with menus, and sure enough, you can cast the object obj to MenuItem and ask for its Text, as suggested there by the MenuItem(obj). So code like that just shown could work.

But now I'm worried about something else. The Form object, in which this menu handler lives, is doing the translation between the menu item and the method to send to the model. That troubles me, as I've mentioned before, because it doesn't feel like the proper function of the Form to do that, and it's hard to test.

Now, in Smalltalk, my favorite language, a common solution would be to use the menu item to look up the name of the method in a hash table and then just tell the model to perform that method. That would be much nicer. Transformed to C#, it would let our current method look like this:

```
void MenuInsertSection(object obj, EventArgs ea) {
  model.SetLines(textbox.Lines);
  model.SelectionStart = textbox.SelectionStart;
  model.Perform("InsertSectionTags");
```

```
  PutText(textbox, model.LinesArray(), model.SelectionStart);
}
```

And the extension to the method with the if statements is obvious. Of course, we would still need to do something nicer than the if statements, to factor the decision out of the Form, but we already have that problem, so we would be at least a bit better off. It might even be possible to send the textbox to the model and let everything happen over there. That would be good.

You may have noticed that we could *already* send the textbox over to the model, in the original code earlier, and that that would at least push the duplication issue over to the other side. Or we could send a standard message to the model, like InsertSomething(string menuItemText), and let the model decide what to do. If you noticed that, you're doing better than I did, because this particular chapter is a report on something already accomplished, not something I'm working out as I go. And I did not think of that approach.

Further Down the Rat Hole

Well, how could we do that Perform thing? Surely C# has some way to invoke a method given its name. Only a half hour or so of experimentation later, I had this code working:

```
void MenuInsertSection(object obj, EventArgs ea) {
  model.SetLines(textbox.Lines);
  model.SelectionStart = textbox.SelectionStart;

  Type modelType = typeof(TextModel);
  modelType.InvokeMember(
    "InsertSectionTags",
    BindingFlags.Default | BindingFlags.InvokeMethod,
    null,
    model,
    new object[]{});

  PutText(textbox, model.LinesArray(), model.SelectionStart);
}
```

That atrocity in the middle is the code to invoke a method on an object, given the string name of the method. After, I swear, only a little more study, I found that you can say:

```
model.GetType().InvokeMember(
  "InsertSectionTags",
  BindingFlags.Default | BindingFlags.InvokeMethod,
  null,
  model,
  new object[]{});
```

That is ever so much nicer, I'm sure you'll agree. But now, you see, we're only one short step away from what we really want. We can implement the Perform() method on TextModel quite easily, like this:

```
private static object[] noArgs = {};
public void Perform(string methodName) {
  this.GetType().InvokeMember(
    methodName,
    BindingFlags.Public | BindingFlags.InvokeMethod | BindingFlags.Instance,
    null,
    this,
    noArgs);
}
```

Now frankly, I'm pretty proud of this. I've learned how to do Reflection—that's what this is called—well enough to send a message to an object, given only its name. I've implemented a method on TextModel to do that fairly transparently, and I'm all set now to eliminate the duplication that is coming real soon now.

Real Soon Now

And that's the problem. My greatest fear in software development is that I won't ship enough good stuff to my customer and my customer will cancel the project, even though really things are going just fine and really we're doing good work and really we're just about ready to start putting in the features you want and really it's going to be a really great product and you really should be just a little more patient.

For me, this fear is well-founded: I've had more than one project cancelled under me when the team had just the feelings noted above. So the main thing that I like about XP is that it is customer-driven and focused on delivering useful features, not nifty code like that above.

Therefore, even though I have learned something, and even though I don't begrudge the few hours I've spent on it, because after all I'm here to learn things, I've spent those few precious hours not making the product better for my customer.

Furthermore, it isn't clear that this is even the best solution. There are some fairly serious issues with it. It's obscure, and it's probably inefficient, not that I'm very worried about that in this particular case. The code is going to be hard to read when it starts saying Perform(methodName). There may be a much more direct way to do what has to be done, and it might be possible to get rid of the duplication in a much simpler and more obvious way.

But not for me. I've got this cool feature put into the code already. You know I'm going to resist taking it back out—and you know you would resist just as much if you had thought of this cool thing!

Don't Try This at Home

It's good to learn. And I'm glad I have this new capability in my bag of tricks. However, as fond as I am of this newfound capability, I'm at risk of using it when I shouldn't. At risk? I've actually *used* it! Now I'm alert to the possibility that this cute little bit of code I've implemented might not be the best choice, but even so, it's going to be difficult to replace it with something more clear, because it's going to keep leading me down this Perform path.

Keep your eye on this code as we go forward. It's good to learn, but there's a good chance that I've learned the wrong thing. Four hours could have implemented a couple of nice new features. On a real project, that could be the difference between a happy customer and an angry one.

Really cool feature, though. I still like it...

15

Climbing Out of the Rat Hole

In which a faithful reader sends a valuable message and our hero heeds the warning before it's too late. In short, let's clean up this mess.

Pairing at a Distance

Kevin Lawrence, of *Diamond Sky http://www.diamond-sky.com*, was kind enough to send along some ideas about the "Perform" rat hole I went down last time. He pointed out that there is a better way to do it, saying, in part, "I think you are well on your way to reinventing delegates," and providing some code samples.

Delegates still don't fit in my brain very well, while the perform-by-name idea is familiar to me, so this came as no surprise. I took the occasion last night to spend a half-hour playing with Kevin's idea, and it's certainly better. That's what this chapter is about.

What's a Delegate?

That's hard to answer, but I'll try. A delegate in Microsoft .NET is a data type, like a class or string or number. It is the .NET managed equivalent of a C function pointer, or a C++ method pointer, or a procedure of object type in Delphi. Let's look at it from that angle for a moment. In C or C++, if f is a pointer to a function, you can say (*f)("hello", 2); and call that function, passing it the arguments "hello" and 2. Very powerful. In ANSI C and C++, these function pointers are checked by the compiler for correctness. In earlier compilers, they were not and you could type most anything in and have it blow up in really interesting ways.

In .NET, a delegate holds on to a specific method, in a specific object instance. Recall that every method can explicitly or implicitly use "this" to refer to the instance, so a method can't just hang around without being hooked to a specific instance. A delegate might be declared like this:

```
public delegate int Combine(int first, int second);
```

That just means that there's a kind of delegate (think class) named Combine that holds on to methods that take two integer parameters and return an integer result. An instance of Combine could hold on to any such method. We might have something like this (untested):

```
class Pair {
  private int left;
  private int right;

  private int Total(int a, int b) {
    return a + b;
  }

  private int Prod(int a, int b) {
    return a*b;
  }

  private delegate int Combine(int first, int second);

  private Combine action;

  public void MultiplyFromNowOn() {
    action = this.Prod;
  }

  public void AddFromNowOn() {
    action = this.Total;
  }

  public int WhatsTheAnswer() {
    return action(left, right);
  }
}
```

With an instance of this class in hand, if we send it MultiplyFromNowOn, then whenever we ask it WhatsTheAnswer, it will reply with the product of left and right. But if we send it AddFromNowOn, it will return the sum until further notice.

Probably you can see that this is quite analogous to the code in the previous chapter, where we would have used the string "MultiplyFromNowOn" instead of the actual method name. An important difference is that if there happens to be a typo in the string—and as it turns out there is—my approach will discover the error only at run time. If we use delegates, the name of the method is checked at compile time. With my approach, if we used the right name but the wrong kind of function, that too would be discovered only at run time. Delegates check the method prototype, not just its name.

Kevin was right: delegates are a lot better.

Converting XMLNotepad to Use Delegates

Kevin's example actually showed how to duplicate my whole Perform thing using delegates, but a simpler and equally effective approach exists. (As we'll see, "equally effective" is used advisedly.) The XMLNotepad code looked like this:

```
void MenuInsertSection(object obj, EventArgs ea) {
  model.SetLines(textbox.Lines);
  model.SelectionStart = textbox.SelectionStart;
  model.Perform("InsertSectionTags");
  PutText(textbox, model.LinesArray(), model.SelectionStart);
}
```

Going to a delegate approach, we add a delegate definition and use it this way:

```
private delegate void MenuAction();
void MenuInsertSection(object obj, EventArgs ea) {
  model.SetLines(textbox.Lines);
  model.SelectionStart = textbox.SelectionStart;
  MenuAction action = new MenuAction(model.InsertSectionTags);
  action();
  PutText(textbox, model.LinesArray(), model.SelectionStart);
}
```

Now, of course, in this mode, the whole thing makes no sense. We could imagine some future day when there was a general MenuHandler method where all the menu clicks came in and we selected which function to delegate with some if or switch statements. So the ifs would choose which method to delegate to, and then action() would call it. The thing is, this is still not a very good idea. Instead of writing code that says

```
if(something) action = model.InsertSomething;
else if(other) action = model.InsertOther;
action();
```

why not just write this?

```
if(something) action = model.InsertSomething();
else if(other) action = model.InsertOther();
```

This should make it clear that the Perform I originally wrote, and the delegate approach just used, is a waste of time from a product viewpoint. So I'm going to take it out, right now. The new code (old code) looks like this:

```
void MenuInsertSection(object obj, EventArgs ea) {
    model.SetLines(textbox.Lines);
    model.SelectionStart = textbox.SelectionStart;
    model.InsertSectionTags();
    PutText(textbox, model.LinesArray(), model.SelectionStart);
}
```

Tests run, GUI runs, all's right with the world.

Lesson: My Point, and I Do Have One

I've spent at least one precious programming day messing with Perform, reflection, and delegates. Now I've learned a lot about those things. I predict that in the entire rest of this book, I'll never once have a use for the Perform approach. I suspect that you might see some use of delegates, but it's likely it won't show up for a while. I do feel better knowing those things, and that will make me a little more comfortable writing programs and a little more confident that I can clean up any messes I might make.

But remember: all this was done on speculation. I was concerned that I was going to get duplication when I added more features, and I was concerned that I wouldn't be able to get rid of it. What I wasn't concerned about was adding more features. One precious programming day has gone by. We have a better programmer at the end of it, and that's a good thing, but we don't have a better program and we don't have a happier customer.

Those, I believe, are both bad things. The lesson should be: we should learn as much as we can, all the time. And we should be careful to keep our learning focused on safely delivering the customer the features he needs.

(My technical editors also note that while delegates can be very useful for communicating between separately developed modules, it is almost always clearer to have your objects communicating by direct method calls rather than by delegates, where that's possible. We have learned that here for ourselves.)

Later today, I'm planning to meet with Chet and do some pairing. I'm sure he'll put his customer hat on and be disappointed at my progress. I hope he's nice enough to say that he's glad I'm learning, or I'll feel really bad. And it will be his fault.[1]

---

1. Remember, it's always Chet's fault.

16

Adding the <pre> Tag

Just to get back in the swing of things, we're going to add a new tag, extending the menu a bit in the process. In the course of that, we'll see what kind of duplication we really get, compared to the kind I've been worrying about. **Better yet, we learn something surprising!**

New Stories

We've got a few new stories to work on:

- Add the <pre> tag that we use to display code. Like the <P> tag, cause it to insert itself after the end of the current tag.

- Add all the tags to the menu. Make it an Insert menu with the various tags under it.

- Modify the <section> tag so that it adds only at the end of a preceding section, rather than in the middle like it does now.

This is a good set of stories that will make the product pretty useful. The customer's objective is to get the tool strong enough to use in place of TextPad. These stories might be nearly enough to do the job.

The <pre> Tag

The <pre> tag is pretty simple; just insert it like a <P> tag. Here's the first test:

```
[Test] public void InsertPre() {
  model.SetLines (new String[1] {"<P></P>"});
  model.SelectionStart = 7;
```

```
model.InsertPreTag();
AssertEquals("<pre></pre>", model.Lines[1]);
AssertEquals(14, model.SelectionStart);
}
```

It doesn't compile, of course, so I code it up, copying from the InsertParagraphTag method:

```
public void InsertPreTag() {
  InsertTags(newPre, preSkip);
}
```

And using the requisite new definitions:

```
private static string[] newPre = { "<pre></pre>" };
private static string paragraphSkip = "<pre>";
```

Oops, not as smart as I thought. Can you tell I was using cut and paste? That last line should read

```
private static string preSkip = "<pre>";
```

That works just fine, and I realize that the normal insert of a tag is already after the previous line, so there's no need to do anything special about searching to the end. I decide to rename the test to InsertPre and let it go at that. Time to write a new Customer Acceptance Test. It looks like this:

```
*input
<P>This is the first p|aragraph.</P>
<P>This is the second paragraph.</P>
*end
*AltP
*output
<P>This is the first paragraph.</P>
<pre>|</pre>
<P>This is the second paragraph.</P>
```

That test won't run, of course, since AltP isn't defined anywhere. This reminds me of that confusion we still have between the menu or keyboard command and the real command. Also, while I was scavenging tests to copy, I didn't find a customer test for inserting a section. I think Chet and I are going to have to work on beefing up the customer tests today, both so that they test more end to end and to add the missing ones. First, though, let's make this one work. We have to add a line to the InterpretCommands method of CustomerTest:

```
private void InterpretCommands(String commands, String message) {
  StringReader reader = new StringReader(commands);
  String line = reader.ReadLine();
  CreateModel();
```

```
while ( line != null) {
  if ( line == "*enter")
    model.Enter();
  if ( line == "*altS")
    model.AltS();
  if ( line == "*altP")
    model.AltP();
  if (line == "*display")
    Console.WriteLine("display\r\n{0}\r\nend", model.TestText);
  if (line == "*output")
    CompareOutput(reader, message);
  if (line == "*input")
    SetInput(reader);
  line = reader.ReadLine();
}
```

Now this confuses me! Notice that an altS command is defined—that means the tests must know how to do InsertSection. Maybe I just didn't see the test.

Lesson   When I'm confused, especially when I have no pair to sort me out, I find it's usually best to get unconfused ASAP. So I'm going to comment out the implementation of AltS in the TextModel. If there's a test for it, that test should break, and I'll find out what its name is. While I'm at it—this is risky, doing two things at once, but since I've written it down here I probably won't forget—I'll implement the AltP method. Here's both:

```
      public void AltS() {
//        InsertSectionTags();
      }
      public void AltP() {
        InsertPreTag();
      }
```

OK, good news. There is a section test, named sect1.test. Somehow I just didn't see it. I'll fix that commented line and see what happens.

Well, the test for pre failed, as did a couple of Programmer Unit Tests. I'm not surprised by the programmer tests, but it appears that the pre test didn't insert anything at all. Do you see why? I accidentally capitalized AltP in the test, and the code checks for lowercase. If that happens many more times, I think we might have to beef up our testing, but for now, I'll just fix the test.

Now you remember—and fortunately I remember as well—that Alt+P shouldn't really work because I haven't put the AltP stuff in the GUI. That has to be done using a menu now, but no test exists to check whether it's there, so I'll fix the Form while I'm thinking of it. I know we need that test but I want help to do it, and I can certainly make this work...I think. Here's the new menu code and handlers:

```
MenuItem insertSection = new MenuItem (
  "Insert &Section",
  new EventHandler(MenuInsertSection));
MenuItem insertPre = new MenuItem (
  "Insert &Pre",
  new EventHandler(MenuInsertPre));
this.Menu = new MainMenu(new MenuItem[] {insertPre, insertSection} );
...

void MenuInsertSection(object obj, EventArgs ea) {
  model.SetLines(textbox.Lines);
  model.SelectionStart = textbox.SelectionStart;
  model.InsertSectionTags();
  PutText(textbox, model.LinesArray(), model.SelectionStart);
}

void MenuInsertPre(object obj, EventArgs ea) {
  model.SetLines(textbox.Lines);
  model.SelectionStart = textbox.SelectionStart;         model.InsertPreTag();
  PutText(textbox, model.LinesArray(), model.SelectionStart);
}
```

I gave you both those handlers so that you can see the duplication I was concerned about. I *knew* this was going to happen. But we'll deal with that later. The tool works; here's an image:

Oops, Here's a New Story Coming Out!

I was typing into the XML Notepad the code you just saw in the last section. As soon as I started typing the code into the pre tag, I encountered a problem: code is almost invariably multiple lines long. But if I try to type an Enter (or a Shift+Enter) into the window, I immediately get a new P tag. There's no way to type code in!

Now, this isn't the end of the world. To begin with, most of the code we type in is pasted from a source file anyway. Stories about that are coming up as well, relating to converting less-than (<) signs and ampersands that XML doesn't understand. But in this very chapter, I typed a free return into a pre tag and I typed free code (rather than pasting) into another this morning. Something will have to be done about this, and the customer will have to decide.

Important Lesson

We have a very important lesson here, and it isn't one that I planned, although of course it was bound to happen.

> **Lesson**   The most important value of shipping features to the customer results when the customer learns something. Therefore, ship early and ship often!

That's enough of a lesson to end this chapter. And anyway, I'm hungry...

17

How Do We Do a Test That We Can't Do?

*We encountered a real bug in the system that wasn't caught by our tests. The feature worked, but the GUI wasn't hooked to it. **We don't know how to test that, but our rules of operation say that we must.** What can we do?*

We Need Better Customer Acceptance Tests

You've now witnessed a couple of GUI-related defects. First there was that scrolling problem, and then when I implemented a feature I forgot to hook it up in the GUI, even though the tests said it was working. It worked for everyone except the users! Lately, I've found myself running the GUI quite often, to be sure that it works, and that's bad.

> **Lesson**   Why is that bad, you ask? It breaks the rhythm. The rhythm one tries to set up is write a test and make it work, running the NUnit tests after every small change. The cycle is just a couple of minutes, and except for typing in code, it's all pretty automatic. When the tests run, we're confident that the software is just a little better. Click, click, click, it ratchets forward. If we have to run the GUI before we have that confidence, it slows us down. Running the GUI means we have to start it up, go to the window, type some kind of test stuff, look at it, and then shut the GUI back down. Wasteful, distracting, bad.

Of course, we would like to have a test, if it's easy to write. But we don't know how to write this test. This chapter explores how to think about writing the test, how to write the test, and how to make the learning for this test help us in the future.

It's tempting—oh so tempting—to skip a test when it seems too hard. Much of the time, we'll get away with it. Once we make the software work, even if it's a bug fix, it's not likely that we'll break it again. If we have to check it manually once in a while, well, we'll probably remember, probably have time, and probably see any problems that creep in. Probably. However, because the software is growing and the design is evolving, every missing test is a hole through which bugs can creep, not just the first time, but for the full duration of the project. The more holes we fill, the better the software will be.

At the time I'm writing this, Chet and I have already tried to test the code we're discussing here, and we weren't successful. I'm tempted to give up, and if you knew what we do, I think you'd forgive me. Fix the problem, move on, be more careful in the future. We've all said it, we've all done it, and we've gotten away with it too.

But this is a book. It's about learning and about sticking to principles, pragmatic principles, by all means, but principles nonetheless. So I'm going to push on this issue just a little harder, and we'll see what happens. I think we'll find that it isn't as hard as we fear to write this test and that we'll see the value of it before the end of the book.

Reviewing the Problem

We have customer tests that let us write scripts and let us run the scripts to see if we get correct output. These tests run against the TextModel object. The theory is that the GUI is so simple that these tests are convincing.

Unfortunately, as a customer, I'm no longer convinced that the product is solid. Even though my tests ran, there have been at least two very different defects that showed up only in the GUI. Again, one time the scrolling didn't work, and another time the test ran but the GUI didn't even have the feature built into it. What's up with that? As a customer, I'm losing confidence. That makes me want to call for massive overtime, or reduced pizza rations, or something equally draconian. The programmers ought to be really interested in this issue.

Let's narrow the problem down a bit. Big problems beget big solutions. That way leads either to big "infrastructure" efforts or to manual testing. I forget which one of those is Charybdis, but either way it's bad.

Here's our problem in a nutshell: when the customer writes a test that sends AltS to the XML Notepad, we want to be sure that Alt+S is in the GUI and that it actually does what is intended—in this case, InsertSectionTags.

I'll tell the tale of trying to drive the GUI automatically in a moment, but we couldn't really make it work well. Let's set aside whether we're *driving* the GUI and remember that we want to *test* the GUI to be sure that if the test script runs, the GUI will run as well.

Let's begin with a look at a couple of tests:

```
*altS
*output
<sect1><title>|</title>
</sect1>
---------------------------------
*input
<P>This is the first p|aragraph.</P>
<P>This is the second paragraph.</P>
*end
*enter
*output
<P>This is the first paragraph.</P>
<P>|</P>
<P>This is the second paragraph.</P>
```

Recall that the lines with * are commands and the rest are data. The data lines show a vertical bar character (|) where the cursor is to be set. So the first test says "User types Alt+S. The text window should then look like this." The rest of the stuff is the desired contents of the window. Similarly, the second test says "Start with these two paragraphs, cursor in the first one. User types Enter. Now there are three paragraphs, a new one in the middle, with the cursor in it." The code to execute *enter or *altS looks like this:

```
private void InterpretCommands(String commands, String message) {
  StringReader reader = new StringReader(commands);
  String line = reader.ReadLine();
  CreateModel();
  while ( line != null) {
    if ( line == "*enter")
      model.Enter();
    if ( line == "*altS")
      model.AltS();;
    if ( line == "*altP")
      model.AltP();
    if (line == "*display")
      Console.WriteLine("display\r\n{0}\r\nend", model.TestText);
    if (line == "*output")
```

```
      CompareOutput(reader, message);
    if (line == "*input")
      SetInput(reader);
    line = reader.ReadLine();
  }
}
```

So when the *enter comes along, we just send the message Enter() to the model. That code looks like this:

```
public void Enter() {
  InsertParagraphTag();
}
public void InsertParagraphTag() {
  InsertTags(newParagraph, paragraphSkip);
}


private static string[] newParagraph = { "<P></P>" };
private static string paragraphSkip = "<P>";
```

Note that the model is making the translation here from "enter" to Insert-ParagraphTag. In the GUI, we have this code:

```
public void XMLKeyDownHandler(object objSender, KeyEventArgs kea) {
  Console.WriteLine("Down" + kea.KeyCode);
  model.SetLines(textbox.Lines);
  model.SelectionStart = textbox.SelectionStart;
  if (kea.KeyCode == Keys.Enter) {
    model.Enter();
    kea.Handled = true;
  }
  PutText(textbox, model.LinesArray(), model.SelectionStart);
}
```

The potential bug is that the code for the KeyDown might not support Keys.Enter. If we changed that to Keys.Tab, the tests would still run, but the GUI would not. This isn't as good as we'd like. And it gets worse. Let's look at the Alt+S situation. Alt+S is implemented in the model similarly to Enter. AltS() calls InsertSectionTags(). But in the GUI, oh my! Look at this:

```
  MenuItem insertSection = new MenuItem (
    "Insert &Section",
    new EventHandler(MenuInsertSection));
void MenuInsertSection(object obj, EventArgs ea) {
  model.SetLines(textbox.Lines);
  model.SelectionStart = textbox.SelectionStart;
  model.InsertSectionTags();
  PutText(textbox, model.LinesArray(), model.SelectionStart);
}
```

The menu isn't going through AltS() in the model; it's calling InsertSection-Tags() directly. Now, I think that's a better design, because the mapping from keystroke to menu to model call is more a function of the Form than of the GUI. But it means the test is completely broken. If we changed the AltS() method in the model, we could break the test without breaking the GUI. We could also find a way to break the GUI without breaking the test: one way is just not to implement that menu item at all. What can we do to make it better? Well, Chet and I worked on that.

First Improvements

Our original plan was to create a GUI instance, run it, and pump fake typed characters at it. We tried a number of different ways to do that, and none of them worked. So we decided to do something that moves in that direction but not quite so far. We created an instance of the Form and held on to both the Form and the model in our test. Then we simulated a KeyDown event in the Form, when the test asked for *enter. The code looks like this:

```
if ( line == "*enter")
  form.XMLKeyDownHandler((object) this, new KeyEventArgs(Keys.Enter));
```

That's nearly good! The actual key handler is running and sending model.Enter(). That's as good as it could get for that case, so we went ahead and sent an Alt+S through, to test the EnterSectionTags():

```
if ( line == "*altS")
  form.XMLKeyDownHandler((object) this, new KeyEventArgs(Keys.Alt | Keys.S));
```

How clever and simple. Unfortunately, it doesn't work. Sending the key through that way doesn't drive the menus, which are supporting the accelerators like Alt+S. Gack. Maybe we should give up. We'll just be careful to build all the menus correctly, OK?

Never Give Up...That Ship

I'm not willing to give up, and here's why. First, the enter thing worked pretty well. That gives me at least a small boost of confidence that we could make this happen. Second, this is, at least in part, a book about how we *ought* to go about things, and by the time we're done here, I want it to be clear, one way or the other, whether this test was worth writing. And third, I have a little feeling that if we can crack this one, it will open other doors and make other tests easier.

And I have a fantasy. Suppose that instead of *altS, we had the test say something like, oh, *menu &S. Suppose that the Form would provide to the test a collection of all its menu items. Suppose we searched through the menu items looking for one that had &S in its text. Suppose we issued an error if it wasn't there, and suppose we clicked it somehow if it was. Then the click would run, send the InsertSectionTags() message or whatever, and when we checked the output, it would be right. If I can make that fantasy come true in an hour's work, I think it'll be worth doing. Let's try it, in that simple XP style.

Test the Connection

First, I want to find out whether this idea will work. I'll write a test that will get a MenuItem from the Form, click it, and see what happens. Let's look for a place to put that test. The CustomerTest class has the right setup now, since it already has the Form and model hooked together. I'll just add a new direct test to that class for now, expecting to remove it later, when all the wiring is hooked up:

```
[Test] public void DirectMenu() {
  form.InsertPreMenu().PerformClick();
  AssertEquals("<pre>|</pre>\r\n", model.TestText);
}
```

Something like that should do the trick. I just assumed a new method on the XML Notepad: InsertPreMenu(), which will return the menu. Let's build that. In the initialize, we have this:

```
MenuItem insertPre = new MenuItem (
  "Insert &Pre",
  new EventHandler(MenuInsertPre));
```

I'll promote the insertPre variable to a member and write the accessor. (I could make it a public member and access it directly, but I usually don't. And I'm thinking that although my test would run a bit sooner, that structure is closer to where I'm going. A judgment call—I almost went the other way.)

```
private MenuItem insertPre;
public MenuItem InsertPreMenu() {
  return insertPre;
}
```

OK, that all compiles. Now to test...whoa! The DirectEnter worked—that's cool—but the TestAllFiles broke. It must have been at red bar before I started this. Now what?

> **Lesson**   This is an important topic. Whenever we leave the code—and there's an overnight between the previous section and this one—we should leave the tests at green bar in most cases. There can be a case made for leaving one test written but not coded, as a reminder of what to do next, but I think it's best to have the system working at all times rather than broken. So it's good that this happened, because it lets me make the point. I am truly confused at this moment. I recognize the error message, something about "TestAllFiles: '-1' is not a valid value for 'value'." That's cryptic. The stack trace says it's in PutText, SetSelectionStart, so there must be a -1 in there somehow.

It's irritating that TestAllFiles doesn't say which test failed. As a quick fix, I'll have it just print the file name to the Console. The last one printed will be the problem. It's sect1.test, the test for the InsertSectionTags capability...that sends Alt+S...oh, right! I was trying to send the Alt+S keystroke to the Form, and it didn't work. That's how we got here. I'll change that line back to doing AltS(), and we should be back on track. Right, OK.

> **Lesson**   Now that could have turned into trouble. Even now I'm kind of thrown off the track, and if it had been hard to find the bug I would have lost momentum. OK, important safety tip: [sb]keep the tests green. (Thanks, Egon.)

Back to the main plan. The test of PerformClick() on the returned menu item worked. So if the test gets the right menu item, it can send PerformClick() and go on with the testing. Therefore, the code that now says

```
if ( line == "*altS")
  model.AltS();
```

can be changed to do our new *menu idea or something similar. I'm tempted to take a big bite here, but it's early in the morning and I'm going to go very slowly.

```
if ( line == "*altS")
  ExecuteMenu("&S");
```

I'm imagining a new method, ExecuteMenu(), that will look up a menu item based on its accelerator, which I'll be pulling off the *menu line shortly. I code that as follows:

```
private void ExecuteMenu(string accelerator) {
    form.MenuForAccelerator(accelerator).PerformClick();
}
```

Here I'm assuming that the Form will look up the menu item based on its accelerator and hand it back. I'll just implement that method by using the Insert-PreMenu() that I already wrote. I'll change its name, let the other test fail, and then change it to use ExecuteMenu also.

```
public MenuItem MenuForAccelerator(string accelerator) {
    return insertPre;
}


[Test] public void DirectMenu() {
    form.MenuForAccelerator("&S").PerformClick();
    AssertEquals("<pre>|</pre>\r\n", model.TestText);
}
```

I expect this to compile and go green...and it all does, except that the sect1 test fails again. This time the message is new: the output is <pre>|</pre>. That's what I get for carrying on a business conversation, writing this chapter, and programming all at the same time. MenuForAccelerator returns only that one menu item, so I'm getting the wrong one for Alt+S. And in the DirectMenu, that string should have been &P, not S. Why didn't my pair catch that? I'll fix that, and I'll do a quick hack to MenuForAccelerator. Then we'll discuss it. Here's the code:

```
private MenuItem insertPre;
private MenuItem insertSection;
public MenuItem MenuForAccelerator(string accelerator) {
    if (accelerator == "&S") return insertSection;
    return insertPre;
}
```

Yes! Tests all green. One more change because I'm hot. I'm going to let the customer tests do altP just like altS. Then we'll talk about that hack just above:

```
if ( line == "*altS")
    ExecuteMenu("&S");
if ( line == "*altP")
    ExecuteMenu("&P");
```

OK, tests all green. Now what's up with that obviously dumb implementation of MenuForAccelerator? That is clearly not going to last. Here's my thinking:

> **Lesson**   When I've got a test on red bar, I want to get to green as quickly as possible. I think of how you and I might build a bridge across a small stream. First thing we might do would be put a line of boards across the stream to stand on. Then, using those boards as a scaffold, we'd build up the bridge bit by bit. I'm not sure how well that would work on large-scale bridges, but in software it works just fine.

Look at the structure of the program for a moment. The CustomerTest command interpreter is actually making an appropriate call to the Form, getting the right menu, clicking it, and checking the results. It's not doing it very generally compared to the *menu idea, but it is basically doing the right thing—just not in the best possible way. And in the Form, the code is looking up the correct MenuItem and returning it. Again, not a general solution, but it is actually doing it. That's the most important aspect of things: we have the program in the right "shape," doing the right things. Now we have a few things to make better. That will be a bit time-consuming but not risky; all the hard parts are now laid in. Best of all, our tests are now better, and they are all green.

> **Lesson**   There's an old saying in programming: [sb]"Make it work, make it right, make it fast." Get the code into the right overall shape quickly: make it work. Then, as the need for a more general solution shows up, improve and refactor the code: make it right. Finally, if and only if a performance measurement shows that you need to, make it fast.

We need to change the Form to save the menu items in a list of some kind, maybe a hashtable, and return them based on their accelerator. We need to deal with the likelihood that the one we're looking for won't be found. Maybe we'll return a null and check for it. And we need to change the Customer Acceptance Test scripting language to have the *menu command, so that we don't have to add code to the CustomerTest class every time the customers ask for a new menu item.

I'll work on those in the next chapter, which should be pretty short unless something else exciting happens. I'll display some big chunks of code at that time so that you can get the big picture if you want it.

Lesson: Let's Sum Up

First and most important, I think, is that a small effort has resulted in a large improvement in the quality of our Customer Acceptance Tests. They are actually going through the keystroke and menu logic of the Form now, such that more of the code is checked. Our customer should feel more confident now after running the tests.

I was ready to give up on this. On a real project, I think I might have. I pushed forward only because this is a book and I feel that I have to let you see how things turn out when we do things right, not just when, as I so often do, I do things wrong. The lesson I learned is that I am too willing to skip testing something if it looks difficult. And frankly, I'm a fanatic about testing, especially customer tests, compared to a lot of folks I know. My fear about how hard it would be was high. The actual effort was quite low, and we now have tests that work better, and a new and simple testing technique for our bag of tricks.

Second, there was that wake-up call when the test didn't run. I had gotten a little careless and walked away from the machine on a red bar, and it took a few minutes to get back up to speed. If I had run the tests before changing anything, it might have been better. I wouldn't have gotten my thoughts all wrapped around getting the menu and then had to reset. But the best thing, I think, is to always stop on a green bar. Lesson learned, again. We'll see how many more times I have to learn it.

Third, we solved this problem in short, almost stupid steps. Now, I'm still pretty new to C#, and I was uncertain about getting the menu item and clicking it, but frankly I go in steps almost that small all the time. It works well for me. When I go in bigger steps, my stress level goes up and sometimes I have a lot of debugging to do before I get things working.

Some people get concerned that going in these small steps means that a lot of rework happens. Well, formally speaking, maybe it is rework, but most of what we're doing is adding, not replacing. The total typing isn't much larger than if we did the whole job, and the advantage is that we never have to fit the whole job into our tiny little heads. To me, that's a powerful advantage.

Three lessons this time. ^{sb}Push a little when something seems to hard; keep the tests on green; ^{sb}build simple scaffolding and then improve it. Enough for this time; see you in the next chapter.

Wait! Wait, Wait, Wait![1]

Before us we have two basic tasks: we want to generalize the MenuForAccelerator a bit, and we want to put the *menu feature into the CustomerTest class. I was just about to start the chapter about doing that, because I know just how to do it and I'm on a roll, but that would be wrong. Why? Because right now, the code is the simplest code that could possibly work, and it does work. I have no feature-driven need to generalize it.

(I'm sure) I'm going to ask for features that will break this code. So why shouldn't we do this? We shouldn't do this because it's more important to focus on delivering real customer value. The existing code is solid, tested, and clear. It's just not super-general. If it needs to get general, we can do that just as well later as we can now. We should turn our attention back to pleasing our customer. That's what keeps the paychecks rolling in.

I know we always like to say it'll be easier to do it now than it will be to do it later. Not likely: I plan to be smarter later than I am now, I plan to have the same tests, and I plan to have an actual need that will direct what I do, not my current fantasy about what's needed. I think it'll be just as easy later, maybe even easier. Why pay now when we can pay later? There's no interest charge running.

My advice, and I'm going to follow it, is to leave well enough alone. We'll probably see this code again, and when we do, we'll improve it. If somehow we don't see it again, well then it certainly doesn't need improving now.

Keep an eye out. See if when we come back to this code, it takes us somehow longer to improve than it would right now. I'm betting that we'll be just fine.

---

1. Ann Anderson, personal communication.

18

A Simple Feature Teaches Some Lessons

Our customer discovered the need to insert a return inside a <pre> tag.
Implementing this turns out to be fairly simple, but we learn some lessons
about how to test and build even a simple feature.

Shift Return Inside <pre> Tags

When we built the <pre> tag, the customer discovered there was no way to type in multiple lines of code, which is kind of the point of the tag, so they've asked us for a way to do that. We suggested, and they agreed, or maybe it was the other way around, that the standard way in Microsoft Windows to enter a return without any special action is to type Shift+Enter. That's what we'll do. The basic plan will be to write a programmer test, make it work, and then write a customer test and show that it works.

You may be wondering why we would do both, especially since today I'm all the programmers, and all the customers, rolled into one. To me, the customer test is of paramount importance, because I'm always concerned about keeping my customers happy. So I can't skip that one. In this case, the customer test will probably serve as a decent test for programming as well, but in general that's not so. I would usually recommend that the programmers write their own finer-grain tests as a matter of practice, and that's what I'll do.

Now, as well, I've noticed that the customer tests don't provide much good information when they fail. We might want to address that later on, but for now, it's another reason why we should start with a programmer test.

First, however, we'll load up Microsoft Visual Studio, and we'll run all the tests to make sure that everything is in good order. It's been a while since any work was done on this project, and it's best to be careful. It only takes a moment...right. Everything works fine. Let's change that.

Shift+Enter Test

We've already got a test for the <pre> tag:

```
[Test] public void InsertPre() {
  model.SetLines (new String[1] {"<P></P>"});
  model.SelectionStart = 7;
  model.InsertPreTag();
  AssertEquals("<pre></pre>", model.Lines[1]);
  AssertEquals(14, model.SelectionStart);
}
```

My first inclination is just to enhance this test by doing the shift enter action. This raises a question for the customer: should Shift+Enter work all the time or just inside the <pre> tags? The answer is that it's harmless elsewhere but might be nice for making the textbox more readable, so we'll let it work anywhere. With that definition, I might have to write more tests to be sure that it works, but I don't think so. Here's our enhanced test including Shift+Enter:

```
[Test] public void InsertPre() {
  model.SetLines (new String[1] {"<P></P>"});
  model.SelectionStart = 7;
  model.InsertPreTag();
  AssertEquals("<pre></pre>", model.Lines[1]);
  AssertEquals(14, model.SelectionStart);
  model.InsertReturn();
  AssertEquals("<pre>", model.Lines[1]);
  AssertEquals("", model.Lines[2]);
  AssertEquals("</pre>", model.Lines[3]);
  AssertEquals(16, model.SelectionStart);
}
```

I'm assuming here that the *model* action will be called InsertReturn and that the GUI action will be the typing of the Shift+Enter character. The naming is a bit awkward here because the user types the Enter key, but I'm thinking about inserting a carriage return character into the lines. Also notice that we've not been entirely orderly about which way we name commands: some of the model methods have had names that sound like keystrokes. We'll take a look and see if any of that needs cleaning up; it's certainly best if the model thinks in terms of what it does, not how what it does is invoked. For this case, this way seems best to me.

We build, to get the message that InsertReturn isn't implemented on Text-Model. We knew that, of course. You might prefer to fix it first; I prefer to let the computer guide me.

> **Lesson**   There may actually be a lesson here. Recall that Watts Humphrey recommends serious desk-checking before compiling or fixing a test, and although we wanted to try his recommendation, Chet and I haven't been able to bring ourselves to do it. The issue might be that we are really combining our thoughts with the "thoughts" of the computer in a substantially different way from what Watts suggests. I believe that by letting the computer deal with some of the more trivial matters, we may be freeing up our thoughts for bigger issues.
>
> Of course, it's possible that I'm kidding myself, but I'm sure that things go more smoothly for me than ever before when I use this simple test/code/refactor cycle. It's working for me!

False Start Number One

To implement InsertReturn, we review other insert methods in TextModel. Here's one and its helper methods and data:

```
private static string[] newSection = {"<sect1><title></title>","</sect1>" };
private static string sectionSkip = "<sect1><title>";

public void InsertSectionTags() {
  InsertTags(newSection, sectionSkip);
}
private void InsertTags(string[] tagsToInsert, string tagsPrecedingCursor) {
  int cursorLine = LineContainingCursor();
  lines.InsertRange(cursorLine+1, tagsToInsert);
  selectionStart = NewSelectionStart(cursorLine + 1, tagsPrecedingCursor);
}
```

This seems custom-made for our purposes, except of course that in our case we aren't going to insert much of anything. Still, it ought to work, and if it doesn't, we should make it work, to avoid duplicating any logic.

The InsertTags method is simple enough: it inserts a new line containing the "tagsToInsert" input array and then sets the selection based on skipping the tagsPrecedingCursor string. It seems like we should be able to do what we want with a couple of empty strings. Let's try it. Here's my attempted code:

```
private static string[] emptyLine = { "" };
private static string emptyLineSkip = "";

public void InsertReturn() {
  InsertTags(emptyLine, emptyLineSkip);
}
```

Oops! That doesn't work. The test fails, with this message: "expected '<pre>' but was '<pre></pre>'". Silly me. It isn't enough to insert a new line after the current line: the Shift+Enter has to insert a new line right in the middle of the current line, wherever the cursor is. So this is actually going to amount to *replacing* a line in our terms, from

```
1: <pre></pre>
```

to this:

```
1: <pre>
2:
3: </pre>
```

Our InsertTags feature may come in there, but there's going to be more to it than that. I'm going to program this one by intention, because it feels a little tricky to me and I'm working without a pair.

False Start Number Two

I coded the following, which isn't exactly by intention. In fact, it isn't much of anything:

```
public void InsertReturn() {
  int cursorLine = LineContainingCursor();
  string cursorString = (string) lines[cursorLine];
  int lineCursorPosition = LineCursorPosition();
  string front = cursorString.Substring(0, lineCursorPosition);
  string back = cursorString.Substring(lineCursorPosition+1);
  lines[cursorLine] = front;
  string[] linesToInsert = { "", back };
  InsertTags(linesToInsert, "");
}
```

Frankly, this is pretty awful code. Worse yet, it's based on an incorrect plan, and even if it worked, and even if it was clear, it would still be wrong. We don't want to add a blank line, as shown in that 1, 2, 3 thing in the last section. We just want to insert a return, but no blank line, to get this:

```
1: <pre>
2: </pre>
```

> **Lesson**   What happened here? Two attempts and they both fail. The only good thing we can say is that because I'm working in such small steps, there's not much harm done before I discover I'm all wet. The lesson: if you're prone to failure, be sure to fail early and often. Another lesson might be that when you set out to program by intention, don't write ugly procedural code instead!

If I had had a pair, maybe the bad plan would have been recognized, or maybe my pair would have seen how awful that code is and stopped me. Neither happened, but I did get lucky. I got a phone call, interrupting my train of thought, and then I decided to change locations from one restaurant to another. That let me think a little more clearly about what has to happen.

New Plan

When we get the Shift+Enter signal, what we have to do is to *split* the line containing the cursor. Everything to the left of the cursor stays on that line; everything after the cursor goes to the next line. This is a much simpler problem. To make this happen, I can envision code much like that earlier, that will split off the front and back of the line, replace the cursor line with the front, and insert just the back. The earlier code, though not clear, might work. However, I'm going to throw that last code away and write it again, this time *really* programming by expressing my intention. To help with that, I'll figure out in words what I want to do:

1.   Get the front part of the line containing the cursor.

2.   Get the back part of the line containing the cursor.

3.   Replace the line containing the cursor with the front part.

4.   Insert the back part as the next line.

5.   Move the cursor to the "right" by the size of a newline.

OK, what does that code look like?

```
public void InsertReturn() {
  string front = FrontOfCursorLine();
  string back = BackOfCursorLine();
  lines[LineContainingCursor()] = front;
  lines.Insert(LineContainingCursor()+1, back);
  selectionStart += Environment.NewLine.Length;
}
```

This time I did program my intention. Can you see that this code makes sense and follows the narrative plan I just described? We get the two line parts, replace the current line with the front, insert the back after it, and update the selection start. Looks good to me. Of course we haven't implemented the FrontOfCursorLine and BackOfCursorLine methods. I'll code one of those by intention as well:

```
private string FrontOfCursorLine() {
  string line = lines[LineContainingCursor()];
  int position = PositionOfCursorInLine();
  return line.Substring(0, position);
}
```

Are you beginning to get the picture here? We get the line, we get the position of the cursor in the line, and we split off the front of the string. One part is left unsolved: PositionOfCursorInLine(). Our variable SelectionStart is the position of the cursor in *all* the lines, counting the newlines. So if we subtract that number from selectionStart, what's left will be the position in our line. It turns out that we have a method to return that number: SumLineLengths(), which looks like this:

```
private int SumLineLengths(int cursorLine) {
  int length = 0;
  for (int i = 0; i < cursorLine; i++)
    length += ((String)lines[i]).Length + Environment.NewLine.Length;
  return length;
}
```

We'll just implement PositionOfCursorInLine() by using that method, like this:

```
private int PositionOfCursorInLine() {
  return selectionStart - SumLineLengths(LineContainingCursor() -1);
}
```

And then we'll build BackOfCursorLine similarly to FrontOfCursorLine:

```
private string BackOfCursorLine() {
  string line = lines[LineContainingCursor()];
  int position = PositionOfCursorInLine();
  return line.Substring(position+1);
}
```

Now frankly, this is pretty scary. I've built four methods in a row without a green bar. But I expect this to work, or at least to be close. Time to build and test. If this doesn't work pretty quickly, I'm going to back the code out and proceed in smaller steps, but I might get away with it this time.

Well, the code doesn't compile because I forgot to cast the lines to string. Templates in C# can't come along fast enough for me. So the methods become

```
private string FrontOfCursorLine() {
  string line = (string) lines[LineContainingCursor()];
  int position = PositionOfCursorInLine();
  return line.Substring(0, position);
}
private string BackOfCursorLine() {
  string line = (string) lines[LineContainingCursor()];
  int position = PositionOfCursorInLine();
  return line.Substring(position+1);
}
```

And we try again...build succeeds, but the test fails. The message is telling me that in InsertPre, in FrontOfCursorLine, calling Substring, the length has to be inside the string. So the position is coming out too large. I'm tempted to debug. Fortunately, I've gone out of my way not to learn how to set a break-point and then run the NUnit tests. I'll probably ask someone how to do that later today, because I'd really like to look around. But a better practice is probably to proceed in smaller steps. I'll leave those methods in, but I'll write a couple of tests against them. I'll have to declare them public to do that, which probably bothers you more than it does me. Let's talk about it later. Here's my first new test:

```
[Test] public void CursorPosition() {
  model.SetLines (new String[] { "<P></P>", "<pre></pre>" });
  model.SelectionStart = 12; // after <pre>
  AssertEquals(5, model.PositionOfCursorInLine());
}
```

The test doesn't run. The message is "Expected 5 but was 12." That trivial method PositionOfCursorInLine() must not be working—what's up with that? Well, obviously it returned zero, to subtract from the 12. Clearly an off-by-one error in the calculation: we must be checking none of the lines. Sure enough. Look at SumLineLengths. It sums up to *but not including* its parameter line. And we have called it using LineContainingCursor() -1. I'll change that and things should work.

Wrong again! Expected 5 but was 3. I should probably give up, but I see the error: the test is wrong. The SelectionStart doesn't include the newline at the end of the first line: it should be 14. I'll fix that and that test will work.

Ha! Good, it works. The InsertPre test, however, is still failing. But look at it:

```
[Test] public void InsertPre() {
  model.SetLines (new String[1] {"<P></P>"});
  model.SelectionStart = 7;
```

```
  model.InsertPreTag();
  AssertEquals("<pre></pre>", model.Lines[1]);
  AssertEquals(14, model.SelectionStart);
  model.InsertReturn();
  AssertEquals("<pre>", model.Lines[1]);
  AssertEquals("", model.Lines[2]);
  AssertEquals("</pre>", model.Lines[3]);
  AssertEquals(16, model.SelectionStart);
}
```

I haven't updated it yet, and it's still expecting that blank line. The correct test is

```
[Test] public void InsertPre() {
  model.SetLines (new String[1] {"<P></P>"});
  model.SelectionStart = 7;
  model.InsertPreTag();
  AssertEquals("<pre></pre>", model.Lines[1]);
  AssertEquals(14, model.SelectionStart);
  model.InsertReturn();
  AssertEquals("<pre>", model.Lines[1]);
  AssertEquals("</pre>", model.Lines[2]);
  AssertEquals(16, model.SelectionStart);
}
```

And it "almost" works. The error says that the assert on Lines[2] fails, returning "pre>", not "<pre>". Of course. The BackOfCursorLine method extracts starting at position+1. That should say position. I think I'll beef up my simple test before fixing this obvious bug, as a lesson to myself to do these things correctly:

```
[Test] public void CursorPosition() {
  model.SetLines (new String[] { "<P></P>", "<pre></pre>" });
  model.SelectionStart = 14; // after <pre>
  AssertEquals(5, model.PositionOfCursorInLine());
  AssertEquals("<pre>", model.FrontOfCursorLine());
  AssertEquals("</pre>", model.BackOfCursorLine());
}
```

This test fails, because of the position+1 in BackOfCursorLine. Change that method to the following:

```
public string BackOfCursorLine() {
  string line = (string) lines[LineContainingCursor()];
  int position = PositionOfCursorInLine();
  return line.Substring(position);
}
```

And all the tests run! Whew! Let's pause for a moment to [re]learn some lessons.

Lessons Learned

Lesson   Well, first of all, I'm a good programmer, or at least not a bad one. Even with all this hassle, I got the feature working in only a few tries, and I never went deeply down any rat holes. So I don't have to kill myself. That's good, because I'm sure you are wondering how all this turns out.

Second, I really do work better with a pair. There's no doubt in my mind that any reasonable pair would have seen some of these problems, questioned others, advised simpler tests, and generally made things go more smoothly. I wonder if Chet would consider quitting his job.

Third, programming by intention didn't work as well as it might have. The code was basically correct, but there were a surprising number of off-by-one errors, and the big test didn't show up precisely where those were. That surprised me: programming by intention is one of my favorite techniques. Let's come back to that.

Fourth, although getting into the debugger might have been good, writing the simpler tests was certainly good: it pointed directly to the mistakes, one after another, and the tests will serve as good documentation for later.

Fifth, even with the first small test helping me, I moved quickly to trying to make the big test work, only updating the small one when the big one failed yet again. This may be the most important lesson for me: proceed in smaller, test-driven steps, especially when working alone.

Finally, the off-by-one errors concern me a bit. For this feature, at least, they make me wonder whether the TextModel is quite right for the task. It seems that this particular code was a little bit primitive and not as expressive as we might like. I don't have an answer for that, but I'm putting it on the list of things to stay alert for.

Programming by Intention

Let's look at that code again. It seems pretty simple and nearly good, but something went wrong:

```
public void InsertReturn() {
  string front = FrontOfCursorLine();
  string back = BackOfCursorLine();
```

```
    lines[LineContainingCursor()] = front;
    lines.Insert(LineContainingCursor()+1, back);
    selectionStart += Environment.NewLine.Length;
}
```

Now that code was in fact correct—so far so good. The FrontOfCursorLine method was also correct, but BackOfCursorLine wasn't:

```
public string FrontOfCursorLine() {
    string line = (string) lines[LineContainingCursor()];
    int position = PositionOfCursorInLine();
    return line.Substring(0, position);
}
public string BackOfCursorLine() {
    string line = (string) lines[LineContainingCursor()];
    int position = PositionOfCursorInLine();
    return line.Substring(position);
}
```

BackOfCursorLine referred to "position+1" originally, but "position" was correct. My tests found the problem, and once I wrote small enough tests, pointed right to it. Maybe if I had drawn a little picture and counted the characters I would have stayed out of trouble. But then there was another, prior, problem in PositionOfCursorInLine:

```
public int PositionOfCursorInLine() {
    return selectionStart - SumLineLengths(LineContainingCursor());
}
```

That used to say "LineContainingCursor()-1". I missed the fact that Sum-LineLengths goes up to the line in question, not through it. That method name isn't helping us. What does that method do? What's a better name: SumLine-LengthsUpTo? TotalLineLengthsBeforeLine? NumberOfCharactersBefore? Let's see how else the method is used. It shows up here:

```
private void InsertTags(string[] tagsToInsert, string tagsPrecedingCursor) {
    int cursorLine = LineContainingCursor();
    lines.InsertRange(cursorLine+1, tagsToInsert);
    selectionStart = NewSelectionStart(cursorLine + 1, tagsPrecedingCursor);
}
private int NewSelectionStart(int cursorLine, string tags) {
    return SumLineLengths(cursorLine) + tags.Length;
}
```

Here, again, what we mean it to be is the total size of all the lines up to but not including cursorLine. It definitely needs a better name. NumberOf-CharactersUpToLine? CharacterPositionOfLine? Now that is starting to work.

The value we have is the cursor position of the *beginning* of the line indicated. CursorPositionAtFrontOfLine? CursorPositionOfLine? StartPositionOfLine? FirstPositionOfLine?

> **Lesson**   You're perhaps wondering if it's worth it to rename this method. After all, it's used only twice. On the other hand, it has confused me at least once. One out of two is a pretty bad average for understanding the name. SumLineLengths is how it is computed, but it isn't what it *means*. We need to name things by what they mean, not how they are implemented. I think I like FirstPositionOfLine. I'll change it and read the code again:

```
public int PositionOfCursorInLine() {
  return selectionStart - FirstPositionOfLine(LineContainingCursor());
}
private int NewSelectionStart(int cursorLine, string tags) {
  return FirstPositionOfLine(cursorLine) + tags.Length;
}
private int FirstPositionOfLine(int cursorLine) {
  int length = 0;
  for (int i = 0; i < cursorLine; i++)
    length += ((String)lines[i]).Length + Environment.NewLine.Length;
  return length;
}
```

Yes, I like that better. It might not be the whole cause of the off-by-one errors, but it certainly contributed to one. And it really is an issue with programming by intention, because this method's former name, SumLineLengths, doesn't express our intention as well as the new name, FirstPositionOfLine.

> **Lesson**   Some programmers, and some managers, resist efforts to give things the right names. In my opinion, this is very shortsighted. We can see from this example that reliability and maintainability can be significantly improved by careful attention to naming and to the meaning of the code.

Enough for Now

> **Lesson**   I think we have the model correctly implementing the insertion of a return at the current cursor location. However, my confidence isn't as high as I'd like it to be, because of the rough road getting here. I'm going to do a few additional programmer tests next time, and then I'll build the customer test and make it work. For now, I'm tired, and tired programmers make mistakes. It's time to stop. Tune in next time...

19

Dark Clouds on the Horizon

When Chet and I were pairing, we found a test that didn't communicate.
Working on that, I thought of a bigger problem. ***The Shift+Enter idea is***
breaking a fundamental assumption of our program! *This could get ugly!*

We're in Big Trouble, Guys![1]

My plan today was to clean up and publish the previous chapter about Shift+Enter. I was thinking about it while showering, and I realized that we've got a big problem. Up until now, the basic idea of the TextModel object is that every line begins and ends with the same tag. The paragraphs aren't made up of lots of separate lines with a <P> on the first line and a </P> on the last: they are just one line. So our InsertParagraphTag() method just inserts a line after the current line, with a new paragraph tag on it.

Working on the <pre> tag in the previous chapter, we discovered that we want multiple lines inside that tag, typically lines of code. Fine, no problem. When we're done with the <pre> stuff, we want to hit Enter and get a new <P> tag and get back to typing text. However, if the user has the cursor up somewhere in the middle of the code, hitting Enter won't insert the <P> tags after the <pre> section! The new paragraph will get inserted right in the middle of the code segment.

This is just the sort of thing people fear with this simple design and refactoring stuff: some simple decision at the beginning is incorrect, and we go down some long path assuming that it will all work, and then suddenly bang we get a requirement that breaks everything. We're doomed!

---

1. Ed Anderi, personal communication.

Well, fact is, at this writing, I don't know whether we're doomed or not. I don't see my way out of the problem, and I haven't solved the problem. My belief, of course, is that simple design plus refactoring always works, so the change we need, whatever it is, won't be a big problem. A couple of chapters from now, we'll find out.

We Need a Test

Having figured out that I probably have a bug, I need to write a test to prove it. So I scurried to the computer and opened up Microsoft Visual Studio. I looked around to find the test for the Shift+Enter, and I couldn't find it. That's odd...or is it? Last Wednesday, Chet and I got together and worked on a different story from this one. As part of that, I brought Chet up to speed on what had happened so far on this story. It had been a couple of days since I had worked on this story, and I had difficulty finding the test for inserting the Shift+Enter. The reason: there is no separate test for that. Instead I had enhanced the Insert-Pre to test the Shift+Enter also. It didn't take us long to figure out.

Now again today, only four days later, I couldn't figure out where the Shift+Enter test was. Now a case could be made that I should pay more attention. Or that I'm becoming forgetful. What were we talking about? Oh, right, I couldn't find that test.

The real lesson is that tests are an important way of recording history and bringing ourselves up to speed on what's in the system. Tests are part of the communication that we try to build into the code. And the code isn't doing enough communicating here. Since I'm here to work on the tests, I'll fix that problem as well. Here's the test for InsertPre, which also includes our only test so far for Shift+Enter:

```
[Test] public void InsertPre() {
  model.SetLines (new String[1] {"<P></P>"});
  model.SelectionStart = 7;
  model.InsertPreTag();
  AssertEquals("<pre></pre>", model.Lines[1]);
  AssertEquals(14, model.SelectionStart);
  model.InsertReturn();
  AssertEquals("<pre>", model.Lines[1]);
  AssertEquals("</pre>", model.Lines[2]);
  AssertEquals(16, model.SelectionStart);
}
```

The Shift+Enter part, of course, is the InsertReturn and everything after it, which is just checking that the <pre> line gets split. Since that should be a separate test anyway, as I just mentioned, I'll split it out into a new test. Here's the InsertPre test and the new one:

```
[Test] public void InsertPre() {
  model.SetLines (new String[1] {"<P></P>"});
  model.SelectionStart = 7;
  model.InsertPreTag();
  AssertEquals("<pre></pre>", model.Lines[1]);
  AssertEquals(14, model.SelectionStart);
}
[Test] public void ShiftEnter() {
  model.SetLines (new String[1] {"<pre></pre>"});
  model.SelectionStart = 5;
  model.InsertReturn();
  AssertEquals("<pre>", model.Lines[0]);
  AssertEquals("</pre>", model.Lines[1]);
  AssertEquals(7, model.SelectionStart);
}
```

Now for the test that will fail. Here's what I'm thinking about. When we use the <pre> tag, we create several lines. The first one starts with the <pre>, the intermediate ones have code on them, and the last line has code and ends with </pre>. It looks like this:

```
<pre>    code1
    code2
    code3</pre>
```

The defect I expect is this: if the cursor is on the first line or the second line, and I hit Enter (not Shift+Enter), what I want is new paragraph tags, after the <pre> tags. What I'll get, however, will be paragraph tags right in the middle of the code. Here's a test that I expect to fail:

```
[Test] public void ShiftEnterMultipleLines() {
  model.SetLines (new String[] {"<pre>code1", "code2","code3</pre>"});
  model.SelectionStart = 14; // after 'co' in 'code2'
  model.InsertParagraphTag();
  AssertEquals("code3</pre>", model.Lines[2]);
  AssertEquals("<P></P>", model.Lines[3]);
}
```

I expect that the first assert will fail, finding the <P> tag there rather than in line 3 where it belongs. And sure enough, that's what happens. Houston, we have a problem.

Think about this a second. Our whole model so far is based on the premise that every tagged item, even a very long paragraph, is really just one line that begins with some tag and ends with the matching tag. Allowing the insertion of a return breaks that fundamental design assumption. We might be up against a big problem here. In fact, the problem is bigger than I realized. Remember that when we do the Alt+S operation to insert a section tag, we're actually inserting multiple lines:

```
<sect1><title></title>
</sect1>
```

Typing a title in there and a few paragraphs works just fine, with a result like this:

```
<sect1><title>Some Section</title>
<P>A paragraph about something.</P>
<P>Another paragraph goes here.</P>
</sect1>
```

However, if we do another Alt+S, the new section gets inserted right in the middle of the old one, resulting in this:

```
<sect1><title>Some Section</title>
<P>A paragraph about something.</P>
<P>Another paragraph goes here.</P>
<sect1><title></title>
</sect1>
</sect1>
```

Chet and I talked about this issue a long time ago. We decided then, as the customers, that we could live with having to cursor to the end of the </sect1> before inserting another section. And we expected that we'd write a story to improve that when it started to bug us. But now, as programmers, we're starting to see a big hole in our design. We're concerned that the program doesn't know enough about XML and that bad things might happen because of that.

Now it may seem obvious to you that an XML editor should be based on some kind of data structure that understands XML. It might lead you to start using Microsoft .NET's XML-handling objects right away. And on another day, I might do the same. However, it's my practice in general to do the simplest thing that could possibly work, and working in plain text seems like that to me. I feel that I'm pretty safe starting without XML parsing built in, but of course I could be wrong.

Is this the end of simple design plus refactoring as a design strategy? We'll find out.

Yellow Bar

I've got another chapter to publish, based on other work Chet and I did recently. I can't ship this code on a Red Bar, and I don't really want to comment the test out. Someone reminded me that NUnit has an "Ignore" feature. You can put an Ignore attribute on a test, and that test will not be run. You won't get a Green Bar, however: you get a Yellow Bar. That will suffice to remind me that I've got work to do. So I'm starting a new project policy, subject to revision if it gets us in trouble: a pair can mark a test as "Ignore" if it marks code that needs work but the check-in doesn't break any production code.

That's the situation here. So I've added an Ignore to the test and will check it in:

```
[Test]
[Ignore("New Para in mid-Pre Bug")]
public void ShiftEnterMultipleLines() {
  model.SetLines (new String[] {"<pre>code1", "code2","code3</pre>"});
  model.SelectionStart = 14; // after 'co' in 'code2'
  model.InsertParagraphTag();
  AssertEquals("code3</pre>", model.Lines[2]);
  AssertEquals("<P></P>", model.Lines[3]);
}
```

The Yellow Bar—trust me—is shown here. See you next time...

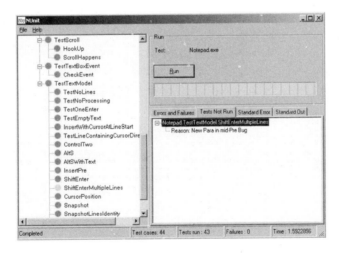

20

Finishing the Shift+Enter Story

The Programmer Unit Tests for the Shift+Enter are working. Chet and I implement the Customer Acceptance Test and install the hooks in the GUI—and in our testing framework—to make it work.

Wrapping Up the Job

We told the customers (ourselves) about our fears with the Shift+Enter: that it will make the neat auto-insertion of paragraph tags insert them in strange places. The customers weren't as concerned as the programmers. They said, "Let us try it. If we don't like it, we'll think of something, or you will." Somewhat relieved, we decided to go ahead and finish the feature so that it could be tried out.

Two things were left to be done. We had to hook up the XMLNotepad Form to process the Shift+Enter properly (calling InsertReturn), and we had to give the customer an acceptance test. We decided that the customer test was a bit time-consuming and that doing it would teach us little, and we felt that putting the feature into the Form might be a bit difficult. We decided to do the implementation first.

Isn't This Against the Rules?

Extreme Programmers all over the world are clamoring now, telling us that this is against the rules: you're supposed to write the test first. Well, that's what the rules say. The rules also say, "They're Only Rules." We're here to report what we did and how it turned out. This is not a highly polished book about a made-up project. This is real people, doing real programming, making real decisions, some good, some bad, learning as we go. Last Tuesday, sitting in the Borders Cafe, that's what we decided to do. Read on, and find out how it turned out.

What's to Do?

The Enter key is handled in the KeyDownHandler code in the XMLNotepad class. When we started, it looked like this:

```
public void XMLKeyDownHandler(object objSender, KeyEventArgs kea) {
  model.SetLines(textbox.Lines);
  model.SelectionStart = textbox.SelectionStart;
  if (kea.KeyCode == Keys.Enter) {
    TypeEnter();
    kea.Handled = true;
  }
  PutText(textbox, model.LinesArray(), model.SelectionStart);
}
public void TypeEnter() {
  model.Enter();
}
```

Our concern, as new C# Microsoft .NET programmers, was that we needed to figure out how to get two different behaviors from typing Enter, depending on whether the Shift key was down. As implemented, Enter inserts a paragraph tag, as you probably remember. So does Shift+Enter, Alt+Enter, Ctrl+Shift+Alt+Function+Enter, and so on. With a little research, we found that the KeyEventArgs (kea) has another property, Modifiers, which can be tested for values like Keys.Shift. Just the thing:

```
public void XMLKeyDownHandler(object objSender, KeyEventArgs kea) {
  model.SetLines(textbox.Lines);
  model.SelectionStart = textbox.SelectionStart;
  if (kea.KeyCode == Keys.Enter && kea.Modifiers == Keys.None) {
    TypeEnter();
    kea.Handled = true;
  }
  PutText(textbox, model.LinesArray(), model.SelectionStart);
}
```

This should change the GUI so that paragraph tags are inserted only when you type Enter with no other keys down. And it worked. This was what we wanted to learn: how to separate out the two similar keystrokes. So we added the code for our new Shift+Enter:

```
public void XMLKeyDownHandler(object objSender, KeyEventArgs kea) {
  model.SetLines(textbox.Lines);
  model.SelectionStart = textbox.SelectionStart;
  if (kea.KeyCode == Keys.Enter && kea.Modifiers == Keys.None) {
    TypeEnter();
    kea.Handled = true;
  }
  else if (kea.KeyCode == Keys.Enter && kea.Modifiers == Keys.Shift) {
    model.InsertReturn();
    kea.Handled = true;
  }        PutText(textbox, model.LinesArray(), model.SelectionStart);
}
```

This worked fine, just like we had hoped! However, in writing the new code, we noticed that odd little method TypeEnter(). It seems useless. We think we wrote it originally as some attempt to break out the human factors action (typing Shift+Enter) from what the system does with that action (send Enter() to the model). We definitely don't like it now, so we removed it, putting the code back in line:

```
public void XMLKeyDownHandler(object objSender, KeyEventArgs kea) {
  model.SetLines(textbox.Lines);
  model.SelectionStart = textbox.SelectionStart;
  if (kea.KeyCode == Keys.Enter && kea.Modifiers == Keys.None) {
    model.Enter();
    kea.Handled = true;
  }
  else if (kea.KeyCode == Keys.Enter && kea.Modifiers == Keys.Shift) {
    model.InsertReturn();
    kea.Handled = true;
  }
  PutText(textbox, model.LinesArray(), model.SelectionStart);
}
```

Now this is certainly a questionable change. Perhaps the broken-out version is better, but we didn't think so. It didn't communicate much more about what was going on, and it increased the general complexity. Your mileage may vary. On your code, use your judgment.

It Works—Now Let's Test It

We may be evil enough to figure out how to make something work—and in fact actually make it work—without writing the customer test, but we're certainly not going to skip the customer test altogether. We've gotten in trouble like that before, and this kind of situation where we drive the GUI is exactly the trouble spot. So we looked for a test to copy or improve, and we found the Insert-Pre.test file:

```
*input
<P>This is the first p|aragraph.</P>
<P>This is the second paragraph.</P>
*end
*altP
*output
<P>This is the first paragraph.</P>
<pre>|</pre>
<P>This is the second paragraph.</P>
```

Perfect! We'll just add a second bit to this test, to test the Shift+Enter:

```
*input
<P>This is the first p|aragraph.</P>
<P>This is the second paragraph.</P>
*end
*altP
*output
<P>This is the first paragraph.</P>
<pre>|</pre>
<P>This is the second paragraph.</P>*shiftEnter *output
<P>This is the first paragraph.</P> <pre> |</pre>
<P>This is the second paragraph.</P>
```

We expect this test to fail, sort of, and it does. This is all well and good, except that the test failed in a really odd way. It seemed to be failing on the first *output section, comparing a perfectly good result against an example that also includes *shiftEnter, and a number of other lines. Chet immediately saw the problem: "The *output command must read all the way to the end." I was sure that it didn't, that it stopped at any line that begins with "*". We discussed it for only a moment or two before looking. Here's the code and the answer:

```
private String ExpectedOutput(StringReader reader) {
  return ReadToEnd(reader);
}
private String ReadToEnd(StringReader reader) {
  String result = "";
  String line = reader.ReadLine();
  while (line != null && line != "*end") {
    result += line;
    result += System.Environment.NewLine;
    line = reader.ReadLine();
  }
  return result;
}
```

Ah. Both wrong. It's reading to "*end". Chet tried vainly to convince me that was what he meant, but I knew better. Anyway, we changed the test. Note the *end:

```
*input
<P>This is the first p|aragraph.</P>
<P>This is the second paragraph.</P>
*end
*altP
*output
<P>This is the first paragraph.</P>
<pre>|</pre>
<P>This is the second paragraph.</P>
*end
*shiftEnter
*output
<P>This is the first paragraph.</P>
<pre>
|</pre>
<P>This is the second paragraph.</P>
```

> **Lesson**   There's a small but important lesson here. Speculate about the code only a little and then read the code. The code knows what it does; we can only guess.

Also, you might be wondering, after we split the Shift+Enter test out in the Programmer Unit Tests, why we put these two tests together in the Customer Acceptance Tests. In the programmer tests, the lack of modularity had left us confused. We generally think of the customer tests as providing assurance to the customer that things are going well, but we don't think of them as providing debugging information to the programmers. Frankly, we could be wrong about this: it could have been sheer laziness that kept us from producing a separate customer test file.

The test fails, as we expect. Why? Because the *shiftEnter line isn't recognized. The CustomerTest command interpreter just ignores commands that it doesn't know. (This could be a problem, but so far it hasn't been.) So now we have to implement the *shiftEnter in the customer test code:

```
private void InterpretCommands(String commands, String message) {
  StringReader reader = new StringReader(commands);
  String line = reader.ReadLine();
```

```
CreateModel();
while ( line != null) {
  if ( line == "*enter")
    form.XMLKeyDownHandler((object) this, new KeyEventArgs(Keys.Enter));
  if ( line == "*shiftEnter")
    form.XMLKeyDownHandler((object) this,
      new KeyEventArgs(Keys.Enter | Keys.Shift));
  if ( line == "*altS")
    ExecuteMenu("&S");
  if ( line == "*altP")
    ExecuteMenu("&P");
  if (line == "*display")
    Console.WriteLine("display\r\n{0}\r\nend", model.TestText);
  if (line == "*output")
    CompareOutput(reader, message);
  if (line == "*input")
    SetInput(reader);
  line = reader.ReadLine();
}
}
```

Note the new item there, with the "*shiftEnter". We took a moment to figure out how to create the right keystroke but then just called the handler like
we did the *enter command. Now the test runs.

Improving the Customer Acceptance Test

However, while working through this, we found a bit of a difficulty. Each customer test is in a file. The files are looped over in the CustomerTest.cs class.
Each test consists of executing some commands and then doing a *output command, which compares the current contents of the model with the expected
value provided. The comparison was being done with a simple Assert, like this:

```
private void CompareOutput(StringReader reader, String message) {
  String expected = ExpectedOutput(reader);
  String result = model.TestText;
  AssertEquals(message, expected, model.TestText);
}
```

NUnit isn't much help here. The test shows up as a failure in Customer-
Test.cs and doesn't really show what happened clearly. You can sort of scroll

through the output in NUnit's little window, but it's not very clear. So we improved the CustomerTest CompareOutput method:

```
private void CompareOutput(StringReader reader, String message) {
  String expected = ExpectedOutput(reader);
  String result = model.TestText;
  if (expected != result) {
    Console.WriteLine(message);
    Console.WriteLine("*Expected");
    Console.WriteLine(expected);
    Console.WriteLine("*Result");
    Console.WriteLine(result);
  }
  AssertEquals(message, expected, model.TestText);
}
```

Now, when a test fails, NUnit's StandardOut window looks like this, showing us just what happened:

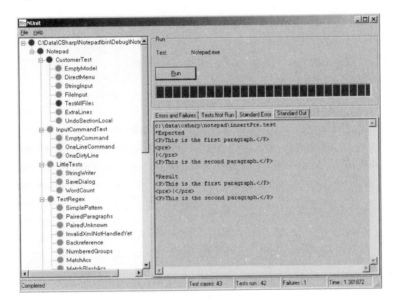

All Done, for Now

The Shift+Enter feature now works and is tested. We improved the Customer-Test framework a little along the way. This is worth a comment:

Lesson   Teams sometimes think that they can't have customer tests because they don't have a framework. We have answered that before and will again: you don't have to have a framework, but you do have to have tests. A framework is helpful, but tests are essential. Back a few chapters, we followed this advice and implemented our first customer tests. We've enhanced the framework a few times to add functionality to it, and we have adjusted our code, especially the XMLNotepad, to make it easier to test things. This time, we have improved the framework to make it easier to understand what has gone wrong. That's what's supposed to happen when you're evolving the system. Small improvements, done in a clean fashion, as needed, add up.

Take a moment to imagine what you might do to the Customer-Test class if your customer wanted a complete report of all the tests: when they were run, whether they worked, and so on. Would it be difficult? HINT: It wouldn't be. You'd just add a little tracing code to the class to output the results to a file, or even to an HTML file, or even, if necessary, to a database of some kind.

You're probably not going to need that, and right now I'm sure that *we* aren't going to need that. But if we did get asked for it, we'd estimate it, our customer would schedule it, and we'd put it in. We know that evolutionary design works, and that it wouldn't be a big problem.

So we've taken a new story, the Shift+Enter idea, and implemented it complete with tests, with little difficulty. We've encountered a worrying problem that still hangs over our head: will the customer decide that they want something special about intelligently inserting tags? We talked with the customers at length, though, and they're not sure whether the current situation is a problem. What they really want is a File\Save and File\Open capability so that they can start using the tool.

Fortunately, we've been working on that, as you'll soon see.

21

Some Things We Ought to Do

Over the weekend, I did a little studying. I was reading Charles Petzold's Programming Microsoft Windows with C# *(Microsoft Press, 2001) and James W. Cooper's* C# Design Patterns: A Tutorial *(Addison-Wesley, 2002). They're both wonderful resources, and I got a lot of ideas. Then today, I took a break from most immediate things and spent a little time at lunch writing ideas on cards about how the XML Notepad should be improved. Here are a few of those ideas, with a little explanation of each one, and some technical discussion.*

Command Pattern

The Command pattern is one where we represent a request or command as an object. It offers the advantage that the Command object carries all the information about what has to be done, and the main line of the code can handle all the commands in a uniform way. (This pattern, and all those mentioned in this chapter, can be found in the excellent book *Design Patterns,* by Erich Gamma, Richard Helm, Ralph Johnson, and John Vlissides [Addison-Wesley, 1995], or in the aforementioned Cooper book.)

The Command pattern is a natural for the XML Notepad. I spent some time thinking about building a subclass of MenuItem that would allow attachment of a Command object, which would then be used to dispatch the action to the TextModel. It should be possible to have all the menu items go to one method, which would init the TextModel, execute the command, and read the

TextModel back into the TextBox. This would eliminate the duplication of the init and de-init that we're seeing now in code like this:

```
void MenuInsertSection(object obj, EventArgs ea) {
  model.SetLines(textbox.Lines);
  model.SelectionStart = textbox.SelectionStart;
  model.InsertSectionTags();
  PutText(textbox, model.LinesArray(), model.SelectionStart);
}
```

Each of the menu items that we have now, and all the future menu items that update the model, have those lines passing stuff back and forth between the model and the TextBox. Use of the Command pattern looks to me like a good way to do this.

Adapter Pattern

The Adapter pattern is used to convert the interface of one class into a more useful interface that a using class expects. We have a bit of a difference between the way the TextBox works and the way our TextModel and Form want to work. Adapter might help us sort that out.

We sort of have Adapter in place now. Note the call to PutText on the TextBox in the code just shown. That's not a native method of TextBox class but a method of our specialized subclass of TextBox, TestableTextBox. This is called the "class adapter" approach. We could also build a separate object to handle the situation, containing a TextBox for which it does translation. That would be called "object adapter."

I've been complaining about the relationship between TextModel and the TextBox for a long time now, and maybe this is a good approach.

Mediator Pattern

The Mediator pattern defines a separate object that encapsulates how two or more objects interact. This can break the coupling between them, making all the objects involved simpler and more clear.

Right now, the Form understands the mapping between the keyboard/menu operations and the specific operations of the TextModel. For example, we have this code:

```
if (kea.KeyCode == Keys.Enter && kea.Modifiers == Keys.None) {
  model.Enter();
  kea.Handled = true;
```

```
}
else if (kea.KeyCode == Keys.Enter && kea.Modifiers == Keys.Shift) {
  model.InsertReturn();
  kea.Handled = true;
}
```

In the second of these cases, the Form knows that Shift+Enter means "Insert Return." In the first of the cases, the Model is told Enter(), and it contains the code to decide what to do:

```
public void Enter() {
  InsertParagraphTag();
}
```

I've been concerned about this for a while. There has been discussion of which way is right, and we have an interaction with the Customer Acceptance Tests as well. We've talked about that before. The Mediator pattern would allow me to break out the translation from form operations like keystrokes and menu actions into a separate class to encapsulate the idea. This could be really good.

Small Boy with a Patterns Book

After spending a bunch of time thinking about these ideas over a few days now, I finally recognized in myself what I call "Small Boy with a Patterns Book." You can always tell when someone on your team is reading the Gang of Four book (Gamma, et al.). Every day or so, this person comes in with a great idea for a place in the system that is just crying out for the use of Composite, or whatever chapter he read last night.

There's an old saying: To a small boy with a hammer, everything looks like a nail. As programmers, we fall into the same trap all too often. We learn about some new technology or solution, and we immediately begin seeing places to apply it. Now I'm not saying that any of these pattern applications is wrong. At this moment, I'm just noting that I've gone into that mode. I'm looking for places in my code to use these good ideas from Cooper's book.

Deriving a File Class

Cooper gave me another good idea. Microsoft .NET has no decent File class. By "decent," I mean a class that represents a file, with a name, and a path, that can be used to open, close, rename, delete, and so on. Instead, there is this all-powerful "Directory" class that can do those things. The implication, however, is that when you want to do anything with files, you have nothing to work with but a collection of strings representing the names of the files. String, of course, has no methods that are anything to do with files.

Cooper suggests building a class to support the kinds of things we need to do with files. Because this Directory to String thing has irritated me for quite a while, I'm thinking it's a good idea.

Rendering the Text More Effectively

The current XML Notepad is pretty rudimentary, and if it's used incorrectly, bad things could happen. If the user cursors into a tag and edits it incorrectly, the text might no longer be valid XML and we might never know it. I thought about a number of ways of making this better.

Use RichTextBox Instead of TextBox

If we used the RichTextBox instead of TextBox, we could do some great things. For example, we could color all the tags a different color from the text so that the user would more readily see where not to type. We could even render the different tag contents in a different font: we could make the section titles large and bold, and the code lines could be in a fixed face, while the regular text was not.

Petzold had some useful information that might help with this. He addressed how to figure out what character was selected when using a variable-width font, and he showed how to know what is and is not scrolled on the screen so that we could render the screen more quickly by rendering only the text that's actually displayed. That would be much more efficient than what we are doing now.

Petzold even showed enough so that we could render not to a RichText-Box but to a pane of our own invention without much difficulty. He even showed how to write some "unsafe" code that accesses the Win32 operations on the caret (that little vertical bar that shows up between the characters you are typing when editing). Using these ideas, we could make a much better experience for the customer.

Keeping the XML Correct

I thought a lot about the user possibly messing up the XML. He might type inside a tag, changing a <P> to a <p> or worse, to <H2>, without changing the corresponding other end. He could get the tags unbalanced, and the file would no longer contain legitimate XML, which of course would be bad.

I thought about displaying the XML not in a TextBox but in some kind of tree browser, showing the shape of the XML in the tree and the details of each paragraph in a separate window. It might be sort of like the Explorer, with the directory tree on the left and the text on the right. The problem with this idea is that on the text side, we want to see all levels in the file, not just one selected one.

I thought about having two columns, one showing the tags and another showing the text. This might make keeping things lined up difficult, because one line on the tag side might consume many lines on the text side, due to word-wrap. I thought about that for a while and couldn't really see any way to make the tags and text line up. I'd like to experiment a little to be sure.

Protect the Tags

It might be possible to catch all the cursor changes. The main way the user could mess up a tag would be to cursor into one and edit it. We could change the program to detect all cursor movements (not forgetting the mouse) and keep him from going inside a tag. This might be a problem if the user actually needed to go in there, but it would be safe. We could maybe add a story to insert a tag that the program doesn't know—that feature would certainly be useful someday. Or perhaps the story should be to add a special command for editing a tag on purpose, which prevents the user from doing it by accident.

Verify the Structure

It might be possible to verify the structure all the time, every time the user does anything. Suppose that on every event we parsed the XML. A simple loop would be sufficient:

```
read the file
  if there's an opening tag, push it on a stack
  if there's a closing tag, pop the stack and compare
  if they match, the syntax is OK, otherwise not.
```

That would be cool to write, not difficult, and it would do a good job, though not a perfect one, of ensuring that nothing is broken in the structure. There could be a red light/green light somewhere in the display, and the light would go red, and probably beep, whenever the structure was broken.

One problem would be a less than sign (<) in the text, but that's already a problem. We haven't had a story for it, but less than in the text needs to be changed to < anyway. We know they're going to ask for that sooner or later, so maybe we should just build it in now.

TextModel as a Tree

An even better solution would be to have the TextModel be a tree of tags, rather than just a bunch of strings. That way, a "sect1" tag would have a "title" tag and a bunch of "P" tags as children. It would be easy to render the tree back to text. A simple pre-order scan of the tree should do it: it would be elementary tree processing.

One issue would arise in reading the text back into the model. But something like the push-down processing described earlier should do it. And we could probably create the tree for the new text, compare it to the old tree, and make sure that nothing too weird had happened.

It might also be possible to check the situation on essentially every keystroke. A quick check of the line that the cursor is on to see if nothing has changed might be sufficient to allow some kind of incremental updating of the TextModel's tree.

XML Support in .NET

XML support in .NET includes XML generation classes, although in my opinion they don't add much to the situation over and above regular string manipulation. You can validate XML with a class named XMLValidatingReader. There's an XMLDocument class that could be used as the base for TextModel instead of the tree. You can load XML into the document with XMLTextReader and then navigate through it.

Using such tools has its pros and cons. Certainly, so far, we've stayed away from them in this book. My reasons aren't just "not invented here." I like to learn how things really work, down at the bits and bytes, so even if we were to use some of the classes just mentioned—and we may well experiment with them before the project is over—I like to start with simple and direct solutions. In addition, it typically takes a lot of learning to get one of these solutions doing anything, especially when you don't know your way around the system very well. I've got a pretty good feeling now for how C# and .NET work, and I feel I can put together some interesting tests of these classes in a few hours. But when I was just starting out, it would have taken much longer and I would have been learning some high-level material but missing out on the basics.

So my practice is to start with the basics. Often, it works just fine to stay there. Other times, it makes sense to move to a more powerful tool, but when we do, we have enough of a grasp of the realities of the problem to enable us to navigate the tool wisely. We'll see how things go this time.

What's the Plan?

All these ideas, and a lot more, came out of a bit of lunchtime reading over the past few days. I'd say that every one of them is worth learning about, and many of them will make our program better. A few probably can't coexist: we can't use both Mediator and Adapter in the TextBox-TextModel interaction. We can't both write our own XML tree and use the .NET XML support like XMLText-Reader. To find out which of these ideas is best, we need to try them both. And, of course, we do want to learn as much as we can, as fast as we can.

On the other hand, we have this customer to keep happy. If we go into a cave to learn everything we might need to know about XML and patterns, the customer isn't going to get any features. And then the customer isn't going to be happy. And then the customer will cancel our project. So what's the best way to handle learning? Well, I don't know, but here are a few ways that learning can happen:

Customer Schedules Learning Stories

Having the customer schedule learning stories is the best possible situation, perhaps with the exception of writing a book that shows how ignorant you are and how you dig your way out of it. The customer allocates a certain amount of the team's time to learning. Sometimes the customer might pick the things that you learn, based on what you tell them might be beneficial. The customer might be more interested in the .NET XML support, which relates to their problem, than they are in Mediator and Adapter. Or the customer might just allow you so much time per week to study and experiment with things that you feel you need to learn. This would be really good. Get paid to learn. It's hard to get this situation, however, because the customer has other things on her mind, like getting her application done.

Manager Schedules Learning Time

Another good deal for the learner is for the team's manager to make a certain amount of time available for learning, holding it back from customer-driven programming time. Maybe the customer gets to schedule four days a week, or four and a half, and the other half day belongs to the team. This can be good for the team and for the manager, of course, because the team becomes more powerful. With a bit of judgment on what to learn, the things we learn this week can help us next week. This situation, too, can be hard to set up. Even the best manager can feel the pressure to make the programmers work more and more, "just this little while," to respond to some urgent need or other.

This is, of course, a shortsighted view. Overworked programmers won't learn, they'll get tired, they'll make mistakes, and quite often the project or the team will falter. But it happens every day. Extreme Programming allocates one of its dozen practices to this issue, with the practice "Sustainable Pace." This practice dictates that the team will work at a pace that can be sustained indefinitely. Sure, you'll sprint once in a while, but by and large, software development is an activity that takes place over months and years, and the team needs to work at a pace that keeps them strong and growing stronger, over the entire term.

Wise team managers provide space, time, and resources for programmers to learn. But often it doesn't happen. What then?

Programmer Schedules Learning Time

Folks, this is our profession. We cannot afford not to learn, not to improve our skills. If time isn't available on the job, we still need to do it. It's hard, ain't it hard, ain't it hard (oh yes), to work on programming in our free time, after slaving over a hot terminal all day long, all week long. Yet we have to find a way to do it, or we'll be left behind.

There are lots of important things in life: our families, our friends, our communities. We have to find room for all of them. Each of us has to find the balance that works for us for learning about our profession, in the context of our lives. I've made mistakes in both directions, but usually my mistake has been to focus too much on work and not enough on the things that were important to me, including learning and family and friends. I'll try hard not to make that mistake again. You—well, you have to find your own balance.

Yes, But What's the Plan?

Enough preaching. We see here that in a few hours, I found out a lot of things that would be good to know about, and I got a lot of ideas that would make the program better. How am I going to put them into effect? Here's my plan, my balance:

I'm going to try a couple of quick experiments with the .NET XML classes, probably XMLTextReader. There seem to be a couple of quick-looking tutorials on it, so I should be able to do something in an hour or so, including the write-up. I'll do that by writing some tests, of course. The test classes will document what I've learned, for later on when and if I want to put what I've learned into the system.

The ideas about validating the XML, beefing up the TextModel to some tree structure, reading every character into the TextModel to keep it up to date, using a RichTextBox, protecting the tags...I'm going to do none of that until the customer stories require it. The code we have is good enough for what it does now. I'm sure it will need to evolve, and I suspect that some upcoming customer stories might even push it in some of the directions I'm foreseeing. But I'm not going to fall into the trap of saying "it will be cheaper if we do it now." Sorry, wrong. The code isn't getting any harder to change while I leave it alone, and I'll make it better when the time comes to edit it. So even though I'm very interested in trying some of these ideas, I'm not going to invest customer time in putting them into the system until I have a customer story that justifies doing so.

There were some other ideas that I'll work on when I get there. The idea for a File object will probably show up in two efforts that I know are coming up. Chet and I have a hanging story to do file load and save, and it might show up there. If the forces so indicate, we'll refactor in the direction of a File object. And I have been doing a little experimentation with .NET's FileSystemWatcher class in conjunction with code manager ideas. The File object might come up there, if we get any more code manager stories.

Your choice might be different. You might choose to push on some of these ideas harder and to put them into the system. That's OK. I'm comfortable that I have a strong focus on learning, and I'm not afraid that the ideas will get lost. Your comfort zone may be different. Just remember that the comfort zone of your customer, or your manager, might be different as well, and keep your eye on the ball, which is shipping well-factored, well-tested, high-quality software to your customer. To do that now and forever, you need to find the balance between completing stories and learning. In this book, you're getting a look at how I try to find my own balance. You get to find yours.

22

The Delegate from Troy

Paul Friedman drove to Ann Arbor from Troy to pair with me. After some
pleasant food and chat, we attacked some code that has been bugging me for a
long time. Using delegates, we reduced duplication and learned a lot.

Finding a Pair and Something to Do

Back in November, I posted to the extremeprogramming list that Chet's new-found gainful employment was making it hard for us to pair, offering to pair with anyone who wanted to meet me in Ann Arbor or vicinity. Paul Friedman allowed as how he would give it a try. After a holiday break, we finally got together last night at Grizzly Peak, where my son is brewmaster.

Paul and I chatted a bit, had a couple of GP's special pizzas, and then sat down to look over the code and find something to do. I showed Paul some of the XML and XSLT tests I had written over the past couple of days, and then we looked at some code that I considered to be the most problematical in the system, in the XMLNotepad form itself.

I've been saying since the early days that I'm not comfortable with the breakout of responsibility between the form and the TextModel. And worse, there's duplication in the code. Let's look at the duplication. The menu item handlers and the KeyDown handler all duplicate some code lines:

```
public void XMLKeyDownHandler(object objSender, KeyEventArgs kea) {
  model.SetLines(textbox.Lines);
  model.SelectionStart = textbox.SelectionStart;
  if (kea.KeyCode == Keys.Enter && kea.Modifiers == Keys.None) {
    model.Enter();
    kea.Handled = true;
  }
```

```
  else if (kea.KeyCode == Keys.Enter && kea.Modifiers == Keys.Shift) {
    model.InsertReturn();
    kea.Handled = true;
  }
  PutText(textbox, model.LinesArray(), model.SelectionStart);
}

void MenuInsertSection(object obj, EventArgs ea) {
  model.SetLines(textbox.Lines);
  model.SelectionStart = textbox.SelectionStart;
  model.InsertSectionTags();
  PutText(textbox, model.LinesArray(), model.SelectionStart);
}

void MenuInsertPre(object obj, EventArgs ea) {
  model.SetLines(textbox.Lines);
  model.SelectionStart = textbox.SelectionStart;
  model.InsertPreTag();
  PutText(textbox, model.LinesArray(), model.SelectionStart);
}
```

You see, of course, that the lines shown in boldface are duplicated three times. Remember back when we first did the menu and I predicted there would be a lot of duplication across menu items? Well, there it is. A while back I did something weird and wonderful with dynamic method dispatch to try to eliminate it, but I backed that code out because it was too complex. My assumption was that sooner or later we'd see what to do.

As we chatted, Paul and I observed that the KeyDown handler has the textual duplication in it but that it is also duplicating the loading and unloading of the TextModel on every single keystroke, because the duplicated lines are outside the if statements. We observed that the code would be more efficient but with even more textual duplication if we moved the lines inside the if. In the absence of a performance measure telling us that we needed that extra efficiency, we didn't make that change.

Lesson   Notice that we have identified two different kinds of duplication here: simple textual duplication (perhaps with a few little changes) and duplication of the same activity repeated many times. All forms of duplication are candidates for removal. The ones relating to efficiency may be less important than the ones relating to clarity.

A Little Refactoring

As we were browsing, Paul noticed a menu item in my copy of Microsoft Visual Studio. The Edit menu had a new item: Refactor. He asked what that was, and I told him that I was trying the C# Refactory from Xtreme Simplicity, *http://www.xtreme-simplicity.net*. To show him how it worked, I tried my first ever Extract Method using the tool. The two lines (SetLines and SelectionStart) that load the model seem to be at a different level of abstraction than the one line (PutText) that loads the TextBox, so I extracted a method with the tool, resulting in

```
void MenuInsertSection(object obj, EventArgs ea) {
  GetText();
  model.InsertSectionTags();
  PutText(textbox, model.LinesArray(), model.SelectionStart);
}
private void GetText() {
  model.SetLines(textbox.Lines);
  model.SelectionStart = textbox.SelectionStart;
}
```

That worked nicely, so I used that method in the other parts of the code, resulting in

```
void MenuInsertPre(object obj, EventArgs ea) {
  GetText();
  model.InsertPreTag();
  PutText(textbox, model.LinesArray(), model.SelectionStart);
}
public void XMLKeyDownHandler(object objSender, KeyEventArgs kea) {
  GetText();
  if (kea.KeyCode == Keys.Enter && kea.Modifiers == Keys.None) {
    model.Enter();
    kea.Handled = true;
  }
  else if (kea.KeyCode == Keys.Enter && kea.Modifiers == Keys.Shift) {
    model.InsertReturn();
    kea.Handled = true;
  }
  PutText(textbox, model.LinesArray(), model.SelectionStart);
}
```

Very nice—that simple change reduces duplication already. Still whining about the remaining duplication of the GetText() and PutText(), I mentioned that I thought delegates would handle the problem and that we'd probably have to subclass MenuItem to get it to work. Paul asked me to explain delegates to him. Like most of us, he had used them in forms, and like me, the concepts wouldn't all fit into his brain at the same time. So we babbled about delegates for a while.

Paul asked why I thought we'd have to subclass MenuItem, and I explained that we would want all the menu items to go to just one handler, and that if we did that, the handler would have to interrogate the menu to find out what method to call in the model. I had been holding off on removing that duplication, because building that subclass seemed like too big a bite and I couldn't see a smaller one.

Add Duplication to Reduce Duplication

As we talked, we felt we wanted to go forward with delegates, to understand them better and to see if we could improve this code. We decided to add some duplication to the KeyDownHandler that we would then try to eliminate. We refactored XMLKeyDownHandler this way:

```
public void XMLKeyDownHandler(object objSender, KeyEventArgs kea) {
  if (kea.KeyCode == Keys.Enter && kea.Modifiers == Keys.None) {
    GetText();
    model.Enter();
    PutText(textbox, model.LinesArray(), model.SelectionStart);
    kea.Handled = true;
  }
  else if (kea.KeyCode == Keys.Enter && kea.Modifiers == Keys.Shift) {
    GetText();
    model.InsertReturn();
    PutText(textbox, model.LinesArray(), model.SelectionStart);
    kea.Handled = true;
  }
}
```

This actually turns out to have been a much more elegant move than it might appear. We just put the duplication in, thinking that if we could get delegates to work, we would move the duplication up and out. As you'll see in a moment, that's what happened, but look what else happened.

The KeyDownHandler originally duplicated the GetText() and PutText() in time, rather than in space. Because we didn't have the methods inside the if statements, they were executed all the time. Now that they are inside the ifs, they are duplicated more in the text, but less often in time. You can think of that refactoring as removing duplication in the time domain and increasing it in the text domain. This might be a trick to remember.

Now, our intention was to remove the duplication by using a delegate, so we used the "fake it till you make it" approach and wrote this:

```
private void HandleKeyboard(KeyboardDelegate kb) {
  GetText();
  kb();
  PutText(textbox, model.LinesArray(), model.SelectionStart);
}
public void XMLKeyDownHandler(object objSender, KeyEventArgs kea) {
  if (kea.KeyCode == Keys.Enter && kea.Modifiers == Keys.None) {
    HandleKeyboard(enterDelegate);
    kea.Handled = true;
  }
  else if (kea.KeyCode == Keys.Enter && kea.Modifiers == Keys.Shift) {
    GetText();
    model.InsertReturn();
    PutText(textbox, model.LinesArray(), model.SelectionStart);
    kea.Handled = true;
  }
}
```

This code won't work, but we typed it in just to look at it. The idea should be clear. We would define a new method, HandleKeyboard, that takes a delegate named kb. That method does the GetText, dispatches the delegate, and does the PutText. The idea is that we would use that same HandleKeyboard method from the other branch of the if, thereby getting rid of the duplication. That would be cool.

We decided we didn't like the name of the delegate, so we immediately refactored our non-working code this way:

```
private void HandleKeyboard(KeyboardDelegate modelAction) {
  GetText();
  modelAction();
  PutText(textbox, model.LinesArray(), model.SelectionStart);
}
```

Now, normally, refactoring is a no-no on a red bar, and what we had here wouldn't even compile, but we were sketching code, not really trying to make anything work, and we felt that better names would help us better figure out what we were really trying to do. Working without any C# documentation, we fumbled our way through a definition of the delegate:

```
private delegate void KeyboardDelegate();
```

We tried to create the actual delegate:

```
private KeyboardDelegate enterDelegate = model.Enter;
```

We wrote a more reasonable syntax for defining the actual delegate:

```
private KeyboardDelegate enterDelegate = new KeyboardDelegate(model.Enter);
```

This makes sense. A delegate definition is basically a type or class, so you have to create a new instance to assign a concrete delegate. But this still didn't compile. Finally, we came to this combination. We defined the delegate type:

```
public delegate void KeyboardDelegate();
```

We defined a member variable of that type:

```
private KeyboardDelegate enterDelegate;
```

And we initialized the delegate, inside the Form's initialize() method:

```
private void initialize(TextModel model) {
  enterDelegate = new KeyboardDelegate(model.Enter);
  this.model = model;
  this.Text = "XML Notepad";
  insertSection = new MenuItem (
    "Insert &Section",
    new EventHandler(MenuInsertSection));
  insertPre = new MenuItem (
    "Insert &Pre",
    new EventHandler(MenuInsertPre));
  this.Menu = new MainMenu(new MenuItem[] {insertPre, insertSection} );
  ... and so on ...
  this.Name = "XMLNotepad";
}
```

It turns out this actually works! The KeyDown method calls HandleKeyboard(enterDelegate), the Get and Put are done, and the tests are green! We go ahead and add another delegate:

```
private KeyboardDelegate shiftEnterDelegate;

private void initialize(TextModel model) {
  enterDelegate = new KeyboardDelegate(model.Enter);
  shiftEnterDelegate = new KeyboardDelegate(model.InsertReturn);
  ...

public delegate void KeyboardDelegate();
private void HandleKeyboard(KeyboardDelegate modelAction) {
  GetText();
  modelAction();
  PutText(textbox, model.LinesArray(), model.SelectionStart);
}

public void XMLKeyDownHandler(object objSender, KeyEventArgs kea) {
  if (kea.KeyCode == Keys.Enter && kea.Modifiers == Keys.None) {
    HandleKeyboard(enterDelegate);
    kea.Handled = true;
```

```
  }
  else if (kea.KeyCode == Keys.Enter && kea.Modifiers == Keys.Shift) {
    HandleKeyboard(shiftEnterDelegate);
    kea.Handled = true;
  }
}
```

This also works. And look, we have removed the duplication in the Key-DownHandler!! By creating and using delegates, we've reduced the code duplication. We'll talk later about whether we have decreased overall complexity, but for now, we're not done yet. First, we decide to rename HandleKeyboard to CallModel, which we think is closer to what it does:

```
private void CallModel(KeyboardDelegate modelAction) {
  GetText();
  modelAction();
  PutText(textbox, model.LinesArray(), model.SelectionStart);
}
public void XMLKeyDownHandler(object objSender, KeyEventArgs kea) {
  if (kea.KeyCode == Keys.Enter && kea.Modifiers == Keys.None) {
    CallModel(enterDelegate);
    kea.Handled = true;
  }
  else if (kea.KeyCode == Keys.Enter && kea.Modifiers == Keys.Shift) {
    CallModel(shiftEnterDelegate);
    kea.Handled = true;
  }
}
```

We decide to go after one of the menu items. We begin with a new delegate:

```
private void initialize(TextModel model) {
  enterDelegate = new KeyboardDelegate(model.Enter);
  shiftEnterDelegate = new KeyboardDelegate(model.InsertReturn);
  insertSectionDelegate = new KeyboardDelegate(model.InsertSectionTags);
  this.model = model;
  ...
```

And we change the MenuHandler for the Insert Section menu. Here's the old:

```
void MenuInsertSection(object obj, EventArgs ea) {
  GetText();
  model.InsertSectionTags();
  PutText(textbox, model.LinesArray(), model.SelectionStart);
}
```

Here's the new:

```
void MenuInsertSection(object obj, EventArgs ea) {
  CallModel(insertSectionDelegate);
}
```

This works! So we do the other menu:

```
void MenuInsertPre(object obj, EventArgs ea) {
  CallModel(insertPreTagDelegate);
}
```

(These uses get the same installation as member variables, with inits in the initialize() method, of course.) In summary, the code looks like the following. We define the member variables:

```
private KeyboardDelegate enterDelegate;
private KeyboardDelegate shiftEnterDelegate;
private KeyboardDelegate insertSectionDelegate;
private KeyboardDelegate insertPreTagDelegate;
```

We initialize them:

```
private void initialize(TextModel model) {
  enterDelegate = new KeyboardDelegate(model.Enter);
  shiftEnterDelegate = new KeyboardDelegate(model.InsertReturn);
  insertSectionDelegate = new KeyboardDelegate(model.InsertSectionTags);
  insertPreTagDelegate = new KeyboardDelegate(model.InsertPreTag);
  this.model = model;
  this.Text = "XML Notepad";
  insertSection = new MenuItem (
    "Insert &Section",
    new EventHandler(MenuInsertSection));
  insertPre = new MenuItem (
    "Insert &Pre",
    new EventHandler(MenuInsertPre));
  ...
```

We use the delegates in the menu and keyboard handlers:

```
void MenuInsertSection(object obj, EventArgs ea) {
  CallModel(insertSectionDelegate);
}

void MenuInsertPre(object obj, EventArgs ea) {
  CallModel(insertPreTagDelegate);
}
public void XMLKeyPressHandler(object objSender, KeyPressEventArgs kea) {
  if ((int) kea.KeyChar == (int) Keys.Enter) {
    kea.Handled = true;
    // this code is here to avoid putting extra enters in the window.
    // if removed, when you hit enter, the new <P> line breaks in two:
    // <P>
    // |</P>  like that.
  }
}
```

```
public delegate void KeyboardDelegate();
private void CallModel(KeyboardDelegate modelAction) {
  GetText();
  modelAction();
  PutText(textbox, model.LinesArray(), model.SelectionStart);
}
```

And we have completely eliminated the duplicate calls to GetText() and PutText()! Now to do some cleanup. We rename KeyboardDelegate to ModelAction, which we think better represents what the delegate is. We extract the delegate inits to a separate method and do a little more renaming of variables, and here's the final code, highlighting the main points of interest:

```
using System;
using System.Drawing;
using System.Windows.Forms;
using NUnit.Framework;
using System.Collections;
using System.Text.RegularExpressions;
namespace Notepad
{
  class XMLNotepad : Form {
    public TestableTextBox textbox;
    private TextModel model;
    private MenuItem insertPre;
    private MenuItem insertSection;
    private ModelAction enterAction;
    private ModelAction shiftEnterAction;
    private ModelAction insertSectionAction;
    private ModelAction insertPreTagAction;
    public delegate void ModelAction();
    public MenuItem MenuForAccelerator(string accelerator) {
      if (accelerator == "&S") return insertSection;
      return insertPre;
    }
    static void Main(string[] args)
    {
      Application.Run(new XMLNotepad());
    }
    public XMLNotepad() {
      initialize(new TextModel());
    }
    public XMLNotepad(TextModel model) {
      initialize(model);
    }
    private void initialize(TextModel model) {
      InitializeDelegates(model);
      this.model = model;
```

```
          this.Text = "XML Notepad";
          insertSection = new MenuItem (
            "Insert &Section",
            new EventHandler(MenuInsertSection));
          insertPre = new MenuItem (
            "Insert &Pre",
            new EventHandler(MenuInsertPre));
          this.Menu = new MainMenu(new MenuItem[] {insertPre, insertSection} );
          this.textbox = new TestableTextBox();
          this.textbox.Parent = this;
          this.textbox.Dock = DockStyle.Fill;
          this.textbox.BorderStyle = BorderStyle.None;
          this.textbox.Multiline = true;
          this.textbox.ScrollBars = ScrollBars.Both;
          this.textbox.AcceptsTab = true;
          this.textbox.KeyDown += new KeyEventHandler(XMLKeyDownHandler);
          this.textbox.KeyPress += new KeyPressEventHandler(XMLKeyPressHandler);
          this.textbox.Visible = true;
          this.AutoScaleBaseSize = new System.Drawing.Size(5, 13);
          this.ClientSize = new System.Drawing.Size(292, 266);
          this.Controls.AddRange(new System.Windows.Forms.Control[]
            { this.textbox});
          this.Name = "XMLNotepad";
      }
      private void InitializeDelegates(TextModel model) {
        enterAction = new ModelAction(model.Enter);
        shiftEnterAction = new ModelAction(model.InsertReturn);
        insertSectionAction = new ModelAction(model.InsertSectionTags);
        insertPreTagAction = new ModelAction(model.InsertPreTag);
      }
      void MenuInsertSection(object obj, EventArgs ea) {
        CallModel(insertSectionAction);
      }
            void MenuInsertPre(object obj, EventArgs ea) {
        CallModel(insertPreTagAction);       }
      public void XMLKeyPressHandler(object objSender, KeyPressEventArgs kea) {
        if ((int) kea.KeyChar == (int) Keys.Enter) {
          kea.Handled = true;
          // this code is here to avoid putting extra enters in the window.
          // if removed, when you hit enter, the new <P> line breaks in two:
          // <P>
          // |</P>  like that.
        }
      }

      private void CallModel(ModelAction modelAction) {
        GetText();
        modelAction();
```

```
    PutText(textbox, model.LinesArray(), model.SelectionStart);      }
  public void XMLKeyDownHandler(object objSender, KeyEventArgs kea) {
    if (kea.KeyCode == Keys.Enter && kea.Modifiers == Keys.None) {
      CallModel(enterAction);
      kea.Handled = true;
    }
    else if (kea.KeyCode == Keys.Enter && kea.Modifiers == Keys.Shift) {
      CallModel(shiftEnterAction);
      kea.Handled = true;
    }
  }
  public void PutText(ITestTextBox textbox, string[] lines,
    int selectionStart) {
    // this is Feature Envy big time.
    textbox.Lines = lines;
    textbox.SelectionStart = selectionStart;
    textbox.ScrollToCaret();
  }
  private void GetText() {
    model.SetLines(textbox.Lines);
    model.SelectionStart = textbox.SelectionStart;
  }
  public void PutText() {
    PutText(textbox, model.LinesArray(), model.SelectionStart);
  }
  }
}
```

All that ugly duplication is gone! And Paul and I know a lot more about how to do delegates than we used to.

Summing Up

Let's ask a few questions in response to the action of this chapter:

Was This a Righteous Change?

Paul and I talked about whether this change is a good one. It certainly cleans up the code substantially from the original, removing a lot of duplication. However, to get rid of that duplication, we had to dig a bit deeper into our bag of tricks and use the delegate feature of C#. Arguing for the defense, Paul pointed out that the code is cleaner and that delegates are quite common in C#, so it's not unreasonable to expect people to know how to use them. Arguing for the prosecution, I pointed out that we didn't understand them until we did this, and as we were surely the two smartest programmers in the room at that moment— 10 P.M. in the back room at Grizzly Peak—it wasn't necessarily fair to expect others to know even more than we did. And I pointed out that of course we liked the solution because we wrote it.

Our conclusion: narrow call, but it is a righteous change. We find the code to be much shorter, and while there's a little mental bump to get over, adding new behavior will be a matter of rote now, duplicating the style of what's there.

Thinking about it this morning, I believe I'll do one more thing: I'll write a couple of tests testing delegates. The idea is that the test cases for the product should be a place where the programmers look to learn things, so we should write tests about things we're learning. I'll do that later, perhaps even today, and bring you up to date.

How Was the Pairing?

Paul said he had a good time and learned some good things, and he wondered how it had been for me. It was very good for me as well. This area had been troubling me for some time. The duplication was there and I couldn't see how to get rid of it. My e-mail advisers had been suggesting delegates for some time, but I foresaw that I was going to have to subclass MenuItem even to get started. (Did you notice that that never happened? We could perhaps eliminate multiple menu handlers if we did it, but it wasn't necessary to eliminate all the duplication we were worrying about. So much for up-front design.)

It was the process of showing Paul the code and making simple little improvements that helped us find a step that seemed safe enough, and small enough, to start with. Recall that we moved duplication *into* a method, then factored it out, in just one place, and made that one place work before moving on. After that, everything followed smoothly.

Even so, we went through a number of false starts trying to figure out who was the delegate, where to declare things, and so on. There were a number of points when, had I been alone, I would have given up and backed out my changes. With Paul pairing with me, his energy carried me over those low points, and he always had another idea for something to try. In short, had I tried this on my own, my memory of how it went, and my knowledge of myself, tells me that I would very likely have given up.

Pairing always makes me better, even when I can't get Paul and have to settle for Chet. Seriously: Pairing makes me better.

What's Left to Do?

Well, lots. One thing is something that I realized on the way back to my car. As you can see in the code, we defined the delegate inside the class. We had tried that in a couple of different ways, and until we found this combination, we kept getting compiler errors. The issue—as you well know if you're ahead of us in the delegate world—is that a delegate is basically a class, a data type. If you declare that type inside a class, it's really only accessible to that class (apparently even if it is defined public). If you want it accessible elsewhere, it needs to be defined at the class level, not inside a specific class.

It might be interesting to put the delegate setup in the MenuItem by making a separate class. As it is, there will be another tiny method for each menu item that we set up, plus the corresponding named delegate and its initializer. We could probably get all the menu items handled in one menu handler method, which would then dispatch back to the menu item to call the actual processing method. At this moment, I'm not sure whether that would be a good idea, but it might be a way to reduce the number of tiny methods. Reducing the number of methods is a priority, but it's the lowest priority on the "Simple Code" list, so I'll just leave it alone for now until the code calls out for it.

Scanning the code, which is now much easier to do, I see that odd PutText() method with no parameters. Is that some vestige? I'll remove it right now to find out. Visual Studio wasn't very helpful in finding the references to it. Turns out it's used in CustomerTest.cs. I think I'll rename it to CustomerTestPutText() and make it protected. Oops, I meant "internal." Protected means only that class and subclasses can access the method. I want other classes in the project to access it—that's "internal." Works fine.

```
internal void CustomerTestPutText() {
  PutText(textbox, model.LinesArray(), model.SelectionStart);
}
```

Why did I do it that way? Why didn't I just use a comment? Well, because comments are code's way of saying that it doesn't communicate well. So I decided to change the method to express the idea instead of adding a comment. You might well choose otherwise—your balance is up to you. Why didn't I leave it public? In this application, it doesn't matter, but I felt it expresses better that this method is specialized for one purpose and not intended for general use. I could be wrong.

Now look at the real PutText method. It has that comment about "feature envy." Feature envy, according to Martin Fowler, is present when a method seems more interested in another class than in its own. We certainly have that here: the PutText method is talking only to the TextBox. We could fix that rather easily, since we already have our own TextBox class. Should we, or shouldn't we? I'd really like to do it, because the change should be so simple. But on the other hand, we were here to do the delegates thing, my pair is long gone, and the code is clearly marked for improvement at some other time. I think I'll ship it as it is.

One Last Thing

In the previous chapter—Chapter 21, "Some Things We Ought to Do"—I was considering some pretty high-powered patterns to clean up the situation between the form and the model. Note that [sb]some very simple refactoring, aimed just at removing duplication, has done most of the job for us. It always seems to turn out that way. Removing duplication is your friend.

23

Planning Interlude

Like every product, this one has a deadline. We need to look at all the things we might do and decide which ones we will do. Here's how we do it.

How Do We Plan to Meet a Deadline

According to Extreme Programming, here's how we should plan all projects for the best results by the deadline:

1. Break down what has to be done into small chunks.

2. Estimate each chunk in terms of value to the project and time needed to do the chunk.

3. Choose chunks to do based on their estimated value and time.

4. Do some chunks.

5. Measure velocity of doing (chunks per unit time).

6. Use velocity to predict how much can really be done by the desired date.

7. Use experience to refine relative precision of estimates.

8. Rinse, repeat.

Managers and customers often resort to pressure or demands when faced with a deadline. As developers, we know that this doesn't work, and if they're paying attention, managers and customers know it too. Despite the pressure, they still don't get quite what they want, and if they put too much pressure on, the quality suffers. The tendency is to blame the developers, but frankly this is silly.

The right approach is to know how hard each feature is and to know how fast the team is at implementing features. Then, using this information, plus the value of each proposed feature, choose what to do next. Teams that use this approach find that they operate with much more knowledge of what's going to happen and with much less stress. They're able to produce code that actually works. And, perhaps most valuable, the team will begin to negotiate the feature content based on information rather than sound volume.

We're using this process *very informally* here in the book, to decide what we should do next for the XML Notepad.

Proposed Stories

We begin by making a list of all the stories (features) that we think we might want to put in the product. Each one is given an estimate of how long it will take to do. In this example, I've estimated in days, but you might prefer to estimate in arbitrary numbers. Just keep them proportional. (We'll come back to the estimating question, and to what I mean by "days," in the next section of this chapter.) Here are the stories, estimates, and descriptions:

- **File Operations: 2 days.** File save, load, save as.

- **File Operations, Recent Files: 1 day.** Recent Files feature, the usual numbered file names in the File menu.

- **WYSIWYG Display: 2 days.** Display the XProgramming.com Web page in a separate Microsoft Internet Explorer window, as editing proceeds. Might require "Validity Indicator."

- **Validity Indicator: 1 day.** Put an indicator on the Notepad page showing whether the XML contained is currently valid. Might be needed to decide when to push to the Internet Explorer window, or we might just let it be invalid.

- **Ordered List: 1 or 2 days.** Ability to insert an "Ordered List" tag and the list items it contains. When the user hits Enter in a list item, give him another one, similarly to how the paragraph tag now works. Will require some work on Enter to make it smarter. Whichever of ordered list and unordered list is done first will require 2 days; the other will require 1 day.

- **Unordered List: 1 or 2 days.** Unordered list. See Ordered List.

- **Proper Menus and Shortcuts: 2 days.** Menus are presently all just spread across the window. They will need to be put under top-level menu headings and such.

- **Copy Cut Paste: 2 days.** Standard Edit menu features.

- **Section Handling: 3 days.** System now handles one level of sections, in a rudimentary fashion. Needs extension to three levels, including proper nesting.

- **Change Enclosing Tag: 2 days.** Put the selection cursor somewhere. Pop up a window to change the enclosing tag to a new tag (for example, change a P tag to H2). Automatically figures out which tag is interesting, and does both ends.

- **Insert Tag Around Selection: 2 days.** Select some text. Pop up a window to enclose the selected text into a user-provided tag.

- **User-Defined Tags: 3 days.** Provide a way for users to define new tag insertions, together with their logic, if any. Sort of like macros. Shouldn't be a big deal, but it's not very defined right now.

- **Insert Starting XML: 1 day.** Start the window with valid XML in it.

- **Insert User-Defined Starting XML: 2 days.** Allow user to select the starting XML patch from a list of scraps stored somewhere.

- **Tabbing: 2 days:** When user presses Tab, cursor goes somewhere reasonable: end of current tag, beginning of next tag, etc.

- **Unit Testing Page: 4 days.** The XProgramming.com unit testing page is a table of unit testing applications made available by various programmers. We need an effective way to keep it up to date. One possibility is to use an XML file. It might even be desirable to use a simple ASP.NET or ADO.NET app to update it, perhaps even allowing contributors to update directly.

- **Book Reviews: 6 days.** The site includes book reviews. These are presently included in articles, one or more reviews per article. Would be nice if they were in some kind of table or other acessible format. They are fully-formatted articles, however, so this might be tricky. The feature needs to include an index of all book reviews and ideally some way of searching for them and viewing a sorted table of contents. Possible XML, or perhaps ADO.NET?

- **XSLT to HTML: 3 days.** Might be desirable to let the user specify an XSL file and then transform the XML to whatever kind of output the XSL specifies. The XProgramming site now runs on HTML, not XML converted on the fly, for compatibility with more browsers. Or, we might convert the whole system to run in ASP.NET, converting the XML behind the scenes. Seems like it would make it slow for no good reason, however.

- **Wiki/Weblog: 4 days.**   Might be desirable to implement a wiki and weblog capability by using ASP.NET. This would allow users to set up discussions on the site and allow the owner to publish short articles more quickly. Could get to be a fairly big app if we pushed it all the way. This estimate is for the simplest initial cases. (Paul Friedman and I actually did this experiment in a few hours, but the report isn't included in this book. The results will appear on my Web site in the future.)

What About These Estimates?

Extreme Programming teams estimate stories in a few different ways:

- **Arbitrary Units.**   Some teams estimate stories in arbitrary units, sometimes called "Gummi Bears." Take a small story, call it a 1. Estimate others proportionally to that small story.

- **Ideal Time.**   Some teams use ideal time, or "bar time." Bar time is the amount of time you would estimate after a few beers, when a programming buddy told you about some hard job he had to do. You might say, "If they'd leave me alone, I could do that in two days." Your ideal time estimate for that story is two days.

- **Elapsed Time.**   Some teams estimate in elapsed time, the expected time actually required to do the job. Note that the previous two estimates are not in elapsed time.

In the previous section, I estimated in "days" and I was thinking in terms of elapsed time. I was assuming that I would not be pairing. If I am able to pair, I'll go much faster. The usual experience is that two people pairing get more effective work done than if they worked alone. Since Chet and Paul are only on the project when they work with me, the effect of pairing with them is to make me go faster. They don't get paid any more for that; it's a good deal for me. Anyway, my figures above are elapsed days, without a pair. That's a conservative number, I hope, and just what I needed at this point.

Teams that use arbitrary or ideal units measure their "velocity," the rate at which they produce units. If the team completes stories adding up to 15 Gummi Bears in a week, their velocity is 15 GB per week, or 15. If the team completes stories adding up to 20 ideal days, their velocity is 20.

Velocity is used to predict how long it will really take to get things done. It's all very well for the team, or its management, to say that everything will be done by January 15th, but it's not likely to come true all by itself. The wise team measures how rapidly progress is really being made, and it reports that information to customers and management on a regular basis. Customers and management adjust what they ask for to get the best possible combination of features by the delivery date they have in mind. The XP "Iteration Planning" practice—see the "Extreme Programming" preliminary chapter at the front of this book—suggests that the team should schedule, in each development iteration, just as much work as they got done in the previous iteration.

Thus, what's important about story estimates is that they should be approximately proportional: a two should take twice as long as a one. If that's the case, we can use velocity to predict how long it will take to get any combination of stories finished. If there's a deadline ahead, some important date, the way to get the best product by that date is to have estimates for all the stories, to know velocity, and to pick the most important stories that the story estimates and the team's velocity indicate you are likely to get done.

It's all very well to rail and fuss over the need to get more done. The wise management move, however, is to manage: based on what the team is able to accomplish, choose the most important work to be done. Measure progress often, and update estimates often. This is how XP customers and managers steer their projects to success.

Our Plan

The purpose here is to show you how to produce a product, the XML Notepad, starting from nothing, delivering capability in small pieces, and winding up with a useful product and maintainable code. And to do this in a book that can be shipped on a suitable date. So I submitted the above stories to my editors and had them wear the customer hat this time. As a first cut, they selected the following ones for implementation:

- File Operations: 2 days

- File Operations, Recent Files: 1 day

- WYSIWYG Display: 2 days

- Validity Indicator: 1 day

- Ordered List: 1 or 2 days

- Unordered List: 1 or 2 days

- Proper Menus and Shortcuts: 2 days

- Copy Cut Paste: 2 days

- Section Handling: 3 days

- Change Enclosing Tag: 2 days

- Insert Tag Around Selection: 2 days

- User-Defined Tags: 3 days

- Tabbing: 2 days

Dropped were these:

- Insert Starting XML: 1 day

- Insert User-Defined Starting XML: 2 days

- Unit Testing Page: 4 days

- Book Reviews: 6 days

- XSLT to HTML: 3 days

- Wiki/Weblog: 4 days

Now, this list isn't final. First, the customers aren't aware yet that some kind of proper starting XML is required in order for WYSIWYG to work. I didn't mention that—in fact, I didn't think of it—when I proposed the story. So we'll probably have to do that one. On the other hand, it probably isn't really a day. I just didn't want to estimate any fractional days. Most likely I'll throw that feature in when the time comes, at a cost of a few lines of code and a few paragraphs in the relevant chapter. Watch for it.

Second, we don't know what my real velocity of implementation will be. I tried to make these estimates in elapsed time. But that's difficult, because I need to take into account my other responsibilities, including consulting time and the like. (That's how I make my living, after all.) The translation from my 2-day estimate to when a feature and its corresponding chapter content is done depends on how good my estimate is, but it also depends on when I get started and how many interruptions I have in the doing. Furthermore, each chapter already written is undergoing improvement and refinement for the book, and that's taking about a half day per chapter. All these things add up to say that we might be able to get more done, if my estimates were pessimistic, or less done, if they were optimistic or something happens to slow me down. Based on what really happens, we'll refine our choices for the book.

Let's emphasize that. Our real purpose here is to examine how to produce running tested software in a situation where we have a lot of learning to do, both about the application and about the environment in which we're working. So while I have a personal desire to see all those stories get done, they won't fit in the book. In fact, there are many additional articles already written, about topics that won't fit in the book. What will fit in the book, I'm sure, are as many lessons as I can find about how I work. Take the ones that work for you, and build them into your own approach.

One last thing: I'm going to miss some of those dropped stories. I am famously poor at updating my unit testing framework page that tells people what unit testing software is available. I had hoped that doing this story would make it easier to update and keep it more current. I hate to lose that feature. Similarly with book reviews. I'd like to do more, but they are very time-consuming to write and to set up on the Web site. I had hoped to improve that process. The XSLT to HTML story might have been interesting to readers of the book, because XSLT is an important technology in the XML family and you might like to know more about how to use it. And it would be valuable to me, because it would let me automate the Web site production all in Microsoft .NET instead of the current mix of .NET and Ruby. Finally, the Wiki/Weblog story would show how to build a wiki—a Web site that can be enhanced by anyone—and to merge it with a Web log. This story, fleshed out, would provide a very nice basis for a team to use to record and communicate their work as they go along.

So we'll miss having these features. Every project is like this: things one would very much like to do cannot be done because resources and time are finite. The advantage to the process we're describing here is that it makes the determination of what we will do and what we will defer, explicit and rather easy to do.

What we have done here is a version of the Extreme Programming "Release Plan." We look at all the stories, estimate them, and see which ones to do first—that is, before the project deadline. There is also an XP plan called the "Iteration Plan," where we plan the work for a week or so. I'm not using that planning step in creating this book, although in retrospect, it might have been helpful. Had I done iteration-level planning, it might have helped me to stay on track better and helped me to stay more motivated. Things have turned out reasonably well, but I could have been more effective and an Iteration Planning practice might have helped me.

We might revise this plan. We may remove more features, add some of these dropped ones back in, or add new ones altogether. Future chapters will show the results of executing the plan and of revising it if need be. The "Planning Game" is done for now. It's time to get back to programming.

24

File Save and Load

If this program is to be of any use to anyone, it needs to be able to save and load files. That shouldn't be too hard, except that this morning I haven't any idea about how we can do it. Let's find out what we know and what we can do.

First the Functionality

As requested by the customer, it's time to implement File menu items, Save and Load, for the XML Notepad. I'm tempted to start with the menu, but I know that if I do it may be hard to focus my attention on the tests that I should write for the functional part of the save and load. I know that once I get programming, it's hard to turn back to tests, and so my best bet is to start with tests.

A long time ago, I wrote a few file-oriented tests, just to learn how files work. I'll take a look at them now. Here's one that looks interesting:

```
[Test] public void SaveDialog() {
  string hello;
  string filename = GetFileName(false);
  using (StreamWriter writer = File.CreateText(filename)) {
    writer.Write("hello");
  }
  using (StreamReader reader = File.OpenText(filename)) {
    hello = reader.ReadLine();
  }
  AssertEquals("hello", hello);
}
private string GetFileName(bool showDialog) {
  if (! showDialog ) return "hello.txt";
  SaveFileDialog dialog = new SaveFileDialog();
  dialog.Filter = "txt files (*.txt)|*.txt|All files (*.*)|*.*"  ;
```

```
  dialog.FilterIndex = 2 ;
  dialog.RestoreDirectory = true ;
  if(dialog.ShowDialog() != DialogResult.OK)
    Assert("dialog failed", false);
  return dialog.FileName;
}
```

I remember writing this test. The GetFileName method accepts a Boolean so that when we run the tests, we don't get the dialog popping up all the time. I'll change it and run it with the dialog just to make sure it still works...and sure enough it pops up a standard Save As dialog. That will come in handy real soon. And the code for writing the file should be good for saving as well.

Examining the tests for TextModel, I find this small test:

```
[Test] public void WriteStream() {
  model.SetLines (new String[] { "<P></P>"});
  StringWriter w = new StringWriter();
  model.Save(w);
  AssertEquals("<P></P>\r\n", w.ToString());
}
```

That was written a long time ago to test saving as well. The corresponding code in the model Save() method is

```
public void Save(TextWriter w) {
  foreach (string line in lines )
    w.WriteLine(line);
}
```

That's good news. We know how to bring up a Save As dialog, and we know how to save the text.

> **Lesson** Let's reflect a moment on what's going on here. I haven't worked for a while on the program, and it has been a very long time since I did any file I/O. You're probably way ahead of me on file I/O, but the principle here applies in any case. If we develop the habit of recording all the little experiments we do as tests, we can refer back to them later. Even simple ones like the Save() method here can give us a start later when we need it. If an experiment is worth doing, it's probably worth recording its result, and the best way I know is to record it as a test. When we need to refresh our memory on how something works or on something we learned in the past and have now forgotten, we can find the tests that will get us going again. That's what happened here, and I'm ready to start moving forward.

Let's write another, somewhat stronger, test of saving and test load at the same time.

```
[Test] public void WriteAndReadFile() {
}
```

The name says what I have in mind. I want to write a file and read it back in to be sure everything is the same. I'm not sure how to proceed—it has been over a week since I have worked on the program—so I'm going to program by intention:

```
[Test] public void WriteAndReadFile() {
  ClearModel();
  VerifyClear();
  GiveModelContents();
  VerifyContents();
  SaveModelToFile();
  ClearModel();
  VerifyClear();
  LoadModelFromFile();
  VerifyContents();
}
```

This code, expressing intention in a kind of "top-down" style, amounts to a plan: Clear the model, make sure it is clear, give it some contents, and make sure they are there. Save the model, clear it, be sure it is clear, and then load it and be sure we got the contents back. I find that things usually go well for me when I express my intention in the code this way, although, as you've seen, I don't always remember to do it. Sometimes we just know what code we want to write, and my habit—frankly, it's not the best habit to have—is to write it. Then I usually have the time and inclination to make it look more expressive. A far better habit would be to start with expressiveness, even when I know what the detailed code should look like. I'll try to remember that. Here, however, I don't know what the detailed code will look like but I'm about to write it to find out. Here goes with the easy ones, ClearModel() and VerifyClear(). I found this test, which looks a lot like ClearModel:

```
[Test] public void TestNoLines() {
  model.SetLines(new String[0]);
  AssertEquals(0, model.Lines.Count);
}
```

That suggests an implementation for ClearModel(), and while I'm at it I'll use it in this test. The easy way to do that is the refactoring "Extract Method." I'll use the refactoring menu, to give me this:

```
[Test] public void TestNoLines() {
  ClearModel();
```

```
    AssertEquals(0, model.Lines.Count);
}
private void ClearModel() {
  model.SetLines(new String[0]);
}
```

That's pretty good. What about VerifyClear()? Well, that other line in Test-NoLines looks like just the thing. We'll extract that also and then run the tests. I'm taking a chance here in not running the tests after the first change, but it seems like a pretty simple refactoring, and since I used the tool to do it, I'm confident. Let's see what happens with this next Extract Method:

```
[Test] public void TestNoLines() {
  ClearModel();
  VerifyClear();
}
private void VerifyClear() {
  AssertEquals(0, model.Lines.Count);
}
```

That looks good. I want to test now, but I know that the new test shown here won't compile with those missing methods. I'll comment them out and then test:

```
    [Test] public void WriteAndReadFile() {
      ClearModel();
      VerifyClear();
//      GiveModelContents();
//      VerifyContents();
//      SaveModelToFile();
      ClearModel();
      VerifyClear();
//      LoadModelFromFile();
//      VerifyContents();
    }
```

No surprises, everything works. Now let's do GiveModelContents and VerifyContents. I bet I can find a test to extract those ideas from. Sure enough, here's something good:

```
[Test] public void TestNoProcessing() {
  model.SetLines(new String[3] { "hi", "there", "chet"});
  AssertEquals(3, model.Lines.Count);
}
```

My plan will be to extract this code into the two methods I need and to beef up the second one to have more asserts in it. Two extracts later I have this:

```
[Test] public void TestNoProcessing() {
  GiveModelContents();
  VerifyContents();
}
private void VerifyContents() {
  AssertEquals(3, model.Lines.Count);
}
private void GiveModelContents() {
  model.SetLines(new String[3] { "hi", "there", "chet"});
}
```

I'll uncomment some of the new test lines and then run the tests. Then I'll enhance the VerifyContents():

```
    [Test] public void WriteAndReadFile() {
      ClearModel();
      VerifyClear();
      GiveModelContents();
      VerifyContents();
//      SaveModelToFile();
      ClearModel();
      VerifyClear();
//      LoadModelFromFile();
//      VerifyContents();
    }
```

Again, the tests run. Let's improve VerifyContents just a bit:

```
private void VerifyContents() {
  AssertEquals(3, model.Lines.Count);
  AssertEquals("hi", model.Lines[0]);
  AssertEquals("there", model.Lines[1]);
  AssertEquals("chet", model.Lines[2]);
}
```

That's not much different, and it was certainly easy to do, but it will give more confidence when the save and load take place. So far this has all been easy, but now I'll have to do a little work. SaveModelToFile() is next, and we can steal that from the two tests at the beginning of this chapter. It goes like this:

```
public void SaveModelToFile() {
  using (StreamWriter writer = File.CreateText("savedmodel.xml")) {
    model.Save(writer);
  }
}
```

I expect this to work, so I'll comment out the SaveModelToFile() line in the test to see what happens. The test runs. I can't resist looking at the file to see what it looks like, and it looks good. It isn't legal XML, of course, but I'm not concerned about that in these tests. Now let's see if we can read the file back in, something like this:

```
public void LoadModelFromFile() {
  String line;
  ArrayList lines = new ArrayList();
  using (StreamReader reader = File.OpenText("savedmodel.xml")) {
    while((line = reader.ReadLine()) != null) {
      lines.Add(line);
    }
  }
  model.Lines = lines;
}
```

That compiles, and the tests run (with the new test fully uncommented, of course). The model is correctly saving itself to the file, but the load is taking place in our code, not in the model. Let's put a Load method in the TextModel, analogous to the Save, and modify the test to use it. In TestTextModel:

```
public void LoadModelFromFile() {
  using (StreamReader reader = File.OpenText("savedmodel.xml")) {
    model.Load(reader);
  }
}
```

And in TextModel itself:

```
public void Load(TextReader r) {
  String line;
  lines = new ArrayList();
  while((line = r.ReadLine()) != null) {
    lines.Add(line);
  }
}
```

It was actually a bit easier in TextModel: I just cleared the lines ArrayList and added directly to it. We now have Save and Load working in TextModel, and we can go ahead and create the menu items to exercise them. We know we should start with a test—maybe even an acceptance test—but honestly I'm not sure how to do that. This is a good stopping point. Let's summarize and take a break.

Lesson   So far this has gone very smoothly, especially since I haven't looked at any of this code for so long. I attribute that success to these things:

First, we began by reviewing old tests and the code they referenced. That refreshed our minds on how to do file I/O in general, and it reminded us what the TextModel already knew about saving. Frankly, I had forgotten that TextModel knew anything at all about I/O, and I suspect that you didn't know either.

Second, we began with a test and coded it by intention: clear and verify the model, give it contents and verify, save it, clear and verify, load and verify. We got a nice simple test, yet it makes us absolutely sure that the save and load are working.

Third, we moved in small steps. This enabled us to make essentially no mistakes. The only mistakes made were typos like missing parentheses that weren't even worth mentioning in the text. They took a moment to correct and didn't slow us down a bit.

Review tests, express intention, small steps. It's working so far.

Lesson   I believe this is the first place where I have used the "using" statement in this book. As I mentioned, I had done some work with files in another context and brought the code over. It was in that other context that I learned about "using" and I really like it. The reason is that it avoids one of my most common errors: forgetting to close the file.

I guess I have a general problem in remembering things that have to be done at the end, and I've developed habits to help me. The using statement helps me close files and do other disposal. When I type an open curly brace, I habitually type the closing one right away, and then go back and edit in the middle so that I won't forget it later. And in Smalltalk, which doesn't complain if you forget a return statement from a function, I developed the habit of using a method "template" that included a return statement to remind me.

If you have some mistakes that you make frequently, see if you can think of simple habits to form that will protect you from yourself.

> **Lesson**   You may be wondering why I couldn't figure out how to do a customer test. Surely it's just a matter of putting *save and *load commands into the interpreter? As you'll see below, that's what finally happened. But I couldn't see that here. Perhaps I was tired. I'm glad I stopped for a break—I might have really messed something up!

Now the Menus

It seems like the basic save and load capability is there now, although I foresee a need to make one change. Right now, the save and load work on an open file. I'm not sure, but it seems to me that we might want to pass the file name to the TextModel and open the file there. We'll see what the code tells us, as we put the menus in.

Over a quick lunch, I read the menu section in Petzold's *Programming Microsoft Windows with C#* (Microsoft Press, 2001), and my plan is to lift his code almost directly.

> **Lesson**   Is this cheating? Well, in a poorly designed ninth grade C# programming class, it might be cheating. In the world of professional software development, it's called learning, research, and reuse. I'm quite serious. There's plenty of new material to figure out in every application we're called upon to write. Where we can find code to borrow, we're wise to do so.
>
> However, there are good ways to borrow and ways that are not so good. We shouldn't allow multiple copies of the same code, or almost the same code, to exist in our own code base. So if I'm going to borrow Petzold's code, I should be sure that I put it in only one place. If I were to need it multiple times, i should turn it into an object or a method and use it multiple times rather than copy it.
>
> In addition, when we copy and paste code, we don't understand it as well as if we type it in ourselves. Also, we understand code that we type in from another source less well than we understand code that we write based on a model or otherwise make our own. As with all things, it's a matter of judgment. Here I chose to follow Petzold's lead, and I gave him the credit so that you'll know where the idea and code came from.

A more serious challenge is the Customer Acceptance Test for this feature. Having made such a big deal about it earlier on, I am honor-bound to write some customer tests. However, I'm not honor-bound to do it first, and in fact my plan is to implement the feature and then test it. We'll see if this gets me in trouble. I'm fairly confident that we'll have no trouble. Here is our menu-related code now, from the XMLNotepad class:

```
class XMLNotepad : Form {
  public TestableTextBox textbox;
  private TextModel model;
  private MenuItem insertPre;
  private MenuItem insertSection;
  ...
  public XMLNotepad() {
    initialize(new TextModel());
  }
  public XMLNotepad(TextModel model) {
    initialize(model);
  }
  private void initialize(TextModel model) {
    InitializeDelegates(model);
    this.model = model;
    this.Text = "XML Notepad";
    insertSection = new MenuItem (
      "Insert &Section",
      new EventHandler(MenuInsertSection));
    insertPre = new MenuItem (
      "Insert &Pre",
      new EventHandler(MenuInsertPre));
    this.Menu = new MainMenu(new MenuItem[] {insertPre, insertSection} );
    this.textbox = new TestableTextBox();
    ...
```

Here, based on Petzold's example but organized to fit into our program, is our first cut at the menuing code. As soon as we get one item typed in, let's compile to check for errors. Here's what we start with:

```
private void initialize(TextModel model) {
  InitializeDelegates(model);
  this.model = model;
  this.Text = "XML Notepad";
  MenuItem fileMenu = new MenuItem("&File");
  MenuItem newFile = new MenuItem("&New");
  newFile.Click += new EventHandler(MenuFileNewOnClick);
  newFile.Shortcut = Shortcut.CtrlN;
  fileMenu.MenuItems.Add(newFile);
  insertSection = new MenuItem (
```

```
    "Insert &Section",
    new EventHandler(MenuInsertSection));
  insertPre = new MenuItem (
    "Insert &Pre",
    new EventHandler(MenuInsertPre));
  this.Menu = new MainMenu(new MenuItem[] {fileMenu, insertPre,
    insertSection} );
  this.textbox = new TestableTextBox();
```

This compiles, except for the missing MenuFileNewOnClick event handler. I'll add that and test the code manually:

```
void MenuFileNewOnClick(object obj, EventArgs ea) {
}
```

This compiles, and when we run it, we get our familiar notepad with the new menu just as expected. Of course, it doesn't do anything, but we didn't expect it to. Let's add some more menu items and then hook them up.

```
private void initialize(TextModel model) {
  InitializeDelegates(model);
  this.model = model;
  this.Text = "XML Notepad";
  MenuItem fileMenu = new MenuItem("&File");
  MenuItem newFile = new MenuItem("&New");
  newFile.Click += new EventHandler(MenuFileNewOnClick);
  newFile.Shortcut = Shortcut.CtrlN;
  fileMenu.MenuItems.Add(newFile);
  MenuItem openFile = new MenuItem("&Open...");
  openFile.Click += new EventHandler(MenuFileOpenOnClick);
  openFile.Shortcut = Shortcut.CtrlO;        fileMenu.MenuItems.Add(openFile);
  MenuItem saveFile = new MenuItem("&Save");
  saveFile.Click += new EventHandler(MenuFileSaveOnClick);
  saveFile.Shortcut = Shortcut.CtrlS;        fileMenu.MenuItems.Add(saveFile);
  MenuItem saveAsFile = new MenuItem("Save &As...");
  saveAsFile.Click += new EventHandler(MenuFileSaveAsOnClick);
  fileMenu.MenuItems.Add(saveAsFile);
  insertSection = new MenuItem (
    "Insert &Section",
    new EventHandler(MenuInsertSection));
  insertPre = new MenuItem (
    "Insert &Pre",
    new EventHandler(MenuInsertPre));
  this.Menu = new MainMenu(new MenuItem[] {fileMenu, insertPre,
    insertSection} );
  ...
void MenuFileNewOnClick(object obj, EventArgs ea) {
}
void MenuFileOpenOnClick(object obj, EventArgs ea) {
```

```
}
void MenuFileSaveOnClick(object obj, EventArgs ea) {
}
void MenuFileSaveAsOnClick(object obj, EventArgs ea) {
}
```

This compiles, runs, and gives a File menu that looks right and does nothing. Things are going well so far. Let's try to make it work. We need a little "think time" first. The program needs to remember the name of the file that it has open, and the Save command should save on that file without comment if the name is known. The Open command should set that name, as should the Save As. If the name is not known, Save should do a Save As. In Save As, we should probably handle a file name that already exists, with a confirmation that we want to write over it. New should clear the name. The customer might ask us to put the file name in the top bar of the window, but unless it's really easy we'll leave that out, because we try always to let the customer decide how to spend our time.

I'm thinking we'll have a member variable fileName to hold the string file name. Load will set it, as will Save As, which will then call Save. Save will just use the file name. New will clear it. And, of course, all these functions will also have to do things to the TextBox and the model. I think I'll start with Save As, because that way I'll have a file to Open. Any one of them would be as good as any other, so I just decided to do Save As even though that will force me to write Save as well. That should be OK. Here goes. I'll start by copying the file dialog code from that earlier test:

```
void MenuFileSaveAsOnClick(object obj, EventArgs ea) {
  SaveFileDialog dialog = new SaveFileDialog();
  dialog.Filter = "xml files (*.xml)|*.xml|All files (*.*)|*.*";
  dialog.FilterIndex = 2 ;
  dialog.RestoreDirectory = true ;
  if(dialog.ShowDialog() == DialogResult.OK) {
    fileName = dialog.FileName;
    SaveFile();
  }
  else {
    MessageBox.Show("File not saved", "XML Notepad");
  }
}
void SaveFile() {
  MessageBox.Show("File saved " + fileName, "XML Notepad");
}
```

This is enough to get the dialog open and enter the file name. The MessageBox in SaveFile() comes up with the correct file name, with the full path, all ready to go. Now I'll enhance SaveFile to open the file and save on it:

```
void SaveFile() {
  using ( StreamWriter writer = File.CreateText(fileName) ) {
    model.Save(writer);
  }
}
```

To test this manually, I typed these three lines into the XML Notepad:

```
<P>one</P>
<P>two</P>
<P>three</P>
```

I saved it to a file and then looked at the file. The result was this:

```
<P>one</P>
<P>two</P>
<P></P>
```

Not good. Clearly what has happened is that the TextModel wasn't updated at the time of the save. This gives us two problems. Naturally, we have to make it work, although we would have expected it to work already, like the other menu items do. There must be something different about how we've set up these items. The more important problem is this: the program has a defect in it when we weren't expecting one. Our process requires me first to write a test to demonstrate that this defect exists and then to fix the defect. I do hate when that happens, but it's good discipline and I know that if I don't do it, you'll all write me nasty e-mails. Let's look around and see what to do.

Show the Bug, Fix the Bug

Browsing around, I quickly see why the model wasn't updated. Remember the refactoring that Paul Friedman and I did at the Michigan Union, with the delegates? All the menu items like Insert Pre now work like this:

```
void MenuInsertPre(object obj, EventArgs ea) {
  CallModel(insertPreTagAction);
}

private void CallModel(ModelAction modelAction) {
  GetText();
  modelAction();
  PutText(textbox, model.LinesArray(), model.SelectionStart);
}
```

```
public delegate void ModelAction();

private void InitializeDelegates(TextModel model) {
  enterAction = new ModelAction(model.Enter);
  shiftEnterAction = new ModelAction(model.InsertReturn);
  insertSectionAction = new ModelAction(model.InsertSectionTags);
  insertPreTagAction = new ModelAction(model.InsertPreTag);
}
```

ModelAction is a delegate in XMLNotepad each of the menu items calls over to the model to get the action done, while the CallModel() method above makes sure that both sides are updated. We need to code our menu items similarly. Let's try it. I'm still living with manual testing here, but I feel it would derail my thought process to write the test. If I had you here with me pairing, maybe you would make me do the right thing. Let's see what happens.

(I'll say "I" for a while here to emphasize that I'm doing this without my pair. I'm sure you would have helped me do a better job here. I'm starting to regret that promise to show you the bad parts as well as the good.) I added a new ModelAction, named Save Action, initialized it in InitializeDelegates, and called it in the SaveAs method. The results look like this:

```
class XMLNotepad : Form {
  public TestableTextBox textbox;
  private TextModel model;
  private MenuItem insertPre;
  private MenuItem insertSection;
  private ModelAction enterAction;
  private ModelAction shiftEnterAction;
  private ModelAction insertSectionAction;
  private ModelAction insertPreTagAction;
  private ModelAction saveAction;
  private String fileName;
  ...
  private void InitializeDelegates(TextModel model) {
    enterAction = new ModelAction(model.Enter);
    shiftEnterAction = new ModelAction(model.InsertReturn);
    insertSectionAction = new ModelAction(model.InsertSectionTags);
    insertPreTagAction = new ModelAction(model.InsertPreTag);
    saveAction = new ModelAction(this.SaveFile);
  }


  void MenuFileSaveAsOnClick(object obj, EventArgs ea) {
    SaveFileDialog dialog = new SaveFileDialog();
    dialog.Filter = "xml files (*.xml)|*.xml|All files (*.*)|*.*";
    dialog.FilterIndex = 2 ;
```

```
    dialog.RestoreDirectory = true ;
    if(dialog.ShowDialog() == DialogResult.OK) {
      fileName = dialog.FileName;
      CallModel(saveAction);
    }
    else {
      MessageBox.Show("File not saved", "XML Notepad");
    }
  }
  void SaveFile() {
    using ( StreamWriter writer = File.CreateText(fileName) ) {
      model.Save(writer);
    }
  }
```

That makes it work, as I would expect. The CallModel is what does the trick; we always want to use CallModel() to keep the TextBox and the TextModel synchronized. It's back to working, but of course this feature is not tested. I'm kind of stressed out because of this unpleasant little surprise. If I try to program right now, I'm going to mess up. I'm going to take a break instead.

My Cunning Plan

After a little reflection on how to test this, I came to the conclusion that using the Customer Acceptance Tests is the best approach. The customer tests are the only ones that create a real, operable XML Notepad, so they are the best place to put the new tests for the file operations. As well, I know that I *must* have customer tests for this capability, so I'll save some duplicated effort. My plan is to do those tests by providing new customer commands to save and load the XML Notepad.

The choice now is whether to do the tests first and let them drive the necessary changes or to complete the changes and then test them. It's always better to do the tests first, and since I've been derelict in not doing them soon enough, let's do the tests now. We'll review the CustomerTest code first:

```
using System;
using System.IO;
using System.Windows.Forms;
using System.Collections;
using NUnit.Framework;
namespace Notepad
{
  [TestFixture] public class CustomerTest : Assertion {
    private TextModel model;
    private XMLNotepad form;
    [SetUp] public void CreateModel() {
```

```
      model = new TextModel();
      form = new XMLNotepad(model);
    }
    [Test] public void EmptyModel() {
      form.XMLKeyDownHandler((object) this, new KeyEventArgs(Keys.Enter));
      AssertEquals("<P>|</P>\r\n", model.TestText);
    }
    [Test] public void DirectMenu() {
      form.MenuForAccelerator("&P").PerformClick();
      AssertEquals("<pre>|</pre>\r\n", model.TestText);
    }


    [Test] public void StringInput() {
      String commands =
@"*input
some line
*end
*enter
*output
some line
<P>|</P>";
      InterpretCommands(commands, "");
    }
    [Test] public void FileInput() {
      InterpretFileInput(@"c:\data\csharp\notepad\fileInput.test");
    }
    [Test] public void TestAllFiles() {
      String[] testFiles = Directory.GetFiles(@"c:\data\csharp\notepad\",
        "*.test");
      foreach (String testFilename in testFiles) {
        InterpretFileInput(testFilename);
      }
    }
    private void InterpretFileInput(String fileName) {
      StreamReader stream = File.OpenText(fileName);
      String contents = stream.ReadToEnd();
      stream.Close();
      InterpretCommands(contents, fileName);
    }
    private void InterpretCommands(String commands, String message) {
      StringReader reader = new StringReader(commands);
      String line = reader.ReadLine();
      CreateModel();
      while ( line != null) {
        if ( line == "*enter")
          form.XMLKeyDownHandler((object) this, new KeyEventArgs(Keys.Enter));
        if ( line == "*shiftEnter")
          form.XMLKeyDownHandler((object) this,
            new KeyEventArgs(Keys.Enter | Keys.Shift));
```

```
        if ( line == "*altS")
          ExecuteMenu("&S");
        if ( line == "*altP")
          ExecuteMenu("&P");
        if (line == "*display")
          Console.WriteLine("display\r\n{0}\r\nend", model.TestText);
        if (line == "*output")
          CompareOutput(reader, message);
        if (line == "*input")
          SetInput(reader);
        line = reader.ReadLine();
      }
    }
    private void CompareOutput(StringReader reader, String message) {
      String expected = ExpectedOutput(reader);
      String result = model.TestText;
      if (expected != result) {
        Console.WriteLine(message);
        Console.WriteLine("*Expected");
        Console.WriteLine(expected);
        Console.WriteLine("*Result");
        Console.WriteLine(result);
      }
      AssertEquals(message, expected, model.TestText);
    }
    private String ExpectedOutput(StringReader reader) {
      return ReadToEnd(reader);
    }
    private String ReadToEnd(StringReader reader) {
      String result = "";
      String line = reader.ReadLine();
      while (line != null && line != "*end") {
        result += line;
        result += System.Environment.NewLine;
        line = reader.ReadLine();
      }
      return result;
    }
    private void SetInput(StringReader reader) {
      InputCommand input = new InputCommand(reader);
      model.Lines = input.CleanLines();
      model.SelectionStart = input.SelectionStart();
      form.CustomerTestPutText();
    }
    private void ExecuteMenu(string accelerator) {
      form.MenuForAccelerator(accelerator).PerformClick();
    }
  }
}
```

Our mission, and we have decided to accept it, is to add commands to the interpreter, implement them, and make them work. There's one special issue to deal with: I really don't want to pop up a file dialog in the middle of the tests, so we'll have to provide the file name somehow as part of the command. We'll see how that goes. The lines in boldface in the code just shown are the core of command interpretation. Let's add a loadfile and savefile command:

```
private void InterpretCommands(String commands, String message) {
  StringReader reader = new StringReader(commands);
  String line = reader.ReadLine();
  CreateModel();
  while ( line != null) {
    if ( line == "*enter")
      form.XMLKeyDownHandler((object) this, new KeyEventArgs(Keys.Enter));
    if ( line == "*shiftEnter")
      form.XMLKeyDownHandler((object) this,
        new KeyEventArgs(Keys.Enter | Keys.Shift));
    if ( line == "*altS")
      ExecuteMenu("&S");
    if ( line == "*altP")
      ExecuteMenu("&P");
    if (line == "*display")
      Console.WriteLine("display\r\n{0}\r\nend", model.TestText);
    if (line == "*output")
      CompareOutput(reader, message);
    if (line == "*input")
      SetInput(reader);
    if (line == "*loadfile")
      LoadFile();
    if (line == "*savefile")
      SaveFile();
    line = reader.ReadLine();
  }
}
private void SaveFile() {        form.SetFileName("customertestxmlfile.xml");
  ExecuteMenu("^S");
}
private void LoadFile() {        form.SetFileName("customertestxmlfile.xml");
  ExecuteMenu("^O");
}
```

The idea so far is that the *loadfile command and the *savefile command will privately set the file name in the form to the file name shown above and then execute the menu associated with Ctrl+O or Ctrl+S, respectively. I'm going to make the hat character "^" mean "control," just as "&" now means "alt."

Making this test run will be a bit tricky, I think, but it should all come down to getting access to the right menu item and executing its code. I happen to remember that the MenuForAccelerator code that supports ExecuteMenu is quite weak right now—that will have to be improved a lot. This code doesn't compile because SetFileName() isn't defined. I'll implement it this way, in XML-Notepad:

```
internal void SetFileName(String name) {
  fileName = name;
}
```

The tests all run, so our next step is to write a customer test using these new commands and make it fail. Then we'll make it work. The first part should be easy:

```
*input
<P>uno</P>
<P>duo</P>
<P>tres</P>
*end
*savefile
*input
*end
*output
*end
*loadfile
*output
*enter
*output
<P>uno</P>
<P>duo</P>
<P>tres</P>
*end
```

In this test, we enter three lines and save them. Then we give the model new empty input and check that it's empty. Then we load the file back up and check that we get the same thing back. I'll save that file and run the tests, expecting big trouble of some kind.

Well, I got big trouble, but I don't know what it means. I have an exception in the test, and the message says "TestAllFiles: '-2' is not a valid value for 'value'." Oh, OK, that's referring to the code that sets the selection. I didn't put the vertical bar anywhere in the input, so it couldn't set the cursor. I'll put it at the end of the last line:

```
*input
<P>uno</P>
<P>duo</P>
```

```
<P>tres</P>|
*end
*savefile
*input
*end
*end
*loadfile
*enter
<P>uno</P>
<P>duo</P>
<P>tres</P>|
*end
```

That didn't fix it. I'm going to have to resort to the debugger. I hate that, but I see no easier choice. I'm a little concerned that the defect isn't coming from where I think it is, even though it seems like it has to be. No, wait. I see it. The program can't deal with empty input. I'll have to put a line into the test in the middle:

```
*input
<P>uno</P>
<P>duo</P>
<P>tres|</P>
*end
*savefile
*input
<P>|<P>
*end
*output
<P>|<P>
*end
*loadfile
*output
*enter
*output
<P>uno</P>
<P>duo</P>
<P>tres|</P>
*end
```

That gives me an error that's more like what I expect:

```
c:\data\csharp\notepad\saveload.test
*Expected
*enter
*output
```

```
<P>uno</P>
<P>duo</P>
<P>tres|</P>
*Result
<P><P>
<pre>|</pre>
```

I'm a little surprised there were no exceptions. What happened, however, was due to the weak code in MenuForAccelerator. We'll fix that and see what happens next. Here's the old code:

```
public MenuItem MenuForAccelerator(string accelerator) {
  if (accelerator == "&S") return insertSection;
  return insertPre;
}
```

This isn't quite up to our needs. It understands &S only and then assumes that if it isn't S, it's P. We need to make that a lot stronger. Fortunately, we can do that pretty readily:

```
public MenuItem MenuForAccelerator(string accelerator) {
  if (accelerator == "&S") return insertSection;
  if (accelerator == "&P") return insertPre;
  if (accelerator == "^O") return openFile;
  if (accelerator == "^S") return saveFile;
  return null;
}
```

I've changed it to return null if it doesn't find the menu sought. That should make any further mistaken tests fail in a more obvious way. This code won't compile, however, until I make openFile and saveFile member variables. Recall that they were temporary variables in the form initialization up until now. I'll promote them and change the init:

```
class XMLNotepad : Form {
  public TestableTextBox textbox;
  private TextModel model;
  private MenuItem insertPre;
  private MenuItem insertSection;
  private MenuItem openFile;
  private MenuItem saveFile;
  private ModelAction enterAction;
  private ModelAction shiftEnterAction;
  private ModelAction insertSectionAction;
  private ModelAction insertPreTagAction;
  private ModelAction saveAction;
  private String fileName;
  public delegate void ModelAction();
  public MenuItem MenuForAccelerator(string accelerator) {
```

```
      if (accelerator == "&S") return insertSection;
      if (accelerator == "&P") return insertPre;
      if (accelerator == "^O") return openFile;
      if (accelerator == "^S") return saveFile;
      return null;
   }
  private void initialize(TextModel model) {
     InitializeDelegates(model);
     this.model = model;
     this.Text = "XML Notepad";
     MenuItem fileMenu = new MenuItem("&File");
     MenuItem newFile = new MenuItem("&New");
     newFile.Click += new EventHandler(MenuFileNewOnClick);
     newFile.Shortcut = Shortcut.CtrlN;
     fileMenu.MenuItems.Add(newFile);
     openFile = new MenuItem("&Open...");
     openFile.Click += new EventHandler(MenuFileOpenOnClick);
     openFile.Shortcut = Shortcut.CtrlO;
     fileMenu.MenuItems.Add(openFile);
     saveFile = new MenuItem("&Save");
     saveFile.Click += new EventHandler(MenuFileSaveOnClick);
     saveFile.Shortcut = Shortcut.CtrlS;
     fileMenu.MenuItems.Add(saveFile);
     MenuItem saveAsFile = new MenuItem("Save &As...");
     saveAsFile.Click += new EventHandler(MenuFileSaveAsOnClick);
     fileMenu.MenuItems.Add(saveAsFile);
     ...
```

I expect this to be close enough to get a new error, and it might even work. Let's find out. The error is

```
c:\data\csharp\notepad\saveload.test
*Expected
*enter
*output
<P>uno</P>
<P>duo</P>
<P>tres|</P>
*Result
<P>|<P>
```

What's this telling us? Well, first of all I don't see where that *enter is coming from. Oh—there's one in the test. Look at it:

```
*input
<P>uno</P>
<P>duo</P>
<P>tres|</P>
*end
*savefile
```

```
*input
<P>|<P>
*end
<P>|<P>
*end
*loadfile
*enter
<P>uno</P>
<P>duo</P>
<P>tres|</P>
*end
```

That's basically wrong. I'll remove that and try the test again:

```
*input
<P>uno</P>
<P>duo</P>
<P>tres|</P>
*end
*savefile
*input
<P>|<P>
*end
*output
<P>|<P>
*end
*loadfile
*output
<P>uno</P>
<P>duo</P>
<P>tres|</P>
*end
```

Now it says

```
c:\data\csharp\notepad\saveload.test
*Expected
<P>uno</P>
<P>duo</P>
<P>tres|</P>
*Result
<P>|<P>
```

It looks like the loadfile got completely the wrong thing, or else the file never got saved. I'll look for the file next. I don't see it anywhere. Now it's definitely time for the debugger. I'll set a breakpoint in the SaveFile method and run the tests. The breakpoint fires, and we find the right menu, saveFile. But when we do the PerformClick(), nothing happens; it just returns. What's up with that? Oh. That's not so mysterious—look at the code for that menu item:

```
void MenuFileSaveOnClick(object obj, EventArgs ea) {
}
```

It says to do nothing, and nothing happens. That's to be expected. Time for some reflection, however.

Lesson   Remember that I decided to write the test rather than complete the functionality of saving and loading. My thought was that I had already seen the need for the test and that the test would help me be sure things were right. However, going down the testing path caused me to lose my train of thought on the implementation for a moment. Thus my surprise.

Some people keep a note card by their side where they make notes about what they're up to, crossing things off when they're done, looking back at the card to see what to do next. Something like that might have saved me a moment's confusion, and I suspect that a pair programmer would have helped me as well.

The real problem, however, is just that this was too big a step. When I get confused in the middle of some operation, that's a good sign that it was too big a bite. We'll press on for now, but then let's remember to see what we could have done that was a bit smaller.

For now, we'll go ahead and implement the MenuFileSaveOnClick() method. I'm going to take a shortcut for now, knowing that the file name will be present. In the final implementation, we have to check whether we have a file name and run the Save As dialog if not. For now, this should do the job:

```
void MenuFileSaveOnClick(object obj, EventArgs ea) {
  CallModel(saveAction);
}
```

I'm surprised to find that that didn't work. Same message. Breakpoint again. The PerformClick() still doesn't do anything. I'm confused. A little stepping and a breakpoint inside the MenuFileSaveOnClick method tells me that it is executing and in fact it is saving correctly. I'm just guessing that you can't step into a PerformClick() method, possibly because they are triggering events. Anyway, the code is working so far, and it's time to make the load work also. This will be tricky. Load should unconditionally open a dialog. To make this test run correctly, I'm going to have to work around that. For now, I'll just short-circuit it like I did with the save:

```
class XMLNotepad : Form {
  public TestableTextBox textbox;
  private TextModel model;
  private MenuItem insertPre;
  private MenuItem insertSection;
  private MenuItem openFile;
  private MenuItem saveFile;
  private ModelAction enterAction;
  private ModelAction shiftEnterAction;
  private ModelAction insertSectionAction;
  private ModelAction insertPreTagAction;
  private ModelAction saveAction;
  private ModelAction loadAction;
  private String fileName;
  ...
  private void InitializeDelegates(TextModel model) {
    enterAction = new ModelAction(model.Enter);
    shiftEnterAction = new ModelAction(model.InsertReturn);
    insertSectionAction = new ModelAction(model.InsertSectionTags);
    insertPreTagAction = new ModelAction(model.InsertPreTag);
    saveAction = new ModelAction(this.SaveFile);
    loadAction = new ModelAction(this.LoadFile);
  }
  ...
  void LoadFile() {
    using ( StreamReader reader = File.OpenText(fileName) ) {
      model.Load(reader);
    }
  }
}
```

The test still fails, but in a happy way:

```
c:\data\csharp\notepad\saveload.test
*Expected
<P>uno</P>
<P>duo</P>
<P>tres|</P>
*Result
<P>|uno</P>
<P>duo</P>
<P>tres</P>
```

The only remaining problem is that the cursor isn't set correctly. We'll fix that and be done. My plan is to fix it by changing the test for now. I don't much care where the cursor goes, and I don't have customer input on it. So we'll change the test, stop for now, and see what happens next time. Here's the changed test, which passes:

```
*input
<P>uno</P>
<P>duo</P>
<P>tres|</P>
*end
*savefile
*input
<P>|<P>
*end
*output
<P>|<P>
*end
*loadfile
*output
<P>|uno</P>
<P>duo</P>
<P>tres</P>
*end
```

Finishing Up

I'm hoping that we can finish up the file operations, in rudimentary but reliable condition, in one more phase. We need to get the dialogs to open up, and I'm thinking that instead of providing the file name, or in addition to providing the file name, we need to set a private flag that suppresses the dialogs for testing purposes. We'll see how that goes. Now that the tests are running, I'll proceed by putting in the dialogs and see whether that implies changes to the tests. I believe it will.

I was thinking also about the cursor-setting trick we saw earlier. What is clearly happening is that the selection is left where it was before the file load. We should change the file load to set it explicitly, probably to zero. We'll keep that in mind as we go forward. Here's the new MenuFileOpenOnClick method:

```
void MenuFileOpenOnClick(object obj, EventArgs ea) {
  OpenFileDialog dialog = new OpenFileDialog();
  dialog.Filter = "xml files (*.xml)|*.xml|All files (*.*)|*.*";
  dialog.FilterIndex = 1;
  dialog.RestoreDirectory = true ;
  if(dialog.ShowDialog() == DialogResult.OK) {
    fileName = dialog.FileName;
    CallModel(loadAction);
  }
}
```

This just brings up an OpenFileDialog and opens the file if you hit OK. I set the FilterIndex to 1 (which is for some reason the first entry in the list) to make it default to .xml files. This code works in the XML Notepad and reads the file in correctly. However, I expect that the tests will not run correctly now. I expect them to open this dialog. If I give it the right file, however, it might still work. Let's run the tests and see. Yes, that's exactly what happens. If I give it customertestxmlfile.xml, the test runs, and if I give it some other file, it does not. Now to change things so that the dialog doesn't come up if we're testing. I'm planning to do it with a testing flag in the Form. A better idea might exist, but none comes to mind right now and this should work just fine. In CustomerTest.cs, we add these lines:

```
private void SaveFile() {
  form.SetFileName("customertestxmlfile.xml");
  form.SetNoFileDialog();
  ExecuteMenu("^S");
}
private void LoadFile() {
  form.SetFileName("customertestxmlfile.xml");
  form.SetNoFileDialog();
  ExecuteMenu("^O");
}
```

And we implement the method, with a private Boolean flag, and use the flag, as follows:

```
void MenuFileOpenOnClick(object obj, EventArgs ea) {
  if (displayDialog) {
    OpenFileDialog dialog = new OpenFileDialog();
    dialog.Filter = "xml files (*.xml)|*.xml|All files (*.*)|*.*";
    dialog.FilterIndex = 1;
    dialog.RestoreDirectory = true ;
    if(dialog.ShowDialog() == DialogResult.OK) {
      fileName = dialog.FileName;
      CallModel(loadAction);
    }
  }
  else {
    CallModel(loadAction);
  }
  displayDialog = true;
}

void MenuFileSaveAsOnClick(object obj, EventArgs ea) {
  if (displayDialog) {
    SaveFileDialog dialog = new SaveFileDialog();
    dialog.Filter = "xml files (*.xml)|*.xml|All files (*.*)|*.*";
```

```
    dialog.FilterIndex = 1;
    dialog.RestoreDirectory = true ;
    if(dialog.ShowDialog() == DialogResult.OK) {
      fileName = dialog.FileName;
      CallModel(saveAction);
    }
  }
  else {
    CallModel(saveAction);
  }
  displayDialog = true;
}
```

Note that I'm unconditionally setting the displayDialog flag back to true after each use of it. That's to make sure that the Form doesn't get stuck in test mode somehow. Also, I notice some duplication in this code, and I'm inclined to get rid of it if possible. Removing the duplicate CallModel from each of those methods seems unlikely to work well, as it would require a complex conditional, checking the displayDialog flag again and the DialogResult. Is there some way to combine the two methods entirely? It looks like there is. The code is all the same except for the initial dialog setup. Let's extract a method:

```
void MenuFileSaveAsOnClick(object obj, EventArgs ea) {
  if (displayDialog) {
    SaveFileDialog dialog = new SaveFileDialog();
    FileAction(dialog, saveAction);
  }
  else {
    CallModel(saveAction);
  }
  displayDialog = true;
}
private void FileAction(SaveFileDialog dialog, ModelAction action) {
  dialog.Filter = "xml files (*.xml)|*.xml|All files (*.*)|*.*";
  dialog.FilterIndex = 2 ;
  .RestoreDirectory = true ;
  if(dialog.ShowDialog() == DialogResult.OK) {
    fileName = dialog.FileName;
    CallModel(action);
  }
}
```

This works fine. Now we can change the other method similarly:

```
void MenuFileOpenOnClick(object obj, EventArgs ea) {
  if (displayDialog) {
    OpenFileDialog dialog = new OpenFileDialog();
    FileAction(dialog, loadAction);
```

```
  }
  else {
    CallModel(loadAction);
  }
  displayDialog = true;
}
```

That doesn't compile, because the FileAction method expects a SaveFile-Dialog. We'll use the common abstract superclass, FileDialog:

```
private void FileAction(FileDialog dialog, ModelAction action) {
  dialog.Filter = "xml files (*.xml)|*.xml|All files (*.*)|*.*";
  dialog.FilterIndex = 2 ;
  dialog.RestoreDirectory = true ;
  if(dialog.ShowDialog() == DialogResult.OK) {
    fileName = dialog.FileName;
    CallModel(action);
  }
}
```

That works, but the two methods, MenuFileSaveAsOnClick and MenuFile-OpenOnClick, still look too similar. Look at them side by side:

```
void MenuFileOpenOnClick(object obj, EventArgs ea) {
  if (displayDialog) {
    OpenFileDialog dialog = new OpenFileDialog();
    FileAction(dialog, loadAction);
  }
  else {
    CallModel(loadAction);
  }
  displayDialog = true;
}
void MenuFileSaveAsOnClick(object obj, EventArgs ea) {
  if (displayDialog) {
    SaveFileDialog dialog = new SaveFileDialog();
    FileAction(dialog, saveAction);
  }
  else {
    CallModel(saveAction);
  }
  displayDialog = true;
}
```

Let's extract all that as a method. We'll wind up creating the dialog unconditionally, but I'm not deeply concerned about that because in the normal running of the program, we always do anyway. Here's the extraction, in both places:

```
void MenuFileOpenOnClick(object obj, EventArgs ea) {
  FileOperation(new OpenFileDialog(), loadAction);
}
void MenuFileSaveAsOnClick(object obj, EventArgs ea) {
  FileOperation(new SaveFileDialog(), saveAction);
}
private void FileOperation(FileDialog dialog, ModelAction action) {
  if (displayDialog) {
    FileAction(dialog, action);
  }
  else {
    CallModel(action);
  }
  displayDialog = true;
}
private void FileAction(FileDialog dialog, ModelAction action) {
  dialog.Filter = "xml files (*.xml)|*.xml|All files (*.*)|*.*";
  dialog.FilterIndex = 2 ;
  dialog.RestoreDirectory = true ;
  if(dialog.ShowDialog() == DialogResult.OK) {
    fileName = dialog.FileName;
    CallModel(action);
  }
}
```

That's pretty good. I'm inclined to rename the FileAction method to DialogFileAction and then call it a night.

Lesson   One of my technical editors was particularly fond of the refactoring above, pointing out that it is rare to see code that talks to GUI components turn out to be well-factored. I share the observation that it's rare, and looking at it now, it did turn out rather nice. At the time I just went after it because I observed the duplication and it seemed like a good idea to hammer home the notion of eliminating duplication wherever we find it.

Removing duplication almost always produces very nice code, and it has the benefit of putting each decision in one place, for easy modification later. If, as sometimes happens, a later change undoes the convergence, so be it. It happens less often than you might think, and the code, even as changed, is usually better than what you started with.

Reflection

Lesson We'll take a look at all the code in a moment. It looks rather good for a few hours' work. It's not entirely robust, however. A wise programmer might enclose the file operations in try/catch to handle unexpected exceptions like running out of storage or other unexpected problems. And I would like to have more tests. In particular, we don't have a customer test for Save, which could leave a problem undetected later. However, I tested Save manually, and it works. Other refinements are also possible. The customer didn't ask for it, but there's probably a need for a dialog popping up with a save warning when the program terminates. I would make it clear to the customer that we did not plan to do it, and didn't do it, and let them schedule it when they want it.

We got in a little trouble by deferring a test. You'd think that I would learn my lesson about that: whenever I skimp on tests, I wind up with defects, or confusion, or both. I hope that you are smarter than I am and that you rely on tests more consistently.

And another force is acting on me. As I started working on this, my editor was pressuring me to get everything about the XML Notepad done by a particular deadline. My estimates showed that the deadline was unlikely, and I replied reasonably—as appears elsewhere in the book—that I would provide estimates for the work and would track my estimates and that our management challenge was to find the right balance between new features and revision of old chapters. I pointed out that we might decide that the date was wrong, so as to have the book be good enough, or that we might reduce scope to make the date.

Nonetheless, even after pointing out that I'm working as effectively as I know how and that the management mission is to manage scope for an ideal product by the desired date, I've been feeling pressure to go fast all day. The effects are subtle. Under too much pressure, I'll start making mistakes and getting into trouble. That didn't happen today. What did happen, I believe, is that this story and the code supporting it are not as "refined" as they would usually be. They're good enough to get by, but they don't feel sufficiently polished. Take a look at what we have wrought and see what you think. Then decide your own proper response to pressure.

The XML Notepad Form

```
using System;
using System.Drawing;
using System.IO;
using System.Windows.Forms;
using NUnit.Framework;
using System.Collections;
using System.Text.RegularExpressions;
namespace Notepad {
  class XMLNotepad : Form {
    public TestableTextBox textbox;
    private TextModel model;
    private MenuItem insertPre;
    private MenuItem insertSection;
    private MenuItem openFile;
    private MenuItem saveFile;
    private ModelAction enterAction;
    private ModelAction shiftEnterAction;
    private ModelAction insertSectionAction;
    private ModelAction insertPreTagAction;
    private ModelAction saveAction;
    private ModelAction loadAction;
    private String fileName;
    private Boolean displayDialog = true;
    public delegate void ModelAction();
    public MenuItem MenuForAccelerator(string accelerator) {
      if (accelerator == "&S") return insertSection;
      if (accelerator == "&P") return insertPre;
      if (accelerator == "^O") return openFile;
      if (accelerator == "^S") return saveFile;
      return null;
    }
    [STAThread]
    static void Main(string[] args) {
      Application.Run(new XMLNotepad());
    }
    public XMLNotepad() {
      initialize(new TextModel());
    }
    public XMLNotepad(TextModel model) {
      initialize(model);
    }
    private void initialize(TextModel model) {
      InitializeDelegates(model);
      this.model = model;
      this.Text = "XML Notepad";
      MenuItem fileMenu = new MenuItem("&File");
```

```
        MenuItem newFile = new MenuItem("&New");
        newFile.Click += new EventHandler(MenuFileNewOnClick);
        newFile.Shortcut = Shortcut.CtrlN;
        fileMenu.MenuItems.Add(newFile);
        openFile = new MenuItem("&Open...");
        openFile.Click += new EventHandler(MenuFileOpenOnClick);
        openFile.Shortcut = Shortcut.CtrlO;
        fileMenu.MenuItems.Add(openFile);
        saveFile = new MenuItem("&Save");
        saveFile.Click += new EventHandler(MenuFileSaveOnClick);
        saveFile.Shortcut = Shortcut.CtrlS;
        fileMenu.MenuItems.Add(saveFile);
        MenuItem saveAsFile = new MenuItem("Save &As...");
        saveAsFile.Click += new EventHandler(MenuFileSaveAsOnClick);
        fileMenu.MenuItems.Add(saveAsFile);
        insertSection = new MenuItem (
          "Insert &Section",
          new EventHandler(MenuInsertSection));
        insertPre = new MenuItem (
          "Insert &Pre",
          new EventHandler(MenuInsertPre));
        this.Menu = new MainMenu(new MenuItem[] {fileMenu, insertPre,
          insertSection} );
        this.textbox = new TestableTextBox();
        this.textbox.Parent = this;
        this.textbox.Dock = DockStyle.Fill;
        this.textbox.BorderStyle = BorderStyle.None;
        this.textbox.Multiline = true;
        this.textbox.ScrollBars = ScrollBars.Both;
        this.textbox.AcceptsTab = true;
        this.textbox.KeyDown += new KeyEventHandler(XMLKeyDownHandler);
        this.textbox.KeyPress += new KeyPressEventHandler(XMLKeyPressHandler);
        this.textbox.Visible = true;
        this.AutoScaleBaseSize = new System.Drawing.Size(5, 13);
        this.ClientSize = new System.Drawing.Size(292, 266);
        this.Controls.AddRange(new System.Windows.Forms.Control[] {
            this.textbox});
        this.Name = "XMLNotepad";
      }
    private void InitializeDelegates(TextModel model) {
      enterAction = new ModelAction(model.Enter);
      shiftEnterAction = new ModelAction(model.InsertReturn);
      insertSectionAction = new ModelAction(model.InsertSectionTags);
      insertPreTagAction = new ModelAction(model.InsertPreTag);
      saveAction = new ModelAction(this.SaveFile);
      loadAction = new ModelAction(this.LoadFile);
      }
    void MenuInsertSection(object obj, EventArgs ea) {
```

```
      CallModel(insertSectionAction);
}

void MenuInsertPre(object obj, EventArgs ea) {
  CallModel(insertPreTagAction);
}
void MenuFileNewOnClick(object obj, EventArgs ea) {
}
void MenuFileSaveOnClick(object obj, EventArgs ea) {
  CallModel(saveAction);
}
void MenuFileOpenOnClick(object obj, EventArgs ea) {
  FileOperation(new OpenFileDialog(), loadAction);
}
void MenuFileSaveAsOnClick(object obj, EventArgs ea) {
  FileOperation(new SaveFileDialog(), saveAction);
}
private void FileOperation(FileDialog dialog, ModelAction action) {
  if (displayDialog) {
    DialogFileAction(dialog, action);
  }
  else {
    CallModel(action);
  }
  displayDialog = true;
}
private void DialogFileAction(FileDialog dialog, ModelAction action) {
  dialog.Filter = "xml files (*.xml)|*.xml|All files (*.*)|*.*";
  dialog.FilterIndex = 2 ;
  dialog.RestoreDirectory = true ;
  if(dialog.ShowDialog() == DialogResult.OK) {
    fileName = dialog.FileName;
    CallModel(action);
  }
}
void SaveFile() {
  using ( StreamWriter writer = File.CreateText(fileName) ) {
    model.Save(writer);
  }
}
void LoadFile() {
  using ( StreamReader reader = File.OpenText(fileName) ) {
    model.Load(reader);
  }
}
public void XMLKeyPressHandler(object objSender, KeyPressEventArgs kea) {
  if ((int) kea.KeyChar == (int) Keys.Enter) {
    kea.Handled = true;
```

```
      // this code is here to avoid putting extra enters in the window.
      // if removed, when you hit enter, the new <P> line breaks in two:
      // <P>
      // |</P>  like that.
    }
  }

  private void CallModel(ModelAction modelAction) {
    GetText();
    modelAction();
    PutText(textbox, model.LinesArray(), model.SelectionStart);
  }
  public void XMLKeyDownHandler(object objSender, KeyEventArgs kea) {
    if (kea.KeyCode == Keys.Enter && kea.Modifiers == Keys.None) {
      CallModel(enterAction);
      kea.Handled = true;
    }
    else if (kea.KeyCode == Keys.Enter && kea.Modifiers == Keys.Shift) {
      CallModel(shiftEnterAction);
      kea.Handled = true;
    }
  }
  internal void PutText(ITestTextBox textbox, string[] lines,
    int selectionStart) {
    // this is Feature Envy big time.
    textbox.Lines = lines;
    textbox.SelectionStart = selectionStart;
    textbox.ScrollToCaret();
  }
  private void GetText() {
    model.SetLines(textbox.Lines);
    model.SelectionStart = textbox.SelectionStart;
  }
  internal void CustomerTestPutText() {
    PutText(textbox, model.LinesArray(), model.SelectionStart);
  }
  internal void SetFileName(String name) {
    fileName = name;
  }
  internal void SetNoFileDialog() {
    displayDialog = false;
  }
  }
}
```

25

Tagging Along

As we add some new tags, we notice that it's a complex and awkward task. Tempted to document how to do it, we improve the code instead. It looks like a win all around.

Setting Direction

One thing that happens on XP projects is that as time goes on, certain things start looking easy. I recall several visits with one client that make my point. One aspect of their project was that they had to compare a series of inputs from one source with a series from another. From each source, a number of values had to be picked up and summed, and the total had to be compared with the summed values from the other sources. But the key values in the two streams were not the same. The team had to create a hand-crafted query to make each comparison group.

When I first visited these folks, these comparison groups were estimated at some large number, perhaps five days for each one, because the first one they had done required five days. A few weeks later, I visited them, and in the planning meeting they were estimated at a day each. I asked why, and the programmer who was working on them told me that he was getting pretty good at it. A few weeks later, I visited them again for the planning meeting. The customer mentioned that she wanted to schedule as many of these comparisons as could be fit in after other things she needed. The programmer said, "Give me the rest of them. I'll do them all." We were all surprised and asked what happened. He said that he had gotten bored doing them manually and had created a tool to help him.

You probably remember similar situations, where at first something you needed to program was slow and time-consuming, but you got better and better at it. It's a common effect in most every project, even without building any specialized tools.

I think we're at a point like that here. My customer wants some stories about inserting new tags, and some of them are rather tricky. But I'm feeling as if the code and I both have a good grasp of how to do tags, so I'm signing up today, not for a specific number, but for as many as I can do. I'm promising to do at least the <UL> and <OL> tags, the ones for ordered lists. In Chapter 23, "Planning Interlude," I originally estimated them as requiring two days for the first one and one day for the second, but I have a good feeling about them right now and I think I can do them both, and maybe more, in one day's session. We'll see what happens.

> **Lesson**   The code we'll be looking at in this chapter will receive quite a bit of well-deserved refactoring. In a perfect world, the changes we'll make here might have been discovered sooner and done sooner. In my world, which is very imperfect, that doesn't always happen. It is tempting, when we run across some code that needs improving, to go ahead and improve it. In small doses, that's probably a good practice. I would be concerned, however, about starting an effort to clean up a lot of code on general principles. It's probably better to wait until the code needs changes and to clean it up as part of a customer-driven effort.

The Basic Approach

Lists involve at least two issues. We need to insert the starting XML, which will look like this:

```
<UL>
  <LI>|</LI>
</UL>
```

Then, every time the user types an Enter while inside the <LI> tags, we want to generate another pair of tags and set the cursor inside, like this:

```
<UL>
  <LI>I was just typing in here, and hit enter here.</LI>
  <LI>I got this item. One more enter, to get this:</LI>
  <LI>|</LI>
</UL>
```

The tag insertion should be easy. We'll just copy what we did for the <section> tag. Getting the <LI> elements to generate will be a bit more difficult: we'll have to make the code that generates new <P> elements be smarter.

We'll do one thing at a time. First we'll get the initial list structure in place, and then we'll work on generating the <LI> items. Let's begin by reviewing the current code. In XMLNotepad.cs, we have the menu-related code. These are the declarations:

```
class XMLNotepad : Form {
  public TestableTextBox textbox;
  private TextModel model;
  private MenuItem insertPre;
  private MenuItem insertSection;
  private MenuItem openFile;
  private MenuItem saveFile;
  private ModelAction enterAction;
  private ModelAction shiftEnterAction;
  private ModelAction insertSectionAction;
  private ModelAction insertPreTagAction;
  private ModelAction saveAction;
  private ModelAction loadAction;
  private String fileName;
  private Boolean displayDialog = true;
  public delegate void ModelAction();
  ...
```

The MenuItem variables hold the actual menu items for the operation. As we'll see in a moment, these are looked up by their accelerators to trigger the insertions. The ModelAction delegate is used to define the specific action to be taken for each item. Let's trace the insertSection code, since it's a lot like what we'll need. Here's the relevant code from the Form's creation and initialization:

```
class XMLNotepad : Form {
  public TestableTextBox textbox;
  private TextModel model;
  private MenuItem insertPre;
  private MenuItem insertSection;
  private MenuItem openFile;
  private MenuItem saveFile;
  private ModelAction enterAction;
  private ModelAction shiftEnterAction;
  private ModelAction insertSectionAction;
  private ModelAction insertPreTagAction;
  private ModelAction saveAction;
  private ModelAction loadAction;
  private String fileName;
  private Boolean displayDialog = true;
```

```
public delegate void ModelAction();
public XMLNotepad() {
  initialize(new TextModel());
}
public XMLNotepad(TextModel model) {
  initialize(model);
}
private void initialize(TextModel model) {
  InitializeDelegates(model);
  this.model = model;
  this.Text = "XML Notepad";
  ... (File menu not shown)
  insertSection = new MenuItem (
    "Insert &Section",
    new EventHandler(MenuInsertSection));
  insertPre = new MenuItem (
    "Insert &Pre",
    new EventHandler(MenuInsertPre));
  this.Menu = new MainMenu(new MenuItem[] {fileMenu, insertPre,
    insertSection} );
  this.textbox = new TestableTextBox();
  ...
```

What's important here is that we are creating the menu item and saving it. We'll of course need to create other menu items for our list elements. Let's remember to look for duplication in the menu code—we can already see some—and see if we can remove it. But for now we'll just make a note of that. Browsing on, let's look at how MenuInsertSection and the related code work:

```
void MenuInsertSection(object obj, EventArgs ea) {
  CallModel(insertSectionAction);
}

private void CallModel(ModelAction modelAction) {
  GetText();
  modelAction();
  PutText(textbox, model.LinesArray(), model.SelectionStart);
}

sprivate void InitializeDelegates(TextModel model) {
  enterAction = new ModelAction(model.Enter);
  shiftEnterAction = new ModelAction(model.InsertReturn);
  insertSectionAction = new ModelAction(model.InsertSectionTags);
  insertPreTagAction = new ModelAction(model.InsertPreTag);
  saveAction = new ModelAction(this.SaveFile);
  loadAction = new ModelAction(this.LoadFile);
}
```

This is a good refresher on how the delegates work. The menu click handler, MenuInsertSection, uses CallModel. CallModel takes care of updating the model with GetText(), performs the model action called for by its parameter, and then updates the TextBox with PutText().

We see that the model action for insert section is a method on the Text-Model, InsertSectionTags(). The code in TextModel looks like this:

```
class TextModel {
  private static string[] newParagraph = { "<P></P>" };
  private static string paragraphSkip = "<P>";
  private static string[] newSection = {"<sect1><title></title>","</sect1>" };
  private static string sectionSkip = "<sect1><title>";
  private static string[] newPre = { "<pre></pre>" };
  private static string preSkip = "<pre>";
  private static string[] emptyLine = { "" };
  private static string emptyLineSkip = "";
  private static object[] noArgs = {};
  private ArrayList lines;
  private int selectionStart;

  public void InsertSectionTags() {
    InsertTags(newSection, sectionSkip);
  }

  private void InsertTags(string[] tagsToInsert, string tagsPrecedingCursor) {
    int cursorLine = LineContainingCursor();
    lines.InsertRange(cursorLine+1, tagsToInsert);
    selectionStart = NewSelectionStart(cursorLine + 1, tagsPrecedingCursor);
  }
}
```

Here, the newSection string shows everything that needs to be inserted, and the sectionSkip string is the part to be skipped over. That's used to calculate the new cursor position. We should be able to add our menu item just like the others, almost by a copy and paste kind of process. We have a plan, so let's go forward.

Lesson: A Little Reflection

Whenever we start a new task, we review the code to get our bearings. There's nothing special about this: you probably do it yourself. It is, of course, possible to do this review from memory, but I find it useful to do it by looking explicitly at the code, for three reasons. First, my memory is fallible. Second, in a team project with team code ownership, the code might be different from the way it looked when I last saw it. Third...third...I forgot what I was going to say. I told you my memory was fallible. It's best to review the code.

As we put our plan together, we're speculating about what we will do. This is a plan, not a commitment. Our actual experience will guide us within this overall scheme. We'll try to do as little speculation in the code as possible: we'll put in what we need and nothing more. But we're always looking ahead in our mind, trying to see what is coming up.

To me, this process is a little like planning a short trip in the car. I plan to drive from my house out to Shehan Road, hang a left, go over to McGregor. There I'll turn right, up to M-36, then left to the drug store. I might vaguely reflect that if Shehan is blocked to the left, I'll go right and around Whitewood and up to M-36 that way. If McGregor right is blocked, I'll go left and over to Dexter-Pinckney Road and up. Mostly, I think I know what I'll do. If as I drive down Shehan, there's a kid on a bike, I'll slow way down. But I don't go super slowly if there is clear visibility: the limit on Shehan is 45. That car coming the other way might decide to pass the guy in front of him. I don't pull off the road because it might happen, but I'm ready in case it does happen.

The same is true with our programming plans. We have a general idea of where we will go, and we plan to stay alert and to modify that plan as things happen. Too much planning wastes time. Too little and we might go off in the wrong direction. How much planning you need depends on your own level of comfort. My own view is that a delicate sense of whether we're going in the right direction reduces the need for planning, and it's useful as well during the course of our work. Suppose we were great at planning but had no sense of direction. The first thing that goes wrong—and we all know something will go wrong—will completely throw us. As soon as we get off course, we're doomed. Suppose we were bad at planning but had a perfect sense of direction. We might get off course, but our knowledge of local roads and our certainty about the general direction of the area would let us adapt quickly to changing situations.

When we plan our trip to the drug store, we don't think much. We just "know" what we're going to do, and we trust our ability to adapt to get us there. In our code, we're trying to do the same thing. A quick review, some direction setting, and we're off.

Lesson: Copy and Paste?

One last thing, and an important one. We are planning to implement our new feature by copying and modifying the code that's already there. Isn't "copy and paste" programming the lowest form of software development? Doesn't it lead to code that contains duplication, lacks modularity, and causes ridicule to be heaped on our heads? Well, yes. Shouldn't we figure out how to build these new features without copy and paste? Shouldn't we figure out some general way to do this, something table-driven, or something that keeps all the menus in a database or uses Web Services to find out what to do? Well, no, I don't think so.

As I've mentioned, Extreme Programming folks have a "rule" called YAGNI: You Aren't Gonna Need It. When tempted to put in some code more general than what we have and what we need right now, we often say, "We're going to need this later; we might as well do it now." The YAGNI rule reminds us that maybe we're going to need it, but maybe we aren't. It expresses that idea in the typical extreme XP way: directly and with certainty. So the YAGNI principle tells us to wait.

Andy Hunt and Dave Thomas, the Pragmatic Programmers, give us lots of advice in their book, and in their columns, about techniques that are useful, and when to use them. Concerned that the YAGNI principle can be overused, in one of their columns they offer a new principle, DOGBITE: Do it Or Get Bitten In The End. The idea they offer is that if we put off generalizing too long, we'll wind up with bad code, code that is hard to modify and that will slow us down in the long run.

Andy and Dave are correct: If we do not generalize soon enough, we will get in trouble. And YAGNI is correct: If we generalize too soon, we will make mistakes and waste time. How do we decide?

(continued)

In my own practice, I choose to decide always in favor of YAGNI. However, I try to be very sensitive to code smells such as duplication, and I have a pretty good sense of direction, owing to my years of experience. So YAGNI works for me, in part because I tend to start in a decent direction, and I'm ready to notice the signs that things are going wrong. In this book, I'm trying to follow YAGNI exclusively, never putting in anything until I really need it. Part of the experiment in the book is to see whether this gets us in trouble.

In the case of our current stories, it's easy to see that we're going to get duplication, because the features are so much alike. I'm going to let the duplication occur if it wants to and then remove it. I believe that if I speculate about what is needed, my guess will be wrong and waste time. If I look at the duplication that I create, it should become more clear exactly what, if anything, needs to be done. Let's watch and see what happens.

The Actual Work

Enough warmup, let's code. We'll do...flip a coin...the UL tag, for Unordered List. The first challenge, of course, is whether to write a test. I find it easy to take the simple copy and paste approach. I feel resistance to writing a test, especially when, like this time, I know just what I need to do to make things work. At least I think I know. I want to code. But my readers are watching, so even though I don't have a pair to prod me this morning, let's at least look at some related tests in TestTextModel.cs to check whether we can borrow anything. We find two tests for the InsertSection code:

```
[Test] public void AltS() {
  model.Lines = new ArrayList(new String[0]);
  model.AltS();
  AssertEquals("<sect1><title></title>", model.Lines[0]);
  AssertEquals("</sect1>", model.Lines[1]);
  AssertEquals(14, model.SelectionStart);
}
[Test] public void AltSWithText() {
  model.SetLines (new String[1] {"<P></P>"});
  model.SelectionStart = 7;
  model.AltS();
  AssertEquals("<sect1><title></title>", model.Lines[1]);
  AssertEquals("</sect1>", model.Lines[2]);
  AssertEquals(23, model.SelectionStart);
}
```

The first one is pretty dull, but the second one is a bit more challenging. Let's be good and write a test for the LI tag. Here goes:

```
[Test] public void UnorderedList() {
  model.SetLines (new String[1] {"<P></P>"});
  model.SelectionStart = 3;
  model.InsertUnorderedList();
  AssertEquals("<UL>", model.Lines[1]);
  AssertEquals("<LI></LI>", model.Lines[2]);
  AssertEquals("</UL>", model.Lines[3]);
  AssertEquals(19, model.SelectionStart);
}
```

I'm not sure about the 19. I always have this problem counting out where the cursor will have to go. This may be calling for one of those tools I was talking about. One possibility is that instead of writing this test, I should work with a customer test instead. I'll have to write one anyway, pretty soon now. Or maybe there should be some blend of the customer test and programmer test technology. For now, our mission is to implement this feature. We'll make a note to do these other things. We'll compile the test, get the error on Insert-UnorderedList, and proceed from there. My first attempt looked like this. Bear with me on the ugly string for a moment, please:

```
class TextModel {
  private static string[] newParagraph = { "<P></P>" };
  private static string paragraphSkip = "<P>";
  private static string[] newSection = {"<sect1><title></title>","</sect1>" };
  private static string sectionSkip = "<sect1><title>";
  private static string[] newUnorderedList = {"<UL>","<LI></LI>","</UL>"};
  private static string unorderedListSkip = @"<UL><LI>>";
  private static string[] newPre = { "<pre></pre>" };
  private static string preSkip = "<pre>";
  ...
  public void InsertUnorderedList() {
    InsertTags(newUnorderedList, unorderedListSkip);
  }
```

It took me a moment to remember that the newUnorderedList should contain a string for each line to be inserted. The unorderedListSkip is a string used to calculate where the cursor goes. That code looks like this:

```
private void InsertTags(string[] tagsToInsert, string tagsPrecedingCursor) {
  int cursorLine = LineContainingCursor();
  lines.InsertRange(cursorLine+1, tagsToInsert);
  selectionStart = NewSelectionStart(cursorLine + 1, tagsPrecedingCursor);
}
private int NewSelectionStart(int cursorLine, string tags) {
  return FirstPositionOfLine(cursorLine) + tags.Length;
}
```

Note that the "tagsPrecedingCursor" variable is just checked for length, so I had to put the return in the tags. I could have used \r\n, but I have been trying to avoid that because I'm worried about systems where the return isn't set to Microsoft Windows style. I suspect that has been a waste of my time—a perfect example of YAGNI perhaps.

The test doesn't quite run. It returns 20, not 19. Let me recount the characters again: I'm still getting 19. I'll have to run the program. This is bad; the tests aren't helping me enough. That has to be fixed, but first let's get green. My first instinct is to run the program, but since we haven't implemented the new menu yet, we can't do that. One way to go is just to do the menu. Is there a quicker way? Well, how about a look at the code? Hah, got it? See the extra ">" in unorderedListSkip? That's the problem. I'll remove it and we should go green...and we do.

> **Lesson**   I'm going to take a short break in celebration, but that ugly string has some explaining to do. I'm sure it is implicated in my mistake. This part of the process wasn't as quick as it should have been, so it's time to improve my tools a bit, when I get back.

Improving the Platform

We're on a mission to build features, so we can't spend too much time. But we have a responsibility to produce clean code, and this isn't it. My suggestion is that we change the skip tags to be like the insert tags—an array. Then we'll make the count calculation a little stronger than just ".Length". Since I have all those tests, I'm just going to change all the skip tags to be arrays and then make the tests run. Here are the tag changes:

```
class TextModel {
    private static string[] newParagraph = { "<P></P>" };
    private static string[] paragraphSkip = { "<P>" };
    private static string[] newSection = {"<sect1><title></title>","</sect1>" };
    private static string[] sectionSkip = { "<sect1><title>" };
    private static string[] newUnorderedList = {"<UL>","<LI></LI>","</UL>"};
    private static string[] unorderedListSkip = { "<UL>", "LI" };
```

```
private static string[] newPre = { "<pre></pre>" };
private static string[] preSkip = { "<pre>" };
private static string[] emptyLine = { "" };
private static string[] emptyLineSkip = { "" };
...
```

This won't compile, of course. I'll compile to find out why, so I won't have to guess. Right, InsertTags expects a scalar and we want to give it an array:

```
private void InsertTags(string[] tagsToInsert, string tagsPrecedingCursor) {
    int cursorLine = LineContainingCursor();
    lines.InsertRange(cursorLine+1, tagsToInsert);
    selectionStart = NewSelectionStart(cursorLine + 1, tagsPrecedingCursor);
}
```

We can see that we'll have to change NewSelectionStart as well. It looks like this:

```
private int NewSelectionStart(int cursorLine, string tags) {
    return FirstPositionOfLine(cursorLine) + tags.Length;
}
```

I'll just change the parameter to be an array and posit a new method to return the length, like this:

```
private void InsertTags(string[] tagsToInsert, string[] tagsPrecedingCursor) {
    int cursorLine = LineContainingCursor();
    lines.InsertRange(cursorLine+1, tagsToInsert);
    selectionStart = NewSelectionStart(cursorLine + 1, tagsPrecedingCursor);
}
private int NewSelectionStart(int cursorLine, string[] tags) {
    return FirstPositionOfLine(cursorLine) + TotalTagLength(tags);
}
```

That compiles, as expected, with just the message about TotalTagLength not being defined.

Lesson   You might have written TotalTagLength before compiling, and on another day so might I. Today, I decided to let the compiler tell me to do it. I'm trying to use my brain as little as possible so that it won't wear out.

Now for TotalTagLength:

```
private int TotalTagLength(string[] tags) {
  int result = (tags.Length -1) * Environment.NewLine.Length;
  foreach (string tag in tags) {
    result += tag.Length;
  }
  return result;
}
```

Oddly, or perhaps not oddly, all the tests run except my new one. Now it's getting 17 instead of 19. What's up with that? Oh! Look at the unorderedListSkip definition earlier. I left the angle brackets off the LI. The line should be

```
private static string[] unorderedListSkip = { "<UL>", "<LI>" };
```

Tests all run again. The world is a bit better place. Shall we return to implementing, or should we do a little more cleanup? Let's scan the code a bit to decide. There is duplication in those insert and skip literals: similar strings appear in each. It's almost tempting to use the trick with the vertical bar that we used in the customer tests. I'm held back because I remember that part of our motivation for going to the arrays of strings was that we didn't like the way the multiline strings looked in the code. The multiple lines look OK in the test files, but in the source they would have to be left-justified and they would make the code hard to read.

I notice some duplication in these methods:

```
public void InsertParagraphTag() {
  InsertTags(newParagraph, paragraphSkip);
}

public void InsertPreTag() {
  InsertTags(newPre, preSkip);
}
public void InsertSectionTags() {
  InsertTags(newSection, sectionSkip);
}
public void InsertUnorderedList() {
  InsertTags(newUnorderedList, unorderedListSkip);
}
```

We have a number of methods that are each calling InsertTags, the only difference being the parameters. Each of those methods is called by a different menu action. We might do something more sophisticated there, but I think it's best not to. The Form should know as little as possible about how the model is going to do things, so moving knowledge of the model over to the Form wouldn't be a good idea. We might consider passing the menu item itself, or some parameter that was attached to the menu item, over to the TextModel to identify it. That doesn't seem quite right.

One possibility might be to have a single TextModel operation, pretend it's called TagInsertion for now, and pass it a parameter saying what kind of tags to insert, something like this:

```
private void InitializeDelegates(TextModel model) {
  enterAction = new ModelAction(model.Enter);
  shiftEnterAction = new ModelAction(model.InsertReturn);
  insertSectionAction = new ModelAction(model.TagInsertion("section");
  insertPreTagAction = new ModelAction(model.TagInsertion("pre");
  saveAction = new ModelAction(this.SaveFile);
  loadAction = new ModelAction(this.LoadFile);
}
```

Then we could look up the tags to insert and to skip over in the Text-Model. My intuition is that this will make the code more complex at this point, and so I'm going to hold off on that. The end result is that we have considered some possible directions for code improvement, but we're not going to do any. I think it's time for the menu.

ˢᵇBegin with a Test

I'm going well now, so I'm not going to break the rhythm. I'll create a new Customer Acceptance Test and make it work. The only point of that test—besides convincing the customer that things are working—is to drive the implementation of the menu. Here's the new test and associated code:

```
*altU
*output
<UL>
<LI>|</LI>
</UL>
```

That should fail...and sure enough it does. So I'll add the menu item and its support. First the item:

```
insertSection = new MenuItem (
  "Insert &Section",
  new EventHandler(MenuInsertSection));
insertPre = new MenuItem (
  "Insert &Pre",
  new EventHandler(MenuInsertPre));
insertUnorderedList = new MenuItem (
  "Insert &UL",
  new EventHandler(MenuInsertUnorderedList));
  this.Menu = new MainMenu(new MenuItem[] {fileMenu, insertPre, insertSection,
    insertUnorderedList} );
```

To support that, I need the MenuItem member variable, the new method
MenuInsertUnorderedList, and the adjustment to the menu lookup code:

```
class XMLNotepad : Form {
  public TestableTextBox textbox;
  private TextModel model;
  private MenuItem insertPre;
  private MenuItem insertSection;
  private MenuItem insertUnorderedList;
  private MenuItem openFile;
  private MenuItem saveFile;
  private ModelAction enterAction;
  private ModelAction shiftEnterAction;
  private ModelAction insertSectionAction;
  private ModelAction insertPreTagAction;
  private ModelAction insertUnorderedListAction;
  private ModelAction saveAction;
  private ModelAction loadAction;
  private String fileName;
  private Boolean displayDialog = true;
  public delegate void ModelAction();
  public MenuItem MenuForAccelerator(string accelerator) {
    if (accelerator == "&S") return insertSection;
    if (accelerator == "&P") return insertPre;
    if (accelerator == "&U") return insertUnorderedList;
    if (accelerator == "^O") return openFile;
    if (accelerator == "^S") return saveFile;
    return null;
  }

  private void InitializeDelegates(TextModel model) {
    enterAction = new ModelAction(model.Enter);
    shiftEnterAction = new ModelAction(model.InsertReturn);
    insertSectionAction = new ModelAction(model.InsertSectionTags);
    insertPreTagAction = new ModelAction(model.InsertPreTag);
    insertUnorderedListAction = new ModelAction(model.InsertUnorderedList);
    saveAction = new ModelAction(this.SaveFile);
    loadAction = new ModelAction(this.LoadFile);
  }
  void MenuInsertUnorderedList(object obj, EventArgs ea) {
    CallModel(insertUnorderedListAction);
  }
}
```

All this compiles, and I expect it to run. However, I forgot to implement
the *altU command in the customer test. That happens almost every time, so I
need to do something about that mistake. More importantly, I think, look at all
the places I had to change or add code to add one menu item. As Andy Hunt

would put it, the dog is biting me. We'll make this one work and then see what we can do to improve the situation. First, implement the *altU:

```
private void InterpretCommands(String commands, String message) {
  StringReader reader = new StringReader(commands);
  String line = reader.ReadLine();
  CreateModel();
  while ( line != null) {
    if ( line == "*enter")
      form.XMLKeyDownHandler((object) this, new KeyEventArgs(Keys.Enter));
    if ( line == "*shiftEnter")
      form.XMLKeyDownHandler((object) this,
        new KeyEventArgs(Keys.Enter | Keys.Shift));
    if ( line == "*altS")
      ExecuteMenu("&S");
    if ( line == "*altP")
      ExecuteMenu("&P");
    if ( line == "*altU")
      ExecuteMenu("&U");
    if (line == "*display")
      Console.WriteLine("display\r\n{0}\r\nend", model.TestText);
    if (line == "*output")
      CompareOutput(reader, message);
    if (line == "*input")
      SetInput(reader);
    if (line == "*loadfile")
      LoadFile();
    if (line == "*savefile")
      SaveFile();
    line = reader.ReadLine();
  }
}
```

That does it! My tests all run. Now for some improvements. First, that irritating thing where the commands don't get implemented. I'll fix the Interpret-Commands method to fail if it doesn't find the item. To begin with, I'll just create some else clauses so that I can do a final assert in the else. Or would a switch statement be better? I think I prefer the else approach because it's easier to get right: I always forget the break statements in switches. The C# compiler will detect that bug, but the code will be longer anyway. Let's do else:

```
private void InterpretCommands(String commands, String message) {
  StringReader reader = new StringReader(commands);
  String line = reader.ReadLine();
  CreateModel();
  while ( line != null) {
    if ( line == "*enter")
```

```
      form.XMLKeyDownHandler((object) this, new KeyEventArgs(Keys.Enter));
    else if ( line == "*shiftEnter")
      form.XMLKeyDownHandler((object) this,
        new KeyEventArgs(Keys.Enter | Keys.Shift));
    else if ( line == "*altS")
      ExecuteMenu("&S");
    else if ( line == "*altP")
      ExecuteMenu("&P");
    else if ( line == "*altU")
      ExecuteMenu("&U");
    else if (line == "*display")
      Console.WriteLine("display\r\n{0}\r\nend", model.TestText);
    else if (line == "*output")
      CompareOutput(reader, message);
    else if (line == "*input")
      SetInput(reader);
    else if (line == "*loadfile")
      LoadFile();
    else if (line == "*savefile")
      SaveFile();
    else
      Assert(line + " command not defined", false);
    line = reader.ReadLine();
  }
}
```

That works fine. I tested it by commenting out the *altU line and running
the tests. I don't see how to test it directly, since it's built to fail, and I'm confident that once implemented, it will continue to work. We'll see if I regret that.
So we have improved the world a little bit: forgetting to create a menu item will
at least give us a clear message.

We'd talked earlier about implementing a generic command, like "*alt U",
with a space, that would allow us to implement any Alt character. That might be
valuable, but I'm not feeling the pressure to do it, especially because this code
is in a test, not in the real program. I'm a bit more casual about keeping my tests
squeaky clean than I am when dealing with the real code. I could be making a
mistake here. For example, in the code just shown, I see some duplication.
Notice all those pairs of lines that deal with *alt something. They all do exactly
the same thing. OK, having noticed it, I guess I'll fix it:

```
private void InterpretCommands(String commands, String message) {
  StringReader reader = new StringReader(commands);
  String line = reader.ReadLine();
  CreateModel();
  while ( line != null) {
    if ( line == "*enter")
```

```
      form.XMLKeyDownHandler((object) this, new KeyEventArgs(Keys.Enter));
    else if ( line == "*shiftEnter")
      form.XMLKeyDownHandler((object) this,
        new KeyEventArgs(Keys.Enter | Keys.Shift));
    else if (line.StartsWith("*alt"))
      ExecuteMenu("&"+line[4]);
    else if (line == "*display")
      Console.WriteLine("display\r\n{0}\r\nend", model.TestText);
    else if (line == "*output")
      CompareOutput(reader, message);
    else if (line == "*input")
      SetInput(reader);
    else if (line == "*loadfile")
      LoadFile();
    else if (line == "*savefile")
      SaveFile();
    else
      Assert(line + " command not defined", false);
    line = reader.ReadLine();
  }
}
```

That was easy, and it handles all the future alt commands automatically. The only thing I'd like to do is move that new bit to the front of the ifs, because it's different from all the others:

```
private void InterpretCommands(String commands, String message) {
  StringReader reader = new StringReader(commands);
  String line = reader.ReadLine();
  CreateModel();
  while ( line != null) {
    if (line.StartsWith("*alt"))
      ExecuteMenu("&"+line[4]);
    else if ( line == "*enter")
      form.XMLKeyDownHandler((object) this, new KeyEventArgs(Keys.Enter));
    else if ( line == "*shiftEnter")
      form.XMLKeyDownHandler((object) this,
        new KeyEventArgs(Keys.Enter | Keys.Shift));
    else if (line == "*display")
      Console.WriteLine("display\r\n{0}\r\nend", model.TestText);
    else if (line == "*output")
      CompareOutput(reader, message);
    else if (line == "*input")
      SetInput(reader);
    else if (line == "*loadfile")
      LoadFile();
    else if (line == "*savefile")
      SaveFile();
```

```
      else
        Assert(line + " command not defined", false);
      line = reader.ReadLine();
    }
  }
```

Good enough, that works. The structure here is suggesting that we need some kind of table, but so far I don't see a way to do it that would actually be better. Good for now. Let's recap, regroup, and take a break.

Lesson: How's It Going So Far?

We've completed the first part of our story, the implementation of the unordered list. We have the list inserting OK, but we haven't done the part about adding a new LI instead of a new P when the user presses Enter inside the LI tags. We'll do that next. We have moved back and forth frequently between reading, testing, implementing, and cleaning up. I feel good about the way that has been going. The world is a little better place because of the cleanup, but we haven't spent large amounts of time avoiding useful work. On the other hand, we've encountered a few places that we haven't cleaned up. The most notable is the fact that we have to make many changes, in many different places, to install a new menu item. That may take a little more time, and I'd like to get this story completely done before addressing it. Now for that break!

Enter the List Item

It's time to get the Enter key to put a ListItem in for us. I was thinking for a moment that we might want that to happen in other places and that perhaps we should just have whatever tag we're inside be replicated. But that's not right: when we're inside a <title> tag, we don't want a new title, we want a paragraph. So I'll curb my DOGBITE instincts for a while, until the code tells me what we need. Here's the code that creates the paragraph tags on Enter, in Text-Model:

```
public void Enter() {
  InsertParagraphTag();
}
public void InsertParagraphTag() {
  InsertTags(newParagraph, paragraphSkip);
}
```

Not much to that. Do you remember, earlier on, when we were worrying about whether the TextModel should understand "Enter" or whether the Form should know to do the translation from Enter to InsertParagraphTag? We decided to let the form keep doing Enter. That makes us happy now, because we can do everything we need to do right here in the TextModel. Waiting paid off that time. It usually does, but this time we happened to notice. I'll program the new feature "by intention":

```
public void Enter() {
  if (InListItem())
    InsertListItemTag();
  else
    InsertParagraphTag();
}
```

That seems clear enough. I would do more, but I just realized that I don't have a broken test. Bad programmer, bad. I'll comment out the above change and then enhance the existing test:

```
[Test] public void UnorderedList() {
  model.SetLines (new String[1] {"<P></P>"});
  model.SelectionStart = 3;
  model.InsertUnorderedList();
  AssertEquals("<UL>", model.Lines[1]);
  AssertEquals("<LI></LI>", model.Lines[2]);
  AssertEquals("</UL>", model.Lines[3]);
  AssertEquals(19, model.SelectionStart);
  model.Enter();
  AssertEquals("<LI></LI>", model.Lines[3]);
}
```

That gives us the failure we need: we get a P line instead of an LI line. The test needs a cursor count as well. I'm putting off adding that, since I always get them wrong. Remind me about that in a little while. Here's what I write next:

```
private Boolean InListItem() {
  return ((string) lines[LineContainingCursor()]).StartsWith("<LI>");
}
public void InsertListItemTag() {
  InsertTags(newListItem, listItemSkip);
}
```

Two things about that. Look at that horrible string cast and access to the lines array. It turns out that we use that construction in several places. As soon as this works, I'm going to improve that. But first, I have to write those new tag variables:

```
private static string[] newListItem = { "<LI></LI>" };
private static string[] listItemSkip = { "<LI>" };
```

Excellent! The test runs! We might want to write another customer test, or extend this one, but basically we have completed our first story. It's time to reflect and to do some cleanup.

What's the Opposite of Simple?

Complex, complicated, elaborate, difficult, Byzantine, labyrinthine. Bewildering. The opposite of simple is "wrong." Putting in this simple and common operation, inserting some XML tags, required me to change code in a number of places. The places were not all obvious, and changes were required all over the code, in more than one source file. This is nature's way of telling us that we have screwed up.

Moving along here, involved in the book, perhaps you have been dragged along in my wake, with the feeling that each change has made sense and with a general feeling that you understand how the menus work. Or, perhaps, you have felt a growing feeling that this isn't right. That has been my own situation: I have been going along feeling that everything is OK and we can easily enough add new things, yet with a growing feeling that this can't be right. That's good. We stick with what we have and what we know while it serves us, and we remain open to learning that it isn't good enough. Today, facing making several changes like this one, we see that this just isn't right. If you're like me, you're not even sure you could write down what has to be done to add a tag-inserting menu item. With the help of the code, let's make that list:

1. Declare a MenuItem member variable, and initialize it:

    ```
    private MenuItem insertUnorderedList;
    ...
    private void initialize(TextModel model) {
      ...
      insertUnorderedList = new MenuItem (
        "Insert &UL",
        new EventHandler(MenuInsertUnorderedList));
      ...
    }
    ```

2. Implement the EventHandler referred to in the MenuItem:

    ```
    void MenuInsertUnorderedList(object obj, EventArgs ea) {
      CallModel(insertUnorderedListAction);
    }
    ```

3. Declare the ModelAction variable referred to in the EventHandler, and initialize it:

```
private ModelAction insertUnorderedListAction;
...
private void InitializeDelegates(TextModel model) {
    enterAction = new ModelAction(model.Enter);
    shiftEnterAction = new ModelAction(model.InsertReturn);
    insertSectionAction = new ModelAction(model.InsertSectionTags);
    insertPreTagAction = new ModelAction(model.InsertPreTag);
    insertUnorderedListAction = new ModelAction(model.InsertUnorderedList);
    saveAction = new ModelAction(this.SaveFile);
    loadAction = new ModelAction(this.LoadFile);
}
```

4.   Implement, in the TextModel class, the insert method referred to in
the ModelAction:

```
public void InsertUnorderedList() {
    InsertTags(newUnorderedList, unorderedListSkip);
}
```

5.   Define the tag lists referred to in the insert method:

```
private static string[] newUnorderedList = {"<UL>","<LI></LI>","</UL>"};
private static string[] unorderedListSkip = { "<UL>", "<LI>" };
```

6.   Oh, and I almost forgot: change the menu search logic, back in the
XML Notepad, to find the new menu:

```
public MenuItem MenuForAccelerator(string accelerator) {
    if (accelerator == "&S") return insertSection;
    if (accelerator == "&P") return insertPre;
    if (accelerator == "&U") return insertUnorderedList;
    if (accelerator == "^O") return openFile;
    if (accelerator == "^S") return saveFile;
    return null;
}
```

Even now, I'm not sure that I have them all. Wait—and I really did forget
this until now—we have to do another thing: we have to add our menu item to
the main menu:

```
this.Menu = new MainMenu(new MenuItem[]
  {fileMenu, insertPre, insertSection, insertUnorderedList} );
```

No wonder we're confused. No wonder it always takes us a few extra tests
to get a new menu item right. And imagine how difficult it's going to be for some
other programmer to come along and install a new insertion item. She might be
able to follow along, one step at a time, starting from an existing MenuItem, but
she is almost certain to miss the menu search logic and she might well miss the
addition of her new menu to the main menu. This isn't good.

We Have to Do Something

What should we do? Well, our first reaction is to put some comments in the code. A big block comment listing the six or seven or eight items it takes to do the job might help. Except that I keep forgetting two of the steps, and I wrote this stuff. We might write it up and hand everyone who has to maintain this code a copy of this chapter of the book, or even a special document, "Instructions for Adding a New Inserted Tag." That's what we might do, and it's what many wise people might tell us to do. But that's not what we're going to do: we're going to fix it.

The need for comments, and the need for documents, is the code's way of telling us that it isn't finished, that it isn't simple enough. We're going to make it simple, and two things are going to happen. First, I bet that it won't take any longer than writing the document we think we need. Second, it will make our own job easier as well as that of the programmer who comes after us. Third, it's going to be a lot more fun than writing a document. Fourth, we'll feel proud of what we have done, instead of vaguely ashamed. Wow, four things instead of just two. We're exceeding expectations already. Let's plan.

Some Starting Ideas

Our problem is that the code to define a new tag insertion is spread all over. There are seven steps, if I have remembered them all this time, and I have to edit at least two files. This is a serious indication that something is wrong. Let's think about what we would like.

Well, what I would like would be to put all the information together. To specify the strings to insert, the lines, and where the cursor goes should be at least as easy as that trick with the two strings. (See newUnorderedList and unorderedListSkip in the "The Actual Work" section earlier.) Since I'm just dreaming, why not make it as easy as specifying a customer test? Remember the test for unordered list:

```
*altU
*output
<UL>
<LI>|</LI>
</UL>
```

I'd like to have something about that easy to specify. We want to specify the menu item as well, so maybe something like this:

```
Insert &Unordered List, <UL>\<LI>|</LI>\<UL>
Insert &Ordered List, <OL>\<LI>|</LI>\<OL>
```

The backslash (\) would mean to put a new line in, and the vertical bar would represent where the cursor should go. What could we do that would be something like that, and how can we do it without much investment?

Lesson   Doing it without much investment is important for two reasons. First of all, our mission is always to deliver real value to our customer. We need to be careful when we make improvements like this that they really do pay off for the customer. If we can make the system better with a very small investment, that's a good thing. Second, it's important to the premise of this book that it's practical to design and build software incrementally, with the confidence that we won't get into a situation where it's a big deal to get back out again. If this doesn't work, I have to cancel the book!

Now all the methods and steps we have to go through have a purpose that is essentially simple: at the end of it all, a given menu click wants to call InsertTags() with the correct two string arrays to do the insert. What if we had a kind of MenuItem that knew the two string arrays, and its EventHandler just passed them directly to the model? Might everything else collapse out? Let's try it.

I'll begin by creating a subclass of MenuItem called NotepadMenuItem. I'll give it a constructor that accepts the two string arrays we need, and I'll use it for one of our menus. Here goes:

```
class NotepadMenuItem : MenuItem {
  private string[] tagsToInsert;
  private string[] tagsToSkip;
  public NotepadMenuItem (String menuString, EventHandler handler,
    string[] inserts, string[] skips)
    :base(menuString, handler) {
    tagsToInsert = inserts;
    tagsToSkip = skips;
  }
  public string[] Inserts {
    get { return tagsToInsert; }
  }
  public string[] Skips {
    get { return tagsToSkip; }
  }
}
```

You may have noticed that I implemented "get" properties for the tags. I did that on speculation, which is a bit against my preferred practice, but I was on a roll and just couldn't stop myself. We'll see whether it causes problems, but I don't expect that it will. Now I'm going to use the new NotepadMenuItem in just one place. I'll change this:

```
...
insertSection = new MenuItem (
  "Insert &Section",
  new EventHandler(MenuInsertSection));
insertPre = new MenuItem (
  "Insert &Pre",
  new EventHandler(MenuInsertPre));
insertUnorderedList = new MenuItem (
  "Insert &UL",
  new EventHandler(MenuInsertUnorderedList));
this.Menu = new MainMenu(new MenuItem[] {fileMenu, insertPre,
  insertSection, insertUnorderedList} );
...
```

so that I get this:

```
insertSection = new MenuItem (
  "Insert &Section",
  new EventHandler(MenuInsertSection));
insertPre = new NotepadMenuItem (
  "Insert &Pre",
  new EventHandler(MenuInsertPre),
  { "<pre></pre>" },
  { "<pre>" } );
insertUnorderedList = new MenuItem (
  "Insert &UL",
  new EventHandler(MenuInsertUnorderedList));
this.Menu = new MainMenu(new MenuItem[] {fileMenu, insertPre,
  insertSection,  insertUnorderedList} );
```

Unfortunately, that doesn't compile. Apparently we can't use that array of string literal notation quite that freely. Oh, we have to create the array with new, like this:

```
insertSection = new MenuItem (
  "Insert &Section",
  new EventHandler(MenuInsertSection));
insertPre = new NotepadMenuItem (
  "Insert &Pre",
  new EventHandler(MenuInsertPre),
  new string[] { "<pre></pre>" },
  new string[] { "<pre>" } );
```

```
insertUnorderedList = new MenuItem (
  "Insert &UL",
  new EventHandler(MenuInsertUnorderedList));
this.Menu = new MainMenu(new MenuItem[] {fileMenu, insertPre,
  insertSection, insertUnorderedList} );
```

This compiles. I'm sure it will run, but let's run the tests...this is embarrassing! A test broke, and it doesn't have anything to do with this change! Somehow I haven't been running all the tests. The error arises in two of the Customer-Tests. One is EmptyModel, which looks like this:

```
[Test] public void EmptyModel() {
  form.XMLKeyDownHandler((object) this,
    new KeyEventArgs(Keys.Enter));
  AssertEquals("<P>|</P>\r\n", model.TestText);
}
```

The error message refers to an invalid or negative subscript in the method InListItem(), which we just implemented. That code looks like this:

```
private Boolean InListItem() {
  return ((string) lines[LineContainingCursor()]).StartsWith("<LI>");
}
```

The bug is clear: If the input is empty, LineContainingCursor() will return -1 and we will try to get that line. And there is no such line to get, causing the exception. This should fix it:

```
private Boolean InListItem() {
  if (LineContainingCursor() < 0 ) return false;
  return ((string) lines[LineContainingCursor()]).StartsWith("<LI>");
}
```

And it does. I must have been running some subset of the tests when I put that last feature in. Very bad.

> **Lesson**   Well, as they say, "Even Homer sometimes nods." I believe they are referring to the Greek Homer, not the yellow television character. We will make mistakes operationally, and I just did. Try not to emulate this feature of your humble author: be sure to run all your tests between tasks. I have often advised people to run the tests *before* starting some new phase, and I didn't follow my own advice. It caused some confusion there for a minute.

However, no harm done. The new NotepadMenuItem works perfectly—and why wouldn't it? We aren't using any of its special features yet. Now we'll do that. The EventHandler for that menu item is MenuInsertPre:

```
void MenuInsertPre(object obj, EventArgs ea) {
  CallModel(insertPreTagAction);
}
```

I believe that the "object obj" parameter to a menu click is the MenuItem itself. I'll test that quickly by trying to print the Inserts array:

```
void MenuInsertPre(object obj, EventArgs ea) {
  NotepadMenuItem item = (NotepadMenuItem) obj;
  Console.WriteLine("Inserts[0] = {0}", item.Inserts[0]);
  CallModel(insertPreTagAction);
}
```

Sure enough, in the Standard Out window of NUnit, I see a couple of lines verifying that we got what we wanted:

```
Inserts[0] = <pre></pre>
Inserts[0] = <pre></pre>
```

Perfect. Now let's see if we can change the MenuInsertPre method to call InsertTags() directly. Remember that the CallModel() method is there to send the text from the TextBox over to the TextModel and to get it back:

```
private void CallModel(ModelAction modelAction) {
  GetText();
  modelAction();
  PutText(textbox, model.LinesArray(), model.SelectionStart);
}
```

We'll just move the GetText() and PutText() into our MenuInsertPre method for now and call the InsertTags directly:

```
void MenuInsertPre(object obj, EventArgs ea) {
  NotepadMenuItem item = (NotepadMenuItem) obj;
  GetText();
  model.InsertTags(item.Inserts, item.Skips);
  PutText(textbox, model.LinesArray(), model.SelectionStart);
}
```

InsertTags() isn't public in TextModel, so I'll promote it:

```
public void InsertTags(string[] tagsToInsert, string[] tagsPrecedingCursor) {
  int cursorLine = LineContainingCursor();
  lines.InsertRange(cursorLine+1, tagsToInsert);
```

We should be good to go. Let's compile and test. The code compiles, and the test runs! This is good. We can now do the following steps:

1. Rename the MenuInsertPre() handler to reflect its more general purpose, probably to MenuInsertTags().

2. Change all the menu items that insert tags to use MenuInsertTags().

3. Remove all the excess code that we no longer need. This will include the handlers in XMLNotepad.cs, the ModelActions, and the string array definitions in TextModel.

Follow me through the steps. When we're finished we'll take a look at the overall results. Here's the renaming of the handler:

```
void MenuInsertTags(object obj, EventArgs ea) {
  NotepadMenuItem item = (NotepadMenuItem) obj;
  GetText();
  model.InsertTags(item.Inserts, item.Skips);
  PutText(textbox, model.LinesArray(), model.SelectionStart);
}


  insertPre = new NotepadMenuItem (
    "Insert &Pre",
    new EventHandler(MenuInsertTags),
    new string[] { "<pre></pre>" },
    new string[] { "<pre>" } );
```

And here I'm changing the other menus to use NotepadMenuItem:

```
insertSection = new NotepadMenuItem (
  "Insert &Section",
  new EventHandler(MenuInsertTags),
  new string[] {"<sect1><title></title>","</sect1>" },
  new string[] { "<sect1><title>" } );
insertPre = new NotepadMenuItem (
  "Insert &Pre",
  new EventHandler(MenuInsertTags),
  new string[] {"<UL>","<LI></LI>","</UL>"},
  new string[] { "<UL>", "<LI>" } );
insertUnorderedList = new NotepadMenuItem (
  "Insert &UL",
  new EventHandler(MenuInsertTags),
  new string[] { "<pre></pre>" },
  new string[] { "<pre>" } );
this.Menu = new MainMenu(new MenuItem[] {fileMenu, insertPre,
  insertSection, insertUnorderedList} );
```

Oops! Tests don't run. Do you see what I did? I changed the Pre menu to insert the UL data. The tests saved me, which is what they are for. The corrected code is

```
insertSection = new NotepadMenuItem (
  "Insert &Section",
  new EventHandler(MenuInsertTags),
  new string[] {"<sect1><title></title>","</sect1>" },
  new string[] { "<sect1><title>" } );
insertPre = new NotepadMenuItem (
  "Insert &Pre",
  new EventHandler(MenuInsertTags),
  new string[] { "<pre></pre>" },
  new string[] { "<pre>" } );
insertUnorderedList = new NotepadMenuItem (
  "Insert &UL",
  new EventHandler(MenuInsertTags),
  new string[] {"<UL>","<LI></LI>","</UL>"},
  new string[] { "<UL>", "<LI>" } );
```

The tests are all running, and the menus are all going through the Menu-InsertTags method. I should be able to delete lots of code. I'll begin by commenting out everything that I would like to delete.

XMLNotepad.cs

```
class XMLNotepad : Form {
  public TestableTextBox textbox;
  private TextModel model;
  private MenuItem insertPre;
  private MenuItem insertSection;
  private MenuItem insertUnorderedList;
  private MenuItem openFile;
  private MenuItem saveFile;
  private ModelAction enterAction;
  private ModelAction shiftEnterAction;
//    private ModelAction insertSectionAction;
//    private ModelAction insertPreTagAction;
//    private ModelAction insertUnorderedListAction;
  private ModelAction saveAction;
  private ModelAction loadAction;
  private String fileName;
  private Boolean displayDialog = true;
  public delegate void ModelAction();
  ...
  private void InitializeDelegates(TextModel model) {
    enterAction = new ModelAction(model.Enter);
    shiftEnterAction = new ModelAction(model.InsertReturn);
```

```
//      insertSectionAction = new ModelAction(model.InsertSectionTags);
//      insertPreTagAction = new ModelAction(model.InsertPreTag);
//      insertUnorderedListAction = new ModelAction(model.InsertUnorderedList);
      saveAction = new ModelAction(this.SaveFile);
      loadAction = new ModelAction(this.LoadFile);
    }
//    void MenuInsertUnorderedList(object obj, EventArgs ea) {
//      CallModel(insertUnorderedListAction);
//    }
//
//    void MenuInsertSection(object obj, EventArgs ea) {
//      CallModel(insertSectionAction);
//    }
  ...
}
```

With these items removed, the system still compiles and the tests run. I'll complete the deletion of these commented-out items. Normally I would delete these lines in one step. Even though I commented them out for your reading convenience only, now I'm tempted to leave them in "just in case." Because all the code is backed up in the code manager, there's no reason to confuse ourselves with dead code. The program still compiles, and the tests run correctly. Now I'd like to remove some code from TextModel. I'll show you what I want to do:

```
class TextModel {
  private ArrayList lines;
  private int selectionStart;
  private static string[] newParagraph = { "<P></P>" };
  private static string[] paragraphSkip = { "<P>" };
  private static string[] newListItem = { "<LI></LI>" };
  private static string[] listItemSkip = { "<LI>" };
  private static string[] emptyLine = { "" };
  private static string[] emptyLineSkip = { "" };
//  private static string[] newSection = {"<sect1><title></title>",
//    "</sect1>" };
//  private static string[] sectionSkip = { "<sect1><title>" };
//  private static string[] newUnorderedList = {"<UL>","<LI></LI>","</UL>"};
//  private static string[] unorderedListSkip = { "<UL>", "<LI>" };
//  private static string[] newPre = { "<pre></pre>" };
//    private static string[] preSkip = { "<pre>" };

//    public void InsertPreTag() {
//      InsertTags(newPre, preSkip);
//    }
//    public void InsertSectionTags() {
//      InsertTags(newSection, sectionSkip);
//    }
```

```
//     public void InsertUnorderedList() {
//         InsertTags(newUnorderedList, unorderedListSkip);
//     }
//     public void AltS() {
//         InsertSectionTags();
//     }
//     public void AltP() {
//         InsertPreTag();
//     }
```

It seems to me that I should be able to remove all this code. However, this time the compiler complains. It seems that tests in TestTextModel.cs are referring to some of these methods. For example:

```
[Test] public void AltS() {
  model.Lines = new ArrayList(new String[0]);
  model.AltS();
  AssertEquals("<sect1><title></title>", model.Lines[0]);
  AssertEquals("</sect1>", model.Lines[1]);
  AssertEquals(14, model.SelectionStart);
}
```

This is a perfectly good test. We've changed the program such that the model can change tags by using its general InsertTags() method but the more specific methods, such as the now oddly-named AltS(), will no longer be hooked up. Similarly, there are tests we wrote for InsertPreTag() and Insert-UnorderedList(), and perhaps others. It's easy enough to change these tests to use InsertTags(), and I expect that we'll do that, but look what happens when I change the AltS test:

```
[Test] public void AltS() {
  model.Lines = new ArrayList(new String[0]);
  model.InsertTags(
    new string[] {"<sect1><title></title>","</sect1>" },
    new string[] { "<sect1><title>" });
  AssertEquals("<sect1><title></title>", model.Lines[0]);
  AssertEquals("</sect1>", model.Lines[1]);
  AssertEquals(14, model.SelectionStart);
}
```

(There is another test, AltSWithText(), that is changed similarly. This one is enough to make my point.) When we make this change, this test runs correctly. However, it's testing less than it did before. In the old form, the test ensured that the strings defining AltS were correctly set up inside TextModel class. Now—since we have deleted the strings—all this test does is assure us that *if* the strings are set up like they are in the test, the insertion will work. The tests are weakened by our refactoring.

Now, it's no surprise that tests often need changing when we refactor the code, especially when, as this time, we are refactoring code across two classes—in our case, XMLNotepad and TextModel. But we don't like to see the tests getting weaker. And they are exposing a real problem, or at least a potential one.

As it happens, the customer tests go all the way through the menu items, so when a customer test calls for an AltS, we know that it is testing the actual string needed in the InsertSectionTags concept. We could enhance these tests to go through the menu, but that would be redundant, and again, it would weaken them. Right now, these tests test the model directly, and we like that. If we put them through the form, they'll be less direct, and if one of them ever breaks, we won't be sure if the problem is in the form, or in the model. The code is trying to tell us something. What is it?

> **Lesson**   Duplication. So often it's duplication that gives us the signal. Here we have duplication between the Form and the tests, regarding the strings to be inserted. We want to insert the sequence for a <pre> tag—what object should know how to do that? Surely not both the Form and the tests. More likely, it's the TextModel, because it's the TextModel's job to know how to format XML. The duplication was the signal.

Removing the Duplication

We know that we want the TextModel to be the only object that knows how to do these things. We have tried pushing in that direction before, by using method names like InsertPreTag, and with AltS, but this led us to a very complex structure in the Form. We like the way the form works now: we just specify a menu item and that item includes enough information to do the job. But in a sense, the NotepadMenuItem has *too much* information. It knows not what to do, but how to do it. Let's change it to know what, not how. Instead of giving the TextModel a string, we'll give it a command.

One possibility is to use a string, like "pre" or "Insert Pre" or even "Insert &Pre", as the command. This leaves open the chance that we would say "pork" or "Insrot Per" and not find out until a test failed or the program breaks. It's better for us if we use commands that can be checked by the compiler, as were the methods in our earlier implementation. I'm thinking that we need a simple list of possible commands, perhaps an Enumeration.

> **Lesson** One of my technical editors objects strongly to what follows. To him, the use of an Enum is an "across-the-room" code smell. He believes that a class would have been a better choice, and based on a few shared e-mails with him, I'm sure he's right. Using a class would let us encapsulate more of the literal constants and would let us move some additional logic inside the resulting new class. Unfortunately for all of us, the history of the project never gave us that discovery. So be warned that, as in other cases in this program, a better way surely exists.

It would be possible to work all this out before doing it. Instead, I'm going to work through it bit by bit, letting the compiler and tests help me. I'm starting from a green bar, with the XMLNotepad converted to use the new Notepad-MenuItem and the TextModel looking like this:

```
class TextModel {
  private ArrayList lines;
  private int selectionStart;
  private static string[] newParagraph = { "<P></P>" };
  private static string[] paragraphSkip = { "<P>" };
  private static string[] newListItem = { "<LI></LI>" };
  private static string[] listItemSkip = { "<LI>" };
  private static string[] emptyLine = { "" };
  private static string[] emptyLineSkip = { "" };
//  private static string[] newSection = {"<sect1><title></title>",
//      "</sect1>" };
//  private static string[] sectionSkip = { "<sect1><title>" };
  private static string[] newUnorderedList = {"<UL>","<LI></LI>","</UL>"};
  private static string[] unorderedListSkip = { "<UL>", "<LI>" };
  private static string[] newPre = { "<pre></pre>" };
  private static string[] preSkip = { "<pre>" };
  public void InsertPreTag() {
    InsertTags(newPre, preSkip);
  }
//  public void InsertSectionTags() {
//      InsertTags(newSection, sectionSkip);
//  }
  public void InsertUnorderedList() {
    InsertTags(newUnorderedList, unorderedListSkip);
  }
//  public void AltS() {
//      InsertSectionTags();
```

```
//    }
//    public void AltP() {
//      InsertPreTag();
//    }
...
```

I've put the InsertPreTag() and InsertUnorderedList() methods back in. The AltS() and AltP() methods aren't needed, because I've left the modified tests in, looking like this:

```
[Test] public void AltS() {
  model.Lines = new ArrayList(new String[0]);
  model.InsertTags(
    new string[] {"<sect1><title></title>","</sect1>" },
    new string[] { "<sect1><title>" });
  AssertEquals("<sect1><title></title>", model.Lines[0]);
  AssertEquals("</sect1>", model.Lines[1]);
  AssertEquals(14, model.SelectionStart);
}
```

Should we back up to a better place, with the the TextModel and tests unmodified, before we started the changes to the TextModel? You might argue that it would be a more stable point to work from. On the other hand, with some tests modified to use the new InsertTags feature, we know that we'll get an immediate look at how our new command idea impacts the tests. It's a judgment call. We'll start from here.

First, let's add an enum. We'll add it inside TextModel:

```
public enum Tags {
  Pre = 1,
  Section = 2,
  UnorderedList = 3
}
```

Now we want to modify the NotepadMenuItem to use the enum instead of the strings that it uses currently. Remember that the code looks like this:

```
  insertPre = new NotepadMenuItem (
    "Insert &Pre",
    new EventHandler(MenuInsertTags),
    new string[] { "<pre></pre>" },
    new string[] { "<pre>" } );
...
void MenuInsertTags(object obj, EventArgs ea) {
  NotepadMenuItem item = (NotepadMenuItem) obj;
  GetText();
  model.InsertTags(item.Inserts, item.Skips);
  PutText(textbox, model.LinesArray(), model.SelectionStart);
}
```

We want to have it look more like this:

```
insertPre = new NotepadMenuItem (
  "Insert &Pre",
  new EventHandler(MenuInsertTags),
  TextModel.Tags.Pre);
...

void MenuInsertTags(object obj, EventArgs ea) {
  NotepadMenuItem item = (NotepadMenuItem) obj;
  GetText();
  model.InsertTags(item.Command);
  PutText(textbox, model.LinesArray(), model.SelectionStart);
}
```

Then, inside TextModel, we'll have to look up the various strings needed. This feels like a big step to me. I can see two ways to do it. The long way will be to do the above, enhancing TextModel to deal with the command to make the tests run. We might be able to get the tests running a bit sooner if we look up the strings on the Form side, as part of the MenuInsertTags method, and pass them to InsertTags(). That will get the tests running again. Then we would change the InsertTags() signature, by using the lookup already implemented, moving to green bar a second time.

Either way would work. I'm tempted to try it in one step, and I'm pretty sure I can make it work. Let's do it in the smaller steps anyway, just as practice in baby steps.

In fact, as soon as I get the baby steps idea, I see an even better plan! I'll look up the two strings in the NotepadMenuItem constructor, not in the MenuInsertTags method as I was first thinking. Like this:

```
class NotepadMenuItem : MenuItem {
  private string[] tagsToInsert;
  private string[] tagsToSkip;
  public NotepadMenuItem
    (String menuString, EventHandler handler, string[] inserts, string[] skips)
    :base(menuString, handler) {
      tagsToInsert = inserts;
      tagsToSkip = skips;
  }
  public NotepadMenuItem (String menuString, EventHandler handler,
    TextModel.Tags tags)
    :base(menuString, handler){
    tagsToInsert = TextModel.InsertString(tags);
    tagsToSkip = TextModel.SkipString(tags);
  }
```

```
public string[] Inserts {
  get { return tagsToInsert; }
}
public string[] Skips {
  get { return tagsToSkip; }
}
}
```

Get the idea? I'll just create the menu item to grab the strings from the TextModel and plug them in. That only requires me to build the InsertString and SkipString methods on TextModel, and then the tests should run:

```
public static string[] InsertString(Tags tag) {
  return newPre;
}
public static string[] SkipString(Tags tag) {
  return preSkip;
}
```

For now, I'll just return this one value and then change only the Pre menu:

```
insertSection = new NotepadMenuItem (
  "Insert &Section",
  new EventHandler(MenuInsertTags),
  new string[] {"<sect1><title></title>","</sect1>" },
  new string[] { "<sect1><title>" } );
insertPre = new NotepadMenuItem (
  "Insert &Pre",
  new EventHandler(MenuInsertTags),
  TextModel.Tags.Pre );
insertUnorderedList = new NotepadMenuItem (
  "Insert &UL",
  new EventHandler(MenuInsertTags),
  new string[] {"<UL>","<LI></LI>","</UL>"},
  new string[] { "<UL>", "<LI>" } );
```

We see how this is shaping up. It looks a bit better to me already. With the current stubbed implementation of InsertString() and SkipString(), it should work. I notice in passing that the methods return arrays of string, so they should be plural, not singular. We'll fix that in a moment. We need to be sure we're on a green bar first...and running the tests shows that we are. The code runs. We'll rename those methods now, using the refactoring tool. Then we'll modify one of the other menus, to get a red bar.

```
"Insert &Section",
new EventHandler(MenuInsertTags),
TextModel.Tags.Section);
```

This breaks a customer test, with this output:

```
c:\data\csharp\notepad\sect1.test
*Expected
<sect1><title>|</title>
</sect1>
*Result
<pre>|</pre>
```

I would be happier if it broke a unit test also, but I didn't change any of them yet. We could do it now or wait. I'm inclined to wait. My plan is to remove the constructor for NotepadMenuItem that accepts the two arrays, and when we do that, we'll get compiler messages for the tests that need changing. We'll let the computer tell us what do to. To make the current test run, we need to improve the lookups:

```
public static string[] InsertStrings(Tags tag) {
  if (tag == Tags.Pre) return newPre;
  else if (tag == Tags.Section) return newSection;
  else return newParagraph;
}
public static string[] SkipStrings(Tags tag) {
  if (tag == Tags.Pre) return preSkip;
  else if (tag == Tags.Section) return sectionSkip;
  else return paragraphSkip;
}
```

To make this work, I had to uncomment the newSection and sectionSkip lines shown following the next Lesson. Note that I also needed to have an else clause. I decided to return the paragraph insert information. An alternative might have been to return null or to throw an exception. We're not finished with this yet, so for now this should work.

> **Lesson** There is a potential problem with this practice: we might forget and leave the code in this awkward state. I haven't looked forward to see whether I got away with it this time, but if you think this is a bad idea, you may be right. The tradeoff is this, however: if we fill in too many of these gaps, it will take us longer to get from test red to test green, and we'll have to think about too many things at once. That will slow us down, but this practice could leave a bug in the system. You might find it valuable to put a TODO in the code, or write a note on a card, or write another test. The main thing is to remain sensitive to what you're doing, and to adjust your practices as you notice problems.

```
private static string[] newParagraph = { "<P></P>" };
private static string[] paragraphSkip = { "<P>" };
private static string[] newListItem = { "<LI></LI>" };
private static string[] listItemSkip = { "<LI>" };
private static string[] emptyLine = { "" };
private static string[] emptyLineSkip = { "" };
private static string[] newSection = {"<sect1><title></title>","</sect1>" };
private static string[] sectionSkip = { "<sect1><title>" };
private static string[] newUnorderedList = {"<UL>","<LI></LI>","</UL>"};
private static string[] unorderedListSkip = { "<UL>", "<LI>" };
private static string[] newPre = { "<pre></pre>" };
private static string[] preSkip = { "<pre>" };
```

The tests do run. Let's do it again with the remaining menu:

```
"Insert &UL",
new EventHandler(MenuInsertTags),
TextModel.Tags.UnorderedList );
```

This, of course, breaks the UnorderedList test, and we fix it with

```
public static string[] InsertStrings(Tags tag) {
  if (tag == Tags.Pre) return newPre;
  else if (tag == Tags.Section) return newSection;
  else if (tag == Tags.UnorderedList) return newUnorderedList;
  else return newParagraph;
}
public static string[] SkipStrings(Tags tag) {
  if (tag == Tags.Pre) return preSkip;
  else if (tag == Tags.Section) return sectionSkip;
  else if (tag == Tags.UnorderedList) return unorderedListSkip;
  else return paragraphSkip;
}
```

Now we can remove the original NotepadMenuItem constructor, deleting this code:

```
public NotepadMenuItem
  (String menuString, EventHandler handler, string[] inserts, string[] skips)
  :base(menuString, handler) {
    tagsToInsert = inserts;
    tagsToSkip = skips;
}
```

> **Lesson**   Try to get the sense of what we're doing here. We are going in tiny steps, one simple change at a time. Each time, either the compiler tells us what to do next or the tests tell us. We change a couple of lines, and everything works again. We're never more than a few moments from a correctly working program.
>
> When you get experienced at working this way, you'll probably notice a couple of things. First, you'll rarely make a serious mistake that has to be backed out. Each step goes forward, rarely back. Second, you'll find that you have a low level of stress as you work. Get used to this feeling, and use the appearance of stress as a clue that your steps may be too big.
>
> My strong advice is to try working like this until you can find these tiny steps. You won't always work that way—you've seen in this book that I don't always work that way—but you will find, I think, that you're working in smaller and more secure steps than ever before. Remember also how often I get into trouble when I take bigger steps. Learn from the "master": don't do as he does.

Moving Responsibility

Right now, the NotepadMenuItem is "translating" between the Form and the TextModel. The translation of the command Tags into string arrays is inside the menu item, and it should be inside the TextModel. The next step, therefore, is to stop translating the strings, send the command over to the TextModel, and let it do the translation. This should be easy. First, we'll change the NotepadMenuItem just to store the command and return it:

```
class NotepadMenuItem : MenuItem {
  private TextModel.Tags command;
  public NotepadMenuItem (String menuString, EventHandler handler,
    TextModel.Tags tag)
    :base(menuString, handler){
    command = tag;
  }
  public TextModel.Tags Command {
    get { return command; }
  }
}
```

The removal of the Inserts and Skips method, of course, breaks the following code:

```
void MenuInsertTags(object obj, EventArgs ea) {
  NotepadMenuItem item = (NotepadMenuItem) obj;
  GetText();
  model.InsertTags(item.Inserts, item.Skips);
  PutText(textbox, model.LinesArray(), model.SelectionStart);
}
```

We change it to

```
void MenuInsertTags(object obj, EventArgs ea) {
  NotepadMenuItem item = (NotepadMenuItem) obj;
  GetText();
  model.InsertTags(item.Command);
  PutText(textbox, model.LinesArray(), model.SelectionStart);
}
```

But there is no InsertTags() method in TextModel that takes a command. So we'll write it:

```
public void InsertTags(Tags command) {
  InsertTags(InsertStrings(command), SkipStrings(command));
}
public void InsertTags(string[] tagsToInsert, string[] tagsPrecedingCursor) {
  int cursorLine = LineContainingCursor();
  lines.InsertRange(cursorLine+1, tagsToInsert);
  selectionStart = NewSelectionStart(cursorLine + 1, tagsPrecedingCursor);
}
```

Note that I just called the old InsertTags method with the converted strings. That compiles, and I think it should run. Let's see...indeed, it does. Now we can declare the InsertStrings() and SkipsStrings() methods private:

```
private static string[] InsertStrings(Tags tag) {
  if (tag == Tags.Pre) return newPre;
  else if (tag == Tags.Section) return newSection;
  else if (tag == Tags.UnorderedList) return newUnorderedList;
  else return newParagraph;
}
private static string[] SkipStrings(Tags tag) {
  if (tag == Tags.Pre) return preSkip;
  else if (tag == Tags.Section) return sectionSkip;
  else if (tag == Tags.UnorderedList) return unorderedListSkip;
  else return paragraphSkip;
}
```

We can remove the second InsertTags() method, folding its behavior into the first one. This should break the unit tests that are relying on knowing those strings directly. They do not compile. This

```
[Test] public void AltS() {
  model.Lines = new ArrayList(new String[0]);
  model.InsertTags(
    new string[] {"<sect1><title></title>","</sect1>" },
    new string[] { "<sect1><title>" });
  AssertEquals("<sect1><title></title>", model.Lines[0]);
  AssertEquals("</sect1>", model.Lines[1]);
  AssertEquals(14, model.SelectionStart);
}
```

becomes

```
[Test] public void AltS() {
  model.Lines = new ArrayList(new String[0]);
  model.InsertTags(TextModel.Tags.Section);
  AssertEquals("<sect1><title></title>", model.Lines[0]);
  AssertEquals("</sect1>", model.Lines[1]);
  AssertEquals(14, model.SelectionStart);
}
```

And so on. There are also a few helper methods inside TextModel that fail to compile. I had forgotten them:

```
public void InsertPreTag() {
  InsertTags(newPre, preSkip);
}
public void InsertUnorderedList() {
  InsertTags(newUnorderedList, unorderedListSkip);
}
public void InsertListItemTag() {
  InsertTags(newListItem, listItemSkip);
}
public void InsertParagraphTag() {
  InsertTags(newParagraph, paragraphSkip);
}
```

They become

```
public void InsertPreTag() {
  InsertTags(Tags.Pre);
}
public void InsertUnorderedList() {
  InsertTags(Tags.UnorderedList);
}
public void InsertListItemTag() {
  InsertTags(Tags.ListItem);
```

```
}
public void InsertParagraphTag() {
  InsertTags(Tags.Paragraph);
}
```

Here, I'm inventing new tags for these methods. This is a good discovery: our new approach is actually picking up and improving functionality that we didn't foresee. It's common that a new capability like this one can improve code elsewhere in the system. Changing the methods to private, which we could have skipped, caused us to find these opportunities. It's a good thing. The code changes include these:

```
public enum Tags {
  Pre = 1,
  Section = 2,
  UnorderedList = 3,
  ListItem = 4,
  Paragraph = 5
}
private static string[] InsertStrings(Tags tag) {
  if (tag == Tags.Pre) return newPre;
  else if (tag == Tags.Section) return newSection;
  else if (tag == Tags.UnorderedList) return newUnorderedList;
  else if (tag == Tags.ListItem) return newListItem;
  else return newParagraph;
}
private static string[] SkipStrings(Tags tag) {
  if (tag == Tags.Pre) return preSkip;
  else if (tag == Tags.Section) return sectionSkip;
  else if (tag == Tags.UnorderedList) return unorderedListSkip;
  else if (tag == Tags.ListItem) return listItemSkip;
  else return paragraphSkip;
}
```

There's still one compiler message, for this code:

```
[Test] public void AltSWithText() {
  model.SetLines (new String[1] {"<P></P>"});
  model.SelectionStart = 7;
  model.InsertTags(
    new string[] {"<sect1><title></title>","</sect1>" },
    new string[] { "<sect1><title>" });
  AssertEquals("<sect1><title></title>", model.Lines[1]);
  AssertEquals("</sect1>", model.Lines[2]);
  AssertEquals(23, model.SelectionStart);
}
```

You'll recall me mentioning earlier that more than one test had broken when I commented out all that material in TextModel. This was the other one, and you can see that I changed it to use the strings. Now, of course, the change is similar to all the others:

```
[Test] public void AltSWithText() {
  model.SetLines (new String[1] {"<P></P>"});
  model.SelectionStart = 7;
  model.InsertTags(TextModel.Tags.Section);
  AssertEquals("<sect1><title></title>", model.Lines[1]);
  AssertEquals("</sect1>", model.Lines[2]);
  AssertEquals(23, model.SelectionStart);
}
```

Everything compiles now...and the tests all run!

A Bit More Cleanup

There were some helper methods that I modified, like this one:

```
public void InsertPreTag() {
  InsertTags(Tags.Pre);
}
```

I'd like to get rid of those, because they don't communicate much and they're complicating the interface to the TextModel. Let's see what's using these methods and what we can do about it. In this case, there's just one test:

```
[Test] public void InsertPre() {
  model.SetLines (new String[1] {"<P></P>"});
  model.SelectionStart = 7;
  model.InsertPreTag();
  AssertEquals("<pre></pre>", model.Lines[1]);
  AssertEquals(14, model.SelectionStart);
  model.InsertReturn();
  AssertEquals("<pre>", model.Lines[1]);
  AssertEquals("</pre>", model.Lines[2]);
  AssertEquals(16, model.SelectionStart);
}
```

Simple enough. We can and should use our new method directly:

```
[Test] public void InsertPre() {
  model.SetLines (new String[1] {"<P></P>"});
  model.SelectionStart = 7;
  model.InsertTags(TextModel.Tags.Pre);
  AssertEquals("<pre></pre>", model.Lines[1]);
  AssertEquals(14, model.SelectionStart);
```

```
model.InsertReturn();
AssertEquals("<pre>", model.Lines[1]);
AssertEquals("</pre>", model.Lines[2]);
AssertEquals(16, model.SelectionStart);
}
```

Let's remove the other helper methods similarly:

```
public void InsertUnorderedList() {
  InsertTags(Tags.UnorderedList);
}
public void InsertListItemTag() {
  InsertTags(Tags.ListItem);
}
public void InsertParagraphTag() {
  InsertTags(Tags.Paragraph);
}
```

I do these each in the same way: I copy the operational line from the method, delete the method, compile, and see where the errors are. I paste the operational line over the offending call. A couple of the uses of the helpers were inside TextModel itself, and some were in the tests. It was a matter of a couple of minutes, with the help of the compiler. When everything compiled, the tests ran.

Reflection

This chapter has been long, and you might have lost track of the code. I'll include the current listings below, but in a sense losing track of the code is part of the message here.

> **Lesson**   We've made a very important set of changes to the system. We have improved the encapsulation of TextModel and removed many unnecessary methods. We have made the menu creation process, and the creation of new tag insertions, far simpler than they were, as we'll see in a few moments. Most important, even though there were many steps, as we see from the length of this chapter, each step was simple and straightforward. Our first steps improved the XMLNotepad class, but when we tried to improve TextModel, we didn't get all the benefits we expected. We could have stopped there—and perhaps I should have stopped the chapter there—but we went on, in tiny steps until we reached a much better point. Is it a better point? I think so, but let's find out before we close.

Ordered List

We have another story that we agreed to do: Ordered List. Take a look back at the seven steps (in the "What's the Opposite of Simple?" section) we used to have to do to implement a new set of tags, and let's see what we have to do now. We'll begin with a Customer Acceptance Test:

```
*alt0
*output
<OL>
<LI>|</LI>
</OL>
```

Simple enough. We need a new menu item, which wants to look like this:

```
insertOrderedList = new NotepadMenuItem (
  "Insert &OL",
  new EventHandler(MenuInsertTags),
  TextModel.Tags.OrderedList );
this.Menu = new MainMenu(new MenuItem[]
  {fileMenu, insertPre, insertSection, insertUnorderedList,
    insertOrderedList} );
```

We must add the new variable:

```
private MenuItem insertPre;
private MenuItem insertSection;
private MenuItem insertUnorderedList;
private MenuItem insertOrderedList;
```

With the previous implementation, we also had to add a new EventHandler method, add a new ModelAction variable, and initialize that variable to call a method inside the TextModel. We save all that effort, and perhaps more important, we don't have to remember to do it!

Our new code doesn't compile so far, with the message that Text-Model.Tags doesn't include OrderedList. We build that and the support for it, as follows:

```
class TextModel {
  private ArrayList lines;
  private int selectionStart;
  private static string[] newParagraph = { "<P></P>" };
  private static string[] paragraphSkip = { "<P>" };
  private static string[] newListItem = { "<LI></LI>" };
  private static string[] listItemSkip = { "<LI>" };
  private static string[] emptyLine = { "" };
  private static string[] emptyLineSkip = { "" };
  private static string[] newSection = {"<sect1><title></title>","</sect1>" };
  private static string[] sectionSkip = { "<sect1><title>" };
```

```
private static string[] newUnorderedList = {"<UL>","<LI></LI>","</UL>"};
private static string[] unorderedListSkip = { "<UL>", "<LI>" };
private static string[] newOrderedList = {"<OL>","<LI></LI>","</OL>"};
private static string[] orderedListSkip = { "<OL>", "<LI>" };
private static string[] newPre = { "<pre></pre>" };
private static string[] preSkip = { "<pre>" };
public enum Tags {
  Pre = 1,
  Section = 2,
  UnorderedList = 3,
  ListItem = 4,
  Paragraph = 5,
  OrderedList = 6     }
private static string[] InsertStrings(Tags tag) {
  if (tag == Tags.Pre) return newPre;
  else if (tag == Tags.Section) return newSection;
  else if (tag == Tags.UnorderedList) return newUnorderedList;
  else if (tag == Tags.OrderedList) return newOrderedList;
  else if (tag == Tags.ListItem) return newListItem;
  else return newParagraph;
}
private static string[] SkipStrings(Tags tag) {
  if (tag == Tags.Pre) return preSkip;
  else if (tag == Tags.Section) return sectionSkip;
  else if (tag == Tags.UnorderedList) return unorderedListSkip;
  else if (tag == Tags.OrderedList) return orderedListSkip;
  else if (tag == Tags.ListItem) return listItemSkip;
  else return paragraphSkip;
}
```

This almost works, but not quite: the customer test fails at this line:

```
private void ExecuteMenu(string accelerator) {
  MenuItem mi = form.MenuForAccelerator(accelerator);
  mi.PerformClick();
}
```

We've still forgotten one thing (but only one). We haven't picked up the new menu here:

```
public MenuItem MenuForAccelerator(string accelerator) {
  if (accelerator == "&S") return insertSection;
  if (accelerator == "&P") return insertPre;
  if (accelerator == "&U") return insertUnorderedList;
  if (accelerator == "&O") return insertOrderedList;
  if (accelerator == "^O") return openFile;
  if (accelerator == "^S") return saveFile;
  return null;
}
```

With this change, the tests run perfectly. We have added OrderedList in a couple of minutes!

Things still are not perfect. I'm most troubled by the fact that I had to remember to add that menu to the MenuForAccelerator() method, and I'm a little troubled by the fact that I had to change five lines in the TextModel, even though they were all adjacent and pretty obvious. But for sure, things are much improved.

Think about it. This is really a rather large "design" change, yet it went largely without difficulty, and in very little time.

Lesson: Incremental Design and Development

Up until now, the incremental changes we've been making have been simple, and most of them have been localized. The delegate changes we made in Chapter 22, "The Delegate from Troy," were a bit larger, but even they were done in a short evening at the Michigan Union. This time the changes were far more significant, involving three significant classes, the XMLNotepad, the TextModel, and the tests. We implemented a new class, NotepadMenuItem, a subclass of MenuItem. We implemented an enumeration to encapsulate the idea of a command between Form and Model and between tests and Model. We refactored all those classes extensively and simplified them significantly.

Most important, we did it in small steps, never more than a moment or two from running tests. If we needed to ship the code, we could have done so at any moment, because the tests were always running, even if the code improvement wasn't finished yet.

Could we have done a better job earlier? Could we have seen that we should build this structure way back at the beginning? Well, perhaps you could have. I myself could not, new as I was to C# and to this application. And, frankly, if we had invested in this design, I fear that we would have spent a lot of time on it and still probably have gone down some wrong paths. As it is, we shipped running, tested software to our customer, and we kept it running, tested, and improving as we went. We have reached a better point—though not a perfect one—where it is now much easier and more reliable to add new tags.

Lesson: Open Questions

There are still some open questions, of course. There always will be. The ones that I see include these:

- **How can we be sure to find new accelerators more automatically?** I'm thinking in terms of storing all the menus in an array, instead of separate scalars, and looking them up in a simple loop. Then each new menu would automatically be found.

- **How can we simplify setting up and accessing the strings in the TextModel?** At this writing, I'm not sure. Perhaps we could do some kind of subscripting into tables of the insertion strings and the skip strings. Perhaps we could go to a more compact string notation like the one we envisioned earlier, with all the information in one string. Perhaps the commands would return these strings, or perhaps there is some new object waiting to be created.

- **How can we build user-defined tags?** We have a story for user-defined tags. I'm not sure whether we'll be called upon to implement it, but it is on the table. We will need a more sophisticated structure for looking up the values if we have to do this story.

- **Should we keep tag strings in a table?** Right now, we have a nested if statement to find the tag strings. For a handful of items, this is probably fine. It does mean that we have to remember to update the list every time we add an item, which leads to a possible error. Using the tests in a disciplined way will find that error, but it is still a potential problem.

The Code at This Point

XNLNotepad.cs

```
using System;
using System.Drawing;
using System.IO;
using System.Windows.Forms;
using NUnit.Framework;
using System.Collections;
```

```
using System.Text.RegularExpressions;
namespace Notepad {
  class NotepadMenuItem : MenuItem {
    private TextModel.Tags command;
    public NotepadMenuItem (String menuString, EventHandler handler,
      TextModel.Tags tag)
      :base(menuString, handler){
      command = tag;
    }
    public TextModel.Tags Command {
      get { return command; }
    }
  }
  class XMLNotepad : Form {
    public TestableTextBox textbox;
    private TextModel model;
    private MenuItem insertPre;
    private MenuItem insertSection;
    private MenuItem insertUnorderedList;
    private MenuItem insertOrderedList;
    private MenuItem openFile;
    private MenuItem saveFile;
    private ModelAction enterAction;
    private ModelAction shiftEnterAction;
    private ModelAction saveAction;
    private ModelAction loadAction;
    private String fileName;
    private Boolean displayDialog = true;
    public delegate void ModelAction();
    public MenuItem MenuForAccelerator(string accelerator) {
      if (accelerator == "&S") return insertSection;
      if (accelerator == "&P") return insertPre;
      if (accelerator == "&U") return insertUnorderedList;
      if (accelerator == "&O") return insertOrderedList;
      if (accelerator == "^O") return openFile;
      if (accelerator == "^S") return saveFile;
      return null;
    }
    [STAThread]
    static void Main(string[] args) {
      Application.Run(new XMLNotepad());
    }
    public XMLNotepad() {
      initialize(new TextModel());
    }
    public XMLNotepad(TextModel model) {
      initialize(model);
    }
```

```
private void initialize(TextModel model) {
  InitializeDelegates(model);
  this.model = model;
  this.Text = "XML Notepad";
  MenuItem fileMenu = new MenuItem("&File");
  MenuItem newFile = new MenuItem("&New");
  newFile.Click += new EventHandler(MenuFileNewOnClick);
  newFile.Shortcut = Shortcut.CtrlN;
  fileMenu.MenuItems.Add(newFile);
  openFile = new MenuItem("&Open...");
  openFile.Click += new EventHandler(MenuFileOpenOnClick);
  openFile.Shortcut = Shortcut.CtrlO;
  fileMenu.MenuItems.Add(openFile);
  saveFile = new MenuItem("&Save");
  saveFile.Click += new EventHandler(MenuFileSaveOnClick);
  saveFile.Shortcut = Shortcut.CtrlS;
  fileMenu.MenuItems.Add(saveFile);
  MenuItem saveAsFile = new MenuItem("Save &As...");
  saveAsFile.Click += new EventHandler(MenuFileSaveAsOnClick);
  fileMenu.MenuItems.Add(saveAsFile);
  insertSection = new NotepadMenuItem (
    "Insert &Section",
    new EventHandler(MenuInsertTags),
    TextModel.Tags.Section);
  insertPre = new NotepadMenuItem (
    "Insert &Pre",
    new EventHandler(MenuInsertTags),
    TextModel.Tags.Pre );
  insertUnorderedList = new NotepadMenuItem (
    "Insert &UL",
    new EventHandler(MenuInsertTags),
    TextModel.Tags.UnorderedList );
  insertOrderedList = new NotepadMenuItem (
    "Insert &OL",
    new EventHandler(MenuInsertTags),
    TextModel.Tags.OrderedList );
  this.Menu = new MainMenu(new MenuItem[]
    {fileMenu, insertPre, insertSection, insertUnorderedList,
      insertOrderedList} );
  this.textbox = new TestableTextBox();
  this.textbox.Parent = this;
  this.textbox.Dock = DockStyle.Fill;
  this.textbox.BorderStyle = BorderStyle.None;
  this.textbox.Multiline = true;
  this.textbox.ScrollBars = ScrollBars.Both;
  this.textbox.AcceptsTab = true;
  this.textbox.KeyDown += new KeyEventHandler(XMLKeyDownHandler);
  this.textbox.KeyPress += new KeyPressEventHandler(XMLKeyPressHandler);
```

```
        this.textbox.Visible = true;
        this.AutoScaleBaseSize = new System.Drawing.Size(5, 13);
        this.ClientSize = new System.Drawing.Size(292, 266);
        this.Controls.AddRange(new System.Windows.Forms.Control[] {
          this.textbox});
        this.Name = "XMLNotepad";
    }
    private void InitializeDelegates(TextModel model) {
      enterAction = new ModelAction(model.Enter);
      shiftEnterAction = new ModelAction(model.InsertReturn);
      saveAction = new ModelAction(this.SaveFile);
      loadAction = new ModelAction(this.LoadFile);
    }
    void MenuInsertTags(object obj, EventArgs ea) {
      NotepadMenuItem item = (NotepadMenuItem) obj;
      GetText();
      model.InsertTags(item.Command);
      PutText(textbox, model.LinesArray(), model.SelectionStart);
    }
    void MenuFileNewOnClick(object obj, EventArgs ea) {
    }
    void MenuFileSaveOnClick(object obj, EventArgs ea) {
      CallModel(saveAction);
    }
    void MenuFileOpenOnClick(object obj, EventArgs ea) {
      FileOperation(new OpenFileDialog(), loadAction);
    }
    void MenuFileSaveAsOnClick(object obj, EventArgs ea) {
      FileOperation(new SaveFileDialog(), saveAction);
    }
    private void FileOperation(FileDialog dialog, ModelAction action) {
      if (displayDialog) {
        DialogFileAction(dialog, action);
      }
      else {
        CallModel(action);
      }
      displayDialog = true;
    }
    private void DialogFileAction(FileDialog dialog, ModelAction action) {
      dialog.Filter = "xml files (*.xml)|*.xml|All files (*.*)|*.*";
      dialog.FilterIndex = 2 ;
      dialog.RestoreDirectory = true ;
      if(dialog.ShowDialog() == DialogResult.OK) {
        fileName = dialog.FileName;
        CallModel(action);
      }
    }
```

```
void SaveFile() {
  using ( StreamWriter writer = File.CreateText(fileName) ) {
    model.Save(writer);
  }
}
void LoadFile() {
  using ( StreamReader reader = File.OpenText(fileName) ) {
    model.Load(reader);
  }
}
public void XMLKeyPressHandler(object objSender, KeyPressEventArgs kea) {
  if ((int) kea.KeyChar == (int) Keys.Enter) {
    kea.Handled = true;
    // this code is here to avoid putting extra enters in the window.
    // if removed, when you hit enter, the new <P> line breaks in two:
    // <P>
    // |</P>  like that.
  }
}

private void CallModel(ModelAction modelAction) {
  GetText();
  modelAction();
  PutText(textbox, model.LinesArray(), model.SelectionStart);
}
public void XMLKeyDownHandler(object objSender, KeyEventArgs kea) {
  if (kea.KeyCode == Keys.Enter && kea.Modifiers == Keys.None) {
    CallModel(enterAction);
    kea.Handled = true;
  }
  else if (kea.KeyCode == Keys.Enter && kea.Modifiers == Keys.Shift) {
    CallModel(shiftEnterAction);
    kea.Handled = true;
  }
}
internal void PutText(ITestTextBox textbox, string[] lines,
  int selectionStart) {
  // this is Feature Envy big time.
  textbox.Lines = lines;
  textbox.SelectionStart = selectionStart;
  textbox.ScrollToCaret();
}
private void GetText() {
  model.SetLines(textbox.Lines);
  model.SelectionStart = textbox.SelectionStart;
}
internal void CustomerTestPutText() {
  PutText(textbox, model.LinesArray(), model.SelectionStart);
```

```
      }
      internal void SetFileName(String name) {
        fileName = name;
      }
      internal void SetNoFileDialog() {
        displayDialog = false;
      }
    }
}
```

TextModel.cs

```
using System;
using System.IO;
using System.Collections;
using System.Reflection;
using System.Text;
using System.Text.RegularExpressions;
namespace Notepad {
  class TextModel {
    private ArrayList lines;
    private int selectionStart;
    private static string[] newParagraph = { "<P></P>" };
    private static string[] paragraphSkip = { "<P>" };
    private static string[] newListItem = { "<LI></LI>" };
    private static string[] listItemSkip = { "<LI>" };
    private static string[] emptyLine = { "" };
    private static string[] emptyLineSkip = { "" };
    private static string[] newSection = {"<sect1><title></title>",
      "</sect1>" };
    private static string[] sectionSkip = { "<sect1><title>" };
    private static string[] newUnorderedList = {"<UL>","<LI></LI>","</UL>"};
    private static string[] unorderedListSkip = { "<UL>", "<LI>" };
    private static string[] newOrderedList = {"<OL>","<LI></LI>","</OL>"};
    private static string[] orderedListSkip = { "<OL>", "<LI>" };
    private static string[] newPre = { "<pre></pre>" };
    private static string[] preSkip = { "<pre>" };
    public enum Tags {
      Pre = 1,
      Section = 2,
      UnorderedList = 3,
      ListItem = 4,
      Paragraph = 5,
      OrderedList = 6
    }
    private static string[] InsertStrings(Tags tag) {
      if (tag == Tags.Pre) return newPre;
      else if (tag == Tags.Section) return newSection;
```

```
      else if (tag == Tags.UnorderedList) return newUnorderedList;
      else if (tag == Tags.OrderedList) return newOrderedList;
      else if (tag == Tags.ListItem) return newListItem;
      else return newParagraph;
    }
    private static string[] SkipStrings(Tags tag) {
      if (tag == Tags.Pre) return preSkip;
      else if (tag == Tags.Section) return sectionSkip;
      else if (tag == Tags.UnorderedList) return unorderedListSkip;
      else if (tag == Tags.OrderedList) return orderedListSkip;
      else if (tag == Tags.ListItem) return listItemSkip;
      else return paragraphSkip;
    }
      public TextModel() {
      lines = new ArrayList();
    }
    public ArrayList Lines {
      get {
        return lines;
      }
      set {
        lines = value;
      }
    }
    public void SetLines(String[] lines) {
      this.Lines = new ArrayList(lines);
    }
    public String[] LinesArray() {
      return (string[])lines.ToArray(typeof(string));
    }
    public String TestText {
      get {
        StringBuilder b = new StringBuilder();
        foreach(String s in lines) {
          b.Append(s);
          b.Append(System.Environment.NewLine);
        }
        b.Insert(SelectionStart,"|");
        return b.ToString();
      }
    }
    public int SelectionStart {
      get {
        return selectionStart;
      }
      set {
        selectionStart = value;
      }
```

```
  }
  public void Enter() {
    if (InListItem())
      InsertTags(Tags.ListItem);
    else
      InsertTags(Tags.Paragraph);
  }
  private Boolean InListItem() {
    if (LineContainingCursor() < 0 ) return false;
    return ((string) lines[LineContainingCursor()]).StartsWith("<LI>");
  }
  public void InsertReturn() {
    string front = FrontOfCursorLine();
    string back = BackOfCursorLine();
    lines[LineContainingCursor()] = front;
    lines.Insert(LineContainingCursor()+1, back);
    selectionStart += Environment.NewLine.Length;
  }
  public string FrontOfCursorLine() {
    string line = (string) lines[LineContainingCursor()];
    int position = PositionOfCursorInLine();
    return line.Substring(0, position);
  }
  public string BackOfCursorLine() {
    string line = (string) lines[LineContainingCursor()];
    int position = PositionOfCursorInLine();
    return line.Substring(position);
  }
  public int PositionOfCursorInLine() {
    return selectionStart - FirstPositionOfLine(LineContainingCursor());
  }
  public void InsertTags(Tags command) {
    int cursorLine = LineContainingCursor();
    lines.InsertRange(cursorLine+1, InsertStrings(command));
    selectionStart = NewSelectionStart(cursorLine + 1, SkipStrings(command));
  }
  private int NewSelectionStart(int cursorLine, string[] tags) {
    return FirstPositionOfLine(cursorLine) + TotalTagLength(tags);
  }
  private int TotalTagLength(string[] tags) {
    int result = (tags.Length -1) * Environment.NewLine.Length;
    foreach (string tag in tags) {
      result += tag.Length;
    }
    return result;
  }
  private int FirstPositionOfLine(int cursorLine) {
    int length = 0;
```

```
      for (int i = 0; i < cursorLine; i++)
        length += ((String)lines[i]).Length + Environment.NewLine.Length;
      return length;
    }
    public void ChangeToH2() {
      ArrayList linesList = Lines;
      String oldLine = (String) linesList[LineContainingCursor()];
      Regex r = new Regex("<(?<prefix>.*)>(?<body>.*)</(?<suffix>.*)>");
      Match m = r.Match(oldLine);
      String newLine = "<H2>" + m.Groups["body"] + "</H2>";
      linesList[LineContainingCursor()] = newLine;
      Lines = linesList;
    }
    private int LineContainingCursor() {
      if (lines.Count == 0)
        return -1;
      int length = 0;
      int lineNr = 0;
      int cr = Environment.NewLine.Length;
      foreach ( String s in lines) {
        if (length <= selectionStart
          && selectionStart < length+s.Length + cr )
          break;
        length += s.Length + cr;
        lineNr++;
      }
      return lineNr;
    }
    public void Save(TextWriter w) {
      foreach (string line in lines )
        w.WriteLine(line);
    }
    public void Load(TextReader r) {
      String line;
      lines = new ArrayList();
      while((line = r.ReadLine()) != null) {
        lines.Add(line);
      }
    }
  }
}
```

TestTextModel.cs

```
using System;
using System.IO;
using System.Collections;
using NUnit.Framework;
```

```
namespace Notepad {
  [TestFixture] public class TestTextModel : Assertion {
    private TextModel model;
    [SetUp] public void CreateModel() {
      model = new TextModel();
    }
    [Test] public void TestNoLines() {
      ClearModel();
      VerifyClear();
    }
    private void VerifyClear() {
      AssertEquals(0, model.Lines.Count);
    }
    private void ClearModel() {
      model.SetLines(new String[0]);
    }
    [Test] public void TestNoProcessing() {
      GiveModelContents();
      VerifyContents();
    }
    private void VerifyContents() {
      AssertEquals(3, model.Lines.Count);
      AssertEquals("hi", model.Lines[0]);
      AssertEquals("there", model.Lines[1]);
      AssertEquals("chet", model.Lines[2]);
    }
    private void GiveModelContents() {
      model.SetLines(new String[3] { "hi", "there", "chet"});
    }
    [Test] public void TestOneEnter() {
      model.SetLines(new String[1] {"hello world" });
      model.SelectionStart = 5;
      model.InsertTags(TextModel.Tags.Paragraph);
      AssertEquals(2, model.Lines.Count);
      AssertEquals(16, model.SelectionStart);
    }
    [Test] public void TestEmptyText() {
      model.Lines = new ArrayList(new String[0]);
      model.InsertTags(TextModel.Tags.Paragraph);
      AssertEquals(1, model.Lines.Count);
      AssertEquals(3, model.SelectionStart);
    }
    [Test] public void InsertWithCursorAtLineStart () {
      model.Lines = new ArrayList(new String[3] { "<P>one</P>", "",
        "<P>two</P>"});
      model.SelectionStart = 14;
      model.InsertTags(TextModel.Tags.Paragraph);
      AssertEquals("<P>two</P>", model.Lines[2]);
```

```
    }
    [Test] public void TestLineContainingCursorDirectly() {
      // todo?
    }
    [Test] public void ControlTwo() {
      model.SetLines(new String[1] {"<P>The Heading</P>" });
      model.ChangeToH2();
      AssertEquals("<H2>The Heading</H2>", model.Lines[0]);
    }
    [Test] public void AltS() {
      model.Lines = new ArrayList(new String[0]);
      model.InsertTags(TextModel.Tags.Section);
      AssertEquals("<sect1><title></title>", model.Lines[0]);
      AssertEquals("</sect1>", model.Lines[1]);
      AssertEquals(14, model.SelectionStart);
    }
    [Test] public void AltSWithText() {
      model.SetLines (new String[1] {"<P></P>"});
      model.SelectionStart = 7;
      model.InsertTags(TextModel.Tags.Section);
      AssertEquals("<sect1><title></title>", model.Lines[1]);
      AssertEquals("</sect1>", model.Lines[2]);
      AssertEquals(23, model.SelectionStart);
    }
    [Test] public void UnorderedList() {
      model.SetLines (new String[1] {"<P></P>"});
      model.SelectionStart = 3;
      model.InsertTags(TextModel.Tags.UnorderedList);
      AssertEquals("<UL>", model.Lines[1]);
      AssertEquals("<LI></LI>", model.Lines[2]);
      AssertEquals("</UL>", model.Lines[3]);
      AssertEquals(19, model.SelectionStart);
      model.Enter();
      AssertEquals("<LI></LI>", model.Lines[3]);
    }
    [Test] public void InsertPre() {
      model.SetLines (new String[1] {"<P></P>"});
      model.SelectionStart = 7;
      model.InsertTags(TextModel.Tags.Pre);
      AssertEquals("<pre></pre>", model.Lines[1]);
      AssertEquals(14, model.SelectionStart);
      model.InsertReturn();
      AssertEquals("<pre>", model.Lines[1]);
      AssertEquals("</pre>", model.Lines[2]);
      AssertEquals(16, model.SelectionStart);
    }
    [Test] public void ShiftEnter() {
      model.SetLines (new String[1] {"<pre></pre>"});
```

```
      model.SelectionStart = 5;
      model.InsertReturn();
      AssertEquals("<pre>", model.Lines[0]);
      AssertEquals("</pre>", model.Lines[1]);
      AssertEquals(7, model.SelectionStart);
    }
    [Test]
    [Ignore("New Para in mid-Pre Bug")]
    public void ShiftEnterMultipleLines() {
      model.SetLines (new String[] {"<pre>code1", "code2","code3</pre>"});
      model.SelectionStart = 14; // after 'co' in 'code2'
      model.InsertTags(TextModel.Tags.Paragraph);
      AssertEquals("code3</pre>", model.Lines[2]);
      AssertEquals("<P></P>", model.Lines[3]);
    }
    [Test] public void CursorPosition() {
      model.SetLines (new String[] { "<P></P>", "<pre></pre>" });
      model.SelectionStart = 14; // after <pre>
      AssertEquals(5, model.PositionOfCursorInLine());
      AssertEquals("<pre>", model.FrontOfCursorLine());
      AssertEquals("</pre>", model.BackOfCursorLine());
    }
    [Test] public void WriteStream() {
      model.SetLines (new String[] { "<P></P>"});
      StringWriter w = new StringWriter();
      model.Save(w);
      AssertEquals("<P></P>\r\n", w.ToString());
    }
    [Test] public void WriteAndReadFile() {
      ClearModel();
      VerifyClear();
      GiveModelContents();
      VerifyContents();
      SaveModelToFile();
      ClearModel();
      VerifyClear();
      LoadModelFromFile();
      VerifyContents();
    }
    public void SaveModelToFile() {
      using (StreamWriter writer = File.CreateText("savedmodel.xml")) {
        model.Save(writer);
      }
    }
    public void LoadModelFromFile() {
      using (StreamReader reader = File.OpenText("savedmodel.xml")) {
        model.Load(reader);
      }
```

```
        }
      }
    }
```

CustomerTests.cs

```csharp
using System;
using System.IO;
using System.Windows.Forms;
using System.Collections;
using NUnit.Framework;
namespace Notepad
{
  [TestFixture] public class CustomerTest : Assertion {
    private TextModel model;
  private XMLNotepad form;
    [SetUp] public void CreateModel() {
      model = new TextModel();
    form = new XMLNotepad(model);
    }
    [Test] public void EmptyModel() {
    form.XMLKeyDownHandler((object) this, new KeyEventArgs(Keys.Enter));
      AssertEquals("<P>|</P>\r\n", model.TestText);
    }
    [Test] public void DirectMenu() {
      form.MenuForAccelerator("&P").PerformClick();
      AssertEquals("<pre>|</pre>\r\n", model.TestText);
    }

    [Test] public void StringInput() {
      String commands =
@"*input
some line
*end
*enter
*output
some line
<P>|</P>";
      InterpretCommands(commands, "");
    }
    [Test] public void FileInput() {
      InterpretFileInput(@"c:\data\csharp\notepad\fileInput.test");
    }
    [Test] public void TestAllFiles() {
      String[] testFiles = Directory.GetFiles(@"c:\data\csharp\notepad\",
        "*.test");
      foreach (String testFilename in testFiles) {
        InterpretFileInput(testFilename);
```

```
      }
    }
    private void InterpretFileInput(String fileName) {
      StreamReader stream = File.OpenText(fileName);
      String contents = stream.ReadToEnd();
      stream.Close();
      InterpretCommands(contents, fileName);
    }
    private void InterpretCommands(String commands, String message) {
      StringReader reader = new StringReader(commands);
      String line = reader.ReadLine();
      CreateModel();
      while ( line != null) {
        if (line.StartsWith("*alt"))
          ExecuteMenu("&"+line[4]);
        else if ( line == "*enter")
          form.XMLKeyDownHandler((object) this, new KeyEventArgs(Keys.Enter));
        else if ( line == "*shiftEnter")
          form.XMLKeyDownHandler((object) this,
            new KeyEventArgs(Keys.Enter | Keys.Shift));
        else if (line == "*display")
          Console.WriteLine("display\r\n{0}\r\nend", model.TestText);
        else if (line == "*output")
          CompareOutput(reader, message);
        else if (line == "*input")
          SetInput(reader);
        else if (line == "*loadfile")
          LoadFile();
        else if (line == "*savefile")
          SaveFile();
        else
          Assert(line + " command not defined", false);
        line = reader.ReadLine();
      }
    }
    private void SaveFile() {
      form.SetFileName("customertestxmlfile.xml");
      form.SetNoFileDialog();
      ExecuteMenu("^S");
    }
    private void LoadFile() {
      form.SetFileName("customertestxmlfile.xml");
      form.SetNoFileDialog();
      ExecuteMenu("^O");
    }
    private void CompareOutput(StringReader reader, String message) {
      String expected = ExpectedOutput(reader);
      String result = model.TestText;
```

```
     if (expected != result) {
       Console.WriteLine(message);
       Console.WriteLine("*Expected");
       Console.WriteLine(expected);
       Console.WriteLine("*Result");
       Console.WriteLine(result);
     }
     AssertEquals(message, expected, model.TestText);
   }
   private String ExpectedOutput(StringReader reader) {
     return ReadToEnd(reader);
   }
   private String ReadToEnd(StringReader reader) {
     String result = "";
     String line = reader.ReadLine();
     while (line != null && line != "*end") {
       result += line;
       result += System.Environment.NewLine;
       line = reader.ReadLine();
     }
     return result;
   }
   private void SetInput(StringReader reader) {
     InputCommand input = new InputCommand(reader);
     model.Lines = input.CleanLines();
     model.SelectionStart = input.SelectionStart();
form.CustomerTestPutText();
   }
   private void ExecuteMenu(string accelerator) {
     MenuItem mi = form.MenuForAccelerator(accelerator);
     mi.PerformClick();
   }
 }
}
```

Selected Customer Tests

saveload.test

```
*input
<P>uno</P>
<P>duo</P>
<P>tres|</P>
*end
*savefile
*input
<P>|<P>
```

```
*end
<P>|<P>
*end
*loadfile
<P>|uno</P>
<P>duo</P>
<P>tres</P>
*end
```

insertOL.test

```
*alt0
*output
<OL>
<LI>|</LI>
</OL>
```

insertAfterPara.test

```
*input
<P>This is the first paragraph.</P>
<P>This is the second| paragraph.</P>
*end
*enter
*output
<P>This is the first paragraph.</P>
<P>This is the second paragraph.</P>
<P>|</P>
```

insertPara.test

```
*input
<P>This is the first p|aragraph.</P>
<P>This is the second paragraph.</P>
*end
*enter
*output
<P>This is the first paragraph.</P>
<P>|</P>
<P>This is the second paragraph.</P>
```

InsertPre.test

```
*input
<P>This is the first p|aragraph.</P>
<P>This is the second paragraph.</P>
*end
```

```
*altP
*output
<P>This is the first paragraph.</P>
<pre>|</pre>
<P>This is the second paragraph.</P>
*end
*shiftEnter
*output
<P>This is the first paragraph.</P>
<pre>
|</pre>
<P>This is the second paragraph.</P>
```

insertUL.test

```
*altU
*output
<UL>
<LI>|</LI>
</UL>
```

paraAfterPara.test

```
*input
<P></P>
*end
*enter
*output
<P></P>
<P>|</P>
```

26

Menu Arrays

*As so often happens when we take a break, I got an idea about how to improve
all that manual creation and searching of the insert menus. So I hurried home
from lunch to share it with you.*

The Pain

Even though we have improved the creation process for new menu items, it's
still not perfect. Every time we create a new insert menu item, we have to deal
with the code that defines the item, the code that adds the item to the menu,
and the code that looks up the item. Check the highlighted items in the following code from the XMLNotepad class, for example:

```
class XMLNotepad : Form {
  public TestableTextBox textbox;
  private TextModel model;
  private MenuItem insertPre;
  private MenuItem insertSection;
  private MenuItem insertUnorderedList;
  private MenuItem insertOrderedList;
  private MenuItem openFile;
  private MenuItem saveFile;
  private ModelAction enterAction;
  private ModelAction shiftEnterAction;
  private ModelAction saveAction;
  private ModelAction loadAction;
  private String fileName;
  private Boolean displayDialog = true;
  public delegate void ModelAction();
  public MenuItem MenuForAccelerator(string accelerator) {
```

```
      if (accelerator == "&S") return insertSection;
      if (accelerator == "&P") return insertPre;
      if (accelerator == "&U") return insertUnorderedList;
      if (accelerator == "&O") return insertOrderedList;
      if (accelerator == "^O") return openFile;
      if (accelerator == "^S") return saveFile;
      return null;
    }

    private void initialize(TextModel model) {
      ...
      insertSection = new NotepadMenuItem (
        "Insert &Section",
        new EventHandler(MenuInsertTags),
        TextModel.Tags.Section);
      insertPre = new NotepadMenuItem (
        "Insert &Pre",
        new EventHandler(MenuInsertTags),
        TextModel.Tags.Pre );
      insertUnorderedList = new NotepadMenuItem (
        "Insert &UL",
        new EventHandler(MenuInsertTags),
        TextModel.Tags.UnorderedList );
      insertOrderedList = new NotepadMenuItem (
        "Insert &OL",
        new EventHandler(MenuInsertTags),
        TextModel.Tags.OrderedList );

      this.Menu = new MainMenu(new MenuItem[]
        {fileMenu, insertPre, insertSection, insertUnorderedList,
          insertOrderedList} );
      ...
```

This is boring and repetitive. It includes duplicated code, and it causes duplication of effort. Plus, the TextModel needs some work as well:

```
class TextModel {
  private ArrayList lines;
  private int selectionStart;
  private static string[] newParagraph = { "<P></P>" };
  private static string[] paragraphSkip = { "<P>" };
  private static string[] newListItem = { "<LI></LI>" };
  private static string[] listItemSkip = { "<LI>" };
  private static string[] emptyLine = { "" };
  private static string[] emptyLineSkip = { "" };
  private static string[] newSection = {"<sect1><title></title>","</sect1>" };
  private static string[] sectionSkip = { "<sect1><title>" };
```

```
private static string[] newUnorderedList = {"<UL>","<LI></LI>","</UL>"};
private static string[] unorderedListSkip = { "<UL>", "<LI>" };
private static string[] newOrderedList = {"<OL>","<LI></LI>","</OL>"};
private static string[] orderedListSkip = { "<OL>", "<LI>" };
private static string[] newPre = { "<pre></pre>" };
private static string[] preSkip = { "<pre>" };
public enum Tags {
  Pre = 1,
  Section = 2,
  UnorderedList = 3,
  ListItem = 4,
  Paragraph = 5,
  OrderedList = 6
}
private static string[] InsertStrings(Tags tag) {
  if (tag == Tags.Pre) return newPre;
  else if (tag == Tags.Section) return newSection;
  else if (tag == Tags.UnorderedList) return newUnorderedList;
  else if (tag == Tags.OrderedList) return newOrderedList;
  else if (tag == Tags.ListItem) return newListItem;
  else return newParagraph;
}
private static string[] SkipStrings(Tags tag) {
  if (tag == Tags.Pre) return preSkip;
  else if (tag == Tags.Section) return sectionSkip;
  else if (tag == Tags.UnorderedList) return unorderedListSkip;
  else if (tag == Tags.OrderedList) return orderedListSkip;
  else if (tag == Tags.ListItem) return listItemSkip;
  else return paragraphSkip;
}
```

This, too, is definitely repetitive and somewhat troublesome. We need to do something about it.

The Plan

When code gets repetitive in this way, with lines that are similar except for the data they contain, it's a good idea to factor out the data. The code is calling for a table of data and a loop, instead of repeated blocks of very similar code. That's the idea we're going to work on here. We'll try to produce a table of data that can be used to define the menu strings and the insert and skip tags, all in one place. Then we'll process the table to produce the menus. We'll put the menus in an array or a list so that we can search them easily for accelerators. And we'll try to eliminate the InsertStrings() and SkipStrings() methods entirely.

Here's a sketch of the kind of data I'm envisioning, not in any language, just to look at:

```
Insert &Pre, { "<pre></pre>" }, { "<pre>" }
Insert &OL, {"<OL>","<LI></LI>","</OL>"}, { "<OL>", "<LI>" }
...
```

I'm envisioning some kind of structure with the menu string and the tag string arrays in it. We would attach that structure to the NotepadMenuItem instead of the current command object. I figure that if I can do this in a couple of hours, it'll be worth it. Let's see.

Menu Array

My first move will be to replace the scalar NotepadMenuItem variables with a single array. I'll do that in small steps so as not to go wrong. First I'll put the menu items into an array and make the MenuForAccelerator() method use the array. Then I'll eliminate the scalars. Just for convenience, I think I'll start with an ArrayList, even though I'm not sure if I can use it in the menu creation. The ArrayList will make for cleaner code—at least I think it will:

```
class XMLNotepad : Form {
  public TestableTextBox textbox;
  private TextModel model;
  private MenuItem insertPre;
  private MenuItem insertSection;
  private MenuItem insertUnorderedList;
  private MenuItem insertOrderedList;
  private ArrayList insertMenus;
  private MenuItem openFile;
  private MenuItem saveFile;
  private ModelAction enterAction;
  private ModelAction shiftEnterAction;
  private ModelAction saveAction;
  private ModelAction loadAction;
  private String fileName;
  private Boolean displayDialog = true;
  public delegate void ModelAction();
  public MenuItem MenuForAccelerator(string accelerator) {
    if (accelerator == "^O") return openFile;
    if (accelerator == "^S") return saveFile;
    foreach( NotepadMenuItem m in insertMenus) {
      if (m.Text.IndexOf(accelerator) >= 0)
        return m;
    }
    return null;
```

```
    }
    private void initialize(TextModel model) {
      ...
      insertMenus = new ArrayList();
      insertSection = new NotepadMenuItem (
        "Insert &Section",
        new EventHandler(MenuInsertTags),
        TextModel.Tags.Section);
      insertMenus.Add(insertSection);
      insertPre = new NotepadMenuItem (
        "Insert &Pre",
        new EventHandler(MenuInsertTags),
        TextModel.Tags.Pre );
      insertMenus.Add(insertPre);
      insertUnorderedList = new NotepadMenuItem (
        "Insert &UL",
        new EventHandler(MenuInsertTags),
        TextModel.Tags.UnorderedList );
      insertMenus.Add(insertUnorderedList);
      insertOrderedList = new NotepadMenuItem (
        "Insert &OL",
        new EventHandler(MenuInsertTags),
        TextModel.Tags.OrderedList );
      insertMenus.Add(insertOrderedList);
      this.Menu = new MainMenu(new MenuItem[]
        {fileMenu, insertPre, insertSection, insertUnorderedList,
          insertOrderedList} );
```

There's no complaining about this. The code is pretty clear, and it works the first time. Now let's use the ArrayList to define the main menu. That makes the above code look like this:

```
insertMenus = new ArrayList();
insertMenus.Add(new NotepadMenuItem (
  "Insert &Section",
  new EventHandler(MenuInsertTags),
  TextModel.Tags.Section));
insertMenus.Add(new NotepadMenuItem (
  "Insert &Pre",
  new EventHandler(MenuInsertTags),
  TextModel.Tags.Pre ));
insertMenus.Add(new NotepadMenuItem (
  "Insert &UL",
  new EventHandler(MenuInsertTags),
  TextModel.Tags.UnorderedList ));
insertMenus.Add(new NotepadMenuItem (
  "Insert &OL",
  new EventHandler(MenuInsertTags),
```

```
    TextModel.Tags.OrderedList ));
this.Menu = new MainMenu(new MenuItem[] {fileMenu} );
this.Menu.MenuItems.
  AddRange((MenuItem[]) insertMenus.ToArray(typeof(NotepadMenuItem)));
```

I don't like that ugly typeof() usage, but it's a small price to pay for the use of the ArrayList elsewhere. We could build a custom class to avoid the typeof, but until Microsoft gives us generics, that seems like too much work for the benefit.

Lesson: Quick Reflection

The work I've done so far in this chapter, including writing this much of the chapter, took me about thirty minutes. Already the code—and the process—is a bit better. Now when we add a new menu item, we don't have to add a private variable for each one or remember to add it to the MenuFor Accelerator() method—a noticeable improvement. Thinking of the private menu items reminds me—let's remove those to get this:

```
class XMLNotepad : Form {
    public TestableTextBox textbox;
    private TextModel model;
//    private MenuItem insertPre;
//    private MenuItem insertSection;
//    private MenuItem insertUnorderedList;
//    private MenuItem insertOrderedList;
    private ArrayList insertMenus;
    private MenuItem openFile;
    private MenuItem saveFile;
    private ModelAction enterAction;
    private ModelAction shiftEnterAction;
    private ModelAction saveAction;
    private ModelAction loadAction;
    private String fileName;
    private Boolean displayDialog = true;
    ...
```

I'm showing them commented out for your convenience, but now I'll delete them for real. And the code compiles, and the tests run correctly.

The Table

Our next step will be to build a table of objects like the list I showed in the "The Plan" section and to build the menu from that. I expect this to be a bit tricky, because I foresee that we'll have to change the code for everyone who is now using that Tags enum:

```
public enum Tags {
  Pre = 1,
  Section = 2,
  UnorderedList = 3,
  ListItem = 4,
  Paragraph = 5,
  OrderedList = 6
}
```

We'll allow the compiler to tell us what to do, and we'll rely on the tests to get things working. First, let's build a little class. This class is so dull that it could even be a struct, but we'll use a class anyway:

```
class InsertAction {
  private string menuString;
  private string[] tagsToInsert;
  private string[] tagsToSkip;
  public InsertAction(string menu, string[] inserts, string[] skips) {
    menuString = menu;
    tagsToInsert = inserts;
    tagsToSkip = skips;
  }
  public string MenuString {
    get { return menuString; }
  }
  public string[] TagsToInsert {
    get { return tagsToInsert; }
  }
  public string[] TagsToSkip {
    get { return tagsToSkip; }
  }
}
```

There's nothing special here; this is just a simple no-behavior structure class. For now, it's actually inside the TextModel.cs file, but we might move it out later. Now let's make a table of these objects in TextModel class:

```
private static InsertAction[] insertActions = new InsertAction[] {
  new InsertAction("Insert &Pre",
    new string[] { "<pre></pre>" },
    new string[] { "<pre>" }),
```

```
new InsertAction("Insert &Section",
  new string[] {"<sect1><title></title>","</sect1>" },
  new string[] {"<sect1><title>" }),
new InsertAction("Insert &UL",
  new string[] {"<UL>","<LI></LI>","</UL>"},
  new string[] {"<UL>", "<LI>" }),
new InsertAction("Insert &OL",
  new string[] {"<OL>","<LI></LI>","</OL>"},
  new string[] {"<OL>", "<LI>" })
};
```

I'm not sure why, but Microsoft Visual Studio can't seem to figure out how to format those lines. The code compiles just fine but formats all over to the right side, the way it does when it thinks there's something wrong. Anyway, that's the table. We'll add a property to get it:

```
public InsertAction[] InsertActions {
  get { return insertActions; }
}
```

Now comes the tricky part. We want to use this table to create our menus. When we do that, some things are likely to break. Let's just go ahead and do it:

```
foreach (InsertAction action in model.InsertActions) {
  insertMenus.Add(new NotepadMenuItem (
    action.MenuString,
    new EventHandler(MenuInsertTags),
    action));
}
```

That's certainly what we want to say: just create a new menu item with the action's string and attach the action to the menu item. Our NotepadMenuItem constructor won't like that. It looks like this:

```
class NotepadMenuItem : MenuItem {
  private TextModel.Tags command;
  public NotepadMenuItem (String menuString, EventHandler handler,
    TextModel.Tags tag)
    :base(menuString, handler){
    command = tag;
  }
  public TextModel.Tags Command {
    get { return command; }
  }
}
```

It needs to look like this:

```
class NotepadMenuItem : MenuItem {
  private InsertAction action;
```

```
public NotepadMenuItem (String menuString, EventHandler handler,
  InsertAction act)
  :base(menuString, handler){
  action = act;
}
public InsertAction Action {
  get { return action; }
}
}
```

We change it that way and compile to see who complains. The compiler points here:

```
void MenuInsertTags(object obj, EventArgs ea) {
  NotepadMenuItem item = (NotepadMenuItem) obj;
  GetText();
  model.InsertTags(item.Command);
  PutText(textbox, model.LinesArray(), model.SelectionStart);
}
```

The NotepadMenuItem no longer understands Command. Here, we'll just pass the action back to the TextModel and require TextModel to deal with it. We start here:

```
public void InsertTags(Tags command) {
  int cursorLine = LineContainingCursor();
  lines.InsertRange(cursorLine+1, InsertStrings(command));
  selectionStart = NewSelectionStart(cursorLine + 1, SkipStrings(command));
}
```

That needs to become this:

```
public void InsertTags(InsertAction action) {
  int cursorLine = LineContainingCursor();
  lines.InsertRange(cursorLine+1, action.TagsToInsert);
  selectionStart = NewSelectionStart(cursorLine + 1, action.TagsToSkip);
}
```

I'm adding that method, not replacing it, because I know that some methods are calling the InsertTags() method that uses a Tags variable. This change makes the compiler messages go away. And the tests run!

Reviewing Where We Are

The XML Notepad is now much improved. Starting from where we were initially, we now have all the insert menus being created by looping over a data structure that TextModel provides. Essentially, TextModel is publishing what it knows how to do, and the Notepad just creates menus for each action. This should mean that we can add a new tag simply by adding one new InsertAction instance to the insertActions variable. We'll try that in a moment. If it works—and I'm sure it will—it will reduce that seven-step process of adding a new item to just one step! Not bad at all!

At this point, counting writing the chapter, I've been working for an hour and twenty minutes, a very good return on my investment. Now let's work on deleting some variables in TextModel, commenting them out as before. I'm sure we'll get some compiler messages or some tests failing.

```
class TextModel {
    private ArrayList lines;
    private int selectionStart;
    private static string[] newParagraph = { "<P></P>" };
    private static string[] paragraphSkip = { "<P>" };
    private static string[] newListItem = { "<LI></LI>" };
    private static string[] listItemSkip = { "<LI>" };
    private static string[] emptyLine = { "" };
    private static string[] emptyLineSkip = { "" };
//    private static string[] newSection = {"<sect1><title></title>",
//    "</sect1>" };
//    private static string[] sectionSkip = { "<sect1><title>" };
//    private static string[] newUnorderedList = {"<UL>","<LI></LI>","</UL>"};
//    private static string[] unorderedListSkip = { "<UL>", "<LI>" };
//    private static string[] newOrderedList = {"<OL>","<LI></LI>","</OL>"};
//    private static string[] orderedListSkip = { "<OL>", "<LI>" };
//    private static string[] newPre = { "<pre></pre>" };
//    private static string[] preSkip = { "<pre>" };
    private static string[] InsertStrings(Tags tag) {
//        if (tag == Tags.Pre) return newPre;
//        else if (tag == Tags.Section) return newSection;
//        else if (tag == Tags.UnorderedList) return newUnorderedList;
//        else if (tag == Tags.OrderedList) return newOrderedList;
        if (tag == Tags.ListItem) return newListItem;
        else return newParagraph;
    }
    private static string[] SkipStrings(Tags tag) {
//        if (tag == Tags.Pre) return preSkip;
//        else if (tag == Tags.Section) return sectionSkip;
//        else if (tag == Tags.UnorderedList) return unorderedListSkip;
//        else if (tag == Tags.OrderedList) return orderedListSkip;
        if (tag == Tags.ListItem) return listItemSkip;
        else return paragraphSkip;
    }
```

Well! That's what we wanted to delete, but we cannot. The reason is that some of the tests are now failing. For example, with those deletions as shown, this test fails:

```
[Test] public void AltS() {
  model.Lines = new ArrayList(new String[0]);
  model.InsertTags(TextModel.Tags.Section);
  AssertEquals("<sect1><title></title>", model.Lines[0]);
  AssertEquals("</sect1>", model.Lines[1]);
  AssertEquals(14, model.SelectionStart);
}
```

Several tests are relying on the old logic in the Tags enum and the Insert-String() and SkipStrings() methods. It's not quite as simple as I thought to remove those methods and the static lists. What can we do? Let's look again at the overloaded method InsertTags():

```
public void InsertTags(Tags command) {
  int cursorLine = LineContainingCursor();
  lines.InsertRange(cursorLine+1, InsertStrings(command));
  selectionStart = NewSelectionStart(cursorLine + 1, SkipStrings(command));
}
public void InsertTags(InsertAction action) {
  int cursorLine = LineContainingCursor();
  lines.InsertRange(cursorLine+1, action.TagsToInsert);
  selectionStart = NewSelectionStart(cursorLine + 1, action.TagsToSkip);
}
```

Looking at both of those gave me an idea. How about changing the first one to use the second, something like this:

```
public void InsertTags(Tags command) {
  InsertTags(ActionForCommand(command));
}
```

The idea is that we will look up the action we need with the Action-ForCommand() method. I'll make the change, and then we'll see about making it work. We know that ActionForCommand() has to look something like this:

```
private InsertAction ActionForCommand(Tags command) {
  // look up and return an InsertAction
}
```

The first thing this tells us is that our InsertAction items need to be accessible, somehow, by Tags. One way would be to build an auxiliary structure such as a hashtable. It would be easier just to put the Tags in the InsertAction object and fill in the table. Here's the updated class:

```
class InsertAction {
  private TextModel.Tags command;
  private string menuString;
  private string[] tagsToInsert;
  private string[] tagsToSkip;
```

```
public InsertAction(TextModel.Tags tag, string menu, string[] inserts,
  string[] skips) {
  command = tag;
  menuString = menu;
  tagsToInsert = inserts;
  tagsToSkip = skips;
}
public TextModel.Tags Command {
  get { return command; }
}
public string MenuString {
  get { return menuString; }
}
public string[] TagsToInsert {
  get { return tagsToInsert; }
}
public string[] TagsToSkip {
  get { return tagsToSkip; }
}
}
```

Now we need to add the tags to the InsertActions array, and we need to add all the tags that are in the scalars but not in the menu. This means that I'll be faced with that horrible formatting bug in Visual Studio. I wonder if there is a way to turn off auto-formatting for a while. Ah, yes: Tools/Options/Text Editor/C#/Formatting has an option. I'll turn it off and then edit that array to look like this:

```
private static InsertAction[] insertActions = new InsertAction[] {
  new InsertAction(
    Tags.Pre,
    "Insert &Pre",
    new string[] { "<pre></pre>" },
    new string[] { "<pre>" }),
  new InsertAction(
    Tags.Section,
    "Insert &Section",
    new string[] {"<sect1><title></title>","</sect1>" },
    new string[] {"<sect1><title>" }),
  new InsertAction(
    Tags.UnorderedList,
    "Insert &UL",
    new string[] {"<UL>","<LI></LI>","</UL>"},
    new string[] {"<UL>", "<LI>" }),
    new InsertAction(
```

```
    Tags.OrderedList,
    "Insert &OL",
    new string[] {"<OL>","<LI></LI>","</OL>"},
    new string[] {"<OL>", "<LI>" })
};
```

This should be enough to make all the tests work again. Let's find out...grrr, not quite. The lookup with the comment in it doesn't compile—probably you remembered that, but I needed the compiler to remind me. Let's code that up now:

```
private InsertAction ActionForCommand(Tags command) {
  foreach ( InsertAction action in InsertActions) {
    if (action.Command == command)
      return action;
  }
  return null;
}
```

This won't work for all cases—some tests should break. But it should compile, and making the rest of the tests run should be accomplished by adding new entries to InsertActions. I'll try it. Sure enough, all but four tests pass. I think they're the four that failed before. I'll add the additional tags to the array:

```
private static InsertAction[] insertActions = new InsertAction[] {
  new InsertAction(
    Tags.Pre,
    "Insert &Pre",
    new string[] { "<pre></pre>" },
    new string[] { "<pre>" }),
  new InsertAction(
    Tags.Section,
    "Insert &Section",
    new string[] {"<sect1><title></title>","</sect1>" },
    new string[] {"<sect1><title>" }),
  new InsertAction(
    Tags.UnorderedList,
    "Insert &UL",
    new string[] {"<UL>","<LI></LI>","</UL>"},
    new string[] {"<UL>", "<LI>" }),
  new InsertAction(
    Tags.OrderedList,
    "Insert &OL",
    new string[] {"<OL>","<LI></LI>","</OL>"},
    new string[] {"<OL>", "<LI>" }),
```

```
new InsertAction(
  Tags.Paragraph,
  null,
  new string[] { "<P></P>" },
  new string[] { "<P>" }),
new InsertAction(
  Tags.ListItem,
  null,
  new string[] { "<LI></LI>" },
  new string[] { "<LI>" })
};
```

You'll notice the nulls I put in there for those last two items. I don't want them to have menus. So we'll enhance the menu-building code just a bit also:

```
foreach (InsertAction action in model.InsertActions) {
  if (action.MenuString != null ) {
    insertMenus.Add(new NotepadMenuItem (
      action.MenuString,
      new EventHandler(MenuInsertTags),
      action));
  }
}
```

Everything compiles, and the tests all run. I should be able to remove all the commented code here:

```
class TextModel {
  private ArrayList lines;
  private int selectionStart;
//    private static string[] newParagraph = { "<P></P>" };
//    private static string[] paragraphSkip = { "<P>" };
//    private static string[] newListItem = { "<LI></LI>" };
//    private static string[] listItemSkip = { "<LI>" };
//    private static string[] emptyLine = { "" };
//    private static string[] emptyLineSkip = { "" };
//    private static string[] newSection = {"<sect1><title></title>",
//    "</sect1>" };
//    private static string[] sectionSkip = { "<sect1><title>" };
//    private static string[] newUnorderedList = {"<UL>","<LI></LI>","</UL>"};
//    private static string[] unorderedListSkip = { "<UL>", "<LI>" };
//    private static string[] newOrderedList = {"<OL>","<LI></LI>","</OL>"};
//    private static string[] orderedListSkip = { "<OL>", "<LI>" };
//    private static string[] newPre = { "<pre></pre>" };
//    private static string[] preSkip = { "<pre>" };
    ...
```

```
//      private static string[] InsertStrings(Tags tag) {
//        if (tag == Tags.Pre) return newPre;
//        else if (tag == Tags.Section) return newSection;
//        else if (tag == Tags.UnorderedList) return newUnorderedList;
//        else if (tag == Tags.OrderedList) return newOrderedList;
//        if (tag == Tags.ListItem) return newListItem;
//        else return newParagraph;
//      }
//      private static string[] SkipStrings(Tags tag) {
//        if (tag == Tags.Pre) return preSkip;
//        else if (tag == Tags.Section) return sectionSkip;
//        else if (tag == Tags.UnorderedList) return unorderedListSkip;
//        else if (tag == Tags.OrderedList) return orderedListSkip;
//        if (tag == Tags.ListItem) return listItemSkip;
//        else return paragraphSkip;
//      }
```

This compiles, and the tests run. I'll delete all that code now. And it still compiles and still runs.

Lesson: Where Are We Now?

The code is much improved. The lookups have been converted to loops, instead of those ugly if/else structures, and all the information about the TextModel's capabilities is encapsulated in one array. We have deleted a lot of code, one of the best signs of progress.

Notice that we have spent only short amounts of time with tests not running. There was one stretch there, filling in the array, that was a few steps long, but it was straightforward and not really difficult. There may have been a way to get the tests running sooner, but I didn't see it; this way was quite simple, and no problems arose.

We created a lot of dead code and removed it. Now I'm wondering if other methods in these classes are not used and therefore are subject to being deleted. I've looked for any indication that the compiler can tell me about things that are unused, but I've found nothing. I guess I'll have to inspect the code manually. That's no fun at all, but I'll take a few minutes and see if I find anything. A quick inspection doesn't turn anything up. I think I'll post a question on some of the lists, however. I'll let you know if I find out anything. [Added in editing: I found no tools for finding dead code. Someone should write one.]

TextModel Code

Here's a summary of TextModel as it stands now. I think you'll agree that it's much better. Was it worth a couple of hours? I think so. What do you think?

```csharp
using System;
using System.IO;
using System.Collections;
using System.Reflection;
using System.Text;
using System.Text.RegularExpressions;
namespace Notepad {
  class InsertAction {
    private TextModel.Tags command;
    private string menuString;
    private string[] tagsToInsert;
    private string[] tagsToSkip;
    public InsertAction(TextModel.Tags tag, string menu, string[] inserts,
      string[] skips) {
      command = tag;
      menuString = menu;
      tagsToInsert = inserts;
      tagsToSkip = skips;
    }
    public TextModel.Tags Command {
      get { return command; }
    }
    public string MenuString {
      get { return menuString; }
    }
    public string[] TagsToInsert {
      get { return tagsToInsert; }
    }
    public string[] TagsToSkip {
      get { return tagsToSkip; }
    }
  }
  class TextModel {
    private ArrayList lines;
    private int selectionStart;
    private static InsertAction[] insertActions = new InsertAction[] {
      new InsertAction(
        Tags.Pre,
        "Insert &Pre",
        new string[] { "<pre></pre>" },
        new string[] { "<pre>" }),
      new InsertAction(
```

```
      Tags.Section,
      "Insert &Section",
      new string[] {"<sect1><title></title>","</sect1>" },
      new string[] {"<sect1><title>" }),
    new InsertAction(
      Tags.UnorderedList,
      "Insert &UL",
      new string[] {"<UL>","<LI></LI>","</UL>"},
      new string[] {"<UL>", "<LI>" }),
    new InsertAction(
      Tags.OrderedList,
      "Insert &OL",
      new string[] {"<OL>","<LI></LI>","</OL>"},
      new string[] {"<OL>", "<LI>" }),
    new InsertAction(
      Tags.Paragraph,
      null,
      new string[] { "<P></P>" },
      new string[] { "<P>" }),
    new InsertAction(
      Tags.ListItem,
      null,
      new string[] { "<LI></LI>" },
      new string[] { "<LI>" })
    };
public InsertAction[] InsertActions {
  get { return insertActions; }
}
public enum Tags {
  Pre = 1,
  Section = 2,
  UnorderedList = 3,
  ListItem = 4,
  Paragraph = 5,
  OrderedList = 6
}
public TextModel() {
  lines = new ArrayList();
}
public ArrayList Lines {
  get { return lines; }
  set { lines = value; }
}
public void SetLines(String[] lines) {
  this.Lines = new ArrayList(lines);
}
public String[] LinesArray() {
  return (string[])lines.ToArray(typeof(string));
```

```
    }
    public String TestText {
      get {
        StringBuilder b = new StringBuilder();
        foreach(String s in lines) {
          b.Append(s);
          b.Append(System.Environment.NewLine);
        }
        b.Insert(SelectionStart,"|");
        return b.ToString();
      }
    }
    public int SelectionStart {
      get { return selectionStart; }
      set { selectionStart = value; }
    }
    public void Enter() {
      if (InListItem())
        InsertTags(Tags.ListItem);
      else
        InsertTags(Tags.Paragraph);
    }
    private Boolean InListItem() {
      if (LineContainingCursor() < 0 ) return false;
      return ((string) lines[LineContainingCursor()]).StartsWith("<LI>");
    }
    public void InsertReturn() {
      string front = FrontOfCursorLine();
      string back = BackOfCursorLine();
      lines[LineContainingCursor()] = front;
      lines.Insert(LineContainingCursor()+1, back);
      selectionStart += Environment.NewLine.Length;
    }
    public string FrontOfCursorLine() {
      string line = (string) lines[LineContainingCursor()];
      int position = PositionOfCursorInLine();
      return line.Substring(0, position);
    }
    public string BackOfCursorLine() {
      string line = (string) lines[LineContainingCursor()];
      int position = PositionOfCursorInLine();
      return line.Substring(position);
    }
    public int PositionOfCursorInLine() {
      return selectionStart - FirstPositionOfLine(LineContainingCursor());
    }
```

```csharp
public void InsertTags(Tags command) {
  InsertTags(ActionForCommand(command));
}
public void InsertTags(InsertAction action) {
  int cursorLine = LineContainingCursor();
  lines.InsertRange(cursorLine+1, action.TagsToInsert);
  selectionStart = NewSelectionStart(cursorLine + 1, action.TagsToSkip);
}
private InsertAction ActionForCommand(Tags command) {
  foreach ( InsertAction action in InsertActions) {
    if (action.Command == command)
      return action;
  }
  return null;
}
 private int NewSelectionStart(int cursorLine, string[] tags) {
  return FirstPositionOfLine(cursorLine) + TotalTagLength(tags);
}
private int TotalTagLength(string[] tags) {
  int result = (tags.Length -1) * Environment.NewLine.Length;
  foreach (string tag in tags) {
    result += tag.Length;
  }
  return result;
}
private int FirstPositionOfLine(int cursorLine) {
  int length = 0;
  for (int i = 0; i < cursorLine; i++)
    length += ((String)lines[i]).Length + Environment.NewLine.Length;
  return length;
}
public void ChangeToH2() {
  ArrayList linesList = Lines;
  String oldLine = (String) linesList[LineContainingCursor()];
  Regex r = new Regex("<(?<prefix>.*)>(?<body>.*)</(?<suffix>.*)>");
  Match m = r.Match(oldLine);
  String newLine = "<H2>" + m.Groups["body"] + "</H2>";
  linesList[LineContainingCursor()] = newLine;
  Lines = linesList;
}
private int LineContainingCursor() {
  if (lines.Count == 0)
    return -1;
  int length = 0;
  int lineNr = 0;
  int cr = Environment.NewLine.Length;
```

```
        foreach ( String s in lines) {
          if (length <= selectionStart
            && selectionStart < length+s.Length + cr )
            break;
          length += s.Length + cr;
          lineNr++;
        }
        return lineNr;
      }
    public void Save(TextWriter w) {
      foreach (string line in lines )
        w.WriteLine(line);
    }
    public void Load(TextReader r) {
      String line;
      lines = new ArrayList();
      while((line = r.ReadLine()) != null) {
        lines.Add(line);
      }
    }
  }
}
```

27

Displaying the Article

The editor is going pretty well, and the customers have been asking about displaying the article in its final form. After some reading and some experimentation, we have something working. Is this a triumph of the process, am I really clever, or was I just lucky?

Today's Process

The current process for writing and displaying an article goes like this:

1. Type the article into the XML Notepad or some other editor.

2. Run the article generation process. This is a fairly complex job stream now: it generates the article using XSLT, scans all the articles for indexing information, sorts it down, generates the index, scans for books reviewed, generates the book list, and so on.

3. Open a Web browser.

4. Navigate to the XP Web site debug location (the index HTML for the site).

5. Click the new article's reference in the index.

6. View the article.

On subsequent edits, it's not so bad. But you still have to run the article generation process. Then you just switch to the Web browser and refresh to see the updated article. The easiest way to run the process is to use the macros and accelerator keys I've built in TextPad. Even then it takes over 30 seconds to see the result.

The fact that most of the process involves TextPad macros means that it's actually inconvenient to use the XML Notepad, even though it is already more help for editing. The result is that the customer (me) isn't using the tool that he has asked for and received. Seeing the result as I go is pretty important to me, so I suffer somewhat more difficult editing to make the overall process less awkward. This is probably not a good tradeoff, frankly, but it's one of the obstacles that a new product like the XML Notepad has to overcome: the inertia of the user base (me).

It's not really important that the whole site get regenerated on every one of these quick looks—in fact, it's a disadvantage. I could probably write a new script and macro that would just update the article, but that would be a hassle and wouldn't really advance my Web site, this book, or the XML Notepad product's chances in the market (me).

The result is that I've been wondering how to get a quick view of the article in finished form, so as to see how I'm doing. We've had that as part of the vision all along. Remember how, way back in the beginning, our "vision" stories called for a WYSIWYG editor and the programmers talked the customers into holding off on that. Now the pressure for that story is increasing.

Possibilities

The perfect vision idea is for an editor that displays the article just as it would be on the Web site and that lets you edit it in place. We have estimated that as being quite difficult. The best way we can think of to do it would be to use a RichTextPane in a Windows Form and to render all the XML into that pane. Even then, we couldn't do a really good job.

The Web site is generated using XSLT. Briefly, XSLT is a langauge from the XML family that specifies a transformation from XML into essentially any other format. The particular format I've chosen is, of course, HTML so that I can display the articles on the Web site. As we'll see when we look at it in more detail, that transformation is rather complex, in two regards: First, the semantic tags, such as <sect1>, with its embedded <title> tag, get translated into some moderately complex HTML. In principle, it can be very complex, and right now, some of it is pretty tricky. Second, the rendering of HTML is itself quite complex. The XProgramming Web site layout includes tables, graphics, horizontal rules, and a variety of fonts. To look good, our program would have to know enough about both the XSLT and HTML rendering to produce all the right layouts, fonts, and so on. This is all possible, but it would be expensive. The customer can't afford that; we need a better idea.

One possibility is to have a separate preview pane, with a Web browser in it. At this stage in the process, I couldn't estimate that one, but it seems that it shouldn't be too difficult. I need to find out more so that my customer can decide whether to order the feature.

Research and Experimentation

Well, with all this coming down from the customer, I was feeling a fair amount of stress over the weekend, thinking that I needed to build this capability pretty soon, but knowing that I can't give the customer a good estimate of how hard it is. So I started doing some research. Here's what happened.

Explorer Pane in Microsoft .NET

If the world really loved me, there would be a Microsoft Internet Explorer pane already built into .NET's toolbox. I looked and looked, and it's just not there. I searched the Microsoft Visual Studio help and found nothing of use. I searched MSDN and found some articles on how to use the Microsoft Web Browser COM object in a Windows Form, but not for .NET. I searched microsoft.public.whatever and found that a lot of people had asked the question, and the answers all came back sounding like they were using the COM object. If you know about COM, that might not hold you back, but I'm the new kid on the block and it sounded daunting to me.

I posted a description of my problem to the group, hoping that someone would come up with something easier, and in so doing, I came to realize that there might be an even easier way to do this: I could use a freestanding browser.

Launch a Browser

We could run the XSLT transformation inside the XML Notepad, producing the HTML, and then launch a copy of Internet Explorer to view the page. After that, the user could refresh the browser whenever he wants to see how things look.

This idea is far from perfect, but it's close to what the user is doing now, and if it would execute in less than the 30 seconds it takes now, we might be able to get the user to do this and use our program. I can estimate this one as probably taking a day or less, depending on whether I have to refresh the browser automatically, and so on. But I don't really know how to do it.

Serendipity Strikes

I had been thinking that, even to use the browser solution, I'd have to take the user's typed XML, run the XSLT script on it to generate the HTML, and then let the user browse the result. Not difficult, but you can see how it could lead to a fair number of new features in the program as we provide ways for the user to tell us what XSLT file to use and so on. Then something I had read in my search slapped me in the face.

Internet Explorer can display XML!! Given a legal raw XML file, it will display it in a simple indented format. That's not very useful to me (or, I would imagine, to anyone), but where I was reading that, it went on to say that the XML file can specify an XSLT transformation to be applied to it and that in that case Internet Explorer will display the result of applying the transformation. To me that meant: If I put a pointer to my XSLT into my XML, maybe Internet Explorer will display a page that looks like my article!

That's easy enough to try. I dug around and found the information again and added the necessary line, which goes second from the top in your XML file. The top of the file looks like this:

```
<?xml version="1.0"?>
<?xml-stylesheet type="text/xsl" href="magazine.xsl"?>
```

The "magazine.xsl" is the name of the file containing the XSLT to convert my articles. So I did this experiment:

1. I opened Internet Exlorer and pointed it at the XML files for one of my articles. Internet Explorer dutifully displayed the XML, all nicely indented, but not looking much like an article.

2. I edited the XML file and entered the xml-stylesheet line, saved the file, and refreshed Internet Explorer. Wow! Something came up that looked like an article! The graphics weren't there, and the fonts were wrong, but it had the header and the underlines and the menus and all the stuff. Nearly worked!

3. The images on my Web site are taken from a directory named "images" that is parallel to the magazine directory. I copied the images directory to the corresponding place beside the XML directory. I refreshed the browser, and the graphics were there!

4.   The fonts and layouts on the site are controlled by a Cascading Style Sheets file named style.css, which needs to be in a standard place relative to the article. I put the style sheet in the right place, and voila! the article looked almost right!

There was a little hassle with the menu items that appear in the upper right of my pages, next to the logo. These were running off to the right, instead of folding to the size of the page as they are supposed to. It took me a good half hour or more to figure out what was happening there. I'm still not entirely sure of the fix, but basically Internet Explorer wasn't seeing the spaces between the items, concluded they were all one big long string, and displayed it accordingly. I seem to remember an XSLT option saying how to treat white space, and I think that's probably implicated in this. In any case, I changed the lines in question to have identifiable space, and the problem went away.

This Is Really Cool!

So, what have I discovered? If the user has legal XML in his Notepad, and if it includes a pointer to the right XSL stylesheet, and if a few files are in the right directories, he can just open the XML file and look at it in Internet Explorer to see how it's shaping up. He can press refresh at any time for a fresh view.

This means that we won't have to do the XSL transformation inside XML Notepad and we won't have to provide any new features. The user can view the file easily after every save by just refreshing the browser. He'll probably want some handy features, but this is definitely better than what he has now. We might be done!

Am I Cheating?

Now, I originally thought that this story would turn out to be a really challenging test of my programming process. Introduced late in the project like this, it might require us to completely change the way things worked. It would address the fear we all have in an incremental project: that something will come along later that destroys our design. But instead we aren't getting a fair test of whether this process could really work. You feel ripped off—heck, *I* feel ripped off! This wasn't hard enough.

Lesson Still, there's a lesson here. When you're working with the real users and they are faced with actually spending money for features, they'll quite often decide to take something that isn't quite perfect but that costs them almost nothing, like this solution. "So, Mr. Customer, we can do this in an hour. This other thing is a bit neater, but will take a couple of days. This third thing will take a couple of weeks. You choose." A customer who's working well with you will almost always say, "Give me the hour thing. We'll try that a while and if it doesn't work out, we'll try something else." They do this because they trust us, trust our estimates, and—most important—because they know they can come back.

When we're dealing with the guy in Marketing asking for features, it's more difficult. The end users now can't come back for a quick improvement if they don't like the simple feature. The Marketing guy rightly fears delivering too little to the customer, and he (not so rightly) often chooses to err on the side of asking for too much. We can help him out, however, in much the same way, by making the cost of features clear to him. Both time and money matter when you're trying to ship a product, and if we can make those costs visible to those who serve as our customer, it will always help.

So maybe it's not cheating after all.

(It turns out that there is another special request coming up later in the book, and that one as well turns out to be almost trivial to implement. Could it be that when we build well-structured code in an incremental fashion, almost all the things we have to do turn out to be fairly straightforward? My experience is that things do happen that way.)

The Power of Reflection

This morning, I received my standard 8 A.M. phone call from Chet, who apparently thinks that if he's up, everyone should be up. Fortunately, I was. I told him about the Internet Explorer solution and was kind of whining because it seems like a cheat. In the course of the conversation I told him about all the options I had learned about, including hooking up to the COM object. That got me thinking.

I went back to microsoft.public.whatever and found that someone had said that
if I would hook up to the COM object, I could drag it into a .NET Windows Form.
I decided it would do no harm to try it and decided to go ahead.

I made a new solution and project. Then I clicked the Visual Studio Toolbox and chose Customize. This brings up, in practically no time, a huge list of
COM objects that you could add to the box. I searched for a while and found
Microsoft Web Browser, so I added it. Visual Studio asks no more questions; it
just plunks "Explorer" into the Toolbox.

Then I created a Windows Forms project and dragged the Explorer into it.
Sure enough, it displayed a little rectangle representing where the pane would
be. I looked around a bit and then double-clicked it. Visual Studio put a new
method in my source code called Form1_Load. I guess that's the main event for
the pane. (I have yet to find any really useful documentation on it.) I surfed
MSDN and found some example C++ code that looks like this:

```cpp
CRect rect;
GetClientRect (&rect);
// Create the control.
m_pBrowser = new CWebBrowser;
ASSERT (m_pBrowser);
if (!m_pBrowser->Create(NULL,NULL,WS_VISIBLE,rect,this,NULL))
{
    TRACE("failed to create browser\n");
    delete m_pBrowser;
    m_pBrowser = NULL;
    return 0;
}
// Initialize the first URL.
COleVariant noArg;
m_pBrowser->Navigate("www.microsoft.com",&noArg,&noArg,&noArg,&noArg);
return 0;
```

That was pretty cryptic, being in C++ and all, but the Navigate method
looked pretty interesting. So I decided to try it. Into the Form1_Load, I type

```
private void Form1_Load(object sender, System.EventArgs e) {
  axWebBrowser1.Navigate("http://www.xprogramming.com");
}
```

That won't compile. Navigate() wants five arguments. The IntelliSense
says: "string URL, ref object flags, ref object targetFrameName, ref object post-
Data, ref object headers". I have no idea what any of those are. I type

```
private void Form1_Load(object sender, System.EventArgs e) {
  axWebBrowser1.Navigate("http://www.xprogramming.com", 0, 0, 0, 0);
}
```

The compiler doesn't like that; it can't convert from int to ref object. Now I see in the code above that they are declaring a COleVariant noArg. There is no COleVariant listed in the Visual Studio Help. I try

```
private void Form1_Load(object sender, System.EventArgs e) {
  object noArgs;
  axWebBrowser1.Navigate("http://www.xprogramming.com", &noArgs, &noArgs,
    &noArgs, &noArgs);
}
```

I was thinking that the noArgs would initialize to null and that & might be the way to do a reference in a call. (Remember, I really am new to C#!) Wrong on both counts. So I try

```
private void Form1_Load(object sender, System.EventArgs e) {
  object noArgs = null;
  axWebBrowser1.Navigate("http://www.xprogramming.com", ref noArgs, ref noArgs,
    ref noArgs, ref noArgs);
}
```

This compiles; I run it. It takes a long time to start up, and then a window comes up with my little Internet Explorer pane in it. Nothing is inside the pane; I'm about to give up. Then an hourglass appears. Then it goes away. Then the little pane has my Web site's home page in it!

Now the Sky Is Clear

The sun comes out and shines on us. Here's what is now possible, and straightforward, that a few hours ago seemed impossible:

We can add an Internet Explorer pane to the notepad. We can use a tabbed window, or two panes on one big page, or any other layout. If the XML in the notepad is legal and includes the right xsl-stylesheet line, we can write the XML to a file and tell the Internet Explorer pane to navigate to it. We can do that any time we think is the right time—we could do it on every character the user types if we want to.

We might even be able to find a way to avoid writing the file out. It looks like the browser COM object may be able to accept its input as a string. Or the customer might decide that every time he saves, we should refresh the browser pane. We could even create a separate little window, with a browser pane in it, and a FileWatcher watching for file updates. We could use asynchronous delegates (whatever those are) to make the panes or windows communicate but run in separate threads! And every one of those ideas is close enough to understandable that we can estimate it, giving our customer a fair chance to decide if he wants to buy it.

The sky's the limit, the world is our oyster, we're in the money. With a couple of hours' work, we've taken a problem from "could be impossible" and broken it down into a fairly manageable number of options that we understand reasonably well. Time well spent.

And Then, as if by Magic

After completing this article, I was sitting at lunch reading one of my favorite C# books, *Professional C#, 2nd Edition,* by Robinson et al. (WROX Press, 2002). Right there on page 963—it was a long lunch—is "Displaying Output as an HTML Page." They provided two patches of code to compare with mine above.

To launch a separate Internet Explorer, they recommend using the Process class in System.Diagnostics namespace, like this:

```
Process p = new Process();
p.StartInfo.FileName = "iexplore.exe";
p.StartInfo.Arguments = "http://www.XProgramming.com";
p.Start();
```

I haven't typed that in and tried it yet, but now I know a little more about how to do it when I need to. They then go on to talk about using the browser as a control. They put it in the toolbox just as we did in this chapter, and their code looks similar, but a little better than mine, like this:

```
int zero = 0;
object oZero = 0;
string emptyString = "";
 object oEmptyString = emptyString;
wb.Navigate("http://www.XProgramming.com",
  ref oZero,
  ref oEmptyString,
  ref oEmptyString,
  ref oEmptyString);
```

They describe the five parameters as representing the URI, flags to modify browser behavior, the name of the target frame (if any), POST data to send with the request, and additional HTTP header information. I don't expect to need any of those things. And there's lots more material than I expect to need in the same chapter ("Accessing the Internet"). The book is like that. It has lots of material in its nearly 1200 pages, but it always seems to include some starting material that is enough to get me going.

It's good to have confirmation that we weren't completely off the rails with the ideas here. With the process idea, I'm wondering if I can hold on to the process and send it more messages. But if not, I can surely do the same thing with my own little private browser window or a pane in the current XML Notepad. I'm tempted to work on that a bit, since the customers really do want to see what they're getting. I'll do it as soon as they give me that story to work on. Right now, they would really like some file saving and loading and a few more tags in the notepad.

Lesson: Is There a Lesson Here?

You bet there is, and it's an important one. When a problem looks tricky and difficult, this is more often due to our ignorance than it is to anything inherently tricky and difficult in the problem. We are well-served to step back, try to think about simple ways of solving the problem, and learn enough to estimate those simple ways. The desired solution might still require a lot of work, but more knowledge lets it be just work, not high-risk speculation.

And at the same time, our ability to estimate the cost of the alternatives makes it easier for our customer to decide what we should do. Instead of sounding like scared or recalcitrant programmers, with "Ohh, that COM stuff is really difficult—we would need a lot of time to work on that," we can approach the question professionally: "We've tried these alternatives. We can give you This right now. We can add That with two days' work. If you want to go to This Big Thing, it will take another week or week and a half." Approaching the question professionally, we're more likely to get a professional answer, instead of "Stop whining and program."

What's Next?

Well, in terms of our product, I think the customer is likely to ask us to do the embedded COM object, partly because it might work a bit better, but mostly because our customer wants us to have to solve a hard problem here in the book. (As you'll see, this was not the hard problem we ended up having to solve.) So I've done one more thing. I've browsed the book sites for "COM .NET" and found at least two books in existence that describe how to do COM-.NET interoperation. I'm going to see if I can find one or both of those in Ann Arbor, and I'll take a look at them. On another day, I'd just order one, but I happen to be heading to the bookstore.

You might be thinking that that's a pretty expensive way to do business. Those books will cost me forty or fifty dollars each. What's up with that? In my opinion, that's a pretty cheap way to provide myself with information on how to do what I have to do. How many good ideas do you need to get from a book before it's worth the price? Not many. In the case of COM and .NET, I'll settle for one or two, and I'm sure to find that many.

Still, I'm almost sorry that this didn't turn out to be harder to do. Yet that's often the way of it. We take a seemingly hard program, chip at it with a little surfing and a spike or two, and the next thing you know, we don't have a hard problem anymore. That might be the real lesson of this chapter. For those who want to see me suffer, I promise: I know there are some hard ones coming up.

28

Oh No! Undo!

Everyone thinks that if you don't plan ahead—and code ahead—for things like "undo," you're doomed. Are we doomed?

The Final Exam

One of the biggest concerns with incremental development, such as we've been practicing in this book, is that there may be "cross-cutting" concerns that the design will not easily accommodate, resulting in a lot more work than if one had done "more" design. A favorite example, first raised to me by Gary Pollice of Rational, is "What if you're writing an editor, and you don't plan for Undo, and then they want it?"

Well, I won't lie to you, Chet and I knew we were going to ask for Undo at the end of this exercise. But we have tried hard not to design for it or plan for it. You've been along with us, and I think you can see that we didn't put anything in that is custom-made to support the Undo capability. We have made many design changes along the way—that's what incremental development is about—but they have all been motivated by producing well-structured code for the system as it stands.

Now we're going to find out what really happens. Will Undo go in easily, or will it be very difficult, such that we will wish we had provided for it earlier? At this moment, I don't know. Let's talk about what we need and how it might be done.

The Requirement

The customers aren't sure just what the details of the Undo will be. They want to try it in action and refine it. The basic starting idea is that there will be an unlimited number of levels of Undo and that each character typed should be capable of being backed out, one at a time, by typing Ctrl+Z or selecting the Undo menu item. They aren't certain about whether they'll want a bigger blob undone at a time, like a whole word, sentence, or paragraph. I figure that if we can undo each character typed and each menu action, that will be sufficient. Then, if they ask for word or sentence chunks, we can put that in. And my guess is that going one character at a time will be perfectly satisfactory.

Possible Solutions

As far as I am aware, the best-known implementation for Undo is to have the program create a centralized list of edit actions, or commands, that retain enough information to undo the action. To be honest, I can't think of another good way to do it. Chet and I talked on the phone this morning about how this might be implemented. I wish he were here pairing with me, because frankly I'm a bit scared that this could be tricky, but I feel the need to get started even though I'll be on my own. Well, the worst that can happen is that I'll learn something, and I promise to tell the truth about what happens in this chapter.

In XP, we like to ask, [sb]"What is the simplest thing that could possibly work?" and in fact I often like to do the simplest thing that could possibly work. The original question is intended to get us thinking simply, while I have adopted a general strategy of actually doing something very simple, given that it just might work. I have wanted to learn what happens when we push simple design plus refactoring to the limit. So far, my experience has been that it works just fine. In that spirit I suggested the following implementation of Undo in my phone call with Chet: "OK, on every keystroke, we make a copy of the entire contents and cursor location of the TextBox and save it away. Then for Undo, we just go back through the list, slamming the entire contents back."

I was concerned that doing it that way would seem like cheating. No one would really do Undo by saving a copy of a whole file on every keystroke. I was worried that you would miss the lesson that incremental design works because you might feel that the solution wasn't realistic. Chet felt that it might be OK to do it that way. There's no evidence that it would be overly costly in real cases, though of course it wouldn't take long to come up with a test that showed it was too much. He wasn't worried about the solution not seeming fair, and he reminded me of that great line in Paul Newman's movie, *Judge Roy*

Bean, where the judge shoots a would-be attacker, Dirty Bad Bob the Albino, in the back. The observers say, "He never had a chance." Judge Bean replies, "If he wanted a chance, he should have gone somewhere else."

Still, we do want the book to be credible. So we talked a bit further, and I came up with some observations that might be useful, while thinking about how awful the "copy everything" solution is. Imagine that the user is typing along, and we're duly copying the whole text buffer and cursor position every time. Generally speaking, the text buffer doesn't change much—usually only by one character. Maybe we could reduce the storage burden by doing some kind of "diff" on each pair of buffers, to see what happened.

Almost always, on every keystroke, one character is inserted into the text. Sometimes a character is deleted (on backspace or Delete), and sometimes a character is replaced, when the TextBox is in overstrike mode. That would collapse the recorded action down from something the size of the whole document to something more like the size of a single character. But the differencing could be difficult.

But wait. Most of the time as the user edits, what's really happening is something like this:

```
...
With cursor at 20, user types "H";
With cursor at 21, user types "e";
With cursor at 22, user types "l";
With cursor at 23, user types "l";
With cursor at 24, user types "o";
...
```

That makes me think that we might be able to "compress" the stream of actions into something quite livable. It might possibly work, so we'll do it.

What About Tests?

I'm having great difficulty thinking of a way to test the interesting parts of Undo. Even the Customer Acceptance Test language isn't strong enough to represent the typing of individual characters. Yet I have an idea for what the system should actually do to get the job done. I'm going to take a bit of a risk. I'll implement parts of this idea, and I'll do them test-first. But I'll hold off a bit on writing the top-level programmer tests or customer tests until I know more. That means there's a chance this will all be wasted or that I'll get into too much debugging. With that awareness, I'm hoping that I'll test enough to be sure that the code works. And of course, this whole idea is a bit experimental, with the possibility of turning out to be a bad idea. The sooner we find out, the better, so let's press on.

Begin with a Test

I've got Microsoft Visual Studio loaded up on the XML Notepad app, and I've run the tests. They are green; we're good to go. I'm envisioning a Programmer Unit Test for TextModel along these lines: Set the TextModel to some contents. Take a snapshot. Set the model to some other contents. Verify that they're there. Undo the snapshot, show that things are back as they were. Simple enough, and a step along the way. In TestTextModel, I find a test that looks like this:

```
[Test] public void CursorPosition() {
    model.SetLines (new String[] { "<P></P>", "<pre></pre>" });
    model.SelectionStart = 14; // after <pre>
    AssertEquals(5, model.PositionOfCursorInLine());
    AssertEquals("<pre>", model.FrontOfCursorLine());
    AssertEquals("</pre>", model.BackOfCursorLine());
}
```

I'll use that concept to create a new test. I'll skip the use of legal tags, because they are hard to type in and don't really improve the quality of the test in this case:

```
[Test] public void Snapshot() {
    model.SetLines(new String[] { "before", "snapshot" });
    model.SelectionStart = 8; // after before ;->
    AssertEquals("before", model.Lines[0]);
    model.Snapshot();
    model.SetLines(new String[] {"a", "new", "contents", "list"} );
    model.SelectionStart = 4; // after n in new
    AssertEquals("contents", model.Lines[2]);
    model.Restore();
    AssertEquals("before", model.Lines[0]);
    AssertEquals(8, model.SelectionStart);
}
```

Lesson   We'll see later on that this test is weak, in that it's not a good example of anything that's likely to happen in a real editing situation. It amounts to "Copy All/Paste Something Entirely Different," which is not a common activity. The test will support us fairly well, but not as well as one that would have been more like real editing.

There is a bit of a lesson lurking here. All through this part of the book, we're going to be feeling a little pressure because it's difficult to set up the programmer tests. We have to count the location of the caret manually, and so on. We might have done a little better had we paid a bit more attention to making testing a bit easier.

Model doesn't understand Snapshot() and Restore(), as referred to in our new test, so first we implement them trivially to get the red bar:

```
public void Snapshot() {
}
public void Restore() {
}
```

No surprises—we get the red bar, because the methods don't save or restore anything. But building the methods that way has given me an idea for an easy implementation. How about if we just save the text and selection start in a couple of new member variables:

```
private ArrayList savedLines;
private int savedSelectionStart;

public void Snapshot() {
  savedLines = new ArrayList(lines);
  savedSelectionStart = SelectionStart;
}
public void Restore() {
  lines = savedLines;
  SelectionStart = savedSelectionStart;
}
```

This actually makes the test run! Whee, we have implemented Undo. Not a very good Undo yet, but Undo nonetheless.

Lesson: Let's Reflect

This is a frightening story, so let's reflect early and often. What do we need to keep in mind? Well, first of all, I'm a little worried about not retaining the selection length. In our current implementation we have never used the selection length for anything, but it seems possible that Undo should be saving and restoring it. I'm not very worried, however, because the extension is pretty clear—we'll just save it and restore it.

Second, we can foresee that as we build a stack of Undo operations, we will need a stack that contains the lines and one for the selections. These stacks will be in parallel. This calls for an object that combines the text lines and the selection information. Should we create such an object?

As soon as I thought this thought, I realized that there already is such an object! TextModel itself is an object that contains exactly those variables, and up until now, no other ones. Here's the head of TextModel class as it stands now, just as a reminder:

(continued)

```
class TextModel {
  private ArrayList lines;
  private int selectionStart;
  private ArrayList savedLines;
  private int savedSelectionStart;
  public TextModel() {
    lines = new ArrayList();
  }
  ...
}
```

What about just using the TextModel as our saved object? Wouldn't that be "too big" an object somehow? Well, no. It is true that the Text-Model has a lot of methods that we might not use in the stacked items, but they won't take up any extra space. The TextModel instances have just exactly the storage we want: one ArrayList of lines, and the selection information. Let's give TextModel a new constructor and use it in our Snapshot() and Restore() methods.

Using TextModel as the Saved Object

```
class TextModel {
  private ArrayList lines;
  private int selectionStart;
  private TextModel savedModel;
  public TextModel() {
    lines = new ArrayList();
  }
  public TextModel(TextModel m) {
    lines = m.Lines;
    selectionStart = m.SelectionStart;
  }
  ...
  public void Snapshot() {
    savedModel = new TextModel(this);
  }
  public void Restore() {
    lines = savedModel.Lines;
    selectionStart = savedModel.SelectionStart;
  }
```

The test still runs. Let's extend the test to require us to build the stack:

```
[Test] public void Snapshot() {
  model.SetLines(new String[] { "before", "snapshot" });
  model.SelectionStart = 8; // after before ;->
  AssertEquals("before", model.Lines[0]);
  model.Snapshot();
  model.SetLines(new String[] {"a", "new", "contents", "list"} );
  model.SelectionStart = 4; // after n in new
  AssertEquals("contents", model.Lines[2]);
  model.Snapshot();
  model.SetLines(new String[] { "here", "is", "yet", "another", "version" } );
  model.SelectionStart = 7;
// before is
  AssertEquals("yet", model.Lines[2]);
  model.Restore();
  AssertEquals("contents", model.Lines[2]);
  model.Restore();
  AssertEquals("before", model.Lines[0]);
  AssertEquals(8, model.SelectionStart);
}
```

As we expect, this test doesn't run. I'll change TextModel to have an Array-List of TextModels as its stack of saved versions:

```
class TextModel {
  private ArrayList lines;
  private int selectionStart;
  private ArrayList savedModels;
  private ArrayList SavedModels {
    get {
      if(savedModels == null)
        savedModels = new ArrayList();
      return savedModels;
    }
  }

  public void Snapshot() {
    SavedModels.Add(new TextModel(this));
  }
  public void Restore() {
    TextModel savedModel = RemoveLastModel();
    lines = savedModel.Lines;
    selectionStart = savedModel.SelectionStart;
  }
```

```
private TextModel RemoveLastModel() {
int last = SavedModels.Count-1;
  TextModel lastModel = (TextModel) SavedModels[last];
  SavedModels.RemoveAt(last);
  return lastModel;
}
```

The only tricky bits here are that we did a "lazy init" on savedModels, covering it with a Property that initializes the list if it's empty. Second, we had to do a little messing around to remove the last item in the list and return it, because ArrayList, in its wisdom, doesn't seem to have a method that does that. I wonder if there's a Stack object in Microsoft .NET. I'll look—and it turns out that there is. How nice! I wish I had known that before we used the ArrayList. It would have saved literally minutes. We'll use that instead. The tests are already running, but the change is worth doing, because it will simplify the code substantially.

```
class TextModel {
    private ArrayList lines;
    private int selectionStart;
    private Stack savedModels;
    private Stack SavedModels {
      get {
        if(savedModels == null)
          savedModels = new Stack();
        return savedModels;
      }
    }
    public void Snapshot() {
      SavedModels.Push(new TextModel(this));
    }
    public void Restore() {
      TextModel savedModel = (TextModel) SavedModels.Pop();
      lines = savedModel.Lines;
      selectionStart = savedModel.SelectionStart;
    }
//    private TextModel RemoveLastModel() {
//      int last = SavedModels.Count-1;
//      TextModel lastModel = (TextModel) SavedModels[last];
//      SavedModels.RemoveAt(last);
//      return lastModel;
//    }
```

The commented method, of course, is to be deleted. Our tests still run!

It's about time to step back and think about what we've done. First, though, I suspect there's a bug. The TextModel constructor from another Text-Model looks like this:

```
public TextModel(TextModel m) {
  lines = m.Lines;
  selectionStart = m.SelectionStart;
}
```

I'm pretty concerned that manipulations to the lines of one TextModel will affect the lines of another one that's associated with it, because we have the same lines object in both TextModels. I'll write a test to demonstrate the bug and then fix it if in fact it is a bug:

```
[Test] public void SnapshotLinesIdentity() {
  model.SetLines(new String[] { "before", "snapshot" });
  model.SelectionStart = 6; // after before ;->
  AssertEquals("snapshot", model.Lines[1]);
  model.Snapshot();
  model.InsertTags(TextModel.Tags.Pre);
  AssertEquals("<pre></pre>", model.Lines[1]);
  model.Restore();
  AssertEquals("snapshot", model.Lines[1]);
}
```

I expect this to fail, because the stacked TextModel has the same lines ArrayList as the original. Let's find out...and in fact the test fails, expecting snapshot but getting the "pre" line instead. Here's the fix:

```
public TextModel(TextModel m) {
  lines = new ArrayList(m.Lines);
  selectionStart = m.SelectionStart;
}
```

This gives our stacked TextModel its own lines array so that changes to the original's ArrayList don't bother us. I'm not sure yet whether this could affect us in the final version of the stacking code, but having noticed the problem I decided it was best to fix it.

Lesson: Let's Reflect

We have modified the TextModel to be able to save and restore its contents, in a push-down stack style. This is good—certainly we can back the contents up to any point where the TextModel gets involved—and we can get it involved on every keystroke if we choose to. There is, of course, some more work to do to make this capability provide Undo capability, and there are serious questions about performance.

As it stands, the Snapshot() method makes a copy of the lines ArrayList. That could get large: some of these chapters are many lines long. And I suspect that every time we load the TextModel from the TextBox, we get all new instances of String for each of the lines, even if they are equal to the lines that we got last time. Perhaps we'll write a test to verify that if it seems important. Even the lines ArrayList is large enough, however, to be concerned about memory usage. Each String in the ArrayList probably takes up a dozen bytes of overhead, and the ArrayList cells themselves must have a similar size. A thousand-line Snapshot could include 24,000 or more bytes in addition to the text. (On the other hand, this is still a small proportion of the total size of the text, which would be perhaps 50 times larger.) Suffice to say we can foresee a memory problem.

Before we go further, we should consider again whether this is fatal to our implementation. I believe that it isn't. Let's consider what happens to the text in the lines ArrayList as the user types. For compactness, I'll show lines separated by slash characters, and I'll indicate the caret by a vertical bar. Here's a little editing sequence, as the user types on line 2 (the third line) of the text:

```
abc/def/ghi|/uvw/xyz
abc/def/ghij|/uvw/xyz
abc/def/ghijk|/uvw/xyz
abc/def/ghijkl|/uvw/xyz
```

See what's happening? As the user types, most of the lines in the text buffer are equal from one keystroke to the next. Only a line or two changes at any given time, and even if there's a paste operation, usually only a few lines change. We should be able to take advantage of this to reduce the storage required for a Snapshot.

Having decided that we are not yet doomed, my plan is to continue on this path. The next thing to try might be a spike to make the XML Notepad do a Snapshot() on every character typed, just to see what happens.

Snapshot Every Time

As an experiment, I'd just like to see what happens to performance if we do a Snapshot() operation on every character typed. The KeyDown handler is just the place:

```
public void XMLKeyDownHandler(object objSender, KeyEventArgs kea) {
  model.Snapshot();
  if (kea.KeyCode == Keys.Enter && kea.Modifiers == Keys.None) {
    CallModel(enterAction);
    kea.Handled = true;
  }
  else if (kea.KeyCode == Keys.Enter && kea.Modifiers == Keys.Shift) {
    CallModel(shiftEnterAction);
    kea.Handled = true;
  }
}
```

This doesn't do anything useful, but it should allow me to run the program and see how it behaves. I'll compile and run the tests first—they run, as we would expect. Now I'll launch the XML Notepad and play with it. I'll be right back.

I pasted this entire chapter into the XML Notepad and edited it. Performance was just as fast as you could want. I brought up a TaskManager and watched memory usage, which was around 8 megabytes and bounced up in jumps of 100K or more on every keystroke. The good news is that performance is fine, and we're not surprised that it eats memory madly. Now, just for fun, let's implement Undo. We'll have to override the Ctrl+Z handling of the Text-Box, which might be tricky. We'll see. I suspect that we will have to work hard to override the Ctrl+Z, so I started with this:

```
public void XMLKeyDownHandler(object objSender, KeyEventArgs kea) {
  model.Snapshot();
  if (kea.KeyCode == Keys.Enter && kea.Modifiers == Keys.None) {
    CallModel(enterAction);
    kea.Handled = true;
  }
  else if (kea.KeyCode == Keys.Enter && kea.Modifiers == Keys.Shift) {
    CallModel(shiftEnterAction);
    kea.Handled = true;
  }
  else if (kea.KeyCode == Keys.Z && kea.Modifiers == Keys.Control) {
    MessageBox.Show("Control Z");
    kea.Handled = true;
  }
}
```

Sure enough, the dialog comes up, but the Ctrl+Z is still executed by the TextBox. We'll probably have to capture it in the KeyPress handler as well:

```
public void XMLKeyPressHandler(object objSender, KeyPressEventArgs kea) {
  if ((int) kea.KeyChar == (int) Keys.Enter) {
    kea.Handled = true;
    // this code is here to avoid putting extra enters in the window.
    // if removed, when you hit enter, the new <P> line breaks in two:
    // <P>
    // |</P>  like that.
  }
  else if ((int) kea.KeyChar ==  26) {
    MessageBox.Show("KeyPress Control Z");
    kea.Handled = true;
  }
}
```

This triggers the dialog and does not do the delete. I'll try putting a model.Restore here to see what happens:

```
public void XMLKeyPressHandler(object objSender, KeyPressEventArgs kea) {
  if ((int) kea.KeyChar == (int) Keys.Enter) {
    kea.Handled = true;
    // this code is here to avoid putting extra enters in the window.
    // if removed, when you hit enter, the new <P> line breaks in two:
    // <P>
    // |</P>  like that.
  }
  else if ((int) kea.KeyChar ==  26) {
    model.Restore();
    kea.Handled = true;
  }
}
```

In fact, nothing happens. My guess is that we have done a Snapshot() already, so the Restore() isn't doing anything. I'll try two copies of Restore() to see what happens. Nothing, and the reason becomes clear. It isn't enough to Restore the TextModel; we need to reload the TextBox from it. I'll hack that in—and it still doesn't work. I'm going to resort to a few debugging statements to print the depth of the snapshot stack.

> **Lesson** Debugging statements are evil. Even more evil is actually using the debugger and probing around, but we haven't fallen that low yet. Both these practices are signs that we do not know what is going on. The question is, who is to be the master, you or your program. A

better course here would have been to write some tests aimed at learning or to make the flow of the system more obvious. In the case in hand, I was on a quest to see whether this idea would work, and if it gets a bit inefficient here, we're back on track fairly quickly.

It occurs to me as I write this that we don't have a Customer Acceptance Test for Undo. I've been a bit erratic on that, because I am the customer and I know what I want, but I would be serving as a better example if I had more customer tests.

```
public void Snapshot() {
  SavedModels.Push(new TextModel(this));
  Console.WriteLine("push {0}", SavedModels.Count);
}
public void Restore() {
  Console.WriteLine("prepop {0}", SavedModels.Count);
  TextModel savedModel = (TextModel) SavedModels.Pop();
  Console.WriteLine("postpop {0}", SavedModels.Count);
  lines = savedModel.Lines;
  selectionStart = savedModel.SelectionStart;
}
```

This immediately shows me what's happening: the Ctrl key is repeating, and the SnapShot() is being done on every repeat. If I hold down Ctrl+Z long enough, the Notepad will actually undo and then it blows up, probably because it isn't protected yet against too many pop operations. So I'll need to see what I can do about the Ctrl key.

Lesson   In spite of the fact that this is taking a bit of work, I'd like to point out that it is work that we could not have saved by designing the Undo capability sooner. We just need to learn more about how the keypressing logic works, and that had to be done sooner or later. I'll work on that now.

In addition, in my own defense, it's hard to see how we could have written a test that discovered that Ctrl was repeating any sooner than by putting in the trace. I still think it would be better to have done the test, but it is my practice to forgive myself when I don't do something because I don't have a clue how to do it!

After a little fiddling, here's what the two handlers look like, with the changed and interesting bits highlighted:

```
public void XMLKeyDownHandler(object objSender, KeyEventArgs kea) {
  if (kea.KeyCode != Keys.ControlKey &&
       kea.KeyCode != Keys.Alt &&
       kea.KeyCode != Keys.ShiftKey)
    model.Snapshot();
  if (kea.KeyCode == Keys.Enter && kea.Modifiers == Keys.None) {
    CallModel(enterAction);
    kea.Handled = true;
  }
  else if (kea.KeyCode == Keys.Enter && kea.Modifiers == Keys.Shift) {
    CallModel(shiftEnterAction);
    kea.Handled = true;
  }
  else if (kea.KeyCode == Keys.Z && kea.Modifiers == Keys.Control) {
    Console.WriteLine("keydown z");
    kea.Handled = true;
  }
}

public void XMLKeyPressHandler(object objSender, KeyPressEventArgs kea) {
  if ((int) kea.KeyChar == (int) Keys.Enter) {
    kea.Handled = true;
    // this code is here to avoid putting extra enters in the window.
    // if removed, when you hit enter, the new <P> line breaks in two:
    // <P>
    // |</P>  like that.
  }
  else if ((int) kea.KeyChar ==  26) {
    model.Restore();
    model.Restore();
    PutText(textbox, model.LinesArray(), model.SelectionStart);
    kea.Handled = true;
  }
}
```

This is nearly working. I just noticed the two Restore operations are still there, and I suspect they're necessary. The other oddity is that when we type text in between tags and then issue a Ctrl+Z, all the text disappears on the first Ctrl+Z, and then nothing happens while we type enough more Ctrl+Zs to have deleted the other characters. The reason is that in the KeyDown handler, we're taking a snapshot on every character, but the model isn't updated, so it doesn't know that the characters are there.

But this was just an experiment to see what would happen. What happened is that we have in fact built a rudimentary but operating Undo capability. I'll take a well-deserved break now and then buckle down to putting in the real code.

Building It In

I was able to pair with Chet for a while on this part of the story. I spent some time bringing him up to date on the code and the Undo experiments. I did this by a combination of talking, showing him the code, and a little bit of sketching on paper and moving cards around to show the relationship between the Text-Box and the TextModel.

To start building up more of the real Undo capability, we knew we needed some tests. Testing manually using the GUI is inconvenient, and it's hard to get any useful information out of it. We see what it does, but not why. After a little discussion, we decided to use the CustomerTests.cs way of writing tests, with the little scripts saying what the input and output are. Our reasoning was that those tests go through the GUI, so they can exercise the form and the TextBox and their interaction with the TextModel. Those tests are "end to end" in nature and seem like just what we need.

Lesson   Teams are sometimes concerned about whether the programmers should use the customer testing tools for their tests. It's a matter of judgment about using the best tool for the job. One concern is that sometimes customer tests are time-consuming. It's important that the programmer tests execute very quickly, because if they are slow we will use them less often, program more between running the tests, make more mistakes, and slow ourselves down. Sometimes customer tests are a little less clear about what has gone wrong than are the more usual NUnit-style tests, so tests written in the customer style might need more debugging. Our own tests here have a bit of that character, in fact. Remember that a single CustomerTest method reads all the .test files and executes them one after another. The result of this is that when a test fails, we get a little printout, but not much other information, and it would be difficult to set a breakpoint to stop for just that test. Since we don't use the debugger much, it hasn't been a problem. If it became a problem, we would figure out a way to address it. For now, we decided to write some customer-style tests to support our work on Undo.

Chet and I decided that we would implement a couple of new commands: *undo, of course, and also *type, which will take a string and push it into the XML Notepad one character at a time. With that in mind, we wrote the following test, to type some things into a notepad and then undo them back out:

```
*enter
*type abc
*output
<P>abc|</P>
*end
*undo
*output
<P>ab|</P>
*end
*undo
*output
<P>a|</P>
*end
*undo
*output
<P>|</P>
*end
*undo
*output
|
*end
```

Naturally, this test doesn't run. The command *type isn't understood. We'll code that:

```
private void InterpretCommands(String commands, String message) {
  StringReader reader = new StringReader(commands);
  String line = reader.ReadLine();
  CreateModel();
  while ( line != null) {
    if (line.StartsWith("*alt"))
      ExecuteMenu("&"+line[4]);
    else if (line.StartsWith("*type"))
      TypeCharacters(line.Substring(6));
    else if ( line == "*enter")
      form.XMLKeyDownHandler((object) this, new KeyEventArgs(Keys.Enter));
    else if ( line == "*shiftEnter")
      form.XMLKeyDownHandler((object) this,
        new KeyEventArgs(Keys.Enter | Keys.Shift));
    else if (line == "*display")
      Console.WriteLine("display\r\n{0}\r\nend", model.TestText);
    else if (line == "*output")
      CompareOutput(reader, message);
```

```
    else if (line == "*input")
      SetInput(reader);
    else if (line == "*loadfile")
      LoadFile();
    else if (line == "*savefile")
      SaveFile();
    else
      Assert(line + " command not defined", false);
    line = reader.ReadLine();
  }
}
```

Now we implement TypeCharacters() and a supporting method that we made up by intention:

```
private void TypeCharacters(String s) {
  foreach (char c in s)
    model.InsertCharacter(c);
}
```

Here we implement InsertCharacter:

```
public void InsertCharacter(char c) {
  lines[LineContainingCursor()] = FrontOfCursorLine() + c + BackOfCursorLine();
  selectionStart++;
}
```

Working through this, we encountered a few problems that we aren't showing in detail. We forgot the *end at the end of each *output check, we forgot to show the vertical bar for the caret position, and we forgot to increment the selectionStart. Three errors for about 10 lines of code: about our usual. It's Chet's fault. The test runs down to the *undo operation now. We have to implement that:

```
private void InterpretCommands(String commands, String message) {
  StringReader reader = new StringReader(commands);
  String line = reader.ReadLine();
  CreateModel();
  while ( line != null) {
    if (line.StartsWith("*alt"))
      ExecuteMenu("&"+line[4]);
    else if (line.StartsWith("*type"))
      TypeCharacters(line.Substring(6));
    else if (line == "*undo")
      model.Restore();
    else if ( line == "*enter")
      form.XMLKeyDownHandler((object) this, new KeyEventArgs(Keys.Enter));
    else if ( line == "*shiftEnter")
```

```
      form.XMLKeyDownHandler((object) this,
        new KeyEventArgs(Keys.Enter | Keys.Shift));
    else if (line == "*display")
      Console.WriteLine("display\r\n{0}\r\nend", model.TestText);
    else if (line == "*output")
      CompareOutput(reader, message);
    else if (line == "*input")
      SetInput(reader);
    else if (line == "*loadfile")
      LoadFile();
    else if (line == "*savefile")
      SaveFile();
    else
      Assert(line + " command not defined", false);
    line = reader.ReadLine();
  }
}
```

This fails when the model.Restore() is executed, because we haven't done any Snapshot() operations yet. Where should we put the Snapshot()? Clearly we need one in the TextModel's InsertCharacter() method, but we also need one in the other operations, *enter in this case. We'll begin by putting Snapshot() calls wherever we need them, and then we'll figure out how to remove the duplication. Because we have a broken test, we're taking the shortest reasonable path to making it work:

```
public void InsertCharacter(char c) {
  Snapshot();
  lines[LineContainingCursor()] = FrontOfCursorLine() + c + BackOfCursorLine();
  selectionStart++;
}


public void InsertTags(InsertAction action) {
  Snapshot();
  int cursorLine = LineContainingCursor();
  lines.InsertRange(cursorLine+1, action.TagsToInsert);
  selectionStart = NewSelectionStart(cursorLine + 1, action.TagsToSkip);
}


public void Enter() {
  Snapshot();
  if (InListItem())
    InsertTags(Tags.ListItem);
  else
    InsertTags(Tags.Paragraph);
}
```

These changes cause the new customer test to run, except for that last part with the empty line containing just a vertical bar. We're not too surprised at that because we have never checked for empty output before. Truth is, there should be no lines now, and we don't have a good way to represent that.

Discussing this, we decided that updating the model in the InsertCharacter method is wrong. We have a way in the CustomerTests.cs to send characters through the notepad, and we should use it. We also want to test backspace followed by an undo, Shift+Enter, and other special situations that aren't handled now. If we push characters through the XML Notepad, however, things should work in a more regular fashion.

The code that sends things through the notepad has to create an event and an EventArgs. It looks, for example, like this:

```
form.XMLKeyDownHandler((object) this, new KeyEventArgs(Keys.Enter));
```

This is the code to send an Enter through. Notice that we create the KeyEventArgs with whatever comes back from the enumeration Keys.Enter. But our InsertCharacter() code wants to send a variable character. This took some research. It turns out that a static method on Enum, Parse(), will, given a string, return the appropriate value from the Enum. After much trial and error, we came up with this, in CustomerTest:

```
private void TypeCharacters(String s) {
  foreach (char c in s) {
    form.XMLKeyDownHandler(
      (object) this,
      new KeyEventArgs( (Keys) Enum.Parse(typeof(Keys), c.ToString(), true)));
  }
}
```

The Boolean *true* at the end of the Parse() call tells it to ignore case. For now that will be enough, although if we want our *type command to handle uppercase as well as lowercase, we'll have to do something special. We probably won't need that.

With this change made, the undo test stops working. The reason, of course, is that the snapshot is once again not happening, because we had hard-wired it into the InsertCharacter() method of the TextModel and that is no longer being used. Things are getting a bit messy: it's time to clean up just a bit.

Removing the Experiments

I wish I had checkpointed the source code before putting in all the experiments for speed. Now I'll have to take them out manually, and I'll also remove those new Insert methods from TextModel. No, wait! That might get me in trouble. My customer test for undo is failing because of the new insertion method, going through the notepad. I do want to get there, but if I'm going to clean up code, I need the tests to support me. So first I'll get green again, by reverting to the previous version of the TypeCharacters code in CustomerTest:

```
private void TypeCharacters(String s) {
  foreach (char c in s) {
    model.InsertCharacter(c);
//    form.XMLKeyDownHandler(
//      (object) this,
//      new KeyEventArgs(
//        (Keys) Enum.Parse(typeof(Keys), c.ToString(), true)));
  }
}
```

Now my tests run; it's safe to start removing things. I'm going to look at each reference to Snapshot() and Restore() and check whether I can remove them. Outside the tests, here's where they are:

In XMLNotepad.cs:

```
public void XMLKeyDownHandler(object objSender, KeyEventArgs kea) {
    if (kea.KeyCode != Keys.ControlKey &&
      kea.KeyCode != Keys.Alt &&
      kea.KeyCode != Keys.ShiftKey) {
      GetText();
      model.Snapshot();
    }
    if (kea.KeyCode == Keys.Enter && kea.Modifiers == Keys.None) {
      CallModel(enterAction);
      kea.Handled = true;
    }
    else if (kea.KeyCode == Keys.Enter && kea.Modifiers == Keys.Shift) {
      CallModel(shiftEnterAction);
      kea.Handled = true;
    }
    else if (kea.KeyCode == Keys.Y && kea.Modifiers == Keys.Control) {
      Console.WriteLine("keydown Y");
      kea.Handled = true;
    }
  }
```

In TextModel.cs:

```
public void Enter() {
    Snapshot();
    if (InListItem())
      InsertTags(Tags.ListItem);
    else
      InsertTags(Tags.Paragraph);
  }
  public void InsertTags(InsertAction action) {
    Snapshot();
    int cursorLine = LineContainingCursor();
    lines.InsertRange(cursorLine+1, action.TagsToInsert);
    selectionStart = NewSelectionStart(cursorLine + 1, action.TagsToSkip);
  }
  public void InsertCharacter(char c) {
    Snapshot();
    lines[LineContainingCursor()] = FrontOfCursorLine()
      + c + BackOfCursorLine();
    selectionStart++;
  }
```

The duplication in the TextModel bugs me. And it makes me think. Maybe that code in the KeyDownHandler is almost right: it is doing a Snapshot on every character. I'm not sure whether the GetText() should be done first or second, but that's almost in the right place. What if we just leave that one in and remove all the others. What would break? I'll find out.

The only thing that breaks is the undo test, with this message:

```
c:\data\csharp\notepad\undo.test
*Expected
<P>ab|</P>
*Result
|
```

Look again at the test:

```
*enter
*type abc
*output
<P>abc|</P>
*end
*undo
*output
<P>ab|</P>
*end
*undo
*output
<P>a|</P>
```

```
*end
*undo
<P>|</P>
*end
*undo
|
*end
```

The failure is happening after the first undo. We expect it to erase just the c, but the result is that it erases everything. What's up with that? Well, at this point, we are still using the InsertCharacter() and not going through the notepad event. Let's change that back to the new way:

```
private void TypeCharacters(String s) {
  foreach (char c in s) {
    form.XMLKeyDownHandler(
      (object) this,
      new KeyEventArgs( (Keys) Enum.Parse(typeof(Keys), c.ToString(), true)));
  }
}
```

This nearly works—well, it fails differently:

```
c:\data\csharp\notepad\undo.test
*Expected
<P>abc|</P>
*Result
<P>|</P>
```

Looking at the test, we see that this tells us that the characters abc are not over in the TextModel. I'm not sure why not. I expect this code to move the text from the TextBox to the TextModel on every character:

```
public void XMLKeyDownHandler(object objSender, KeyEventArgs kea) {
  if (kea.KeyCode != Keys.ControlKey &&
    kea.KeyCode != Keys.Alt &&
    kea.KeyCode != Keys.ShiftKey) {
    GetText();
    model.Snapshot();
  }
  ...
```

I'm not sure the characters are ever getting into the TextBox at all. We've always been a bit unclear about which of the events the TextBox itself uses. Updating the undo test as follows gives the answer:

```
*enter
*type abc
*enter
*display
*output
<P>abc|</P>
```

When we run this test, the output is

```
display
<P></P>
<P>|</P>
end
```

As we suspected, the characters aren't being sent over to the TextBox. Very likely the TextBox uses the KeyPress event rather than the KeyDown. We'll change TypeCharacter to use that event:

```
private void TypeCharacters(String s) {
  foreach (char c in s) {
    form.XMLKeyDownHandler(
      (object) this,
      new KeyEventArgs( (Keys) Enum.Parse(typeof(Keys), c.ToString(), true)));
    form.XMLKeyPressHandler((object) this, new KeyPressEventArgs(c));
  }
}
```

This has no effect whatever on the test. The keys still aren't going into the TextModel. I'm not sure if the TextBox isn't seeing them or what.

It Gets Weird for a Moment

To figure out what was happening, I decided to run the notepad in GUI mode. I instrumented the keypress and keydown handlers to show me the characters going by:

```
public void XMLKeyDownHandler(object objSender, KeyEventArgs kea) {
  Console.WriteLine("down  {0} {1} {2}", kea.KeyValue, kea.KeyCode,
    kea.KeyData);
  if (kea.KeyCode != Keys.ControlKey &&
    kea.KeyCode != Keys.Menu &&
    kea.KeyCode != Keys.ShiftKey) {
    GetText();
    model.Snapshot();
  }
  if (kea.KeyCode == Keys.Enter && kea.Modifiers == Keys.None) {
    CallModel(enterAction);
    kea.Handled = true;
  }
```

```
        else if (kea.KeyCode == Keys.Enter && kea.Modifiers == Keys.Shift) {
          CallModel(shiftEnterAction);
          kea.Handled = true;
        }
        else if (kea.KeyCode == Keys.Y && kea.Modifiers == Keys.Control) {
          Console.WriteLine("keydown Y");
          kea.Handled = true;
        }
      }
    public void XMLKeyPressHandler(object objSender, KeyPressEventArgs kea) {
      Console.WriteLine("press {0}", kea.KeyChar);
      if ((int) kea.KeyChar == (int) Keys.Enter) {
        kea.Handled = true;
        // this code is here to avoid putting extra enters in the window.
        // if removed, when you hit enter, the new <P> line breaks in two:
        // <P>
        // |</P>  like that.
      }
      else if ((int) kea.KeyChar ==  26) {
        Console.WriteLine("restoring");
        model.Restore();
        model.Restore();
        PutText(textbox, model.LinesArray(), model.SelectionStart);
        kea.Handled = true;
      }
    }
  }
```

And in TextModel:

```
public void Snapshot() {
    Console.WriteLine("snapping");
    SavedModels.Push(new TextModel(this));
  }
```

Note that there are a couple of changes here. The Down handler now says Keys.Menu instead of Keys.Alt. I learned that when I typed Alt, I didn't get a Snapshot, and the printout called the key Menu in some places, not Alt. Making the change shown got the snapshots to happen. And something else very weird is happening: the Notepad is now doing Undo exactly as we want it to! Typing the various commands—Enter, Alt+S, and so on—inserts tags just like always. We can type inside them as we should be able to. When we do Ctrl+Z, the characters disappear one at a time. When a tag is empty, one more Ctrl+Z removes the tag. The cursor moves around just as we would think it should.

This tells me a couple of things. First, the code we have is nearly right. Second, the way we are pushing characters to the TextBox for testing isn't working. In particular, it seems that adding the KeyPressHandler call for the characters didn't help at all. I'll remove that and see if it changes anything. Sure enough, the test still fails in the same way, so the KeyPress wasn't helping. And the notepad still works just fine. I exercised it pretty hard, even moving the caret with the arrow keys and with the mouse, and Ctrl+Z just goes around deleting just the characters you would expect. The backspace and Delete key work as you would expect. Typing over selections works. It all works, except the test.

There's one odd thing. Look at the code up there for Ctrl+Z, KeyChar == 26. Two restores are there, not one. The reason, of course, is that up where we do the KeyDown, we are snapshotting on every character, including the Ctrl+Z. We would like to fix that, but first let's think a bit about what to do.

Remember that the Form isn't really running when we do our customer tests. We have created a Form and connected it to the model, but the widgets aren't displayed on the screen. We have no event loop running, because we haven't done the Application.Run(). We are sending things to it by calling our handlers directly. Usually our handlers are on an event chain, from the Form to the textbox to us...and if our handler doesn't deal with something and set key.Handled = true, then the TextBox takes it. That's not happening here, and it won't happen without a lot of trouble.

In a different situation, we might want to run things all the way through, with SendKeys(), a function in Microsoft Windows that lets you type into a running application. I don't think that's appropriate here, because it won't add much information, because the feature is already working, and because we're writing a book here and there won't be much to learn about our topic. Instead, what I want to do is modify the tests and the XML Notepad so that we have a very simple testing interface that is as close as possible to the operation of the notepad in real life.

How about this as a possibility: we'll go back to using the model.Insert-Character() function to poke the character in, but we won't allow the Insert-Character() to do the Snapshot(). Instead, we'll also trigger the KeyDown and let it be the only place in the system that does the Snapshot(). We'll be perpetrating a minor hack around the fact that we can't type into the TextBox from our test, but the effect should be the same. Let's build that, make it work, and then look around again.

```
private void TypeCharacters(String s) {
  foreach (char c in s) {
    form.XMLKeyDownHandler(
      (object) this,
      new KeyEventArgs( (Keys) Enum.Parse(typeof(Keys), c.ToString(), true)));
    model.InsertCharacter(c);
    // the handler doesn't really update the TextBox
    form.CustomerTestPutText();
  }
}
```

Note that we had to do the form.CustomerTestPutText() method to force the form to update the TextBox in this case. The reason is, of course, that this time the model knows something that the text box does not. With this change, the tests are all running. Let's see if we can make things just a little bit better.

The way we have it now, functionality is in the KeyDown and in the Key-Press. The original purpose of the KeyPress was just to be sure that the TextBox didn't handle Enter. Let's retain that purpose, with these changes:

```
public void XMLKeyPressHandler(object objSender, KeyPressEventArgs kea) {
  if ((int) kea.KeyChar == (int) Keys.Enter) {
    kea.Handled = true;
    // this code is here to avoid putting extra enters in the window.
    // if removed, when you hit enter, the new <P> line breaks in two:
    // <P>
    // |</P>  like that.
  }
}
public void XMLKeyDownHandler(object objSender, KeyEventArgs kea) {
  if (kea.KeyCode != Keys.ControlKey &&
      kea.KeyCode != Keys.Menu &&
      kea.KeyCode != Keys.ShiftKey) {
    GetText();
    model.Snapshot();
  }
  if (kea.KeyCode == Keys.Enter && kea.Modifiers == Keys.None) {
    CallModel(enterAction);
    kea.Handled = true;
  }
  else if (kea.KeyCode == Keys.Enter && kea.Modifiers == Keys.Shift) {
    CallModel(shiftEnterAction);
    kea.Handled = true;
  }
  else if (kea.KeyCode == Keys.Z && kea.Modifiers == Keys.Control) {
    model.Restore();
    model.Restore();
    PutText(textbox, model.LinesArray(), model.SelectionStart);
    kea.Handled = true;
  }
}
```

That's better. I just noticed that the handlers are public and that they can be internal. In fact, one of them can probably be private. I'll change that. We still have the need to override the Enter in KeyPress, but we don't need to process the Ctrl+Z in KeyPress at all. The tests are green!

Now there's that duplicate call to Restore() highlighted up there. We can make that go away if we check for Ctrl+Z in the code that does the Snapshot().

We do have a small dilemma: we don't have a broken test that tells us we must do this. What if we remove the extra Restore() and see whether any tests break...they do not. Why?? A quick look at the *undo command in the customer tests shows us:

```
...
        if (line.StartsWith("*alt"))
          ExecuteMenu("&"+line[4]);
        else if (line.StartsWith("*type"))
          TypeCharacters(line.Substring(6));
        else if (line == "*undo")
          model.Restore();
        else if ( line == "*enter")
          form.XMLKeyDownHandler((object) this, new KeyEventArgs(Keys.Enter));
        ...
```

We're restoring the model directly, not using a Ctrl+Z character. Let's put the double Restore() back and change that code to use our KeyDownHandler:

```
...
        if (line.StartsWith("*alt"))
          ExecuteMenu("&"+line[4]);
        else if (line.StartsWith("*type"))
          TypeCharacters(line.Substring(6));
        else if (line == "*undo")
          form.XMLKeyDownHandler((object) this,
            new KeyEventArgs(Keys.Z | Keys.Control));
        else if ( line == "*enter")
          form.XMLKeyDownHandler((object) this, new KeyEventArgs(Keys.Enter));
        ...
```

This breaks a test, with an odd diagnostic: "-1" is not a valid value for "value". We weren't expecting anything to break yet. I'm going to go out on a limb a bit here. I'll assume that this broke because of what I want to change, and I'll make the changes to the KeyDownHandler code. If that doesn't fix this test and keep all the others running, I'll have to dig deeper. This is a risk: I'm on the edge of a debugging rathole. Here's my change:

```
internal void XMLKeyDownHandler(object objSender, KeyEventArgs kea) {
  if (kea.KeyCode != Keys.ControlKey &&
    kea.KeyCode != Keys.Menu &&
    kea.KeyCode != Keys.ShiftKey &&
    (kea.KeyCode == Keys.Z && kea.Modifiers == Keys.Control)) {
    GetText();
    model.Snapshot();
  }
  if (kea.KeyCode == Keys.Enter && kea.Modifiers == Keys.None) {
    CallModel(enterAction);
```

```
          kea.Handled = true;
        }
        else if (kea.KeyCode == Keys.Enter && kea.Modifiers == Keys.Shift) {
          CallModel(shiftEnterAction);
          kea.Handled = true;
        }
        else if (kea.KeyCode == Keys.Z && kea.Modifiers == Keys.Control) {
          model.Restore();
//          model.Restore();
          PutText(textbox, model.LinesArray(), model.SelectionStart);
          kea.Handled = true;
        }
      }
```

Arrgh! Tests still fail, but with a new message:

```
c:\data\csharp\notepad\undo.test
*Expected
<P>ab|</P>
*Result
<P>abc|</P>
```

It looks to me like it still needs the double Restore(). I'll check that quickly...no! Putting it back gives me a Stack Empty message. That's kind of good news, but I've overstayed my welcome on this speculation. Fortunately, I took a second look at that complex if statement at the top. It needs a not (!) in front of the last clause. Let's see if that works better...that gets me back to the message about -1 not being a valid value for "value".

I am very tempted to start debugging now. I'm sure that I can find this problem and fix it, but if my pair were here with me, he would make me back out these changes and find that first bug. So that's what I'll do. The error is coming up with this stack trace:

```
at System.Windows.Forms.TextBoxBase.set_SelectionStart(Int32 value)
at Notepad.TestableTextBox.Notepad.ITestTextBox.set_SelectionStart(Int32 )
at Notepad.XMLNotepad.PutText(ITestTextBox textbox, String[] lines,
   Int32 selectionStart)
   in c:\data\csharp\notepad\xmlnotepad.cs:line 221
at Notepad.XMLNotepad.XMLKeyDownHandler(Object objSender, KeyEventArgs kea)
   in c:\data\csharp\notepad\xmlnotepad.cs:line 213
at Notepad.CustomerTest.InterpretCommands(String commands, String message)
   in c:\data\csharp\notepad\customertest.cs:line 69
at Notepad.CustomerTest.InterpretFileInput(String fileName)
   in c:\data\csharp\notepad\customertest.cs:line 56
at Notepad.CustomerTest.TestAllFiles()
   in c:\data\csharp\notepad\customertest.cs:line 48
```

Line 69, we're not surprised to see, is our sending of the Ctrl+Z. Time for a little breakpointing. At the breakpoint, we'll see what's up. Stepping in, we see that the abc is in, we snap (redundantly), we restore twice, and the model has ab, as we expect. This isn't going to be the time through that causes the problem. Let's see...I'll let it proceed once to find the state at the error.

Debugging wasn't helpful. The error occurs, the system hurls, and I don't get a breakpoint in my code, because NUnit catches the exception. However, I learned that it wasn't the first *undo that failed, and I hypothesize that it is the last. So I'll do it again, waiting until the last *undo, which is the fourth one. Hold on...at the last *undo, after the Snapshot(), the model contains empty P tags. We expect it to remove them. I'll inspect the stack, expecting two entries. That's what I find, one with the P tags that we just pushed (redundantly) and then one with nothing in it. I'm vaguely remembering that we put in special code to handle the result of an empty TextModel. Is that the bug???

After the two Restore() calls, we have no lines and a SelectionStart of -1. Ha! I see it. Look at this code:

```
else if (kea.KeyCode == Keys.Z && kea.Modifiers == Keys.Control) {
  model.Restore();
  model.Restore();
  PutText(textbox, model.LinesArray(), model.SelectionStart);
  kea.Handled = true;
}
```

We weren't executing this before in the CustomerTests; we were just calling model.Undo(). So we never tried to push an empty model back to the TextBox. What's happening is that we are telling the TextBox to set its selection to -1, and it doesn't like that. To make things work, I'm going to fix the PutText method not to do that:

```
internal void PutText(ITestTextBox textbox, string[] lines,
  int selectionStart) {
  // this is Feature Envy big time.
  textbox.Lines = lines;
  textbox.SelectionStart = selectionStart<0 ? 0 : selectionStart;
  textbox.ScrollToCaret();
}
```

And this fixes the bug! Let's pause to think about that.

We had been testing *undo just against the model, and we are on a general path of pushing the tests to go more through the Form. In so doing, we did something we have never done before, at least not in this way: we set the Text-Box SelectionStart to -1, because that was the saved value in the TextModel. We need to think about this, however, because we did not see that same problem when running the XML Notepad as an application. In that case, it apparently pushed a zero all on its own. Why is it different when testing?

We now have two problems on our plate. First, we are trying to get rid of the double Restore(), and second, we want to understand why we had to put that glitch in the code for the -1. First things first, let's see if we can now remove the double Restore(). This time the change works:

```
internal void XMLKeyDownHandler(object objSender, KeyEventArgs kea) {
    if (kea.KeyCode != Keys.ControlKey &&
        kea.KeyCode != Keys.Menu &&
        kea.KeyCode != Keys.ShiftKey &&
        !(kea.KeyCode == Keys.Z && kea.Modifiers == Keys.Control)) {
        GetText();
        model.Snapshot();
    }
    if (kea.KeyCode == Keys.Enter && kea.Modifiers == Keys.None) {
        CallModel(enterAction);
        kea.Handled = true;
    }
    else if (kea.KeyCode == Keys.Enter && kea.Modifiers == Keys.Shift) {
        CallModel(shiftEnterAction);
        kea.Handled = true;
    }
    else if (kea.KeyCode == Keys.Z && kea.Modifiers == Keys.Control) {
        model.Restore();
//      model.Restore();
        PutText(textbox, model.LinesArray(), model.SelectionStart);
        kea.Handled = true;
    }
}
```

Lesson   As I read the section just above, it feels to me that I was on the very edge of getting in trouble. The comments about confusion, the extra confusion when things don't work, problems piling on problems: these are all signs of trouble. I'm sure you have felt them yourself. This time I got away with it with very little time spent in the rat hole. I was lucky.

What would be a good way for me to avoid this sort of thing? A great way, of course, is pairing. Our pair will not be very tolerant of this sort of thing, and if he isn't pretty sure that we're on the right track, he'll stop us. What could we do when we're working alone? Maybe set an oven timer? I'm not sure: it's very easy for me to fall into this mode of just hacking around blindly, and it's not an effective use of my time. We'll see a big example of this in an upcoming chapter.

The tests run. However, my confidence is a bit lessened by this trouble. I'm going to run the application manually. I did the same test as the customer one, and it works. We still need more information. We'll add some instrumentation and try it manually and with the tests:

```
public void Snapshot() {
  Console.WriteLine(
    "pushing {0} lines, sel {1}",
    this.Lines.Count,
    this.selectionStart);
  SavedModels.Push(new TextModel(this));
}
public void Restore() {
  TextModel savedModel = (TextModel) SavedModels.Pop();
  Console.WriteLine(
    "popping {0} lines, sel {1}",
    savedModel.Lines.Count,
    savedModel.selectionStart);
  lines = savedModel.Lines;
  selectionStart = savedModel.SelectionStart;
}
```

Running in this mode tells the tale. The first push in the manual mode pushes a selectionStart of zero, while the first push in the automatic mode pushes a selection start of -1. A little searching finds this code:

```
private int LineContainingCursor() {
  if (lines.Count == 0)
    return -1;
  int length = 0;
  int lineNr = 0;
  int cr = Environment.NewLine.Length;
  foreach ( String s in lines) {
    if (length <= selectionStart
      && selectionStart < length+s.Length + cr )
      break;
    length += s.Length + cr;
    lineNr++;
  }
  return lineNr;
}
private Boolean InListItem() {
  if (LineContainingCursor() < 0 ) return false;
  return ((string) lines[LineContainingCursor()]).StartsWith("<LI>");
}
```

There's our hack about -1. We have felt nervous about it more than once. I don't see a really good way to improve it, but let's make it a bit better. Let's first fix InListItem():

```
private Boolean InListItem() {
  if (Lines.Count == 0 ) return false;
  return ((string) lines[LineContainingCursor()]).StartsWith("<LI>");
}
```

The tests still run. Now let's see who else is relying on that -1 in the Line-ContainingCursor(), by making it return zero. We get a bunch of errors, all with a negative index in InsertRange():

```
public void InsertTags(InsertAction action) {
  int cursorLine = LineContainingCursor();
  lines.InsertRange(cursorLine+1, action.TagsToInsert);
  selectionStart = NewSelectionStart(cursorLine + 1, action.TagsToSkip);
}
```

This looks familiar—the -1 glitch was put in a long time ago to let us handle an insertion on an empty file. If the line count is zero, we want to insert at zero. Let's change that:

```
public void InsertTags(InsertAction action) {
  int cursorLine = LineContainingCursor() + 1;
  if (Lines.Count == 0) cursorLine = 0;
  lines.InsertRange(cursorLine, action.TagsToInsert);
  selectionStart = NewSelectionStart(cursorLine, action.TagsToSkip);
}
```

The tests run again. Now we should be able to remove that special code in the PutText():

```
internal void PutText(ITestTextBox textbox, string[] lines,
  int selectionStart) {
  // this is Feature Envy big time.
  textbox.Lines = lines;
  textbox.SelectionStart = selectionStart<0 ? 0 : selectionStart;
  textbox.ScrollToCaret();
}
```

But when we do, a bunch of tests break! A little looking around and we find out why: the TextBox, when it is empty, will give us a SelectionStart of -1, but it won't take one back as input! Thanks, TextBox! If that's the case, what about the changes we just made? InListItem() looks about the same either way. The change to InsertTags() is a little awkward, but at least we're not passing an impossible value around from LineContiningCursor(). However, the result we send back, 0, is just as wrong as -1 if there are no lines. InsertRange handles an insertion at location zero, but if we were to try to subscript into Lines, the zero would be incorrect (as would -1).

There is definitely a code smell here, in our handling of the ArrayList of lines, but it's not really related to our main purpose, the implementation of Undo. Undo is passing all its tests so far.

Are We There Yet?

Not quite. We know there is a problem with an Undo that tries to Undo too much. We know how to fix it: we'll just check whether the stack is empty, and if it isn't, we'll do nothing. But we need a test—let's add one more *undo to the undo.test file:

```
*enter
*type abc
*output
<P>abc|</P>
*end
*undo
*output
<P>ab|</P>
*end
*undo
*output
<P>a|</P>
*end
*undo
*output
<P>|</P>
*end
*undo
*output
|
*end*undo *output | *end
```

This fails, predictably, with the message "Stack Empty". Now we can add the feature:

```
public void Restore() {
  if (SavedModels.Count == 0) return;
  TextModel savedModel = (TextModel) SavedModels.Pop();
  lines = savedModel.Lines;
  selectionStart = savedModel.SelectionStart;
}
```

The tests all run. I believe that functionality is now complete. Let's reflect. In the next chapter—Chapter 29, "The Final Optimized Undo"—we'll turn our attention to efficiency.

Review of What Has Happened So Far

The tests all run. We're nearly there—maybe even there. Close enough, anyway, to reflect on our main concern: would some kind of up-front planning, some big design decisions at the very beginning, have made this job easier? We have run into a number of interesting problems, so we need to reflect carefully. It would have been perfect for my story had we encountered no problems at all, but that didn't happen. Let's first look at the big picture of the implementation and then at the problems we encountered.

Even the detailed flow of the implementation is pretty simple:

1. **First we think.** We thought a bit about what would work, and whether we could get away with saving the whole file on every keystroke. We decided that it might work. We surely would have needed to think first, no matter how much thinking we had already done.

2. **Simple snapshot.** We did a single-level Snapshot and Restore. This got us started and showed that the concept was viable. No wasted time here.

3. **Move to stack.** In a few short steps, we had a Stack implementation in the model. Just what we need, and a very elegant structure. No waste here.

4. **Experiment for viability.** We did a quick experiment where we stacked on every character, just to see whether performance would kill us. We didn't die. No waste here.

5. **Weird character things.** Experimenting with the Undo side, we ran into trouble with the TextBox's handling of characters and with repeating keys that were held down. Once we recognized the problem, we fixed it with a simple guard clause. At this point we had Undo basically working. It was time to build it in. This was tricky but would have occurred in any case.

6. **Build an end-to-end test.** We decided to use the customer test style to build a test. To do this, we needed to add a couple of new features to the framework. We would have to do this for Undo, no matter how prepared we were for it.

7. **Put snapshot calls in.** We began with three or four calls to Snapshot() in a few different Insert methods. We noticed the duplication immediately, of course, since we were typing it it. Might we have avoided typing these three lines by more up-front design early in the project? Frankly I doubt it, but even if so, how much would you pay to avoid typing and later deleting three lines?

8. **Removing the experiments.** I wasted a tiny bit of time removing the experiments: it would perhaps have made more sense to revert the code, but I didn't think of it. Not likely that more design weeks ago would have solved that problem.

9. **Remove the duplicates.** The duplication of the Snapshot() calls was irritating, and we found nearly the right place for a single call: in the keyboard handler. If we had started end to end, we might have done this initially. Perhaps we would have saved typing and deleting those three lines by starting with a Customer Acceptance Test instead of our experiment, but frankly we didn't have the courage to commit this approach without trying it.

10. **Keyboard problems.** We went into a bit of a debugging frenzy handling the keyboard issues. This is certainly evidence that we don't know everything we would like to, but it wasn't due to a design problem, just to solid ignorance about how the TextBox really works. It did go on for too long, but I don't see, even now, how we could have "designed" more. We just had to learn things about running and testing the system without opening the GUI.

11. **System works; test does not.** We were in that odd state where the Undo was working fine, but the tests didn't work. It was tempting to let it be, but that would have left us with untested code in a critical area. Better to go on and get the character push to work. That was tricky, but nothing to do with Undo.

12. **Negative one in cursor line.** This took us a bit of time, and there can be no doubt that it is a design issue. But it's not a design issue related to Undo; rather, it's a hack that has been with us for a while. It is fundamentally due to the interface between the TextBox and the TextModel, and the TextBox's insistence on handing out a value that it can't take back. Irritating, but not entirely our fault. I'm inclined to put it on the list to clean up just because the code is a bit tricky.

The Big Picture

The big picture is even simpler:

1. We found a single place to put a Snapshot() call and a single place to put a Restore().

2. We implemented a Snapshot() method that pushes a copy of the editor onto a stack and a Restore() method that pops it back off the stack.

There was a little fumbling around with the installation, but no major refactoring was required. We didn't need to make changes "all over" the implementation. All the problems we encountered were typical of working with reasonably well-designed objects, not of working in a system that wasn't ready to receive the changes we needed to make. Frankly, it went quite well.

Does This Prove Anything?

I believe that this experience indicates something but does not prove it. This is just an example, and it's possible to argue that somehow, as we were refactoring along, we accidentally pushed the design in a direction that just happened to be good for Undo, or maybe we even subconsciously did so, knowing that Undo was coming. Or, maybe I cheated somehow, by making design decisions that I knew were good for Undo, while giving other flimsy reasons for doing so, in an attempt to bamboozle you, pull the wool over your eyes, and flim-flam you. But would I do that? I don't think so, since I'm trying to help, and I won't get paid extra if you get in trouble following my advice.

Therefore, I think those explanations are less compelling than this simpler one: Writing clean code and removing as much duplication as we can almost inevitably leads to a program where the thing we want to do next needs to be done in just one, or a very few, places. We have seen that happen throughout this book, and we have just seen it happen in one of the most challenging situations people can imagine: needing to put Undo into a program that wasn't designed for it.

That's important because when we worry that an unexpected change will be more expensive unless we prepare for it, we are really saying that we're worried that the change will have to be made in lots of places and that lots of code will have to be changed around. It seems quite plausible to me that this can happen only if an "idea" in our heads is represented in many places in the code and that idea needs to be changed. But our simple style of development focuses on putting every idea we have into the code and on removing all the duplication. The result is that the ideas tend all to be in just one place. So even if the idea is wrong, there tends to be only one place needing to be changed.

Ultimately, you need to do your own experimentation and make up your own mind. Build up skills in recognizing duplication and expressing ideas, and as you practice those skills, you can work on reducing how much up-front preparation you do in support of things you see coming. I'm comfortable doing very little preparation, as a result of many years of general experience and around five years of working in this simple evolutionary style. Your point of balance will surely be different, but I'm sure you'll find a balance that will let you focus a bit more on results for your customer and a bit less on preparing for a future that may never come.

Lesson   One of my technical editors thinks that I'm a bit too happy with the result so far. He points out that this marvelous Undo implementation is consuming memory madly, and that's just not good enough. True enough, it is using too much memory, but that is a matter that's internal to the implementation. We'll address that in a moment. My point here is that more design of the rest of the editor was not needed to put Undo in the right place. I'm happy because no matter what happens next, we did not have to redesign the whole program to support Undo, and now it's clear that we will not need to do so.

Another editor points out that there is something a bit odd about using the TextModel as the object that gets pushed on the stack of the TextModel. It is a bit asymmetric or something. In particular, the Undo stack of the pushed TextModels never gets used. This is a good observation: we have two ideas here tied up in one object. One idea is "holding the text that is being edited," and the other is "holding the stack of things to be undone." When one object has two functions, the code is not expressing our ideas as well as it should. I didn't see that issue while writing the code, and neither did my pairs. No excuses, sir. It would have been better another way. I hope this is the worst mistake I ever make in the rest of my life. However, because at this writing I know what is coming up, I am sorry to say that a bigger mistake is coming.

Finally, one of my editors points out that all this was made much easier because the editor's data is primarily stored in a model class that is part of the application, not just a graphical control (TextBox). This is certainly true, true enough that I consider it a necessary design step for every system: separate model from view. You recall that we did this way back in Chapter 4, "Extracting the Model."

Now please read on about optimizing this effective but inefficient Undo and the problems that came up as we did it.

29

The Final Optimized Undo

With a few simple considerations, we come up with a good way to reduce the storage requirements of our original Undo. However, as you'll read in the chapter that follows this one, first came some false starts. Here, we'll take a look at how well things turned out, and then we'll explore the dead ends.

Deciding to Begin Again

This chapter is out of chronological order. Following it is a dark chapter about the false starts I made trying to optimize Undo. This one is moved forward for three reasons: first, it will be easier to understand if placed in proximity to the initial Undo that you just read about in Chapter 28, "Oh No! Undo!"—the one that snapshots everything. Second, with knowledge of how truly simple the optimization turns out to be, you'll benefit more from the false-start chapter that follows—Chapter 30, "The Long Dark Teatime of the Soul." Third, you may wish to skip over much of the false-start material. It's quite painful—to me, at least, who made all the mistakes—but I promised to show you most everything in this book.

We came up with three basic approaches to optimizing our initial Undo:

■ **First, do nothing.** This could be a perfectly viable solution. We have a working Undo that happens to waste a lot of memory. However, it seems to cause no problems in actual use. Our main motivation for "fixing" it wasn't that it was hurting the program, but that the simple implementation almost seemed like "cheating," so we wanted to show how to evolve it to something better.

- **Second, compare the lines.**   There will be more discussion of this in Chapter 30, but here's the idea: Most changes affect only a line or two. If we compared all the lines from the beginning down until the first line that didn't match, and then we compared all the lines from the end until the first line that didn't match, we could limit our considerations to those in between. It seems that these would invariably be just exactly the lines that were changed, and that rarely, if ever, would there be anything extra in there. We would have to consider deletions carefully, to be sure we handled them correctly, but that should be no problem. One concern is that this might be quite costly, but it would be easy to write a test to decide that.

- **Third, handle the most common case only.**   The most common case, by far, is the user typing one ordinary character into an existing line. Looking at this book as an example, there are typically around 500 characters in each paragraph—and I write very short paragraphs. It seems likely that handling this one case—insert a character into the current line—would reduce the storage requirements by well over 99 percent.

I must reflect on these options and counsel with Chet to find out what I really think. And I'll have to gird my loins to delete all that code, although now that I'm sure it really cannot work, it's a lot easier. Read on...

Clearing a Space to Work

Remember that we're starting in the middle here. We have had some false starts, to be described below, and we have accepted that what we did won't work; we have given it enough chances. It's time to start with a better idea. To do that, we need a clean space to work. One way to do this might be to revert the code. I have every version saved in the source manager, and it would be easy to back it up to the point before we started with the Optimized thing. But although it might take a bit longer, I've decided to go "forward" by removing the unnecessary code from the current version. I think that will give me a better view of the terrain, in preparation for starting again. It's a judgment call. We'll begin by removing all the old optimization material. You can follow along or skip to the next heading. What you'll see, if you stay with me, is an example of scavenging through bad code trying to preserve some good bits.

> **Lesson**   From my later perspective, it looks to me as if backing out would have been better. The ideas were all in my head, and the code was at best only partly good. Still, no real harm done. Read on...

I begin by removing the Interface, OptimizedTextModel, and UnoptimizedTextModel from the system. The compiler will tell me what to do next. It says that OptimizedTextModel can't be found, in TextModel's MostRecentlySavedModel method. The method is used in a lot of tests, so I'd rather not remove it. I believe, though, that I will add an interface for the Undo operation. I'll call it IUndoRestore, just like before.

```
public interface IUndoRestore {
}
```

and in TextModel:
```
    public IUndoRestore MostRecentlySavedModel(){
      return (IUndoRestore) SavedModels.Peek();
    }
```

This triggers a lot of error messages about methods not in IUndoRestore; I'm not surprised. I'll remove most of them without remarking here. Some of what needs removal are tests for the old optimize. I'll comment them out for now, but they really need to die. In other cases, I'll just make sure that the test will fail, and then I'll revise it when I know more about what's going on. Here's one example:

```
[Test] public void SectionUndo() {
  ShowLines("empty");
  model.Snapshot();
  model.InsertTags(model.SectionCommand());
  ShowLines("section");
  model.Snapshot();
  model.InsertCharacter('x');
  ShowLines("x");
  model.Restore();
  ShowLines("no x");//
  AssertEquals(2,
    model.MostRecentlySavedModel().NumberOfLinesToRemove());
  model.Restore();
  ShowLines("no section");
  AssertEquals(99, model.Lines.Count);
}
```

The next test I look at tells me that I need to add Restore() to IUndoRestore:

```
public void Restore() {
  Console.WriteLine("Restore {0}", SavedModels.Count);
    if (SavedModels.Count == 0) return;
  Console.WriteLine("  non-empty");
  IUndoRestore opt = (IUndoRestore) SavedModels.Pop();
  opt.Restore(this);
}
```

which begs:

```
  public interface IUndoRestore {
    void Restore(TextModel model);
  }
```

This, of course, is exactly what we had before, but now we know that we need it.

There are many calls to OptimizeSavedModel in the tests. I hate to remove them, but they are in fact mostly useless, as they are testing that feature and we're not going to have that feature any more. Out they go! The Snapshot() method itself refers to OptimizedTextModel. I change it back to using Text-Model, the way it originally did:

```
public void Snapshot() {
  SavedModels.Push(new TextModel(this));
}
```

The system compiles. Some unused methods are probably around, but let's see about the tests. Various Undo-related tests fail. I'll look at them and see what to do. I expect that after we fix a few, the rest will work. They are all failing on a cast, in line 313:

```
public void Restore() {
  Console.WriteLine("Restore {0}", SavedModels.Count);
    if (SavedModels.Count == 0) return;
  Console.WriteLine("  non-empty");
  IUndoRestore opt = (IUndoRestore) SavedModels.Pop();
  opt.Restore(this);
}
```

No surprise: TextModel, which is now on the stack, doesn't implement IUndoRestore. I'll fix that:

```
public class TextModel : IUndoRestore {
  ...
  public void Restore() {
    IUndoRestore opt = (IUndoRestore) SavedModels.Pop();
```

```
    opt.Restore(this);
  }
  public void Restore(TextModel model) {
    model.ReplaceAllLines(
      this.Lines,
      this.SelectionStart,
      this.SelectionLength);
  }
  ...
```

This last method is the callback that we used to have in UnoptimizedText-Model. We'll be calling back to ourselves. This might seem odd, but I think it's right. This is taking a little more time than I would like, a sign that starting over might have been better. Let's see what fails now—SnapshotLinesIdentity():

```
[Test] public void SnapshotLinesIdentity() {
  model.SetLines(new String[] { "before", "snapshot" });
  model.SelectionStart = 6; // after before ;->
  AssertEquals("snapshot", model.Lines[1]);
  model.Snapshot();
  model.InsertTags(TextModel.Tags.Pre);
  AssertEquals("<pre></pre>", model.Lines[1]);
  model.Restore();
  AssertEquals("snapshot", model.Lines[1]);
}
```

This is failing because it expects snapshotxxx (which I changed just to be sure the test would fail) and gets snapshot. This test is working now!

SectionUndo() is also failing. That's the method I put the 99 into:

```
[Test] public void SectionUndo() {
  ShowLines("empty");
  model.Snapshot();
  model.InsertTags(model.SectionCommand());
  ShowLines("section");
  model.Snapshot();
  model.InsertCharacter('x');
  ShowLines("x");
  model.Restore();
  ShowLines("no x");
  model.Restore();
  ShowLines("no section");
  AssertEquals(99, model.Lines.Count);
}
```

The zero is correct, and when we put it back, the test runs. I'll remove all that tracing, and while I'm at it, I'll add some sorely needed assertions.

```
[Test] public void SectionUndo() {
  ShowLines("empty");
  model.Snapshot();
  model.InsertTags(model.SectionCommand());
  model.Snapshot();
  model.InsertCharacter('x');
  model.Restore();
  AssertEquals("<sect1><title></title>", model.Lines[0]);
  AssertEquals("</sect1>", model.Lines[1]);
  model.Restore();
  AssertEquals(0, model.Lines.Count);
}
```

This test also passes. We are left with one customer test, which is saying "Stack Empty" attempting a Restore(). I got a little too rambunctious when I edited the tracing out of the old Restore() method. It needs to check the stack, and I deleted that when I deleted the Console.WriteLine() calls:

```
public void Restore() {
  if (SavedModels.Count == 0) return;
  IUndoRestore opt = (IUndoRestore) SavedModels.Pop();
  opt.Restore(this);
}
```

All the tests are running again, using the original Snapshot() that just saves a new copy of the TextModel. Now there are a number of methods that are no longer needed, and I'll remove them to clean up the space further. Removed are ReplaceChangedLines(), RemoveNewLines(), PutBackOldLines(), LinesBeforeCursor, BeforeLines, and some tests that use those: the entire UndoAnalyzer.cs and UndoAnalyzerTest.cs.

Again, I discover to my dismay that Microsoft Visual Studio and the compiler won't tell me which public methods are unreferenced. It will be difficult to be sure that I have found all the excess. I find: LineNumberToInsert, NumberOfLinesToRemove, FirstLineToRemove, NewModelLineContainingCursor and its corresponding member variable, newModelLineContainingCursor. I also remove the Boolean debugIsOptimized and its property. There's LinesToPutBack and NumberOfLinesToPutBack. The tests are all running. We have a good place to begin now.

A New Idea

While munching my luncheon chicken strips, I drew the following design picture in my notebook:

The last time I did this design thing, as you'll read about in the next chapter, I worked for a few hours over a period of a few days, going through cases and figuring things out in some detail. And I got it wrong, even after all that thinking. This time, a few things popped out right away:

1. At the time we do the Snapshot(), we can know the character typed. We can get it from the KeyEventArgs that's passed to the KeyPress event.

2. Since Snapshot() is done by the TextModel, before the typing is completed, we will also know the SelectionStart and SelectionLength. This is certainly enough to let us recognize an insert of an ordinary character, and I think a lot more as well.

3. Instead of waiting until "next time" and then "optimizing" the previous snapshot, let's try to get it right the first time. Whose idea was that optimization thing, anyway? It was hard to implement and hard to understand.

4. We'll probably wind up using an Interface like the previous one, but I'm going to delete the whole thing and start over nonetheless. I want the code to reflect the real need, not a foreseen need, so I'll wait and put it back in. It's only a few lines. (Again a sign that starting over might have been better.)

5. It should be possible to do this in a test-driven fashion. I can set up a TextModel with whatever values I want, and I can send it a Snapshot() message with parameters indicating what's happening next.

The design sketch is so small because the idea seems much simpler than the last one and because I feel the need to let the tests and code help me, rather than speculate so much. Speculation got me in trouble last time. Let's begin. The general direction I'd like to take is to move the Undo-related keyboard analysis into the Snapshot processing instead of leaving it in the KeyDown logic. We start with this:

```
internal void XMLKeyDownHandler(object objSender, KeyEventArgs kea) {
  if (kea.KeyCode != Keys.ControlKey &&
    kea.KeyCode != Keys.Menu &&
    kea.KeyCode != Keys.ShiftKey &&
    kea.Modifiers != Keys.Alt &&
    !(kea.KeyCode == Keys.Z && kea.Modifiers == Keys.Control)) {
    GetText();
    model.Snapshot();
  }
  if (kea.KeyCode == Keys.Enter && kea.Modifiers == Keys.None) {
    CallModel(enterAction);
    kea.Handled = true;
  }
  else if (kea.KeyCode == Keys.Enter && kea.Modifiers == Keys.Shift) {
    CallModel(shiftEnterAction);
    kea.Handled = true;
  }
  else if (kea.KeyCode == Keys.Z && kea.Modifiers == Keys.Control) {
    model.Restore();
    PutText(textbox, model.LinesArray(), model.SelectionStart);
    kea.Handled = true;
  }
}
```

And we get to this:

```
internal void XMLKeyDownHandler(object objSender, KeyEventArgs kea) {
  GetText();
  model.KeyboardSnapshot(kea);
```

```
  if (kea.KeyCode == Keys.Enter && kea.Modifiers == Keys.None) {
    CallModel(enterAction);
    kea.Handled = true;
  }
  else if (kea.KeyCode == Keys.Enter && kea.Modifiers == Keys.Shift) {
    CallModel(shiftEnterAction);
    kea.Handled = true;
  }
  else if (kea.KeyCode == Keys.Z && kea.Modifiers == Keys.Control) {
    model.Restore();
    PutText(textbox, model.LinesArray(), model.SelectionStart);
    kea.Handled = true;
  }
}
```

and in textmodel.cs:

```
using System.Windows.Forms;
...
public void KeyboardSnapshot(KeyEventArgs kea) {
  if (kea.KeyCode != Keys.ControlKey &&
    kea.KeyCode != Keys.Menu &&
    kea.KeyCode != Keys.ShiftKey &&
    kea.Modifiers != Keys.Alt &&
    !(kea.KeyCode == Keys.Z && kea.Modifiers == Keys.Control)) {
    this.Snapshot();
  }
}
```

The tests run. I hate that complex if statement. Let's give it some intention:

```
public void KeyboardSnapshot(KeyEventArgs kea) {
  if ( ! ShouldSnapshot(kea)) return;
  this.Snapshot();
}
private Boolean ShouldSnapshot(KeyEventArgs kea) {
  if (kea.KeyCode == Keys.ControlKey) return false;
  if (kea.KeyCode == Keys.Menu) return false;
  if (kea.KeyCode == Keys.ShiftKey) return false;
  if (kea.Modifiers == Keys.Alt ) return false;
  if (kea.KeyCode == Keys.Z
    && kea.Modifiers == Keys.Control) return false;
  return true;
}
```

The tests still run. I observe that Snapshot() is now unconditionally doing a full snapshot of the textmodel, so let's rename it to FullSnapshot():

```
public void FullSnapshot() {
  SavedModels.Push(new TextModel(this));
}

referenced by:
public void KeyboardSnapshot(KeyEventArgs kea) {
  if ( ! ShouldSnapshot(kea)) return;
  this.FullSnapshot();
}

and in XMLNotepad.cs:
void MenuInsertTags(object obj, EventArgs ea) {
  NotepadMenuItem item = (NotepadMenuItem) obj;
  GetText();
  model.FullSnapshot();
  model.InsertTags(item.Action);
  PutText(textbox, model.LinesArray(), model.SelectionStart);
}
```

Now we're ready to handle our case: an ordinary keystroke. Let's limit ourselves also to selection length zero.

```
public void KeyboardSnapshot(KeyEventArgs kea) {
  if ( ! ShouldSnapshot(kea)) return;
  if (SimpleInsertCharacter(kea))
    this.SnapshotInsertCharacter();
  else
    this.FullSnapshot();
}
private Boolean SimpleInsertCharacter(KeyEventArgs kea) {
  if (SelectionLength > 0) return false;
  if (kea.Modifiers != Keys.None) return false;
  char c = (char) kea.KeyValue;
  if (Char.IsLetterOrDigit(c)) return true;
  if (Char.IsPunctuation(c)) return true;
  return false;
}
private void SnapshotInsertCharacter() {
  FullSnapshot();
}
```

All we have done here is break out the case of selection length zero, no modifiers such as control or alt, and letters, digits, and punctuation. (Char doesn't seem to offer an easy way to know whether a graphic is an ordinary character.) This will cover most of our cases anyway, and the learning will be in the next step. In the code so far, of course, we just fall back to the FullSnapshot(). The tests run with FullSnapshot enabled inside SnapshotInsertCharacter(), and they do not if we comment it out. So we know that we're getting there under control of our tests. Now let's make it do something—we'll build a new class, SingleCharacterSnapshot. Since we never create it with SelectionLength greater than zero, I thought it should just need to know SelectionStart, but here's what I wound up with as a first working version:

```
public class SingleCharacterSnapshot : IUndoRestore {
  private int selectionStart;
  private int lineNumber;
  private String oldLine;
  public SingleCharacterSnapshot(TextModel model) {
    selectionStart = model.SelectionStart;
    lineNumber = model.LineContainingCursor();
    oldLine = (string) model.Lines[lineNumber];
  }
  public void Restore(TextModel model) {
    model.Lines[lineNumber] = oldLine;
    model.SelectionStart = selectionStart;
  }
}
```

invoked by:

```
  private void SnapshotInsertCharacter() {
    SavedModels.Push(new SingleCharacterSnapshot(this));
  }
```

What I wanted to do was just remember the selectionStart, and then inside the Restore() method, get the current line, remove the character right after selectionStart, and put the line back. When I started to do that, it turned out to be a bit tricky. We can get the line containing selectionStart easily enough, but no method in textModel will tell us which character within the line we are interested in. I could have programmed it by intention, but I was more interested in keeping the code working, so I took this intermediate step.

The tests now run...and because I forgot to reset model.SelectionStart in my first implementation, I know that they do not work when I don't have that line in. This tells me that the SingleCharacterSnapshot class is being used and that it works. Now we can make it better.

> **Lesson** Now truth is, I can't resist making it better, because I see that we can avoid storing any lines at all by editing the line in place. It's worth noting, however, that this might not be the best idea. First of all, by reducing the storage from all the lines to just one, we have already reduced the storage requirement by a factor of more than 100 for the average file: one line vs. all the lines. Second, while we will save storage by calculating the undo line, we will increase processing time. I'm sure this won't be enough to notice, but we should remain aware of it. I've decided to go ahead, because it should be just a few minutes' work. But is this change necessary? Probably not.

Ha! I was mistaken. (First time that ever happened.) I thought there was no method that tells us our position within the caret line, but there is one after all, PositionOfCursorInLine(), which is just what we need to edit the line. Let's change the class to use that:

```
public class SingleCharacterSnapshot : IUndoRestore {
  private int selectionStart;
  private int lineNumber;
  private int positionInLine;
  public SingleCharacterSnapshot(TextModel model) {
    selectionStart = model.SelectionStart;
    lineNumber = model.LineContainingCursor();
    positionInLine = model.PositionOfCursorInLine();
  }
  public void Restore(TextModel model) {
    String lineToEdit = (String) model.Lines[lineNumber];
    String oldLine = lineToEdit.Remove(positionInLine,1);
    model.Lines[lineNumber] = oldLine;
    model.SelectionStart = selectionStart;
  }
}
```

Using the PositionInLine() method, we record where the caret is within the selected line. In Restore(), we grab the line from the TextModel, remove one character (the one that must have been typed during the edit), and put the line back. Our tests still run.

Where do we stand? In the most common case (probably over 99 percent of the time), we have reduced the storage requirements of an Undo Snapshot from the entire contents of the file to three integers. This is a good thing.

A Minor Setback on the Way to Success

However, I still don't trust the tests completely. This is not a good thing, but it's a true thing. And rightly so: running the notepad manually, I notice some odd behavior when using the arrow keys to cursor around. That complex code to classify whether to do a single-character snapshot is snapping on an arrow key. It turns out that the arrow keys come in looking like shifted numeric characters, % and such. This called my attention to the fact that we have both Key-Press and KeyDown handlers. I like the KeyDown, because it allows us to use the Keys enumeration. On the other hand, we were left with that one check for Enter in the KeyPress handler, and now character classification is getting really tricky in KeyDown.

I did some research: I read about keyboard handling in Petzold's C# book and posted questions on a few lists and newsgroups. What I was advised is that KeyDown isn't a good way to classify characters—the KeyPress handler is recommended. So I removed the KeyDownHandler and moved all its logic to Key-Press, modifying KeyboardSnapshot and its friends along the way:

```
public void XMLKeyPressHandler(object objSender,
  KeyPressEventArgs kea) {
  GetText();
  model.KeyboardSnapshot(kea);
  if ((int) kea.KeyChar == (int) Keys.Enter) {
    kea.Handled = true;
    if (Control.ModifierKeys == Keys.Shift
        || this.TestModifierKeys == Keys.Shift)
      CallModel(shiftEnterAction);
    else if (Control.ModifierKeys == Keys.None)
      CallModel(enterAction);
  }
  else if ( (int) kea.KeyChar == 26 ) { // Control Z
    model.Restore();
    PutText(textbox, model.LinesArray(), model.SelectionStart);
    kea.Handled = true;
  }
}
public void KeyboardSnapshot(KeyPressEventArgs kea) {
  if ( ! ShouldSnapshot(kea)) return;
  if (SimpleInsertCharacter(kea))
    this.SnapshotInsertCharacter();
  else
    this.FullSnapshot();
}
private Boolean ShouldSnapshot(KeyPressEventArgs kea) {
  if (kea.KeyChar == (char) 26)
    return false;
  else
```

```
      return true;
   }
private Boolean SimpleInsertCharacter(KeyPressEventArgs kea) {
   if (SelectionLength > 0) return false;
   if (Control.ModifierKeys != Keys.None
      && Control.ModifierKeys != Keys.Shift)
      return false;
   char c = kea.KeyChar;
   if ( Char.IsLetterOrDigit(c) || Char.IsPunctuation(c))
      return true;
   else
      return false;
}
```

These were all fairly straightforward changes. I don't like having to refer to Ctrl+Z as "26", but it was the best I had at the moment. Let's fix that while we're thinking of it:

```
public class TextModel : IUndoRestore {
   private static char controlZ = (char) 26;
   ...
   private Boolean ShouldSnapshot(KeyPressEventArgs kea) {
      return (! (kea.KeyChar == controlZ) );
   }
}
```

That seems a bit nicer. To make this change work, we needed to modify the way our testing works. Recall that we were calling the KeyDown handler directly in the customer tests, so we have to change that to use KeyPress instead:

```
private void InterpretCommands(String commands, String message) {
   StringReader reader = new StringReader(commands);
   String line = reader.ReadLine();
   CreateModel();
   while ( line != null) {
      if (line.StartsWith("*alt"))
         ExecuteMenu("&"+line[4]);
      else if (line.StartsWith("*type"))
         TypeCharacters(line.Substring(6));
      else if (line == "*undo") {
         form.XMLKeyPressHandler((object) this,
            new KeyPressEventArgs( (char) 26 ));
      }
      else if ( line == "*enter") {
         form.XMLKeyPressHandler((object) this,
            new KeyPressEventArgs ( (char) 13 ));
      }
      else if ( line == "*shiftEnter") {
         form.TestModifierKeys = Keys.Shift;
         form.XMLKeyPressHandler((object) this,
            new KeyPressEventArgs ( (char) 13 ));
```

```
      form.TestModifierKeys = Keys.None;
    }
    else if (line == "*display")
      Console.WriteLine("display\r\n{0}\r\nend", model.TestText);
    else if (line == "*output")
      CompareOutput(reader, message);
    else if (line == "*input")
      SetInput(reader);
    else if (line == "*loadfile")
      LoadFile();
    else if (line == "*savefile")
      SaveFile();
    else
      Assert(line + " command not defined", false);
    line = reader.ReadLine();
  }
}
```

Note those boldface references to TestModifierKeys. Because of the way the KeyPress event works, we don't get modifier bits for the Ctrl key and Shift key and so on as part of the KeyPressEventArgs. Instead, we have to ask Ctrl whether the key is down, during the event. (This is a rather serious flaw in the design of KeyPress events, in my opinion, but we have to deal with it.) So we add a special flag just for testing, TestModifierKeys, that looks like this:

```
class XMLNotepad : Form {
  ...
  private Keys testModifierKeys;
  public Keys TestModifierKeys {
    get { return testModifierKeys; }
    set { testModifierKeys = value; }
  }
  public void XMLKeyPressHandler(object objSender,
    KeyPressEventArgs kea) {
    GetText();
    model.KeyboardSnapshot(kea);
    if ((int) kea.KeyChar == (int) Keys.Enter) {
      kea.Handled = true;
      if (Control.ModifierKeys == Keys.Shift
        || this.TestModifierKeys == Keys.Shift)
        CallModel(shiftEnterAction);
      else if (Control.ModifierKeys == Keys.None)
        CallModel(enterAction);
    }
    else if ( kea.KeyChar == controlZ ) {
      model.Restore();
      PutText(textbox, model.LinesArray(), model.SelectionStart);
      kea.Handled = true;
    }
  }
```

TestModifierKeys is, of course, a pure hack to support testing. In view of the importance of this feature and all the trouble I have had with it, I prefer to have the ability to test it, even at this small cost.

Reviewing this code, we see that we have some more literal integers here representing keys, and we'll fix them as we did the Ctrl+Z:

```
[TestFixture] public class CustomerTest : Assertion {
  private static char controlZ = (char) 26;
  private static char enter = (char) 13;
  ...
    else if (line == "*undo") {
      form.XMLKeyPressHandler((object) this,
        new KeyPressEventArgs( controlZ ));
    }
    else if ( line == "*enter") {
      form.XMLKeyPressHandler((object) this,
        new KeyPressEventArgs ( enter ));
    }
    else if ( line == "*shiftEnter") {
      form.TestModifierKeys = Keys.Shift;
      form.XMLKeyPressHandler((object) this,
        new KeyPressEventArgs ( enter ));
      form.TestModifierKeys = Keys.None;
    }
  ...
```

There are a couple of other references to KeyDown that were changed to KeyPress in just the same way. The change required a bit of book study and less than an hour's programming and writing—and the final code is simpler than we had when we started.

Further Optimizations Are Possible

We have taken the most common case, the user typing an ordinary character, and created an undo that does that efficiently. We could approach other optimizations in the same way. As they say in the textbooks, we'll leave those for the reader, but we'll talk about them briefly here.

Our current version of Undo for single-key typing requires the selection length to be zero. We could deal with single-character typing when the selection length is greater than zero fairly readily. I think we would just observe that the selection is there, and we would grab the characters into the Snapshot object. During undo, after deleting the typed character, we would insert the saved characters back, if there are any. I believe I would extend the existing SingleCharacterSnapshot class to do that.

The tag insertions all insert complete lines. It would be easy to create a snapshot object that for undo just deleted those lines. We would record the current line and the number of lines to be inserted. The tag insertions know that information. The implementation should be simple, and it would go in just one spot, the Insert-Tags area. I believe I would build a new Snapshot class to do that one.

With these changes, I believe that almost all the full snapshots would be eliminated. One remaining area that would trigger a full snapshot would be a cut or paste operation. These would be easy to implement in the TextModel: we would add those characters to those recognized in the KeyPress, and handle them. We would have to learn how to access the clipboard in Microsoft .NET, but the capability is there, in the Clipboard class.

It seems to me that each of these optimizations would be rather straightforward and the structure we have would support them readily.

Summing Up Undo

For the purposes of this book, we're declaring Undo to be done. We built our XML Notepad without preparing in any explicit way for Undo and then called upon ourselves to implement Undo anyway. We started with the simplest Undo we could imagine: make a copy of everything and slam it back when an unUndo is called for. This worked quickly and well, but we felt that it wasn't realistic as a solution, both because it was almost too easy and because it was clearly inefficient in storage. So we decided to optimize it.

Perhaps it was the focus on optimization, perhaps it was my reduced ability to think through pain, or perhaps it was just inexperience with doing Undo, but in any case, there were a couple of false starts, which you can read about in the next chapter. Each of these had the same characteristic, in retrospect. Each of the false starts tried to solve a fairly large problem in a fairly complex way. The problem was "You are given two states of the notepad—find a representation that compactly represents the difference between the states." The solutions started by thinking about what could happen and by drawing conclusions about the state of the lines and selection before and after. Those conclusions were incorrect, and the mistakes in my thinking turned up in the code, usually rather late in the process.

In earlier days, I would have said, ruefully, that "I should have designed more." That's not my view now, and I'd like to suggest that the history here shows why. Again and again during Undo, the best things happened when we thought and programmed at the same time, not first thinking and then trying to do what we thought. Now don't get me wrong—I do think before I start, and I always used to think while I was programming a design that had been thought out beforehand. But I find that when I am working to an existing design, the more I understand that design, the more I try to make it work out—even if in fact it cannot work out. I am less likely to listen to what the code is telling me, because I feel committed to the design.

In the version of "optimized" Undo that worked well, there was also a difference of focus. Instead of thinking of the two big snapshots and how to reconcile them, we looked at what kinds of events we could deal with and then dealt with them. We focused on the biggest improvement first, namely, ordinary typing.

The most important thing to observe about the Undo story is that the system's overall design did not get in the way, and we did not have to make sweeping changes all over the system to make Undo work. Now it might be that we were lucky, or that subconsciously we were somehow preparing for Undo. I don't think that's credible: as you have seen in the course of the book, I can barely program consciously! It might even be that we somehow cheated, but again, I think the evidence is clear that I'm not that clever.

Frankly, I was concerned that the result would be other than it has turned out. Especially with my early attempts at Undo turning out badly, I was starting to worry. Yet even when I was having trouble, the trouble wasn't with the existing design—it was with the inherent difficulty of Undo. Certainly I could have spread the work out over time, but it would have been just as difficult and perhaps more so, when the system's design was more vague. When you read the next chapter, keep in mind that during all that trouble, Undo was already working, and I got in trouble trying to make it better.

I think we see here that incremental development works well, evolving from simple design by refactoring, with our primary focus on removing duplication. I believe that it works because modularity works. When we have good abstractions in the code that make sense, they can usually be assembled in any order that we need, and they can usually be enhanced by adding new abstractions that come up. And simple design plus refactoring creates modularity.

You'll have to draw your own conclusions about your own work, but my conclusions are that simple design, combined with continuous design improvement, results in code that is easy to change when new requirements, even tricky ones like Undo, come along. As I'll talk about in Chapter 31, "Project Retrospective," the code we have isn't perfect by any means. Yet our focus on removing duplication, on making common ideas use common code, has served us well enough. Undo went into the system as an addition and as a rather tricky one at that. But it did not bend or break the design in any way. Undo is difficult on its own, but our design accepted it without needing to be changed in any substantial way.

Your mission is to decide for yourself. This extensive Undo section is evidence that might induce you to experiment. Your own experiments will help you decide the right balance for you. Now read on and look at my mistakes!

30

The Long Dark Teatime of the Soul

Before coming up with the optimized version of Undo in the previous chapter, I made three failed attempts to optimize it. The initial Undo had gone so smoothly, and the ideas seemed so clear in my mind, yet they would not come together. I would like to leave this report out, as it does not reflect my best moments. Still, there are bright spots even in the darkness, and perhaps you can learn from my mistakes as well, so here's a brief summary of what happened.

Recollection

In Chapter 28, "Oh no! Undo!" we saw that Undo fit into our system in exactly one place, an ideal situation. No sweeping edits "all over the system" were needed. I believe that this shows that incremental design can work and can be resilient to change. It's no proof that it will always work, but since Undo is one of the difficult examples that people often raise, it's at least encouraging.

Our first Undo did go in simply, which is encouraging, but it was incredibly inefficient in its use of storage. I might have left optimization as an "exercise for the reader," but that would have weakened my main point about incremental development leading to a design that is easy to change. So in Chapter 29, "The Final Optimized Undo," I showed one simple optimization that reduces the storage by about an order of magnitude. That, too, went in easily, and I feel that the main point is made about as well as it can be from a single demonstration. My belief, demonstrated but not fully proven here, is:

> **Lesson**   Incremental development, with due attention to refactoring, particularly to removal of duplication, leads to designs which are highly modular and therefore resilient to change.

However, as the preceding chapter suggests, things did not go entirely smoothly. Although the XML Notepad's design was demonstrably ready for Undo, in some way I was not ready. I fouled up the optimization feature several times in a row. The full report of those efforts (that is, my first take at this chapter) spans over seventy pages, and I'll send that report to you on request, if you want to read a chronicle of how the old fat guy fouled up his attempts to do something that was in fact quite simple.

In this chapter, we'll save some trees. I'll give you an overview of what happened, but I'll spare you the tedium of slogging through the mud with me. I'll also include some excerpts and snapshots from that original chapter, to illuminate what was going on, to show you signs of trouble that I should have seen, and perhaps even to draw some lessons from the mostly useless work that was done. I'll begin with one of those now:

Lesson: First-Take Excerpt—Dragging On and On...

Perhaps the best sign that we are in trouble is that feeling that something we're doing is just dragging on and on. As you read this chapter, notice the dreadful sameness of what I'm doing, again and again, over and over. There are moments of light and discovery, and the lessons in here are often good. Yet each time, I end where I begin, with perhaps a little more knowledge but with little real progress.

The good news is that each time I finally recognized that I was in trouble, took out my changes, and started over. As you read, try to spot where I went off the road, try to imagine what you could have done as my pair to help me see that I was off the road.

You might find yourself skipping over more and more pages, trying to find something interesting or useful. Think about how I could have recognized that I was doing work that any reasonable person would want to skip over. Think about how you can recognize that slogging situation in your own work. Try to use my time in the weeds to help you recognize your own so that you can get back on the road quickly.

> Also, at this point in the project, I did something bad to my neck. It hurt horribly in my neck and shoulder, and it seemed to be paralyzing my arm. I was partly laid up for about a month. It was very hard to work at the computer, but I wanted to make progress on the Undo optimization. I did what seemed like some pretty good design, but as you'll read here, nothing very good came from it. Good-seeming design that didn't work— that's worth thinking about.

A Repeated Mistake

Throughout the long history of my optimization attempts, I referred over and over again to an idea that I had early on: Given two consecutive full-memory Snapshots, compare all the lines from the beginning toward the end, stopping when you find a difference. Compare all the lines from the end toward the beginning, stopping when you find a difference. Save the lines in between— they are the lines changed by the event that triggered the second Snapshot.

I *refer* to that idea many times, but I never tried it! It seems clear even now that it would work perfectly, thought it might (or might not) be a bit inefficient. If it were inefficient, it would likely be possible to optimize it by limiting what needs to be compared, depending on what the edit action actually was.

A simple, easy, and probably quite useful idea, and in over seventy pages of blather, I never tried it! Why? I'm not sure. It seemed that I was seduced by ideas that were more clever and possibly more efficient. Unfortunately, those clever ideas were also incomplete, wrong, and too difficult to implement.

On the other hand, the line-comparing optimization would probably have been a good small step in the right direction. I never took that step!

Playing with Pain

Just after I got the initial Undo working, I did something bad to my neck. I had terrible pain in my neck and shoulder, and my left arm was partially paralyzed. I was laid up for about a month. Between the drugs and the pain, it was difficult to make progress on the book, but I was able to do what seemed like some pretty good paper design.

In fact, I think the paper design ideas were good but that they gave me too much confidence and induced me to take approaches that were too complex to implement in a half-day or so. My overall productivity drops rapidly if I work in bites bigger than that, and this was no exception. I bogged down, failed to notice mistakes in the original paper design, made new mistakes, and foundered again and again.

Design Thinking

My paper design addressed various editor operations that might take place, with consideration about what's selected, what's typed, and so on. Here are a couple of pages of those notes:

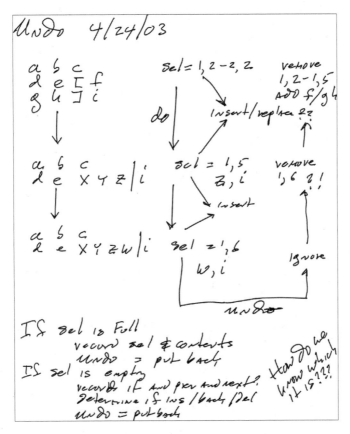

My general thinking was that I would compare two consecutive Snapshots, taking into account the position of the selections in both. The paper reasoning tempted me away from the simple idea of just comparing my lines. In the original chapter, I said:

> *I've talked about comparing all the lines to see if they are different—and I was inclined to try that just to see if it works or if it is terribly inefficient. But I got to thinking about the selection...*

Off I went, chasing a complex solution that didn't hang together, when I had a perfectly good next step staring me in the face. As HAL 9000 put it, "it can only be attributable to human error."

Experiments Without Tests

I wasn't sure just what happened to the selection and selection length during various editing actions, and I felt I needed to know. Rather than record that learning in tests, I put tracing statements into the code, ran the XML Notepad, and observed the results manually.

I do strongly favor experiments when we don't know something, but here I was trying to learn details before nailing down the basics. It was as if I was fumbling around in the dark, not doing a focused experiment. Tracing statements are a strong sign of trouble, and confused experiments are as well. I should have paid more attention to these signs.

An Initial Attempt

Then I got down to work by trying to build an object called UndoAnalyzer. This object didn't do anything useful, but it took two TextModels and compared them, using the selection information as well as the lines. I worked for eight or ten book pages on the Analyzer and never even tried the idea of comparing all the lines, the only really simple idea I had. Instead, I kept fiddling with combinations of the beginning and ending selections of the before and after Snapshots. This was a mistake on the face of it: the object's name alone tells us that it is some kind of assumed infrastructure object or perhaps a test probe.

I pushed on this course for quite a while, three or four hours, trying hard to make it work. I added extra variables to TextModel, to save the lines that I felt were indicated as important by the selection. This, too, was an indicator of trouble, as TextModel had no use for that information and never would have. I was hacking, in the worst sense of the word. At one point in this first push, I slowed down and wrote, "I owe it to myself, when these uncertainties arise, to slow down and consider taking another route."

And after giving myself this good advice? This: "...waist deep in the Big Muddy, the big fool said to press on." I pressed on for a few more pages, took another break, examined the code and finally decided to back it out and start over. All this spans about twenty book pages and about four hours' work. The page count seems high for as much work as got done, probably because I was confused most of the time and had to do a lot of explaining. Toward the end of this section, I said the following. It's good advice, which I should have followed sooner.

Lesson: First-Take Excerpt—The Value of Reflection

I realize now that I haven't been proceeding as effectively as I might have in this last push to come up with the "optimized" TextModel. The work done isn't wasted, but it could have been put off in favor of faster learning.

All this effort of copying the lines around is wasted: we already have the lines in the TextModel. We could have just figured out which lines were interesting and stopped there.

I had been thinking, of course, that we would need these lines in the final version, so it seemed to make sense to get them. But what's important is putting the right lines back when we do the Undo and whether this scheme will work at all. A faster approach with more learning might have been to record the interesting line numbers—the beginning and end lines of the selections in old and new versions—and just use them to get the lines out of the existing TextModel Lines array. That would have been a more effective way to learn whether this approach will work and what it will take to make it work.

The lesson isn't that I made a mistake. I learned a long time ago that I make mistakes, and probably you have as well. The lesson is that the more frequently we take a break to reflect on how things are going, the sooner we are likely to realize when we're off the best track. We can decide, then, whether to backtrack, change direction a bit, or just go ahead. Deciding is the important thing, and to make a real decision, we need to reflect.

A Second Attempt and a Big Mistake

The next time around, I started with a simple mistake that delayed my learning. I wanted to express the operation of Undo as "out with the bad lines, in with the good," so I changed this code:

```
public void Restore() {
  if (SavedModels.Count == 0) return;
  TextModel savedModel = (TextModel) SavedModels.Pop();
  lines = savedModel.Lines;
  selectionStart = savedModel.SelectionStart;
  selectionLength = savedModel.SelectionLength;
}
```

to this:

```
public void Restore() {
  if (SavedModels.Count == 0) return;
  TextModel savedModel = (TextModel) SavedModels.Pop();
  this.RemoveNewLines(savedModel);
  this.AddOldLines(savedModel);
  lines = savedModel.Lines;
  selectionStart = savedModel.SelectionStart;
  selectionLength = savedModel.SelectionLength;
}
private void RemoveNewLines(TextModel savedModel) {
  Lines.RemoveRange(0,Lines.Count);
}
private void AddOldLines(TextModel savedModel) {
  Lines.InsertRange(0,savedModel.Lines);
}
```

The problem, which I didn't see, is the line highlighted in the upper example. I intended to replace it with the boldface lines in the lower example, but I left it in. This means that no matter how badly the RemoveNewLines, AddOldLines pair fouls up, the next line fixes the problem by going back to the original, inefficient but working code. Almost no test we can write is going to fail in operation. It might throw an exception, but as soon as the exceptions are all taken out, the code will appear to work.

If tests start failing all over as we work, it's a sign that we need to start over. This particular mistake masks failures: I never got that sign in this attempt and never could!

This time through I tried to focus more on expressing intention, working more "top down," and I went in much smaller steps. This is always a good idea when one approach has failed: slow down and take smaller bites. Even with the smaller steps I was feeling uncertainty, but I chalked it up to nervousness from the first attempt. Things seemed to be taking too long, but I pressed on, in part because my tests "showed" that I was doing well. Unfortunately, my implementation was cheating on the exams.

I continued my basic mistake: I was still assuming that I could just process the lines indicated by the before and after Snapshots' selections. This is true, but my reasoning about how it would work was faulty. The right insight, or the right simple test, would have sorted me out. I never had that insight nor wrote that test.

The text describing this attempt has things in it like "this is getting scary." I didn't listen to that fear. Instead I slogged on. Finally, two good things happened. First, with all my tests running fine, I ran the XML Notepad manually. It threw exceptions right and left, showing that my tests were weak and off target.

Then Chet showed up to pair with me, and sensing my uncertainty, he talked me into backing out most of the code and starting over. During that exercise, I spotted that fatal line that was obscuring trouble. We agreed to start over, and to use some new tests. Up until Chet arrived, my new attempt had spanned only about seven pages: I was making mistakes much more efficiently now!

The Third Attempt

This time we started with some rather neat tests that expressed little editing scenarios and that checked an OptimizedTextModel object to see if it was going to do the right thing. Here's an example of one of those tests:

```
[Test] public void LinesToRemove() {
  model.SetLines(new String[] { "abc", "def", "ghi" });
  model.SelectionStart = 8; // after e
  model.Snapshot();
  model.SetLines(new String[] { "abc", "deXf", "ghi" });
  model.SelectionStart = 9; // after x, user inserted X
  model.OptimizeSavedModel();
  TextModel oldModel = model.TopSavedModel();
  AssertEquals(1, oldModel.FirstLineToRemove());
}
```

That might seem a bit cryptic still, but it expresses a pretty easy edit, from "abc/de|f/ghi" to "abc/deX|f/ghi", where slash represents a newline and the vertical bar represents the position of the caret. The notation above would have been even better, but we didn't think of it at the time.

We wrote four increasingly difficult tests and made them work, and we were feeling pretty good. However, we were working on low-level functions, not Undo itself, and the result was that we didn't see that our idea was fundamentally flawed. A more top-down approach, or fake it till you make it, would have been better. We were working on infrastructure that we assumed we would need.

Ironically, I am the inventor of the XP motto "YAGNI" meaning "You Aren't Gonna Need It" which we use to remind ourselves to build infrastructure as we need it, not in advance. Why didn't I listen to myself?

Chet and I went on, refactoring and refining our infrastructure for quite some time, about ten book pages, and a few hours' work. We even wrote some new Customer Acceptance Tests, and at the end of the session I concluded:

The answer appears to be that we have successfully built code that knows which lines of the saved TextModel need to be saved and which lines need to be removed and replaced when doing an Undo. We still need to delete the unneeded lines and to wire up the Undo correctly. This has been a good session: the problem seems to be completely caged now.

I'm noticing the weasel words now—"appears to be" and "seems to be"—but at the time I was pretty confident that we were on the right track. At this point, I needed to continue without Chet's help for a while, and my plan was to plug this infrastructure into the product. Good idea, even if a bit late: Infrastructure doesn't please the customer, features do.

I wrote some tests, turned up some problems, put in lots more tracing statements (a telltale sign of corruption), and wrote more detailed tests. I ran into a long series of off-by-one errors and indexes out of range but I didn't recognize these for what they represented: faulty reasoning. In editing the original chapter, I wrote this lesson, which is worth preserving:

> **Lesson** First-take excerpt: Another telltale sign of corruption is that I'm instrumenting the code to print things out. When do we do this? When we don't know what the code is doing. This is a bad sign. I'm resolving to raise my sensitivity to this practice.

Later, I added this signpost and ignored it:

> **Lesson** First-take excerpt: Whenever we have the urge to test the program manually, we need to recognize that this might reflect a lack of confidence in our tests. Since I've been having these little problems with off by one and array out of bounds, I think it's more that I'm not entirely confident in the code—but the fact is that my tests are supposed to give me that confidence. More evidence that the tests need some beefing up.

I fiddled around with improving the tests—for about four pages!—and then discovered that the tests were making assumptions that weren't consistent with the program. Even if they ran, my tests were no assurance that the program would really work.

> **Lesson**   This is an inherent issue with working with infrastructure first: when our assumptions are wrong about what's going to be needed, the result won't work even if it passes all its tests. Outer design should drive inner design, always.

I messed around to try "just fixing" the exceptions that were arising. Special case code indicates bad design. But still I didn't listen.

Finally, Chet came and joined me again and managed to increase my recognition that there was trouble, but we pressed on for a while anyway. We even put in a special object called a Hint and didn't recognize it for what it was. We should have named it Hack! Here's a quote from the chapter, showing that a sufficiently stuck programmer can't even be pulled out by his pair. Chet should have formatted my hard drive, I guess:

It has been a long time since all the tests worked. We like to make them work every ten minutes or so, and we have been working much longer than that. In a phone call setting up another pairing section with Chet, we talked about this. I heard myself saying: "If someone told me this story, I would be advising them to tear out the code and start over. It sounds like they are going down a rat hole. But I'm sure that we're just one problem away from having this work."

There was a long silence, as Chet let me listen to my own words. I would advise anyone else to start over, yet I want to go ahead. We all know that feeling of "just one bug away," and we have all spent a lot of time discovering one more. In the end, we agreed to meet and work on it just a bit more.

We continued on with some very nice double-dispatching code between the TextModel and the new OptimizedTextModel. I was looking forward to showing you how nice it was, until I realized that it was a good implementation of a bad idea.

This part of the original chapter is full of huge blocks of code with very little text. In my work, that's a sign of working but not thinking. If I had been thinking then, I would have told you about it now. Programming without thinking—what good is that?

Over 30 pages later, we hit the fatal flaw. We couldn't handle the Insert-Tags operations. We put in another hack and bashed on the code a bit longer. I put more and more tracing code into the system to try to find out what was going on. Finally, after 32 pages of chapter (although only about six hours of programming), everything worked. Jubilation!

One paragraph and one thoughtful manual test later, I discovered that the whole idea just wouldn't hold water. Cuts, pastes, cursor movements all fatally confused my carefully designed OptimizedTextModel. Despair, weeping, gnashing of teeth!

Enough! Convinced at last, I stopped and started over with more focus on the specifics, and I moved quickly to the version in the preceding chapter, which reduces storage requirements to less than one percent of what they were. As you have seen, that simple approach worked well. It's what I should have done the first time.

Here is the conclusion I wrote for that long, dark chapter. It concludes this chapter as well.

First-Take Excerpt: The Stench of Death

Three attempts at implementing the same idea, and each one fails. Why did I stick to this idea so long? My only explanation is that I had done all that design on it, and I was confident that it should work. Even when the signs arose again and again—examples of perfectly common cases that the design didn't handle—I kept trying to hammer it into shape.

My colleagues Kent Beck and Martin Fowler coined the notion of "code smells," characteristics of the code that tell us that it needs refactoring. As I have a very sensitive sense of smell, the term bothers me. But if a couple of lines of code duplication are a "smell," then what you have just read surely reeks. Three tries, over a number of days, to do the same thing, and all come to nothing. What were the signs that I should have seen? What are the signs that you and I should look for as we go forward? Here are a few ideas:

- **Lack of confidence in tests.**   Many times in this chapter, I feel and express that the tests aren't helping. Yet I never really go to work on the tests. Instead I put it off.

- **Long periods between green bars.**   Instead of going for a few minutes without my tests running, I went for hours. If the tests aren't running, we really don't know whether we are writing good or bad code.

- **Sun setting on bad code.**   Sometimes I even stopped a session with the tests not running. This is never a good idea. If I can't figure it out today, tomorrow isn't likely to be better, since I will have lost the "picture" by then. It's true, sometimes when we get up from the machine, we see our mistake. But it's wiser to get to the green bar, even if we have to do it by removing today's code.

- **Large editing steps.**   There were some very big edits in this series of sessions. Instead of a couple of lines at a time, I was putting in whole classes, whole interfaces, in a blob. This is taking a big risk. Because I'm a smart programmer, that kind of risk often pays off. Because I'm a stupid programmer, instead of pretending it didn't happen, I'm telling the world about it.

- **Console printing.**   Sometimes it does make sense to print out some information to find out what's going on. There was a lot of instrumentation in this chapter, more than I even showed. The need for tracing printouts and the like is a clear sign that we don't understand our own program. How is it going to work if we don't understand it?

- **Debugging.**   The same is true of debugging. Spending time in the debugger tells us that we're confused. I even remember one time during this debacle where I started thinking that I should learn more of the debugger's features! Wrong! Better not to need it, and the rest of this book tells me that I know how to program, and do better without it.

Some of our best lessons come from our worst times, and that's why I decided to leave this part in the book. It would have been easy enough to move from the simple Undo to the nifty optimized one, and to drop this material right out. Truth be told, we see here some real examples of why I try to work in the style this book talks about. When I work in tiny, simple steps, supported by tests, things go smoothly, easily, and well. When I work in bigger chunks, even supported by more up-front design, things don't go so well.

What is most interesting to me is that the way this effort went isn't much different from how my work—and perhaps yours—has often gone in the past. Long, dark times, punctuated by small successes, and finally, through sheer effort and intelligence, we make something work. I'm proud of all the things I have made work—and work well—over the years. And I'm more proud of having learned some better ways to work.

Now if I can just remember to stick to them...

Go now, and sin no more. I'll try to do the same.

31

Project Retrospective

It is time to assess the XML Notepad project, considering what we would do again next time and what we would do differently.

Learning from the Past

We can do many things to learn our craft. We can go to school, read books, take courses, talk with people, and so on. All of these can give us ideas and techniques that can improve our programming. However, the most important thing of all, in my opinion, is reflective practice. We have to use the techniques we read about, and we have to reflect on the results. In the course of this book, we have reflected frequently on how things are going and we have even tried things different ways and thought about that. Now let's look back at the whole XML Notepad project to see what we might have learned.

There are many good ways to reflect. For best results with a project team, I would recommend that you take a look at Norman L. Kerth's landmark book, *Project Retrospectives: A Handbook for Team Reviews* (Dorset House, 2001). Norm begins and ends with what he calls the Prime Directive:

> *Regardless of what we discover, we understand and truly believe that everyone did the best job they could, given what they knew at the time, their skills and abilities, the resources available, and the situation at hand.*

It can be very difficult to do a retrospective for a project and keep the prime directive in mind. For best results on important projects, you may find it best to use an experienced retrospective facilitator. Here, we'll just do our best.

Could We Put This Program into Production?

Our real purpose here, of course, was to write a book about how to develop software in an environment where we have much to learn, and the project was only secondary. Still, we should look at how close the XML Notepad comes to being a production program.

There certainly are features that we would like to add or to improve. File I/O is barely implemented; copy, cut, and paste work, but they are not integrated into our code; the menus aren't organized into a reasonable structure; there is no real ability to view what the resulting document looks like; and the TextBox is limited to 65,000 characters. On the other hand, the program is doing exactly what has been asked of it so far, and it is rather well-tested. We'll come back to the testing issue, and certainly we wish the tests were better, but they're still enough to give us strong confidence that the program works as advertised.

Surprising new features might cause us trouble, although our experience with Undo makes me very confident that we can handle with little difficulty anything that might be thrown at us. Most of the features we can foresee are now just more of the same: more I/O options, more inserts, perhaps a few more intelligent features like adding another P tag or LI tag.

Finally, I suspect that the program may be vulnerable to the user doing things we don't expect. For example, the logic to decide whether to emit a P tag or LI tag looks at the current line to see which to do. A sufficiently complex list item might confuse this logic. If it did, we know exactly where we would have to go to deal with the issue—to the InListItem() method:

```
private Boolean InListItem() {
  if (Lines.Count == 0 ) return false;
  return ((string) lines[LineContainingCursor()]).StartsWith("<LI>");
}
```

We might have to strengthen that method. That would be the only place we'd need to change things.

The feature list might not be as long as the customers would want, but I suggest that the program itself is generally robust and ready to be put into the hands of some interested users. I do suspect that they would find a few problems and that we could write tests for them and fix them fairly readily. Which brings me to my next point.

The Value of Real Customers

Chet and I tried hard to wear two hats, the customer hat and the programmer hat. We tried to demand the features that customers would want and to focus as programmers on quality code and on estimating the costs of things. We tried not to make programmer decisions on "business" topics. Since this is a book about how to learn while producing useful features, I think it worked fairly well. The presence of real customer input would quite likely have changed things, however. I can think of these possibilities:

Real customers would probably have had somewhat different priorities than we imagined. This might have changed the direction of the project in some ways. I think the resulting program, given the same amount of work, might have been better suited to immediate use, because our customers would be trying to use it.

Real customer tests would have helped. I feel sure that we tolerated a cryptic and incomplete testing language, in part because we knew the code and had confidence in it, so we did not feel the need for more, better, or easier customer tests. (In many cases, we were wrong to feel that confident. Programmers are like that.) An independent customer would probably have demanded more tests and different tests. In turn, this would very likely have caused us to recognize problems more easily and to fix them sooner.

Frankly, I am surprised, given that I planned this book and think of it as a book about programming, at how much value an independent customer could have provided. The lesson for you is that contact with real users, or someone who can stand in for real users, is of very great value on your projects as well. Once you have had a good XP "customer," you'll never want to be without them.

Customer Tests

Let's reflect further on the customer tests. I see these key lessons here:

First, the initial customer test was difficult to do. We didn't want to do it, we resisted it, and we had to get a bit creative to figure it out. Once we made the commitment to have the test, however, it took only a couple of hours to do it. This is almost always the way, in my experience. We think we don't need the test, we don't see how do to it, and then it isn't hard to do.

Second, the tests served us well, but not perfectly. They were pretty easy to write, but because they didn't give us good debugging information, we would sometimes skip them when we shouldn't have. So the customer test suite is not as strong as it should be. Of course, if we had a true independent customer, they would be focused on making those tests strong to be sure that the product was working as they wanted. If the customer tests had been stronger, they would have turned up more problems. Had they turned up more problems, we would have had the incentive to improve our ability to get useful information out of them.

Finally, as I learn anew on every project, end to end is further than we think it is. The most effective customer tests test the system from one edge to the other. In the case of the XML Notepad, that means from keyboard to display. We encountered a few cases where the tests ran but the GUI did not. We improved the tests in response to most of those, but my suspicion is that the tests are still a bit weak in some undiscovered areas. End to end is always further than we think it is.

Pair Programming

It's fascinating how much better pair programming made the program and the book. This works for a number of reasons, but the bottom line for me is pretty clear: I work better with someone to collaborate with, and the closer the collaboration, the better things seem to go. Even pairing with someone whom I haven't worked with before makes the code better, and interestingly enough it makes the book better, too. Because I have talked through the design with my pair, I'm a bit better prepared to detail it to you and I'm far less likely to skip over important aspects.

Even bringing my pair up to date—freshening the pair's eyes—helps a lot. It makes me say out loud the things I've been thinking. Often even I can hear how stupid something I'm doing is. The bottom line that I'd offer to you is to try pair programming until you're good at it, and then you can decide whether it helps you as much as it helps me. It just might.

Trends over Time

Early on in the project, we were mostly struggling with C# and Microsoft Visual Studio. We were discussing how to say things in the language and how to use collections, strings, events, and the like. Later on, we had found ways to do most things, and we were working primarily within the objects that we had created and a few standard patterns of use that we had found to work. Although it took a long elapsed time to write this book, most of the chapters represent only about two to four hours of programming. Thus, in the equivalent of a few weeks of full-time working with C#, with no experts around to help us, we have come a long way in our understanding and ability to make progress.

You can see places where "programming by intention" enables us to create objects and methods that really seem to help with solving the problem. The objects become representative of our ideas—abstractions if you will. When we program this way, it really helps.

We also see places where we never got around to creating an object. The interface between Form/TextBox and TextModel is an example. We just kept passing the lines, the selection start, and the selection length around. Worse yet, we kept doing it in three separate steps, like this:

```
private void GetText() {
  model.SetLines(textbox.Lines);
  model.SelectionStart = textbox.SelectionStart;
  model.SelectionLength = textbox.SelectionLength;
}
```

I still don't see what would be better than what we did, so long as we have the separation between the TextBox and the TextModel. This code may be trying to tell us that we should move away from that structure. However, that structure has served us pretty well, so the code isn't speaking loudly as yet.

Sometimes we see projects that program only in terms of the base classes of the language, ints and strings and arraylists and the like. They never build abstractions of their own, like the TextModel or the SingleCharacterSnapshot. Especially as projects get larger, building our own abstractions is a very important technique to keep us going quickly and reliably. One key technique is to ask whether our tests and objects are helping us.

Are the Tests Helping Us?

We'll ask this question whenever we find a defect that wasn't found by the tests. In a perfect world, there should be no defects. Every defect in the system should have been tested for, and prevented, by one or more of our tests. So when we enounter defects, we reflect on how our tests could help us better.

In the case of this application, the tests could have been more help had there been a better connection between testing, TextModel, and TextBox. We started with the assumption that if we tested TextModel, TextBox would take care of itself. This was nearly true but not completely true. TextBox carries too much functionality in the product to be left quite as alone as our tests leave it. This showed up particularly when we were fiddling with getting Undo to work.

The tests could have been more helpful if the customer tests were easier to run one at a time and if it was easier to find out why they failed when they failed. In this case, it was our testing infrastructure that wasn't helping, and we might have profited from making it a bit stronger.

Teams using this test-driven approach are reporting results so good as to seem unbelievable. In one example, I am told of a test-driven C++ project, which included interfacing to hardware, that went into heavy production with zero defects reported. Many test-driven XP teams are reporting similar results: bug lists that used to contain hundreds of defects contain one or two on the XP project. It does take work, and we have to develop skill, but the payoffs being reported are quite exciting.

Are the Objects Helping Us?

We ask this question whenever something seems to be hard to program. If we have to send several messages to an object to accomplish something, maybe that object isn't helping enough. Maybe it needs a method added to it that does more of the job for us. Or perhaps there is another class in there trying to get out. Here's an example from our most recent work, the SingleCharacterSnapshot's Restore() method:

```
public void Restore(TextModel model) {
  String lineToEdit = (String) model.Lines[lineNumber];
  String oldLine = lineToEdit.Remove(positionInLine,1);
  model.Lines[lineNumber] = oldLine;
  model.SelectionStart = selectionStart;
}
```

This method sends three messages to the model, one message to a string, and no messages to itself. This is a lot of work outside the model. In some of our earlier attempts at Undo, we added methods to the TextModel to help out. We might want to do that here, perhaps this way:

```
public void Restore(TextModel model) {
  model.RemoveCharacterForUndo(lineNumber, positionInLine, selectionStart);
}
```

supported in TextModel by:

```
public void RemoveCharacterForUndo(int line, int position, int start) {
  Lines[line] = ((string) Lines[line]).Remove(position,1);
  SelectionStart = start;
}
```

Better? Quite possibly. At least the functionality is now where it belongs, instead of over in the Undo, ripping the guts out of the TextModel and jamming them back. We might want to improve the name, but at this moment I don't have a better idea.

We do ask, of course, "Are the names helping us?" You have seen places where we renamed methods just to make them more expressive.

Did Our Tests and Objects Help Us Enough?

I believe that our tests and objects helped us a lot but perhaps not enough. I'm sure that there are places like the one just above, where a clear head and clear eyes would see the possibility of improvement. The improvement above took just a few minutes to do, by the way, and this is often the case. Often we can afford to improve the code, just a little bit, every day. This adds up over time to a much better program.

For this program, I am satisfied with how well the tests and objects help us, but I'm not delighted. I'm sure it could be better. I hope you have seen places in the code where you know a way to make it better. I'm not saying that I left it there for pedagogical purposes; it's just that I'm not perfect. If you were here pairing with me, we would have done better. Still, the program works and is well-tested. We can be content, if not complacent, about the work we have done.

Eat Your Own Dog Food

We are commonly advised that companies, and software developers, should "eat their own dog food." This means that we should have to use the things we provide. I often wish that airline executives were required to sit in the worst seat, on the longest flight, three or four times a month, eating a dry sandwich, and climbing over two large people to get to the restroom. I think it would improve flying tremendously.

With the XML Notepad, we would have benefited from using it more. I did use it a few times, but until very close to the end, it wasn't as capable as my macros in TextPad and it seemed not to make sense to use it. Had I used it, however, I would surely have found issues and changed priorities.

As programmers, we are often unable to eat our own dog food—we have no use whatsoever for the programs we are called upon to write. That's another reason why it's so important to have an XP customer, a team member who does need the resulting program and who can eat the dog food as soon as we create it.

Code Manager

Although we built a very simple code manager, it was quite valuable to us. There are certainly cases in the book where I needed to show more code than I had at first realized. Since every version that ever got compiled is archived by the code manager, I was always able to find just the snippet I needed.

Knowing that the code was saved gave us the courage to make changes. We knew that we could get back to any previous state with only a little effort. If we had written the tool to roll back to a given point in time, we probably would have used it a few times. If we had needed it more than a time or two, we certainly would have written it.

In short, our code management tool was almost but not quite sufficient for our needs. That's a pretty good place to position tools. We don't want to work on them too much, to the exclusion of customer needs, but we want them to be strong enough to serve us. Once the tool reliably saved all versions, it was good enough. Had we needed to roll back more frequently, we had the information to do so.

Coding Standard

Our coding standard evolved over time as we became more familiar with C#. We didn't pay much attention to the standard, since only a few people were involved and only one of them worked with all the code. Still, we could have done better in certain areas. In particular, I'd point to our use of properties and methods.

We have not been consistent with properties and methods. On the one hand, in Smalltalk and in Ruby, we are used to not needing parentheses or other parameter indicators on methods that don't need parameters. So we were initially inclined to use properties whenever they would work. We often got confused, however, for these reasons: First, in the Microsoft .NET library, some things that seem like properties are in fact methods, and vice versa, so we were often unsure as to what to use in the library. Second, sometimes we felt the need to mimic a similar method in .NET, so we would put parentheses on something where it felt to us that it didn't belong. Third, it seemed that on some days we preferred to put parentheses everywhere.

The bottom line is that we were not consistent, and we never sat down and talked through just what our conventions should be. The code suffers a little because of that, although I hope it doesn't suffer much.

Be Ready to Use Advanced Facilities

We did little subclassing, either from real objects or from interfaces. I think we would benefit from more. In the case of our TextBox, which we did subclass from TextBox, we could have been more aggressive and given it a better interface to the TextModel. Perhaps an event-driven interface would have been good, perhaps just something that better hides the difference between the TextModel's view of things (ArrayList) and the TextBox's (a big string, or an array of strings).

I suspect that we would have done well to create a special collection class for our lines. There are casts to strings sprinkled around in the code, and we could have avoided many of these, perhaps all of them. The need to downcast collection elements is a serious flaw in languages like C#, and it's being addressed in future versions. C# will have templates, for example, which will make it easier to set up collections containing objects of known type.

At one point in the Undo saga, we tried to build one class as a subclass of another. To do this, we needed to override a couple of methods. The compiler didn't like the way we tried to do it, and after a couple of attempts, we just built to an Interface instead. In this case, it was probably a better design anyway, but it's not good to have the design pushed around by ignorance of the language and its syntax. In a future project, I would try to use more of the language facilities sooner. This is a delicate balance, because we don't want to slow down and we don't want to insert gratuitous differences in the code. But at this point I feel that I know parts of the C# and .NET system pretty well and that there are untapped riches that I could use if only I knew a bit more about them.

Is TextModel Too Large?

TextModel has nearly fifty variables, methods, and properties. It is the mainstay of our functionality, and our product is somewhat "transaction-based," so we should not be surprised that it has a broad interface. Indeed, quite a few of the variables, methods, and properties are private, so the situation isn't as bad as it might be. Still, it feels too large to me. There might be things that could be broken out. Here are some thoughts:

- **Base functionality.** We might break out just the amount of capability that is required to interface between the TextBox and the TextModel into a separate class. Perhaps this capability would move over into the TextBox subclass, providing a line-indexed interface to the TextBox. That would almost certainly make for simpler code on both sides of the line.

- **Saving and loading.** We haven't pushed this code very far but it might turn out to want to be off in a separate object that just deals with blobs of text. It would act a bit like a factory, perhaps, transforming files into arrays of lines and back, returning new instances of TextModel.

- **Menu and insert processing.** We have those tag objects that we use to create the menus, and we have the corresponding methods to carry out those operations. Perhaps the generic InsertTags() method would remain on the base object and the others might be broken out into some kind of helper object.

- **Editing primitives.** Quite a few methods exist for breaking lines apart, for figuring out where the caret is, and so on. These might want to be in some other object.

These thoughts aside, one might approach this question in at least two ways. One might design some kind of TextModel constellation of objects, do a little bit of CRC carding or UML design, and come up with a structure that breaks these things out in some way that might be reasonable. Or one could proceed bit by bit, finding bits of code that seem not to belong where they are, and finding—or creating—better places for them to be.

Of course, this book is about focusing on the second approach, incrementally letting the code tell us what it wants to be. And your mission is to learn both ways and how to find your own balance. We could have done more up-front design on this project. Had we done so, we might have a "better" design right now, although I am not convinced of that. I am quite sure, however, that we would have fewer features and therefore a less happy customer, as well. I don't see that the time spent in coming up with a better design would have, as yet, begun to pay off in faster implementation. Frankly, I think it rarely does.

However, our large TextModel object might not be helping us as much as it might, so right now I am feeling the need to improve its design, to invest a bit more in it, because if it isn't slowing us down now, I feel that it will soon. If we were going to carry this project further forward, I'd be looking for ways to do some of the changes listed in this section.

People often ask whether we should "go back" and refactor things like the TextModel. In my opinion, we should learn to do a better job of keeping TextModel clean as we go along, and I will be taking this experience into account as I write more code in C#. However, I would not make a special effort to "go back," unless perhaps the project was truly complete and we had scheduled a few weeks for final preparation of documents for maintenance and for cleaning up the code for archiving. As a matter of course during the actual project, I would use the observations here to guide me in doing smaller refactorings as new features impacted on TextModel.

If this project were continuing, we would be touching TextModel for almost every feature. So as I plan and estimate each feature, I'll reflect on how to fit in a little refactoring to make TextModel a bit better. Perhaps I add an hour or a half-hour of cleanup to each day of programming. For the first couple of features, this might slow me down. But as the structure of TextModel gets better, I will actually speed up. Therefore, the practice I recommend in refactoring is not to make a separate task of it but just to focus a bit more during ordinary work delivering stories.

Think of the analogy of cleaning up the kitchen after each meal. Even if we have good discipline about keeping things clean, every now and again some things pile up. We could take Saturday morning and do a blitz on the kitchen, but that would get in the way of the football game. So instead, after each meal for the next few days, we just clean up a bit more vigorously than before, perhaps one dirty pot or a few of the dishes in that pile over there. Maybe we grab the rough sponge and give the counter an extra scrubbing. Without extending ourselves at all, in a few days the kitchen is back to spotless. The same is true for our code. Just a little extra effort can get us back up to speed.

All of this is about learning new skills and applying them with judgment. We always need to find a balance between design quality and prompt delivery.

The good thing about the incremental approach is that the balance is easy to find, because we are looking at the real code and how well it is coming together, while with more up-front design we are always speculating to a large degree. I think I'm very good at speculating accurately, but I'm better at sensing what is really going on and responding to it as the real needs arise. And the real needs are always somewhat different from what I foresaw.

Premature Optimization

We spent a lot of time optimizing Undo. I would estimate that the optimization cost about as much as three or four new features, or more if they were easy, like new tags. Now, we did have a special motive, to show that our simple Undo wasn't just a trick. We wanted to find out whether Undo really did spell doom for our incremental approach, and we found out that it did not.

But there is a lesson here for a real project, if not for the book project. Had we ignored the storage inefficiency of Undo for a while and shipped a version with a simple but working Undo, we could have put a more useful product in the hands of our users sooner. Optimizing Undo would still have to be done, but it could have been left for a later day. It would have been no more difficult later than it was. Maybe even easier, considering the number of stumbles I made.

As programmers we are sometimes accused of "gilding the lily." Yet we fear leaving things till later, because they might be harder to do. And, of course, no one likes to do less than their best work. I believe, though, that if our code is well-structured and if our ideas are well-explained and well-encapsulated, optimizations like these can be done on customer time. They can be done when requested, and we can deliver more useful capability earlier.

Responding to Pressure

This book is a book about discovery. We discovered our needs as we went along, and we discovered how to fill those needs. As such, it made the book difficult to schedule, because I didn't—and couldn't—know exactly what was coming next. Then, as I was nearing the end, I was seriously slowed down by my neck problems.

From time to time, my acquisitions editor, Linda Engelman, would express concern over how long things were taking. She was always very gentle in these expressions, only rarely mentioning things like "the full weight of my mighty wrath coming down on you," but I always perceived the pressure behind her innocent and delicate queries. Now, it is my view that a comment about how long things are taking is always really a request for information and a request for more control. So I always try to respond with these things:

1. A list of everything I know of that may need to be done

2. An explanation of the possible value of each thing as I understand it

3. An estimate of how long each thing will take

4. My recommended list of the things we should actually do

5. The total estimated time to accomplish those things

6. An expression of willingness to change the list, or the order of the list, as stakeholders might direct

We cannot know the pressures and dates that our customers and managers are subject to. And we should not try to take responsibility for them. What we can do is to lay out the project as we understand it, with costs and recommendations, and let them adjust things to best meet their needs. They must manage: we can provide the information they need to do it.

The results of responding this way are almost always the same:

■ The customer whines a little about how long some things take. I respond by pointing to history to show how I came up with the estimate that it will take that long. I indicate what parts of the thing are time-consuming in case they want to scale back the feature. I never agree to do what I cannot do—that is, make it take less time than it will take.

■ The customer simplifies some things, drops some, and sometimes adds some. I make sure that I understand the changes; I make new estimates where they are now needed; I explain the consequences of their decisions; and I express willingness to do whatever they decide.

The most important result is the increased understanding between us of what is going on and what is needed. I recommend this practice to you as well; I'm sure that it will help you.

Another practice that I think would be good, and that I recommend, is one that I do not reliably do: provide the information above on a regular basis to customers, managers, and other stakeholders. They will get value from the information and will have less need to bring pressure to bear on you. I wish I could learn to do that, but I get so involved in the work that I forget to communicate. You can do better, I'm sure.

There is a name for this list of things to do, by the way. In Extreme Programming, it is called the Release Plan. Use it—it will help you.

Pressure and Productivity

I do find that a little pressure helps keep me going. By a little, I mean an occasional "How ya doin'?" Just that tiny reminder is enough to keep me focused. More pressure than that slows me down. I get angry, I get scared, I think about the pressure instead of the project. It takes me a half day to a full day to get settled back into productive work. The sooner I get to doing my Release Plan, the sooner I get back on track—but I always lose some productivity, and not just the time it takes to do the Release Plan. The plan helps me; the pressure does not.

There's a lesson here for us as recipients of pressure: respond with a Release Plan.

There may be a bigger lesson for us when we think of applying pressure to others: skip the pressure; just ask people to sit down with you and create a Release Plan.

Pressure and Quality

When I feel too much pressure, it affects quality. If you'll look for them in the chapters about optimizing Undo, you'll see places where I saw that the code or the tests needed improving, but I didn't do it. In earlier chapters, faced with the same sort of issues, I more often improved them.

Letting pressure keep us from writing better tests or clear code is shortsighted. It doesn't just affect us later—it probably slows us down right away. We wouldn't have noticed these problems had they not been impacting us now. Still, as much as I try, I can't always keep my eye on quality when I'm feeling pressure. It always slows me down to back off on the quality, yet I continue to do it.

I have no magic solution to offer for this, just the observation that pressure hurts the project. Think about it, try to work around the effects of pressure, and use the Release Plan list. If you have additional practices that help, please drop me an e-mail.

Debugging Techniques

The best debugging technique is not to have any bugs. As unrealistic as it seems, when our test steps are small enough, we very rarely have bugs, and when we do, we encounter them quickly and resolve them quickly. It's fairly easy to program for five minutes without writing a bug. An hour? I'm just not up to it.

When we do encounter a defect, if we can back up a short distance and start over, it usually pays off. As you have seen here, it's difficult to do that—I always want to "find the bug." Yet you have also seen here that when we did start over, things usually went better. It's good to have a pair at these times—your pair is more likely than you to be ready to start over and will usually have a good idea on another approach.

Beyond starting over, however, there is debugging. As you've seen, I'm more inclined to write some information to the console than to use the debugger. It's not just that I'm a Luddite: I know that once I get into the debugger, too often I spend a lot of time there. My mother always told me not to hang out with bad companions, and for me, the debugger smokes, drinks, and shoots pool in sleazy dives, so I try not to spend much time with him.

When we need it, the debugger is a powerful tool. I wish, at least a little, that I knew the Visual Studio debugger a bit better. A little more facility with it might have shortened some of our stays in the debugger and might have reduced some of our need for tracing. I'll put learning about the debugger a bit higher on my list of things to do.

Still, I try always to remember something that a wise manager told me a long time ago: "I never hire anyone who tells me in the interview that he's a really good debugger. There's only one way to get to be a really good debugger."

Design and Code Quality

We should take a look at the overall quality of the design and its expression in the code. Here are a few things that come to mind:

- **The TextBox/TextModel interface.** There seems to be some awkwardness in the interface between the TextBox and the TextModel. This is probably due, in part, to the fact that we decided to divide the work of editing between the TextBox and the TextModel. The idea seems like a good one: let the existing objects do what they can, and extend them as needed. Now, however, we are in an intermediate state, and it seems just a bit off. Moving all the functionality to Text-Model would be a lot of work, however. We have to deal with all the ordinary keys, plus editing keys, plus cursor keys, and so on. I believe that it isn't worth doing yet, but some might disagree. In addition, as we have mentioned before, the Array to ArrayList conversions are awkward. One possibility might be, because we have already built a subclass of TextBox anyway, to extend it to have a better interface and hide all the ugliness inside. If the project were to go forward for a few more weeks, I believe I would push in that direction if the interface continued to annoy me.

■ **Project organization.** You can't see it from here, but I'm not fond of the way that the XML Notepad solution and projects are arranged in Visual Studio. It may be that there was something we should have read before we started, or maybe we just haven't learned some important lesson, but either way I don't like it. The Solution Explorer seems to have all the XML Notepad files at the top, and then it has some other subprojects also at the top (the Notepad Setup, and the Table Experiment that I did with Paul), and then those items appear again. For a project this small, it's livable. For a larger or longer-lived project, we would need a "coding standard" for how to set up solutions and projects, and we would probably have to reorganize this one. A related area is our little tests, like the Regex tests and the tests done for saving and loading. They need to be somewhere accessible, but they shouldn't be in the way as we try to view the important classes and tests in the system.

■ **Method organization.** We used no particular organization for the methods in the source file. In the test files, methods tend to be in chronological order, which seems like the best way to read them. By seeing how the tests build up, the reader could build a sense of how the system builds up. In the functional classes, however, there is no conscious arrangement of method order at all. It's easy enough to find them with the Class View, but it might be easier if they were in the source file in some discernible order, probably alphabetic. We should come up with a standard and bring the source files into line with it.

■ **Tags enumeration is inside TextModel.** Perhaps tags should be public, instead of embedded inside the TextModel class. Since the InsertAction class refers to it, it should more likely be higher in the hierarchy.

■ **Temporary code.** We used a fair number of Console.WriteLine statements, and we have no good way of finding them to remove them. We also used a few temporary variables just to get the value of some complex expression stored, to look at it in the debugger. Sometimes these are worth leaving in, especially if they are given a good "explaining temporary variable name." Sometimes they would be better removed. Again, we have no good way of finding them. We need to figure out some good way of marking these statements for later consideration. The // TODO notation would be good enough if we could remember to use it.

■ **Keyboard handling.** We never really understood the proper use of KeyDown and KeyPress and their cousins. I believe that we are close to having the right structure now, given our use of the TextBox, but we discovered how to do things by experimentation. This can be OK, but I feel that more tests would have helped, and I can't help feeling that there must be someone somewhere who we should have asked or something somewhere that we should have read.

My general impression is that there are certain things we would like to be cleaned up but that there aren't any really bad situations. Things seem to be rather well-tested, with the exceptions I've just mentioned, and fairly well-structured. As the project continued, if we remained sensitive to the issues, we would probably improve some of these things.

In short, I'm not satisfied with the way things are, but it feels to me that things are under control, although not as good as we might like them to be.

Would "More Design" Have Helped?

Would we have benefitted from doing "more" design (by which we probably mean more design before starting)? I don't see it. Indications in the code call for improvement, but more design would not, in my opinion, have reduced them—it would just have consumed more time. There were certainly some design reversals in the optimization of Undo, discussed at length in earlier chapters, but there was far more up-front design there than in any other part of the system. I am inclined to think that doing less up-front design and paying more attention to how things were going would have worked better.

This result would have surprised me some years ago. When things went wrong in my code, I used to say that I wished I had done more design earlier. Now I do not feel that way. I wish that I had done more design while programming—that is, I wish I had refactored the code when it first began to go bad. Personally I grow more comfortable all the time with very little initial design, which I replace with lots of intensive design thinking—and design action—during implementation. Your mission is to try what's been done here and find your own balance. *In a very real sense, this is the point of the whole book.*

Smaller Questions

I've covered in this retrospective the questions that seem important to me. Your retrospective might focus on different ones, and that's just fine. Here are a few short items that I'd like to mention, just so that you'll know that I've thought about them and what I think:

- **Tools.** Would we have gained much from better tools? I'm not aware of any tools that held me back a lot. Still, good programmers are good tool users and tool builders, and maybe we should have thought of more. As it stands, I see the need for improved customer testing tools, but beyond that I feel that our tools were good enough.

- **WYSIWYG.** Would the program have been very different had our customers demanded a WYSIWYG editor? I don't believe that the structure would have been different, but certainly much more effort would have been spent on look and feel, with correspondingly less time available for actual features. I feel we had the tradeoff right.

- **What about rendering instead of TextBox?** If this project goes forward, I believe we'll want to get rid of TextBox, to move all the functionality to TextModel, and to render characters and handle mouse-clicks in a widget of our own invention. I believe that doing this will put some effort into the widget, but I know where there is one to start with, in Petzold's book. We'll add more function to Text-Model, but it shouldn't change the design. I believe our design is fully ready for a hand-rendered display should we want one.

- **Are there other "big" design changes needed?** I don't see them. I feel that the design is rather good for the problem it solves, and there's not much that I would change if I could. One reason for this is that when we see changes we would like to make, we usually make them. So everything important that has shown up has already been reflected in the design.

- **Better use of Visual Studio.** I do wish I knew Visual Studio better. I'm sure there is a book out there I should have read. On a larger project, there would be more people experimenting, and in a larger organization we might find an expert who could teach us a few tricks. I feel sure that we would benefit from a better understanding of Visual Studio, but I can't prove it.

- **Deeper study.** In general, would studying more have helped us? There are probably a few places where a little more book research would have paid off. Visual Studio, just mentioned, is one example, and keyboard handling might be another. But we probably didn't go far off, and while I might in retrospect add in a few half days of study or experimentation, I feel that we drew the balance well, though not perfectly.

The Effect of Illness

I'd like to comment explicitly on the effect of illness. I was "able to work," although in a lot of pain, for about a month during this project. For a couple of weeks, I couldn't stand to sit in front of the computer for more than an hour a day. Yet I felt that I could "design." My paper designs were, frankly, inadequate.

I'm not sure whether to blame that on being ill or on the fact that paper designs, in the absence of feedback, are inherently risky. My philosophy would be to claim the latter, but both were probably part of the equation. In any case, my advice is to focus on getting concrete feedback about designs early and often. And don't assume that working through illness means being "tough." It might well be a time to get more help, rather than a time to be brave and try to push through by force. Force isn't one of our best programming techniques, even in the best of times.

Does Incremental Development Work?

This, of course, is the big question. It's clear to me, and I hope it's clear to you, that it certainly worked for me on this project. Will it work for you on your project? That is for you to determine.

You have seen the techniques used here: test-driven development, starting with simple design, a strong focus on recognizing duplication and other evidence of design problems, a willingness to improve the code when we see the signs, and so on. All of these require skill, which is gained by practice. The skills are valuable in their own right, and they may enable you to find a more flexible way to develop your software.

Incremental development works for me, and I believe it will work for you.

Sound Bites

Here are a few more words on the "sound bite" lines, indicated by ^{sb}, that litter the book, as well as a few on bonus sound bites not found in the book.

Are the objects helping us? (Chapter 31, page 482)
Sometimes as we're programming along, things go very smoothly. It's as if all the objects and methods are reaching out, always ready to help us. Other times, it seems that they are hiding, ducking out of the way, fighting us for every inch. If we're sensitive to these feelings, we can begin to sense when the code we're working with isn't as well-designed or as well-structured as it needs to be. Do you have to tell some object about ten things before it will do anything useful? It's not helping—maybe you can fix it, or find a better helper.

Are the tests helping us? (Chapter 31, page 481)
Usually we'll find that our tests lead us through new areas and protect us as we change things. But sometimes they seem to let us down. Are bugs cropping up in some areas of the code? Even if we are using "Find a bug, write a test," we might see continuing weakness in some area of the code. Code weakness can slow us down profoundly. It can be worthwhile to think about and install a new approach to testing that area.

Are we having trouble creating some new chunk of code, even using a test-driven approach? Are the tests hard to write or hard to make work? Consider turning attention to the tests for a while. Test by using a different approach, attacking a different corner of the problem or from a different angle.

Automated tests record our intelligence for later! (Chapter 5, page 65)
If you're like me, sometimes you write a little patch of code to learn how some object works and to get a sense of how to use it. My habit, formed over many years, is to write a little main program that tries something and perhaps prints a few values. I make it work, learn from it, and then throw it away.

I'm trying to train myself to write a TestFixture instead, which has two advantages. First, using the test-oriented part of my brain seems to help me learn a little more. Second, the test records the use of the object, and the results, in an easy to find form for later. Give it a try—you might like it!

Begin with a test. (Chapter 25, page 323)

As programmers, we tend to think in terms of algorithms and solutions. We see a problem and visualize a way to program it. And there's great joy in putting some sweet little algorithm together. For me, though, that way often leads to debugging. I write a bunch of code, finally get around to testing it, and it doesn't quite work.

The discipline I try to use is to say to myself whenever I sit down to program, "Begin with a test." Sometimes I listen to myself and actually do it. It always works better when I do.

Build simple scaffolding and then improve it. (Chapter 17, page 216)

Because programming is so much fun, it's easy to get carried away, building complex software to support simple needs. Because "infrastructure doesn't please the customer, features do," we'll often be more successful if we build just enough infrastructure to the current situation and don't elaborate it beyond the current need. What we build needs always to be robust, well-tested, well-crafted. But we can leave off the bells and whistles, until the customer calls for ringing and hooting.

See also *YAGNI—You Aren't Gonna Need It.*

Card, Conversation, Confirmation. (Chapter 6, pages 71-72)

XP-style planning is in some ways my favorite part of Extreme Programming, although we barely touched on it in this book. The techniques can help a team focus on what's important and what should be put off, they can help us figure out how long things will take, and they can help us keep track of how we're doing. If you decide to learn more about XP planning, you should keep three things in mind:

- **Card**   The names of stories, and perhaps a few words about them, are written on cards. These cards are tokens representing the requirement, and we can use them to lay out a schedule, to signify that we have accepted responsibility to implement a feature, or as part of a display of what's done and what's left to be done. But the card is not the full requirement, just a token containing the requirement's name.

- **Conversation**   There is an exchange of information between the Customers, the people who understand the need, and the Programmers, the people writing the program. To build a feature, the programmers need a deep understanding of what needs to be done. This knowledge can be provided by written requirements specifications as part of the Conversation, but we call it Conversation to emphasize that understanding comes faster and better in a personal conversation than in passing documents back and forth. So write what you must, and explain as much as you can, face to face.

- ■ **Confirmation** No matter how much we write, and no matter how much we talk, there will be misunderstandings. If we code according to a misunderstanding, the customer won't be happy. Tightening up our documents and lengthening our review cycles really won't help—human language is inherently ambiguous. Therefore, express the details of story requirements unambiguously, in Customer Acceptance Tests. Getting these tests defined and agreed to, you'll nail down the requirements quickly. The tests will help the programmers know when they are done and will help them avoid defects. Finally, running the tests will give the customer a concrete understanding of how things are going. Card, conversation, confirmation—don't do software without them.

Daily builds are for wimps. (Extreme Programming, page xxix)

Most teams now realize that weekly or longer build cycles are a disaster—the build always breaks. I once visited a team that was seven weeks behind on their "weekly" builds! Daily builds are a great improvement, but they only scratch the surface of what can and should be done. Many teams strike down with harsh consequences upon anyone who "breaks the build." They are right to want the build not to break, but I suggest that it is a team issue, not a blame issue, when the build breaks. Stop the whole assembly line, figure out what went wrong, and fix the root cause.

Building many times per day is paradoxically easier than building once. First of all, the changes that can be made in an hour or two don't deviate as wildly as those saved up for a whole day or more, so an hourly build is much less likely to break. Second, if breaking the build is a team issue and we build many times per day, we will get very good at it. Those root causes of breaks will be discovered and corrected quickly.

Design all the time. (Chapter 1, page 8)

Design isn't something that we do just at the beginning of a project or story or task. As we work, we'll encounter design issues all the time, whether we're coding and find something awkward, testing and find something difficult to test, or even if we're just designing. If we can be sensitive to emerging design issues and respond to them immediately, the design will stay closer to good all the time.

Don't fall in love with our own work.

Sometimes we code up something really nifty and we're pretty proud of it. That's good—it's important to practice and to exercise our skills. Sometimes we work really hard on something and finally get it to work. That's good too—sometimes we have to get things done even if they aren't entirely pretty.

But both these situations, and others, can sometimes blind us to the fact that there's a better way to do whatever it is. When we feel ourselves resisting change, defending our code like it was our dearest child, it's more likely time to let go. Don't fight back. Pretend that someone else wrote that piece of junk, and get on board with seeing what's wrong with it and how to make it better. Then decide what to do.

End to end is further than you think. (Chapter 13, page 182)

When we test our product, we always try to test it "from end to end." We want to make sure that inputs come in correctly, get processed correctly, and turn into outputs correctly. Paradoxically, it always seems that the worst problems occur just beyond the current edges of our testing. When this happens, there's not much we can do but push the ends out a bit further. I guess we just have to get used to it...

Expressing Intention. (Chapter 4, page 42)

We always have something in mind as we program, at least I hope we do. When we have finished something, often our intentions changed a bit along the way, as we learned what the code really wanted to do. Therefore, as we finish up some piece of code, let's look back at it, and at what we were trying to do, and see whether the code expresses that intention.

We have all had that joyful experience of reading some stretch of code and suddenly seeing what some part of it does: "Look, this bit updates all the pending requests, then this bit selects one request, then the next bit processes that request!" It's kind of fun to figure out that stuff, but it takes time and energy. Let's change the code to say what it does:

```
UpdatePendingRequests();
Request toDo = SelectNextRequest();
ProcessRequest(todo);
...
```

Sometimes it's even a good idea to program the intentions first and fill in the details later. We call both these practices "Expressing Intention."

Fake it before you make it. Fake it till you make it. (Chapter 11, page 146)

In test-driven development, we do best when we cycle very quickly between writing a test and making it work. One way to speed up this cycle is to send a message to the object under test and, rather than write the code to return a fully robust answer, merely return a constant. Then we write a second test that requires us to fill in the details of the method. This practice seems odd to most people when they first encounter it, but many of us find it a useful approach, especially at the beginning of a new class or method. Give it a try!

Find a bug, write a test. (Chapter 5, page 58)

We don't want bugs in our code, right? We find bugs with tests, right? By writing tests, we prevent other people from embarrassing us by finding bugs, right? Therefore, if a bug is found, we have missed at least one test. Let's write it, think about it, and learn from it to write better tests in the future. And, as a useful side effect, when the new tests run, the bug is probably fixed!

Infrastructure doesn't please the customer; features do. (Chapter 30, page 472)

Of course, we can't do the program without infrastructure. Let's recognize, though, that building infrastructure is a necessary evil, and let's do it as frugally and incrementally as we possibly can. Unused infrastructure is a waste until it is used. Deleted features reduce customer happiness. Put these two facts together and build infrastructure incrementally, as needed, in support of features.

Isolate the unknown.

Often when we're working on something, we know how to do most of it and there's just this one part we don't know how to handle. Isolate that part, via one of two ways:

- We can begin by focusing on that part, writing tests about it, programming it, and solving it. Now, since we understand the rest, everything is easy.

- Or we can pretend that we know the solution, program as if it exists, and get the rest of the program laid out. Now we can focus on the unknown, and often doing what we know has made the unknown more clear.

It's Chet's fault. (Chapter 11, page 139)

"Who broke the build" is a common question but the wrong question. We all broke the build, through omission and commission. When a problem occurs, ask "why," not "who." To help with this, we have Chet. In the early days of Extreme Programming, the team was on a hunt to figure out who to blame for something. Chet Hendrickson stopped the meeting: "Stop! It's *my* fault! Here, look, I'm writing 'It's my fault' on this card and signing it. From now on, everything is my fault." So, when you're wondering whose fault it is, now you know the answer: it's Chet's fault. Now get down to figuring out why it happened and what to do about it.

Keep the tests on green. (Chapter 17, page 213)

As I reflect back on this book, I can see that when my tests were good and all working except for one new one, things went rather well and I was relaxed and more productive. When my tests were weak or not running well, I was tense and less productive. I like relaxed and productive better. That's why I try to begin with a test and why I try to keep all the tests green.

Make it work; make it right; make it fast. (Chapter 17, page 215)

This might be the oldest advice in computing, except for "Mr. Babbage, don't get your tie in the gears!" I can't find the original source, but in any case it's good advice. First make the code get the right answers. Don't spend time honing or optimizing code that doesn't work yet. When it works, hone it to make it clean. Don't waste time optimizing code that is hard to understand. Then—and only then—if a performance test shows that this code is too slow, make it fast.

Outer design should drive inner design, always. (Chapter 30, page 473)

There's not much more irritating than programming with objects that aren't helping us. (See also *Are the objects helping us?*) Tests are one good way to find out how easy or hard an object is to use. If it's hard to test, it's probably hard to use. Plus, it's often best to program top down, to better find out what the objects need to be.

Programming without thinking...what good is that? (Chapter 30, page 473)

Sometimes it feels like we're just "cranking out code" by rote, almost without thinking about it. This can be a sign that what we're doing needs to be automated in some way, or perhaps we should ask, "Are the objects helping us?" If you're programming and not thinking about it, think about it.

Push a little when something seems too hard. (Chapter 17, page 216)

Sometimes I know what I "should" do, but it just seems too hard. When that happens, it's often valuable to push a bit. Sometimes I push myself to start on the difficult-seeming thing. Often once I get started, I can keep going. Other times I push on the idea of why it's hard. Dale Emery refers to "Resistance as a Resource." When what we're doing is resisting us, there can be value in pushing back a bit. Of course, there can also be value in turning aside and going another way. I never said that all this would become obvious!

Reflect on how things are going. (Chapter 30, page 469)

It's good to pause frequently to see how we're doing—another good reason to drink lots of fluids. Sit still for a moment, clear your mind, and pay attention to your body. Is it tense, uncomfortable in some way? Is your neck tight? Are you frowning? Is anything nagging at you? Is the code trying to tell you something? Are we on the right road, going in the right direction?

Removing duplication is your friend. (Chapter 11, page 151)

It's fascinating how valuable it is to observe and remove duplication in the code. Duplicate code represents some idea that is being used over and over. To remove it, we have to clarify that idea and give it a name and a place to be. The code gets better in small, smooth steps. Duplication can occur in space, in time, or in concept. Think about it, observe it, and mindfully remove it.

Solve what you know; leave the parts you don't know for later. (Chapter 6, page 78)

See also *Isolate the unknown*.

Some very simple refactoring...has done most of the job for us. (Chapter 22, page 268)

Sometimes we get to a point where the solution we have been working on turns out to be wrong. Our reaction is often to start over on a new solution, but there is an alternative and it's often better. Parts of our bad solution might well be pretty good; otherwise, we wouldn't have been going that way. Consider refactoring the solution, extracting the good part from the bad or the bad from the good. In doing so, there's a good chance you'll tease apart the known from the unknown. Then just fix the part that needs it without wasting the good bits or doing them over.

Start a new path with something abysmally simple. (Chapter 4, page 45)

See also *Fake it before you make it. Fake it till you make it.* and *What is the simplest thing that could possibly work? Do the simplest thing that could possibly work.*

The story's not done until the customer tests run. (Chapter 6, page 72)

Use Customer Acceptance Tests—the "Confirmation" part of a story—as a means of communicating, but also as a means of feedback. Clearly, we can't call a story done until the tests run, but we should strive also to be done when the tests all run. If the tests run but some functionality still needs to be added, either the tests are incomplete or we're working on something that the customer doesn't want.

If the tests run but there is still a lot of refactoring or cleanup to do, by all means do it, but try also to need only a little code to clean up before the code is ready to go. Refactoring works best in small doses all the time, not in big bites. Use the moment when the tests run as a time to see whether your refactoring is keeping up.

Twenty lines without a successful test is a pretty big change! (Chapter 4, page 45)

Except in rare circumstances, I think I probably write a defect every twenty lines, or at least every forty. Of course, it's an easy defect and after only a few console writes or a few moments in the debugger, I'm back on track. On the other hand, I can almost always write five lines without a defect. How many lines should I write between successful tests?

Two Hats. (Chapter 8, page 95)

Kent Beck taught us to think of two hats: a "new functionality" hat and a "refactoring" hat. He told us to wear only one hat at a time, or we would look stupid. When we start refactoring in the middle of trying to make something work, we seem to make mistakes much more often. Add or fix functionality when the tests are red. Refactor or improve design when the tests are green. Are the hats themselves red and green? You decide. My hat is white.

We don't need a testing framework; we need tests. (Chapter 6, page 73)

Too often I see teams who have few customer tests because they are waiting until they (or QA) build a testing framework. If we have no tests, we don't know whether the program works. If we don't know whether the program works, it doesn't work. It's like driving with your eyes closed until you get sunglasses: a really bad idea. Don't wait for a framework—write a test!

We start new features with large bold strokes. We're intentionally building from rough toward smooth. (Chapter 4, page 47)

You don't build fine furniture by taking triple-zero sandpaper to the nearest tree. The sequence is more like chain saw, band saw, circular saw, hand saw, coarse sandpaper, and finally the triple-aught. Consider coding the same way, first getting the big bits right and then refining and refining until everything is fitted just right. I think you'll save a lot of time, instead of polishing the wrong bits.

See also *Make it work; make it right; make it fast.*

What is the simplest thing that could possibly work? Do the simplest thing that could possibly work. (Chapter 28, page 408)

Often our first approach to a new problem is overly complex. We don't fully understand what we're up against, and we respond by figuring out a big solution or by fumbling around for hours with an ill-conceived idea. When he hears someone imagining a solution that may be too complex, Kent Beck likes to ask, "What is the simplest thing that could possibly work?" When we look at the problem this way, we often see a simpler approach that will get us started, or perhaps, even see us through.

For the past few years, in my own code, I've been taking this idea a step further: I ask myself what the simplest thing is that could possibly work, and then I do it. I don't expect these solutions to hold up till the end of the application, although often they do. But because I try always to keep the shape of the code good, the simple solution is easy to improve later. Meanwhile, I'm free to concentrate on the whole problem, by realizing this detail in a simple, albeit temporary way.

YAGNI—You Aren't Gonna Need It. (Chapter 14, page 192)

We have all been there: We're coding away on something and we see the possibility for a neat generalization or a nifty feature. We don't really need it right now, but "We're gonna need it—might as well do it now." Extreme Programming suggests that "you aren't gonna need it," but not because you aren't going to need it. Sometimes you will need it. We just automatically deny that "we're gonna need it" for a moment, because the issue really isn't the future—the issue is now!

We don't need it now. If we write it now, it will lie unused for some period of time, until we do need it, if we ever do. Leaving aside whether we ever need it, and leaving aside whether it's just right for what we do finally need, face this: our investment of time in that neat feature is *wasted* until that future day when we put it into use, if in fact we ever do. Let's instead use our time now to make our customer happy, with another feature that she actually wants. That's not waste—that's production.

"But," you protest, "it'll be easier and cheaper to put in now."

"We figure the code we'll put in now will be the right code later?" I ask. You assure me that it will.

"So, if we wait, we'll just have to put that same code in there after all?"

"Yes," you tell me.

"Well," I ask, "if it's the same code, why will it be harder later than it is now?" You glare at me for a while and then try, "But I know how to do it now, and I'll have to figure it out again later."

"So, the code we have now is hard to understand? Maybe we should focus on that instead of this new feature?"

Well, probably at this point you kill me, which makes me glad this is a book and not a meeting. But my point remains: it should not be cheaper now than later, and, if it is, we should address that issue, not the new feature.

Now of all the points in this book, this may be the hardest to accept, so in a way I'm glad it's at the end of this list. I hope you believe me, but I'm not asking you to take it on faith. Instead, I'm asking this: When you have one of those ideas and you decide to go ahead and do it, pay attention to what happens. How long does it take to do; does it get used; how long is it until it is used; how close to right is it when it does get used; and how hard does it look to do if you had to do it at that point?

And sometimes, when you have one of those ideas, make note of it, but don't put it in. See whether the time comes when you do need to do it and how hard it is to do at that later time. Adjust your balance as your own experience dictates, and maybe drop me a note about what you learned.

Bibliography

Atchity, Kenneth. *A Writer's Time*. New York: W. W. Norton and Company, 1995.

Austin, Rob, and Lee Devin. *Artful Making: What Managers Need to Know About How Artists Work*. Upper Saddle River, NJ: Prentice Hall, 2003.

Beck, Kent. *Extreme Programming Explained*. Boston: Addison-Wesley, 1999.

———. *Test-Driven Development By Example*. Boston: Addison-Wesley, 2003.

Boehm, Barry, and Richard Turner. *Balancing Agility and Discipline*. Boston: Addison-Wesley, 2004.

chromatic. *Extreme Programming Pocket Guide*. Sebastapol, CA: O'Reilly, 2003.

Cockburn, Alistair. *Agile Software Development*. Boston: Addison-Wesley, 2002.

Crispin, Lisa, and Tip House. *Testing Extreme Programming*. Boston: Addison-Wesley, 2003.

DeMarco, Tom. *Slack: Getting Past Burnout, Busywork, and the Myth of Total Efficiency*. New York: Broadway Books, 2001.

DeMarco, Tom, and Timothy Lister. *Peopleware, Productive Projects and Teams*. New York: Dorset House, 1999, 1987.

Dobson, Terry, and Victor Miller. *Aikido in Everyday Life*. Berkeley, North Atlantic Books, 1993.

DuCharme, Bob. *XSLT Quickly*. Greenwich, CT: Manning, 2001.

Dupré, Lyn. *Bugs in Writing; A Guide to Debugging Your Prose*. Boston: Addison-Wesley, 1998.

Fowler, Martin, with contributions by Kent Beck, John Brant, William Opdyke, and Don Roberts. *Refactoring: Improving the Design of Existing Code*. Boston: Addison-Wesley, 1999.

Friedl, Jeffrey E. F. *Mastering Regular Expressions*. Sebastapol, CA: O'Reilly, 1998, 1997.

Gabriel, Richard P. *Writers' Workshops & the Work of Making Things*. Boston, Addison-Wesley, 2002.

Griffiths, Ian, Jon Flanders, and Chris Sells. *Mastering Visual Studio .NET*. Sebastapol, CA: O'Reilly, 2003.

Gunnerson, Eric. *A Programmer's Guide to C#, Second Edition*. Berkeley: Apress, 2001.

Highsmith, James A. *Adaptive Software Development*. New York: Dorset House, 2000.

Highsmith, Jim. *Agile Software Development Ecosystems*. Boston: Addison-Wesley, 2002.

Holm, Christian, Mike Krüger, and Bernhard Spuida. *Dissecting a C# Application; Inside SharpDevelop*. Birmingham, UK: Wrox Press Ltd, 2003.

Hunt, Andrew, and David Thomas. *The Pragmatic Programmer*. Boston: Addison-Wesley, 2000.

Jay, Ricky. *Cards and Weapons*. New York: Warner Books, 1997.

Jeffries, Ron. *Card Magic for Managers*. Cited in Constantine, Larry L. (ed.) *Beyond Chaos, The Expert Edge in Managing Software Development*. Boston: Addison-Wesley, 2001.

Jeffries, Ron, Chet Hendrickson, Ann Anderson. *Extreme Programming Installed*. Boston: Addison-Wesley, 2000.

Kay, Michael. *XSLT Programmer's Reference*. Birmingham, UK: Wrox Press Ltd, 2000.

Kerth, Norman L. *Project Retrospectives, A Handbook for Team Reviews*. New York: Dorset House, 2001.

Larman, Craig. *Agile & Iterative Development: A Manager's Guide*. Boston: Addison-Wesley, 2004.

Liberty, Jesse. *Programming C#*. Sebastapol, CA: O'Reilly, 2001.

Martin, Robert C. *Agile Software Development: Principles, Patterns, and Practices*. Upper Saddle River, NJ: Prentice Hall, 2003.

McBreen, Pete. *Software Craftsmanship, the New Imperative*. Boston: Addison-Wesley, 2002.

Newkirk, James W., and Alexei A. Vorontsov. *Test-Driven Development in Microsoft .NET*. Redmond, WA: Microsoft Press, 2004.

Petzold, Charles. *Programming Microsoft Windows with C#*. Redmond, WA: Microsoft Press, 2002.

Poppendieck, Mary, and Tom Poppendieck. *Lean Software Development, An Agile Toolkit*. Boston: Addison-Wesley, 2003.

Richter, Jeffrey. *Applied Microsoft .NET Framework Programming*. Redmond, WA: Microsoft Press, 2002.

Robinson, Simon, et al. *Professional C# 2nd Edition*. Birmingham, UK: Wrox Press Ltd., 2002.

Schwaber, Ken, and Mike Beedle. *Agile Software Development with Scrum*. Upper Saddle River, NJ: Prentice Hall, 2001.

Sharp, John and Jon Jagger. *Microsoft Visual C# .NET Step by Step*. Redmond, WA: Microsoft Press, 2002.

Sher, Gail. *One Continuous Mistake: Four Noble Truths for Writers*. New York: Penguin, 1999.

Smith, Les. Writing *Add-ins for Visual Studio .NET*. Berkeley: Apress, 2002.

Sun Tzu. *The Art of War*. London: Oxford University Press, 1963.

Ueshiba, Morihei. *The Art of Peace*. Boston: Shambhala Publications, 2002.

Wake, William. *Refactoring Workbook*. Boston: Addison-Wesley, 2004.

Williams, Laurie, and Robert Kessler. *Pair Programming Illuminated*. Boston: Addison-Wesley, 2003.

Index

Symbols

& (ampersand), 187, 212, 293, 402
* (asterisk), in test code, 25
^ (caret), 293, 410, 423, 431
^ (hat character). *See* caret (^)

A

accelerator keys, 214, 215, 313, 357, 377, 395. *See also*
    Alt+S; MenuForAccelerator method
acceptance tests. *See* Customer Acceptance Tests
ActionForCommand method, 385
Adapter pattern, 246, 250
AddOldLines method, 470
AddRange method, 61, 62, 64–65
Alt key, 181–82, 326, 430. *See also* accelerator keys
Alt+P, 111, 202, 203
Alt+S. *See also* AltS method; AltS test; AltSWithText test
  as accelerator key, 182, 187, 188, 211
  adding to GUI, 148
  beeping sound, 148, 181–82, 188
  vs. Ctrl+S, 148
  vs. Enter, 188
  implementing, 148–51, 234
  testing, 148–49, 209–16
AltS method, 173, 174, 175, 343
AltS test, 318, 319, 340, 343, 350, 385
AltSWithText test, 318–19, 340, 351–52
ampersand (&), 187, 212, 293, 402
ArrayInput test, 73, 76, 78, 80
ArrayList class
  AddRange method, 61, 62
  vs. arrays, 36, 43, 54, 60, 63, 88, 93, 99, 159, 169, 173,
    176, 484, 490
  Count property, 60, 93, 94, 160
  creating object, 169–70
  defined, 54, 60
  line cleaning and, 94–95
  lines, 412, 413, 414, 415, 416, 439
  menu array and, 378–80
  newlines and, 63–64, 66
arrays
  vs. ArrayList, 36, 43, 54, 60, 63, 88, 93, 99, 159, 169,
    173, 176, 484, 490
  empty, 65, 163, 164
  Enter and, 36

  skip tags as, 320–21
  storing menus in, 357, 377–80, 386–87, 389
  string, 57, 60, 63, 64, 88, 92, 93, 99, 169–70, 322, 329,
    333, 334, 337, 345, 348, 378, 484
  TextBox and, 43, 54, 56, 59
ArrayToEnd method, 103
articles
  displaying on Web site, 395–404
  generating with XSLT, 395
AssertEquals method, 20
assertion methods, 20, 79–80, 242, 450
asterisks (*), in test code, 25

B

backing out code, 85, 88–89, 99, 446–47. *See also* code
  manager
BackOfCursorLine method, 224, 225, 228
backreferences, named, 25
backslash, 25
Beck, Kent, xxiii, 51, 95, 474
BeforeLines method, 450
blank lines, 160, 161, 222–23
blank projects vs. built-in projects, 5
book reviews, estimated time to improve
  XProgramming.com Web pages, 271, 275
breakpoints, 26, 27, 29, 225, 298–99, 421, 435
browsers. *See* Internet Explorer
bugs, testing and, 58, 116
built-in projects vs. blank projects, 5
Button, Brian, 182

C

C#
  adding empty projects to Visual Studio .NET
    solutions, 4
  adding new files to projects, 4
  method syntax, 21
  property syntax, 21
  regular expressions and, 18
C# Refactory, 257
CallModel method, 261, 289, 290, 303, 315
caret (^), 293, 410, 423, 431
Cascading Style Sheets (CSS), 399
ChangeToH2 method, 180
class adapters, 246

H

H2 heading tags, 144, 180
HandleKeyboard method, 259, 261
hat character (∧). *See* caret (∧)
heading tags, 144, 180
Hello World
    as console application, 4
    Windows Dialog version, 4–5
Helm, Richard, 245
hindsight vs. forethought, 66
Holmes, Lee, 118
HTML (Hypertext Markup Language), transformations
        from XML, 112–13, 396, 397, 398
Humble Dialog Box article, 182
Humphrey, Watts, 100, 103, 107, 221
Hunt, Andy, 117, 317, 324

I

if statement, 34, 258, 434
Ignore feature, NUnit, 235
incremental development, 462, 463, 464, 494
InitializeComponent method, 185
InitializeDelegates method, 289
InListItem method, 329, 437–38
InputCommand.cs
    code summary, 128–29
    Command metaphor and, 102
    creating, 91–100
    refactoring, 106–7
    similarity to CustomerTest, 102–3
    testing, 129, 142
InputCommandTest.cs, 129
InsertAction class, 381, 385–88, 491
InsertAfterPara test, 141, 372
InsertCharacter method, 423, 424, 425, 428, 431
InsertListItemTag method, 329, 350
InsertOL test, 372
InsertOrderedList method, 322
InsertPara test, 141, 372
InsertParagraphTag method, 52–53, 170, 188, 322, 329,
        350, 351
    calls NewSelectionStart method, 163
    calls SumLineLengths method, 163, 164
    code summary, 176–77
    copying lines into newlines, 64–65
    duplication with InsertSectionTags, 159–64, 165, 166,
        173
    vs. Enter, 210
    as logical method, 175
    refactoring, 59–62, 65
    summary, 66
    what it does, 231

InsertPre test, 201–2, 225–26, 232–33, 352–53
    adding Shift+Enter customer testing to, 240–42
    code summary, 372–73
    enhancing, 220–23
InsertPreMenu method, 212
InsertPreTag method, 202, 322, 340, 350, 352
InsertRange method, 64–65, 162, 170, 438–39
InsertReturn method, 220, 221–23, 232
InsertSection method, 186–87, 203, 318–19
InsertSectionTags method, 154, 169, 188, 211, 315, 322
    duplication with InsertParagraphTag, 159–65, 166,
        173
    duplication with NewSection, 151–53
    as logical method, 175
    testing, 213
InsertString method, 345
InsertStrings method, 349, 377, 385
InsertTags method
    arrays and, 321
    calling, 322
    MenuInsertTags and, 344
    overview, 221, 222
    removing, 350
    revising, 349, 385
    snapshot object and, 461
    Tags variable, 383
    testing, 340, 343
InsertUL test, 373
InsertUnorderedList method, 319, 340, 350
installable software, shipping stories as, 110–11
intention-revealing names, 51–53, 87. *See also*
        programming by intention
interfaces
    building, 120–23
    ITestTextBox interface, 121, 122, 130, 142
    IUndoRestore interface, 447–49
Internet Explorer
    adding to Windows Forms projects, 401
    adding to XML Notepad application, 402–4
    displaying XML, 398–99
    .NET and, 397
InterpretCommands method, 74, 77, 105, 108, 202,
        241–42, 293, 325–28
InterpretFileInput method, 105
iteration plans, 14, 273, 275
iterations, 10, 11
ITestTextBox interface, 121, 122, 130, 142
IUndoRestore interface, 447–49

J–K

Johnson, Ralph, 245
Kerth, Norman L., 477

Ron Jeffries

Ron Jeffries has been writing software longer than most people in the profession have been alive. In spite of academic degrees and help from some of the best software developers in the world, he has learned more from his mistakes, through having made so many of them. Ron's teams have shipped over half a billion dollars worth of commercial software, and he wonders why he didn't get more of the money. He's happy, though, that he has had so much fun.

Get a **Free**
e-mail newsletter, updates,
special offers, links to related books,
and more when you
register online!

Register your Microsoft Press® title on our Web site and you'll get a FREE subscription to our e-mail newsletter, *Microsoft Press Book Connections.* You'll find out about newly released and upcoming books and learning tools, online events, software downloads, special offers and coupons for Microsoft Press customers, and information about major Microsoft® product releases. You can also read useful additional information about all the titles we publish, such as detailed book descriptions, tables of contents and indexes, sample chapters, links to related books and book series, author biographies, and reviews by other customers.

Registration is easy. Just visit this Web page and fill in your information:

http://www.microsoft.com/mspress/register

Microsoft
